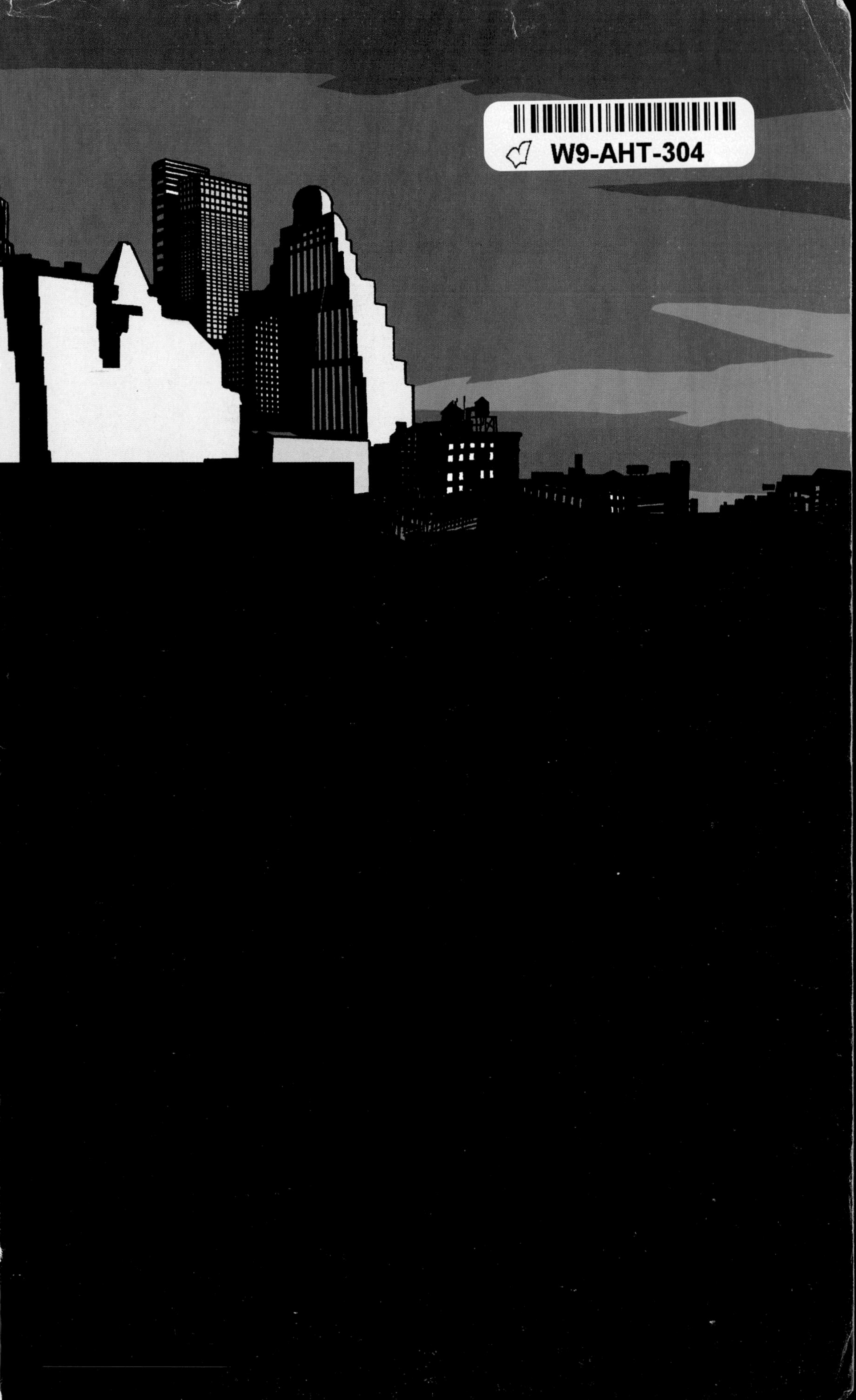

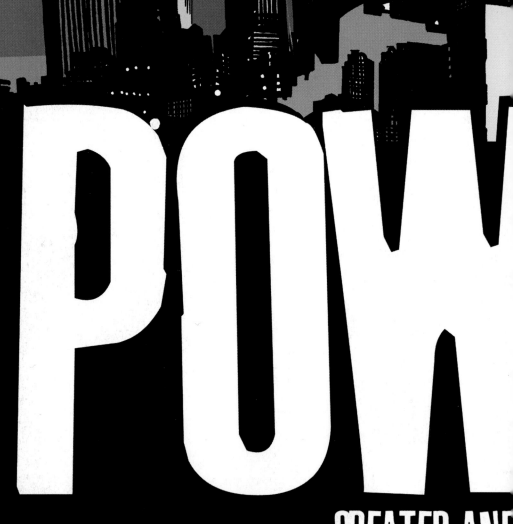

POW

CREATED AND

BRIAN MICHAEL BENDIS

COLOR ART BY
PAT GARRAHY

LETTERING BY
GARRAHY AND BEND

SEPARATION ASSISTS BY O/O CALIENTE STUDIOS

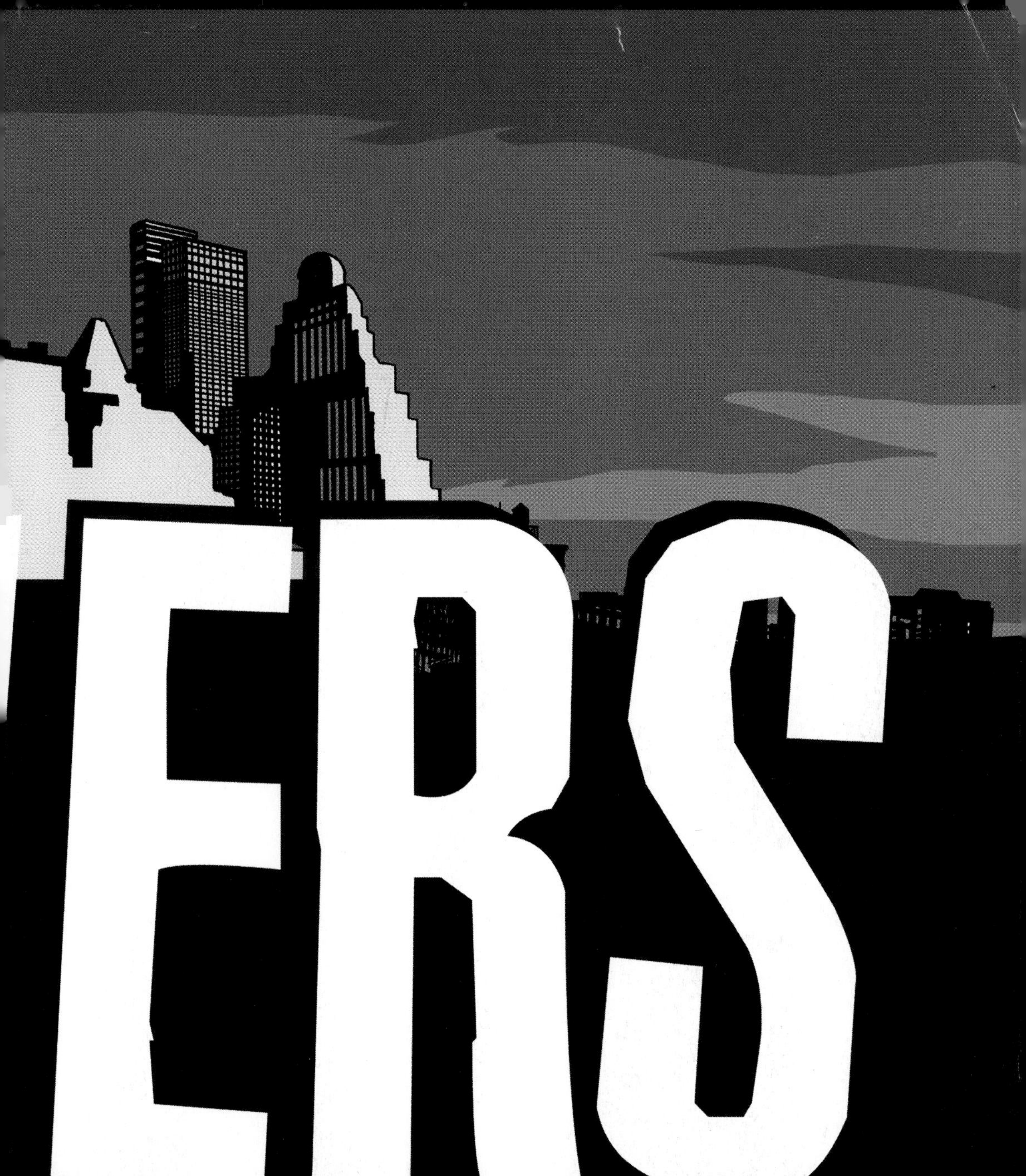
ERS

RODUCED BY

AND MIKE AVON OEMING

EDITOR
KC MCCRORY

BUSINESS AFFAIRS
ALISA BENDIS

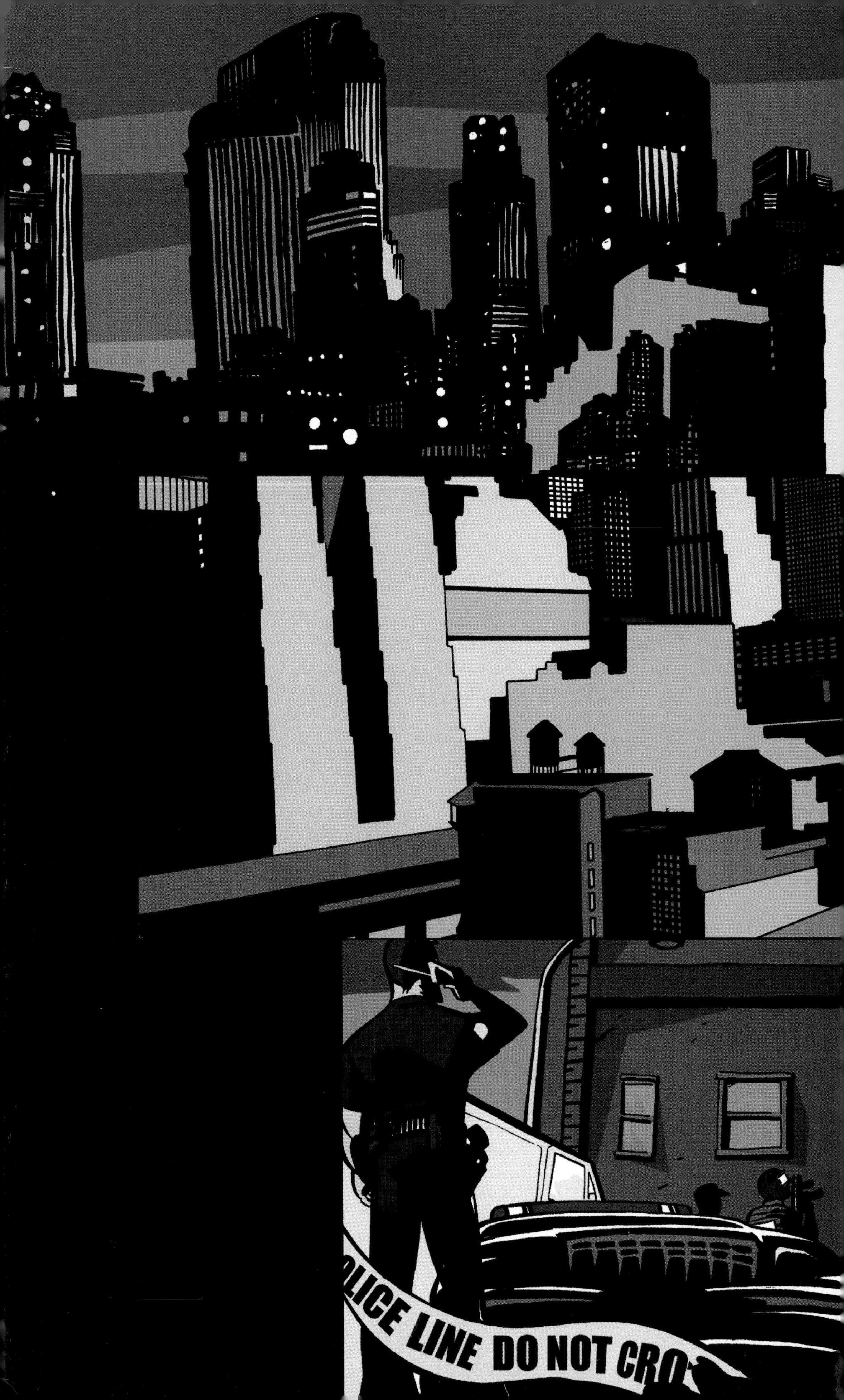
OLICE LINE DO NOT CRO

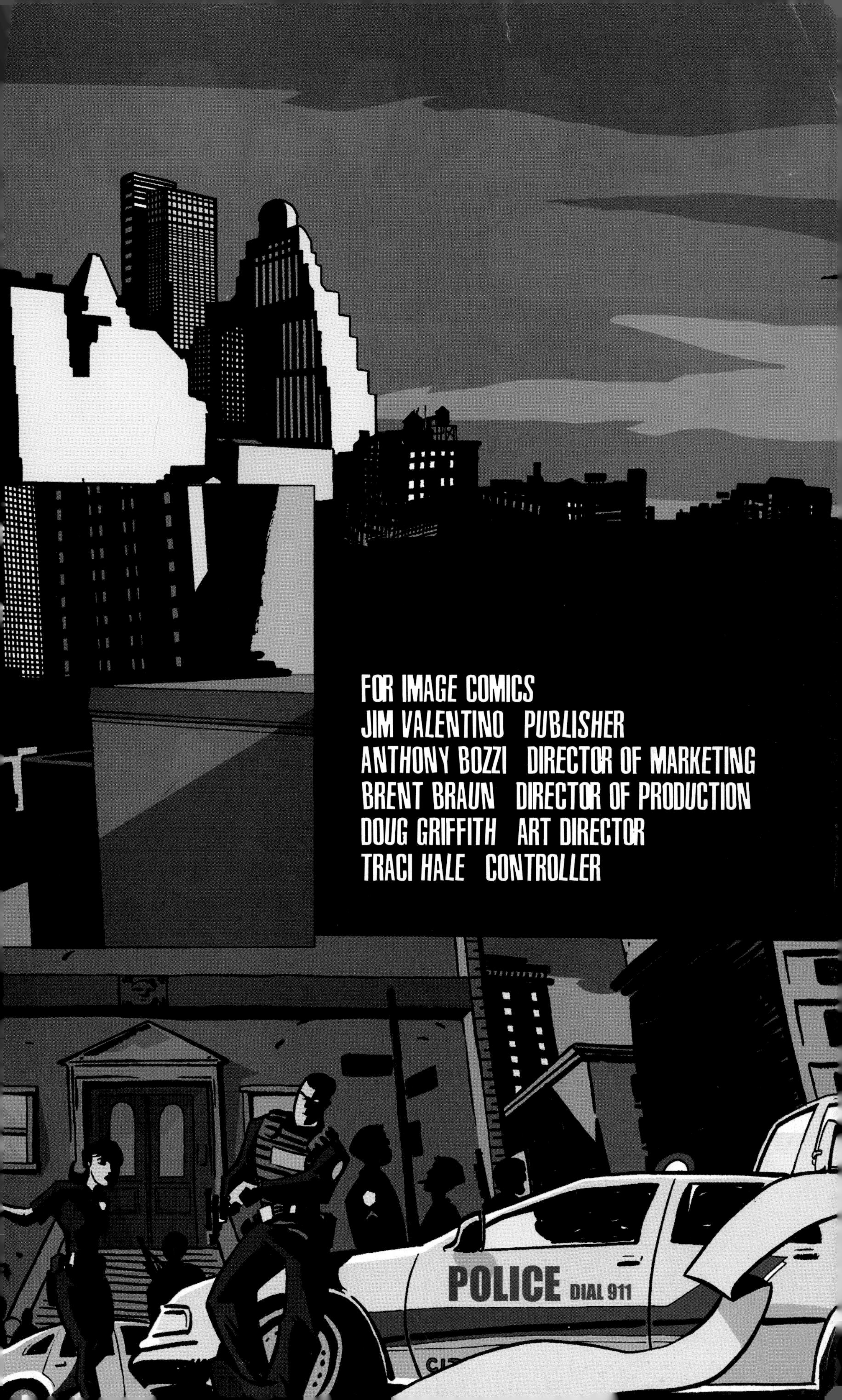
POLICE DIAL 911

FOR IMAGE COMICS
JIM VALENTINO PUBLISHER
ANTHONY BOZZI DIRECTOR OF MARKETING
BRENT BRAUN DIRECTOR OF PRODUCTION
DOUG GRIFFITH ART DIRECTOR
TRACI HALE CONTROLLER

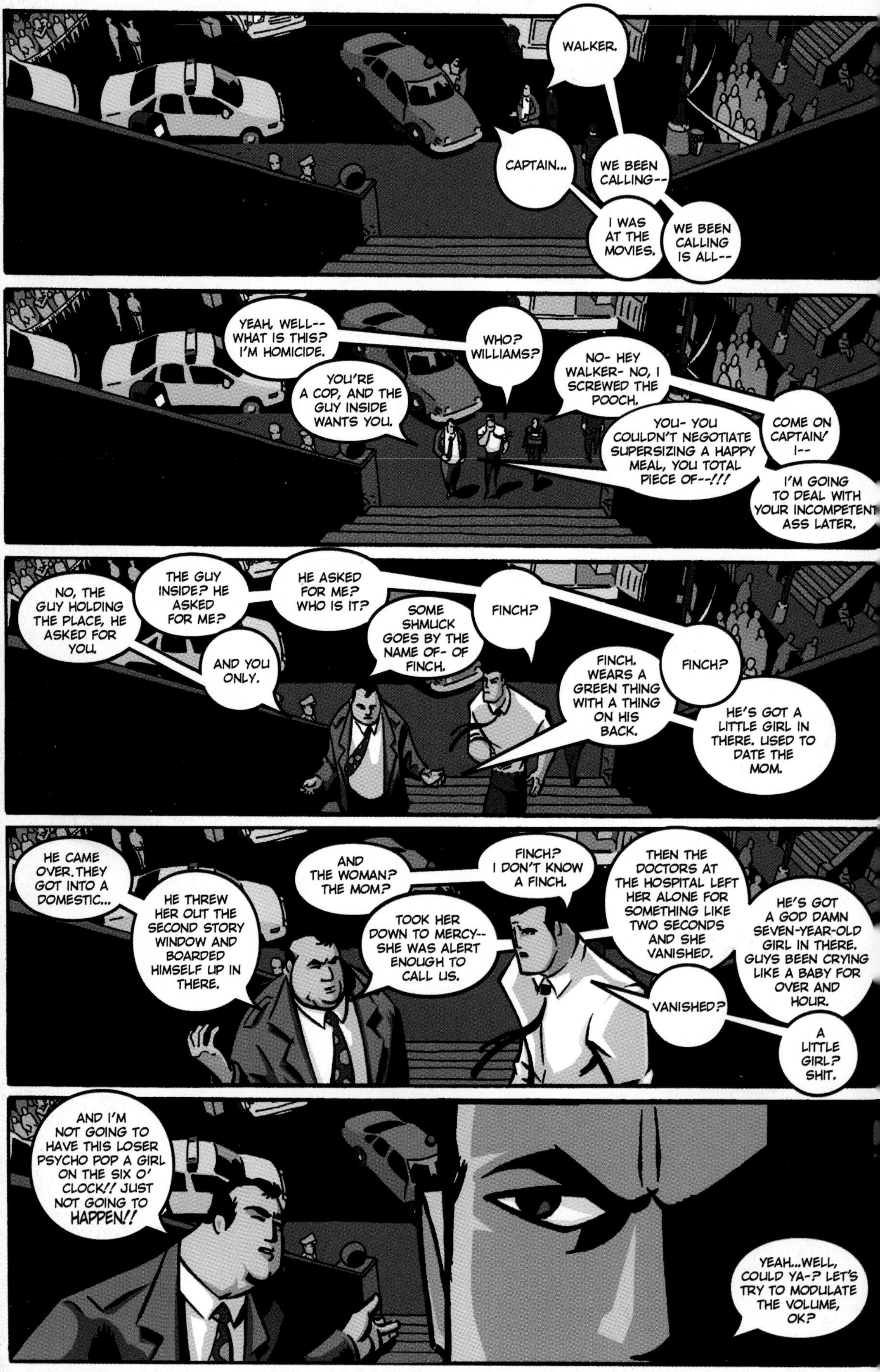
WALKER.
CAPTAIN...
WE BEEN CALLING--
I WAS AT THE MOVIES.
WE BEEN CALLING IS ALL--
YEAH, WELL-- WHAT IS THIS? I'M HOMICIDE.
YOU'RE A COP, AND THE GUY INSIDE WANTS YOU.
WHO? WILLIAMS?
NO- HEY WALKER- NO, I SCREWED THE POOCH.
YOU- YOU COULDN'T NEGOTIATE SUPERSIZING A HAPPY MEAL, YOU TOTAL PIECE OF--!!!
COME ON CAPTAIN! I--
I'M GOING TO DEAL WITH YOUR INCOMPETENT ASS LATER.
NO, THE GUY HOLDING THE PLACE, HE ASKED FOR YOU.
THE GUY INSIDE? HE ASKED FOR ME?
AND YOU ONLY.
HE ASKED FOR ME? WHO IS IT?
SOME SHMUCK GOES BY THE NAME OF- OF FINCH.
FINCH?
FINCH. WEARS A GREEN THING WITH A THING ON HIS BACK.
FINCH?
HE'S GOT A LITTLE GIRL IN THERE. USED TO DATE THE MOM.
HE CAME OVER. THEY GOT INTO A DOMESTIC...
HE THREW HER OUT THE SECOND STORY WINDOW AND BOARDED HIMSELF UP IN THERE.
AND THE WOMAN? THE MOM?
TOOK HER DOWN TO MERCY-- SHE WAS ALERT ENOUGH TO CALL US.
FINCH? I DON'T KNOW A FINCH.
THEN THE DOCTORS AT THE HOSPITAL LEFT HER ALONE FOR SOMETHING LIKE TWO SECONDS AND SHE VANISHED.
VANISHED?
HE'S GOT A GOD DAMN SEVEN-YEAR-OLD GIRL IN THERE. GUYS BEEN CRYING LIKE A BABY FOR OVER AND HOUR.
A LITTLE GIRL? SHIT.
AND I'M NOT GOING TO HAVE THIS LOSER PSYCHO POP A GIRL ON THE SIX O' CLOCK!! JUST NOT GOING TO HAPPEN!!
YEAH...WELL, COULD YA-? LET'S TRY TO MODULATE THE VOLUME, OK?

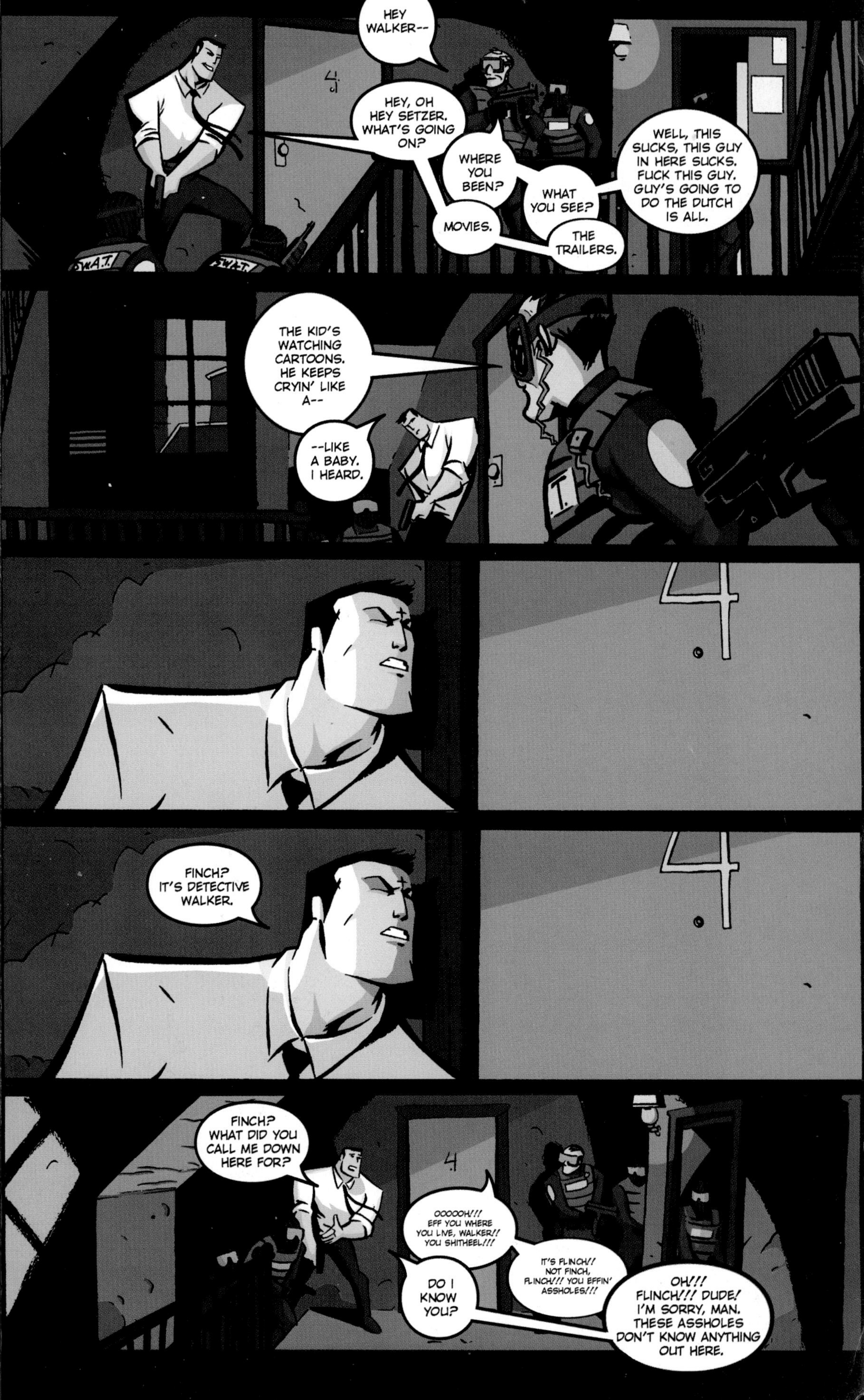

HEY WALKER--
HEY, OH HEY SETZER. WHAT'S GOING ON?
WHERE YOU BEEN?
MOVIES.
WHAT YOU SEE?
THE TRAILERS.
WELL, THIS SUCKS, THIS GUY IN HERE SUCKS. FUCK THIS GUY. GUY'S GOING TO DO THE DUTCH IS ALL.
S.W.A.T.
THE KID'S WATCHING CARTOONS. HE KEEPS CRYIN' LIKE A--
--LIKE A BABY. I HEARD.
FINCH? IT'S DETECTIVE WALKER.
FINCH? WHAT DID YOU CALL ME DOWN HERE FOR?
OOOOOH!!! EFF YOU WHERE YOU LIVE, WALKER!! YOU SHITHEEL!!!
DO I KNOW YOU?
IT'S FLINCH!! NOT FINCH, FLINCH!!! YOU EFFIN' ASSHOLES!!!
OH!!! FLINCH!!! DUDE! I'M SORRY, MAN. THESE ASSHOLES DON'T KNOW ANYTHING OUT HERE.

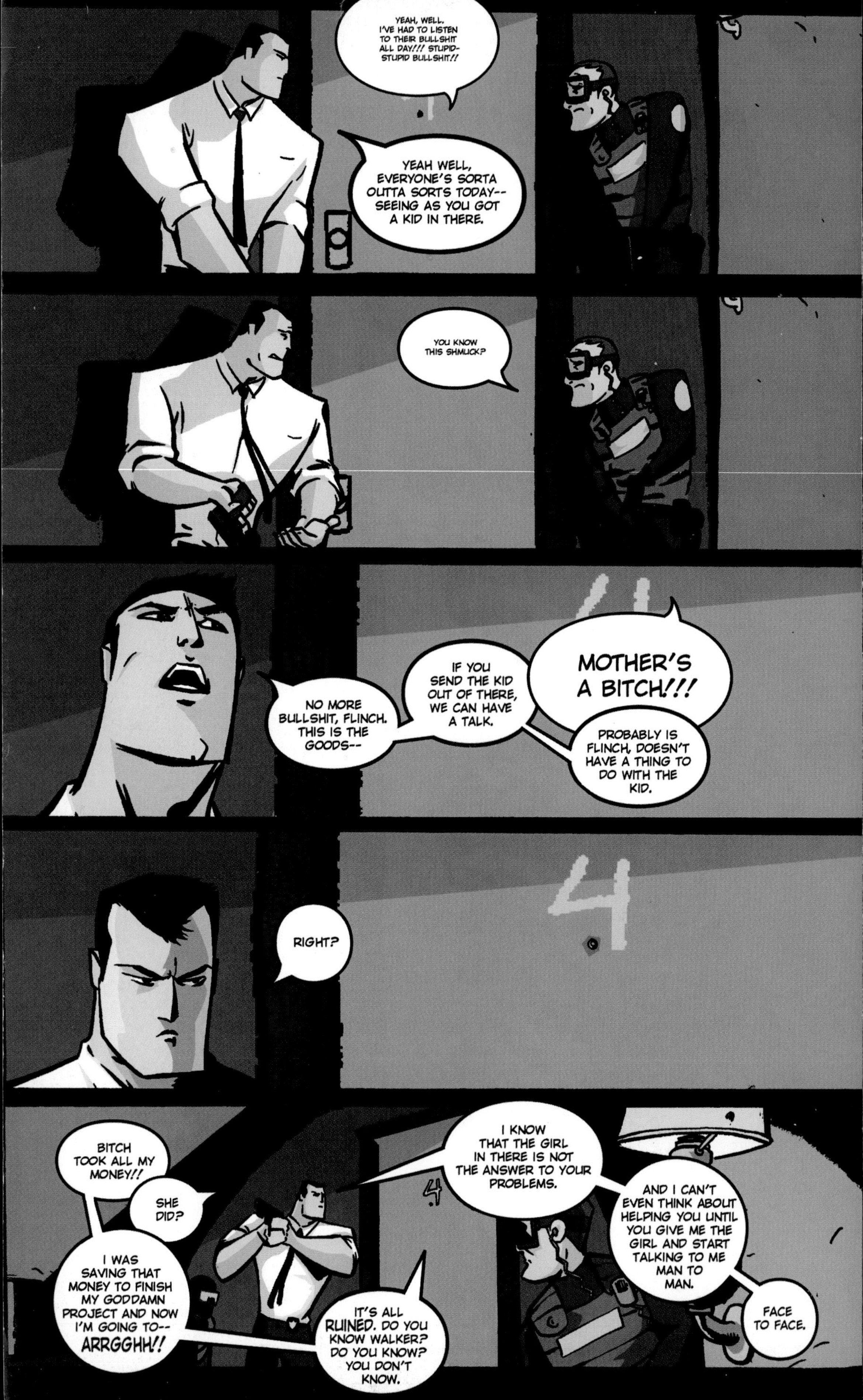
YEAH, WELL. I'VE HAD TO LISTEN TO THEIR BULLSHIT ALL DAY!!! STUPID-STUPID BULLSHIT!!
YEAH WELL, EVERYONE'S SORTA OUTTA SORTS TODAY-- SEEING AS YOU GOT A KID IN THERE.
YOU KNOW THIS SHMUCK?
MOTHER'S A BITCH!!!
IF YOU SEND THE KID OUT OF THERE, WE CAN HAVE A TALK.
NO MORE BULLSHIT, FLINCH. THIS IS THE GOODS--
PROBABLY IS FLINCH, DOESN'T HAVE A THING TO DO WITH THE KID.
RIGHT?
BITCH TOOK ALL MY MONEY!!
SHE DID?
I WAS SAVING THAT MONEY TO FINISH MY GODDAMN PROJECT AND NOW I'M GOING TO-- ARRGGHH!!
IT'S ALL RUINED. DO YOU KNOW WALKER? DO YOU KNOW? YOU DON'T KNOW.
I KNOW THAT THE GIRL IN THERE IS NOT THE ANSWER TO YOUR PROBLEMS.
AND I CAN'T EVEN THINK ABOUT HELPING YOU UNTIL YOU GIVE ME THE GIRL AND START TALKING TO ME MAN TO MAN.
FACE TO FACE.

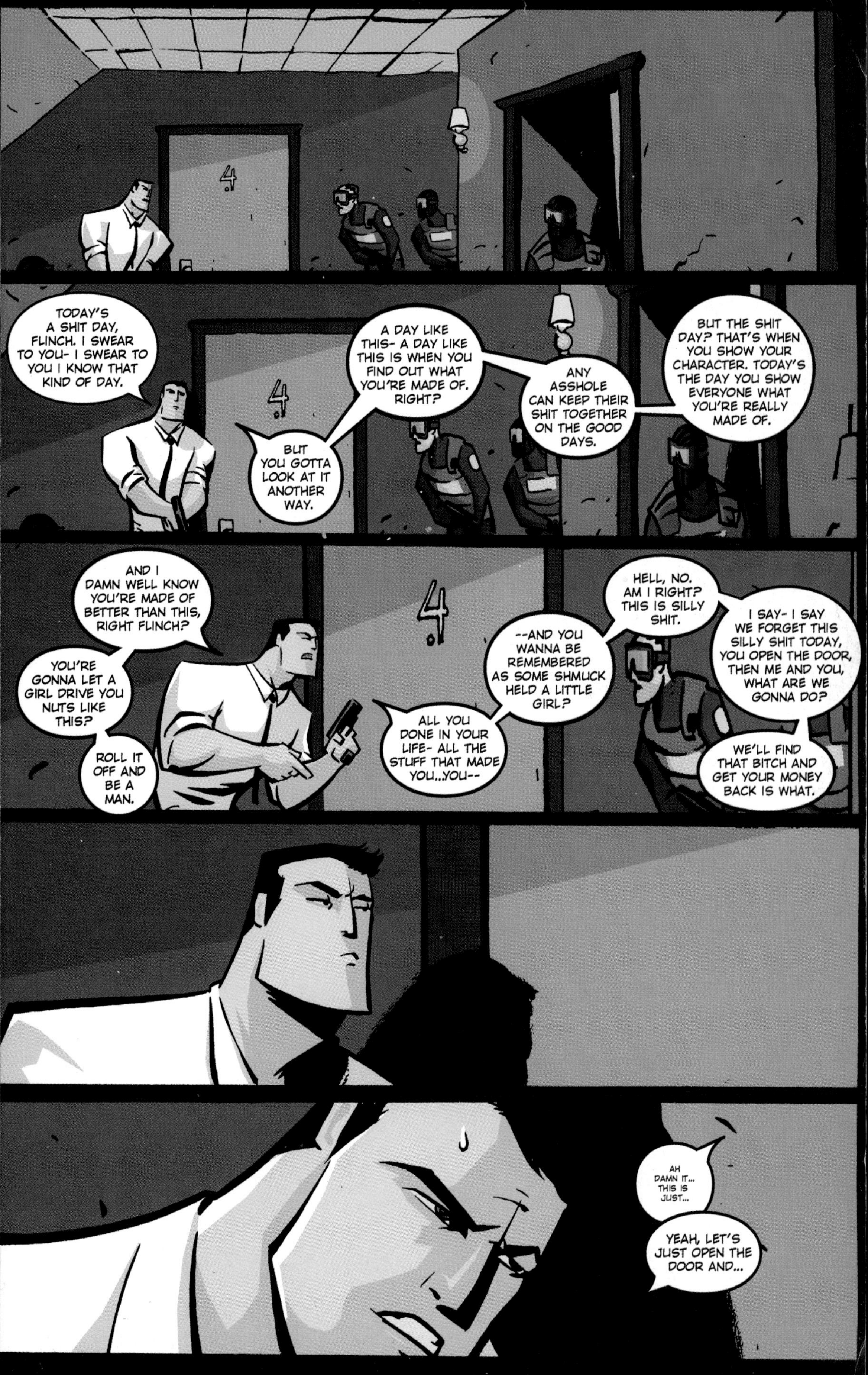
TODAY'S A SHIT DAY, FLINCH. I SWEAR TO YOU- I SWEAR TO YOU I KNOW THAT KIND OF DAY.
A DAY LIKE THIS- A DAY LIKE THIS IS WHEN YOU FIND OUT WHAT YOU'RE MADE OF. RIGHT?
BUT YOU GOTTA LOOK AT IT ANOTHER WAY.
ANY ASSHOLE CAN KEEP THEIR SHIT TOGETHER ON THE GOOD DAYS.
BUT THE SHIT DAY? THAT'S WHEN YOU SHOW YOUR CHARACTER. TODAY'S THE DAY YOU SHOW EVERYONE WHAT YOU'RE REALLY MADE OF.
AND I DAMN WELL KNOW YOU'RE MADE OF BETTER THAN THIS, RIGHT FLINCH?
YOU'RE GONNA LET A GIRL DRIVE YOU NUTS LIKE THIS?
ROLL IT OFF AND BE A MAN.
ALL YOU DONE IN YOUR LIFE- ALL THE STUFF THAT MADE YOU...YOU--
--AND YOU WANNA BE REMEMBERED AS SOME SHMUCK HELD A LITTLE GIRL?
HELL, NO. AM I RIGHT? THIS IS SILLY SHIT.
I SAY- I SAY WE FORGET THIS SILLY SHIT TODAY, YOU OPEN THE DOOR, THEN ME AND YOU, WHAT ARE WE GONNA DO?
WE'LL FIND THAT BITCH AND GET YOUR MONEY BACK IS WHAT.
AH DAMN IT... THIS IS JUST...
YEAH, LET'S JUST OPEN THE DOOR AND...

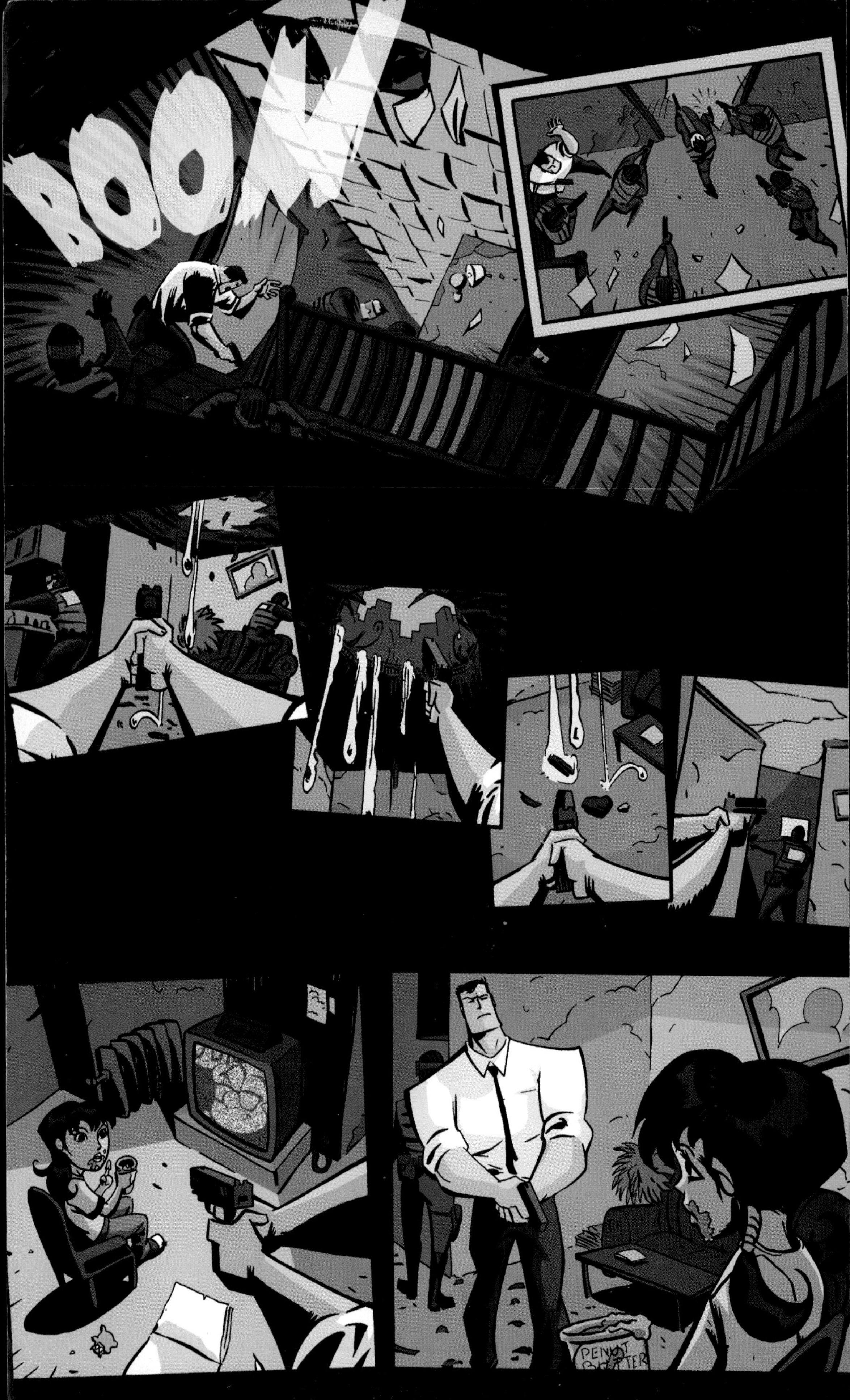
BOOM!

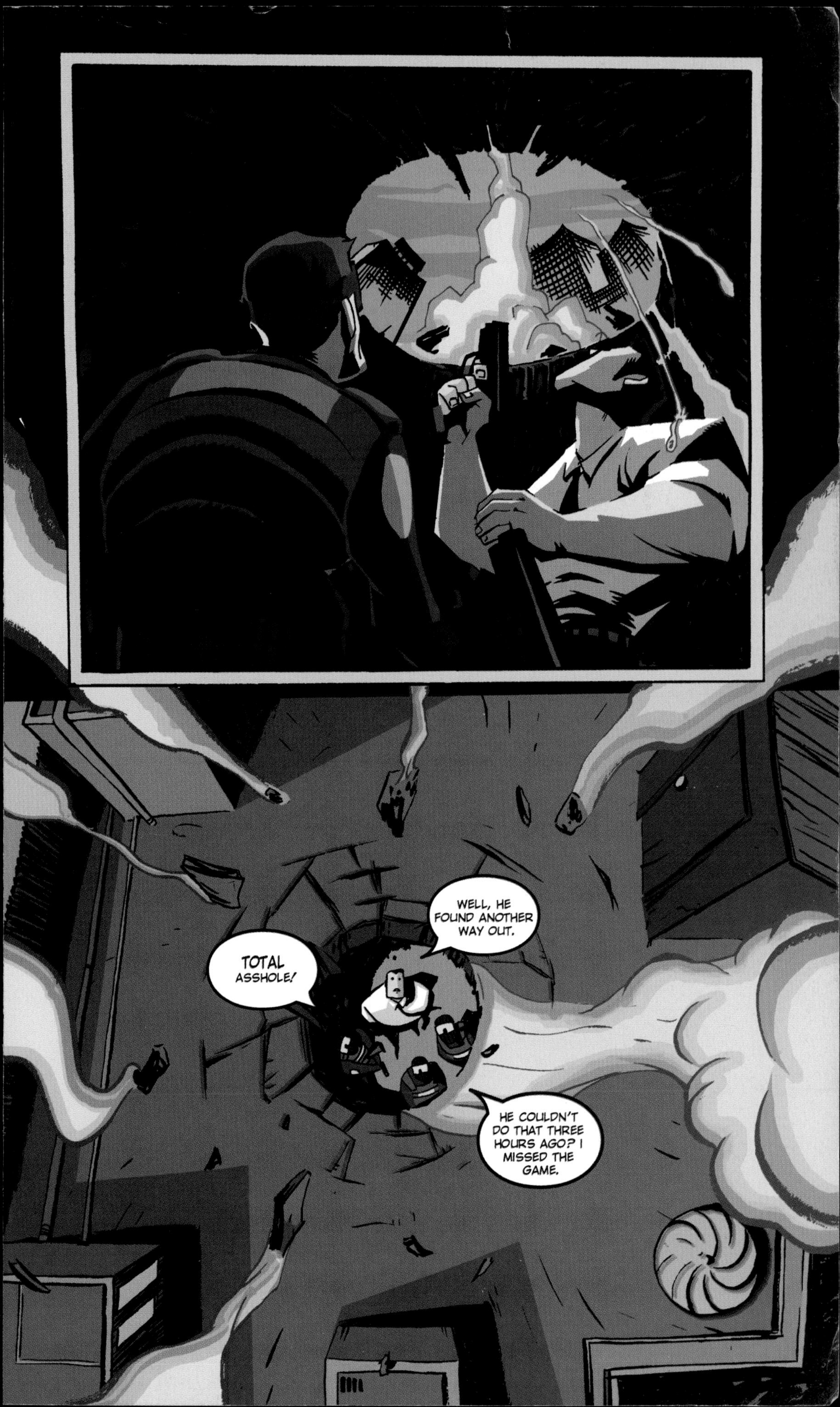
WELL, HE FOUND ANOTHER WAY OUT.
TOTAL ASSHOLE!
HE COULDN'T DO THAT THREE HOURS AGO? I MISSED THE GAME.

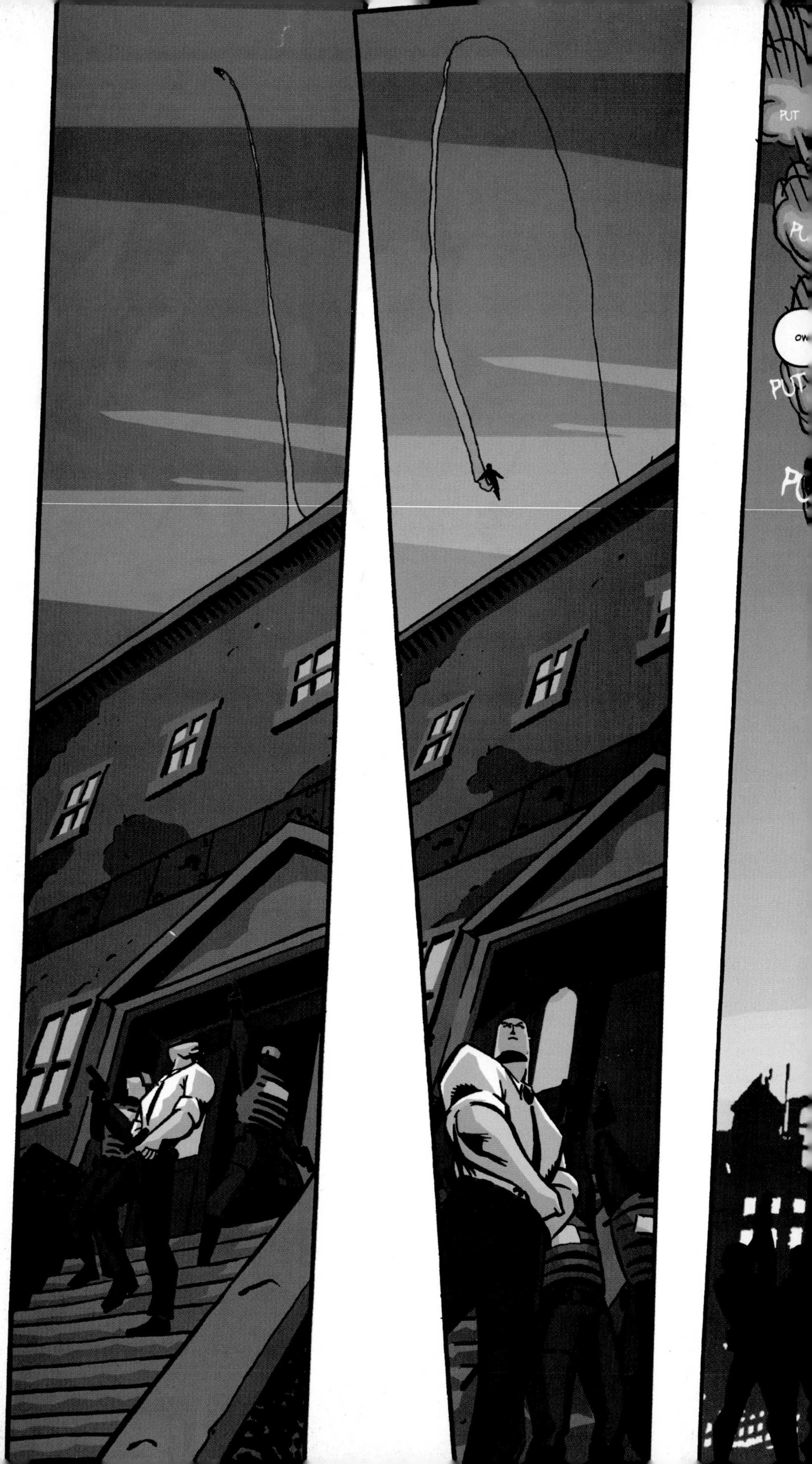
PUT
PUT

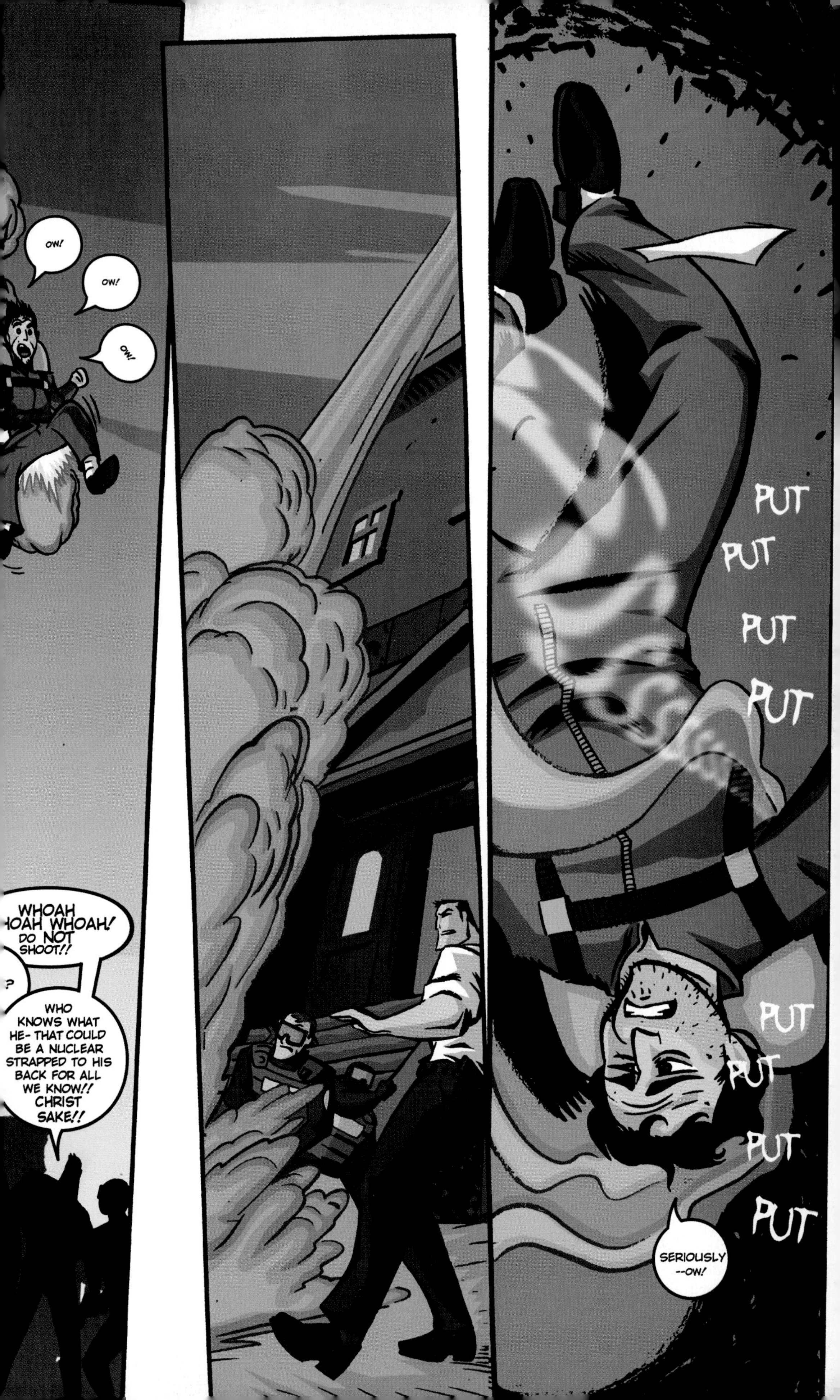

OW!
OW!
OW!
WHOAH
OAH WHOAH!
DO NOT
SHOOT!!
WHO
KNOWS WHAT
HE- THAT COULD
BE A NUCLEAR
STRAPPED TO HIS
BACK FOR ALL
WE KNOW!!
CHRIST
SAKE!!
PUT
PUT
PUT
PUT
PUT
PUT
PUT
PUT
SERIOUSLY
--OW!

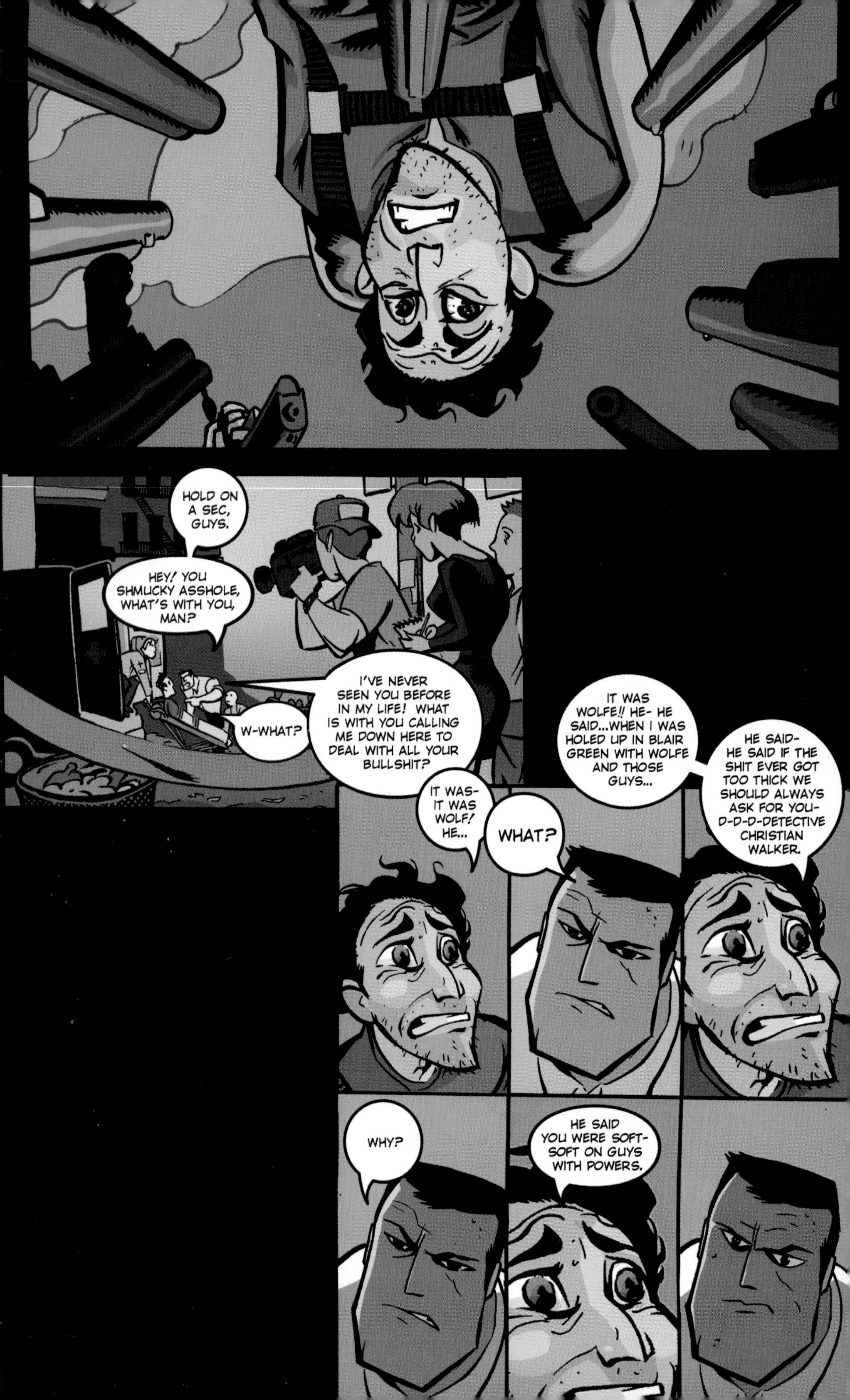

HOLD ON A SEC, GUYS.
HEY! YOU SHMUCKY ASSHOLE, WHAT'S WITH YOU, MAN?
I'VE NEVER SEEN YOU BEFORE IN MY LIFE! WHAT IS WITH YOU CALLING ME DOWN HERE TO DEAL WITH ALL YOUR BULLSHIT?
W-WHAT?
IT WAS- IT WAS WOLF! HE...
WHAT?
IT WAS WOLFE!! HE- HE SAID...WHEN I WAS HOLED UP IN BLAIR GREEN WITH WOLFE AND THOSE GUYS...
HE SAID- HE SAID IF THE SHIT EVER GOT TOO THICK WE SHOULD ALWAYS ASK FOR YOU- D-D-D-DETECTIVE CHRISTIAN WALKER.
WHY?
HE SAID YOU WERE SOFT- SOFT ON GUYS WITH POWERS.

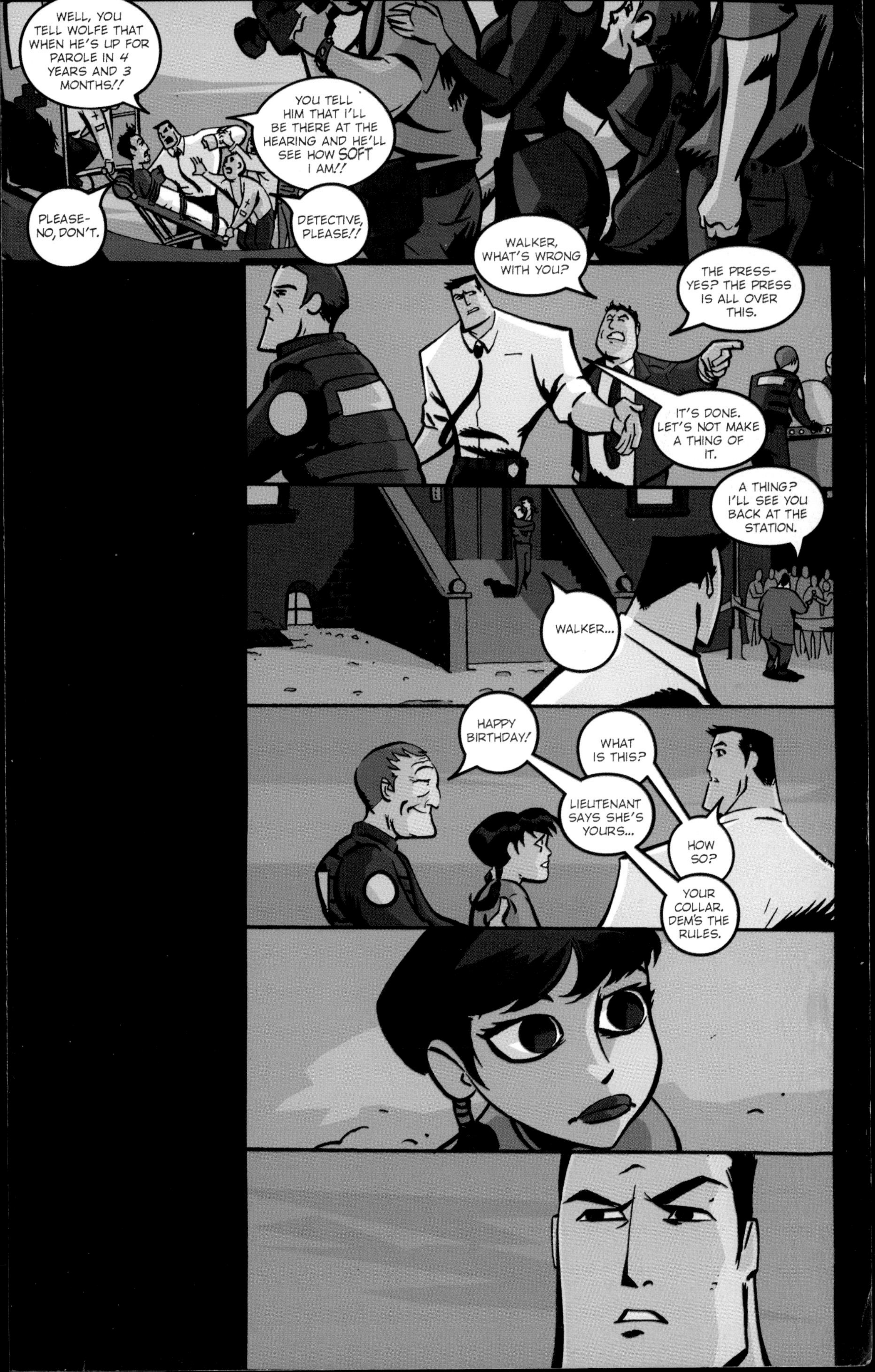
WELL, YOU TELL WOLFE THAT WHEN HE'S UP FOR PAROLE IN 4 YEARS AND 3 MONTHS!!
YOU TELL HIM THAT I'LL BE THERE AT THE HEARING AND HE'LL SEE HOW SOFT I AM!!
PLEASE- NO, DON'T.
DETECTIVE, PLEASE!!
WALKER, WHAT'S WRONG WITH YOU?
THE PRESS- YES? THE PRESS IS ALL OVER THIS.
IT'S DONE. LET'S NOT MAKE A THING OF IT.
A THING? I'LL SEE YOU BACK AT THE STATION.
WALKER...
HAPPY BIRTHDAY!
WHAT IS THIS?
LIEUTENANT SAYS SHE'S YOURS...
HOW SO?
YOUR COLLAR. DEM'S THE RULES.

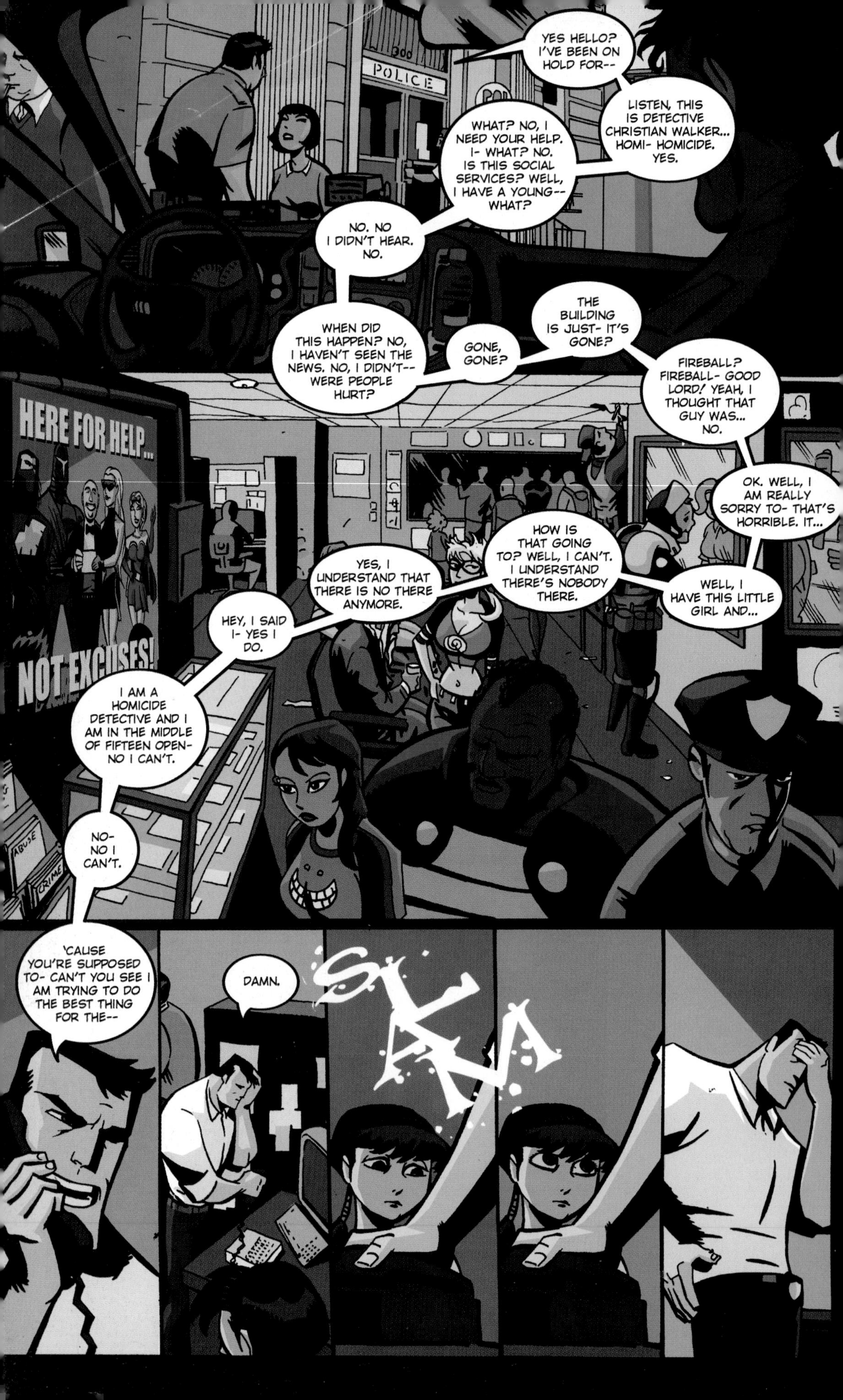
POLICE
YES HELLO? I'VE BEEN ON HOLD FOR--
LISTEN, THIS IS DETECTIVE CHRISTIAN WALKER... HOMI- HOMICIDE. YES.
WHAT? NO, I NEED YOUR HELP. I- WHAT? NO. IS THIS SOCIAL SERVICES? WELL, I HAVE A YOUNG-- WHAT?
NO. NO I DIDN'T HEAR. NO.
WHEN DID THIS HAPPEN? NO, I HAVEN'T SEEN THE NEWS. NO, I DIDN'T-- WERE PEOPLE HURT?
GONE, GONE?
THE BUILDING IS JUST- IT'S GONE?
FIREBALL? FIREBALL- GOOD LORD! YEAH, I THOUGHT THAT GUY WAS... NO.
OK. WELL, I AM REALLY SORRY TO- THAT'S HORRIBLE. IT...
WELL, I HAVE THIS LITTLE GIRL AND...
HOW IS THAT GOING TO? WELL, I CAN'T. I UNDERSTAND THERE'S NOBODY THERE.
YES, I UNDERSTAND THAT THERE IS NO THERE ANYMORE.
HEY, I SAID I- YES I DO.
I AM A HOMICIDE DETECTIVE AND I AM IN THE MIDDLE OF FIFTEEN OPEN- NO I CAN'T.
NO- NO I CAN'T.
HERE FOR HELP...
NOT EXCUSES!
ABUSE
CRIME
'CAUSE YOU'RE SUPPOSED TO- CAN'T YOU SEE I AM TRYING TO DO THE BEST THING FOR THE--
DAMN.
SLAM

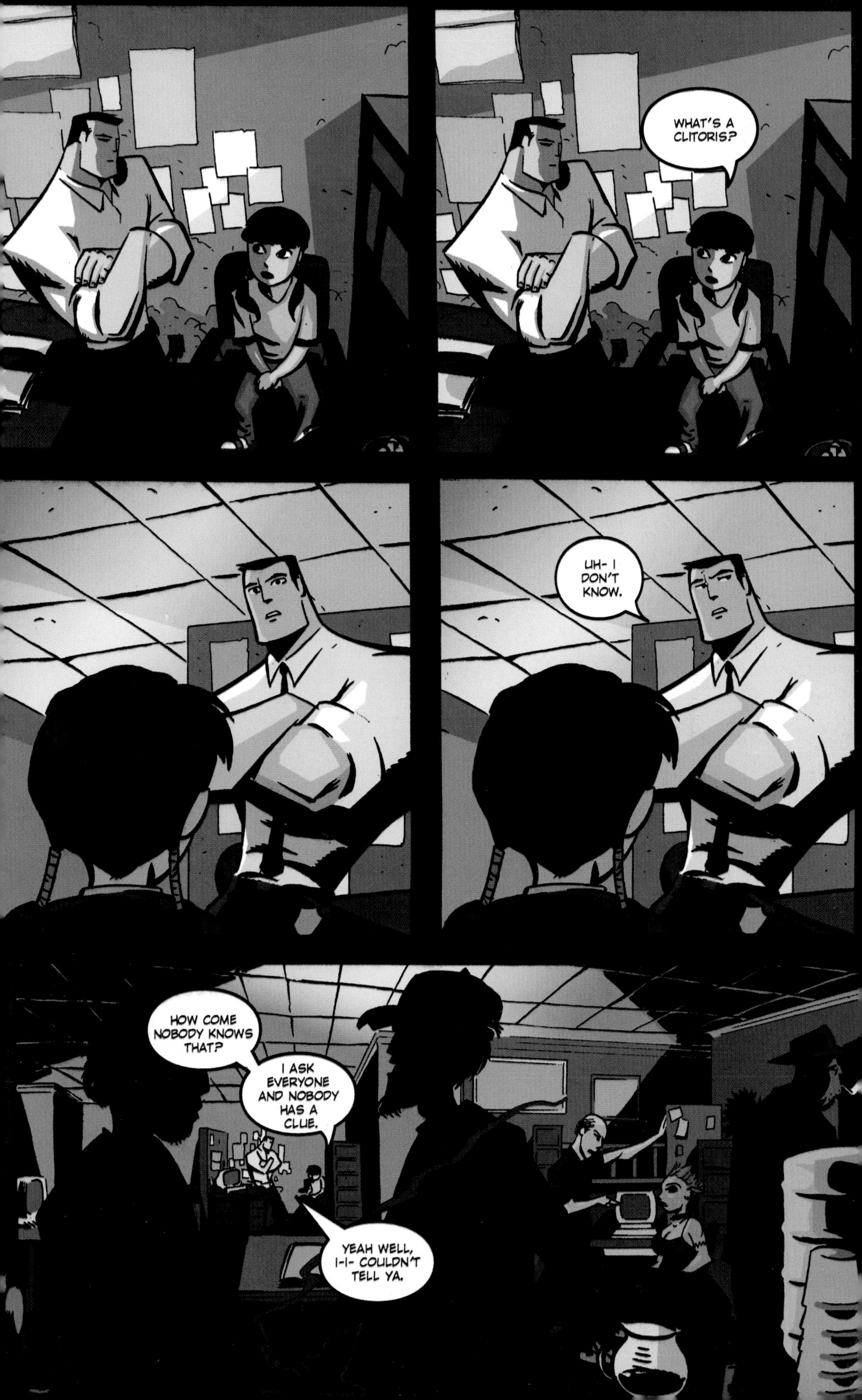
WHAT'S A CLITORIS?
UH- I DON'T KNOW.
HOW COME NOBODY KNOWS THAT?
I ASK EVERYONE AND NOBODY HAS A CLUE.
YEAH WELL, I-I- COULDN'T TELL YA.

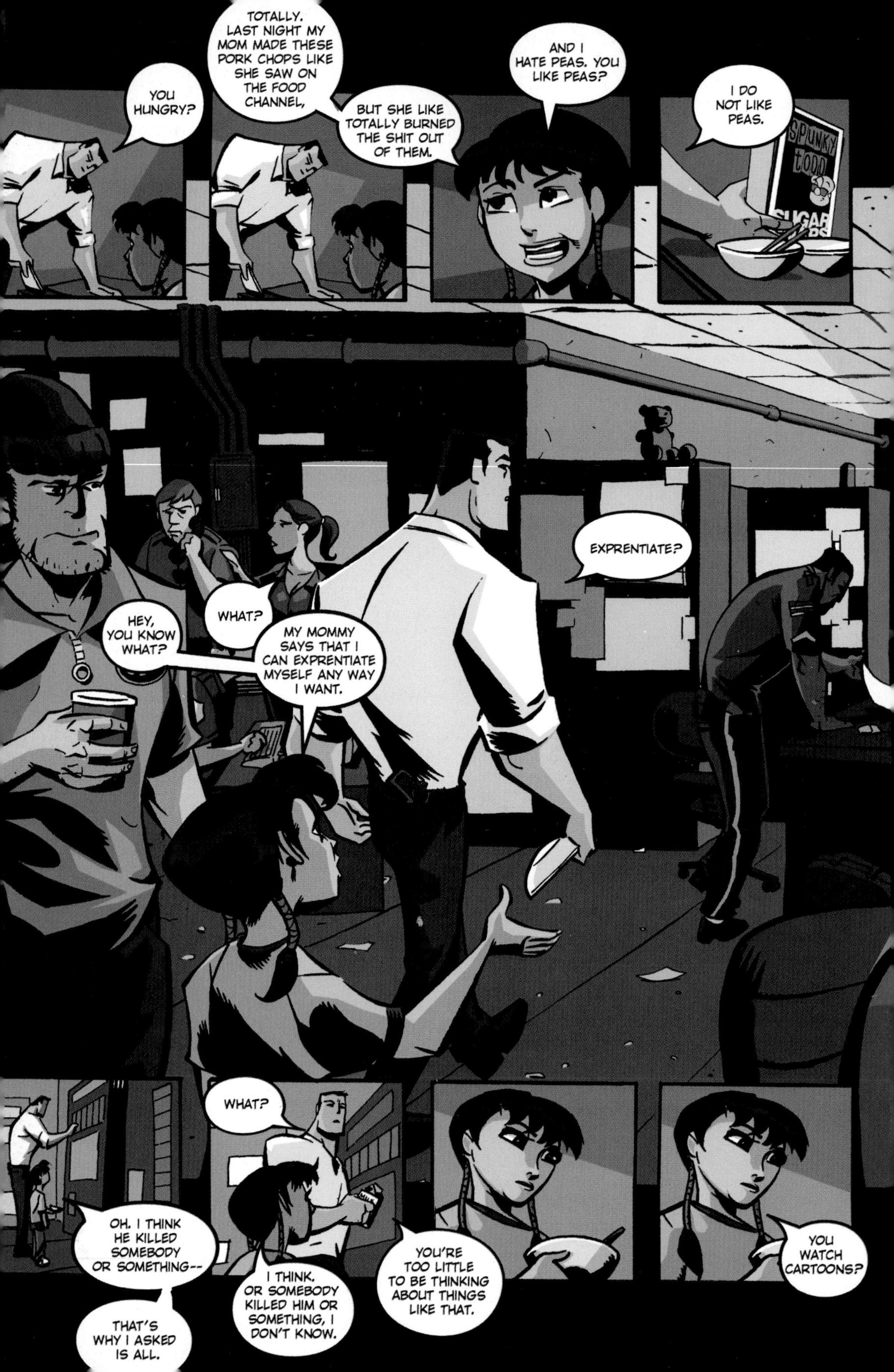
YOU HUNGRY?
TOTALLY. LAST NIGHT MY MOM MADE THESE PORK CHOPS LIKE SHE SAW ON THE FOOD CHANNEL,
BUT SHE LIKE TOTALLY BURNED THE SHIT OUT OF THEM.
AND I HATE PEAS. YOU LIKE PEAS?
I DO NOT LIKE PEAS.
SPUNKY TODD
SUGAR
HEY, YOU KNOW WHAT?
WHAT?
MY MOMMY SAYS THAT I CAN EXPRENTIATE MYSELF ANY WAY I WANT.
EXPRENTIATE?
WHAT?
OH. I THINK HE KILLED SOMEBODY OR SOMETHING--
THAT'S WHY I ASKED IS ALL.
I THINK. OR SOMEBODY KILLED HIM OR SOMETHING, I DON'T KNOW.
YOU'RE TOO LITTLE TO BE THINKING ABOUT THINGS LIKE THAT.
YOU WATCH CARTOONS?

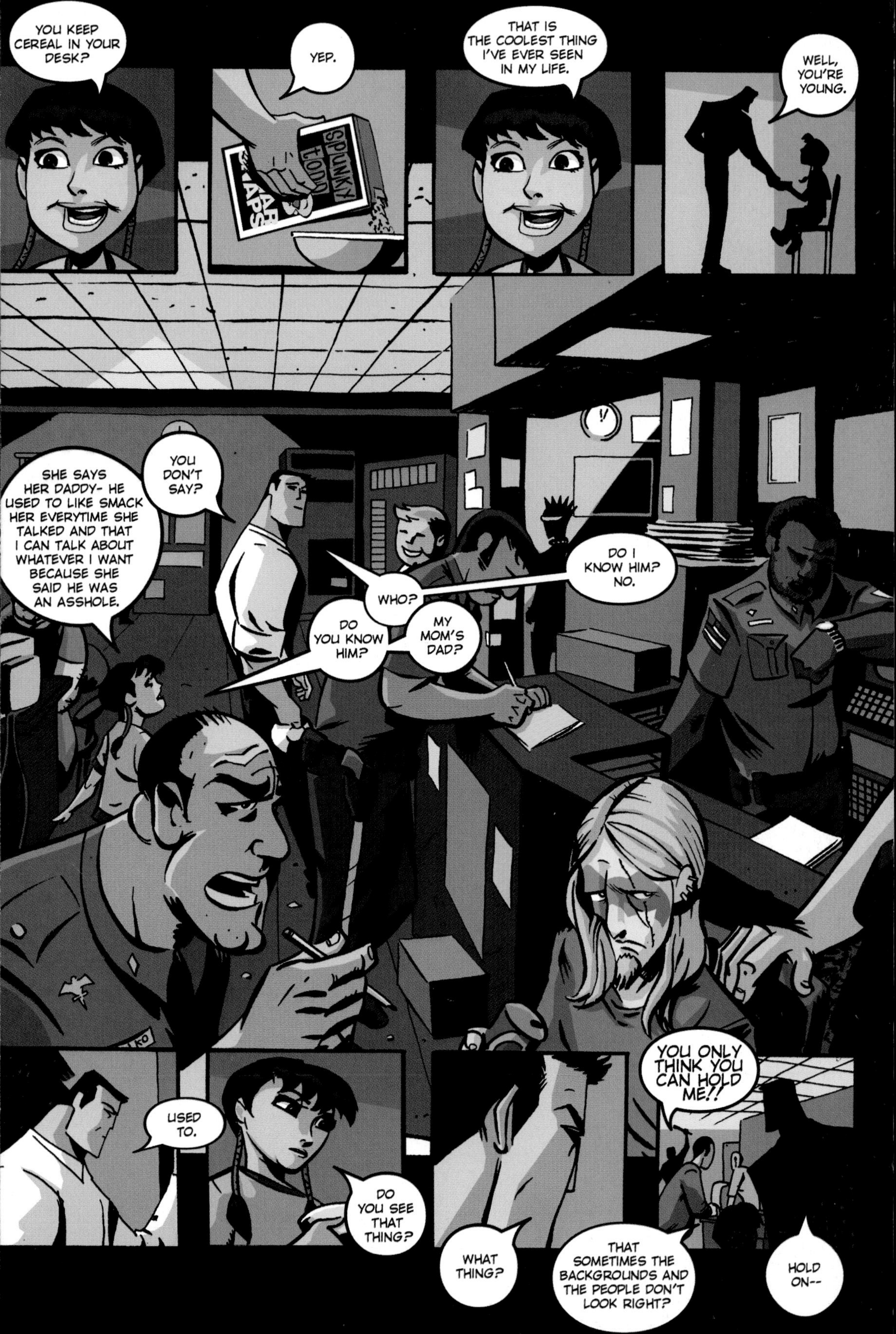
YOU KEEP CEREAL IN YOUR DESK?
YEP.
SPUNKY TODD
THAT IS THE COOLEST THING I'VE EVER SEEN IN MY LIFE.
WELL, YOU'RE YOUNG.
SHE SAYS HER DADDY- HE USED TO LIKE SMACK HER EVERYTIME SHE TALKED AND THAT I CAN TALK ABOUT WHATEVER I WANT BECAUSE SHE SAID HE WAS AN ASSHOLE.
YOU DON'T SAY?
WHO?
DO I KNOW HIM? NO.
DO YOU KNOW HIM?
MY MOM'S DAD?
USED TO.
DO YOU SEE THAT THING?
YOU ONLY THINK YOU CAN HOLD ME!!
WHAT THING?
THAT SOMETIMES THE BACKGROUNDS AND THE PEOPLE DON'T LOOK RIGHT?
HOLD ON--

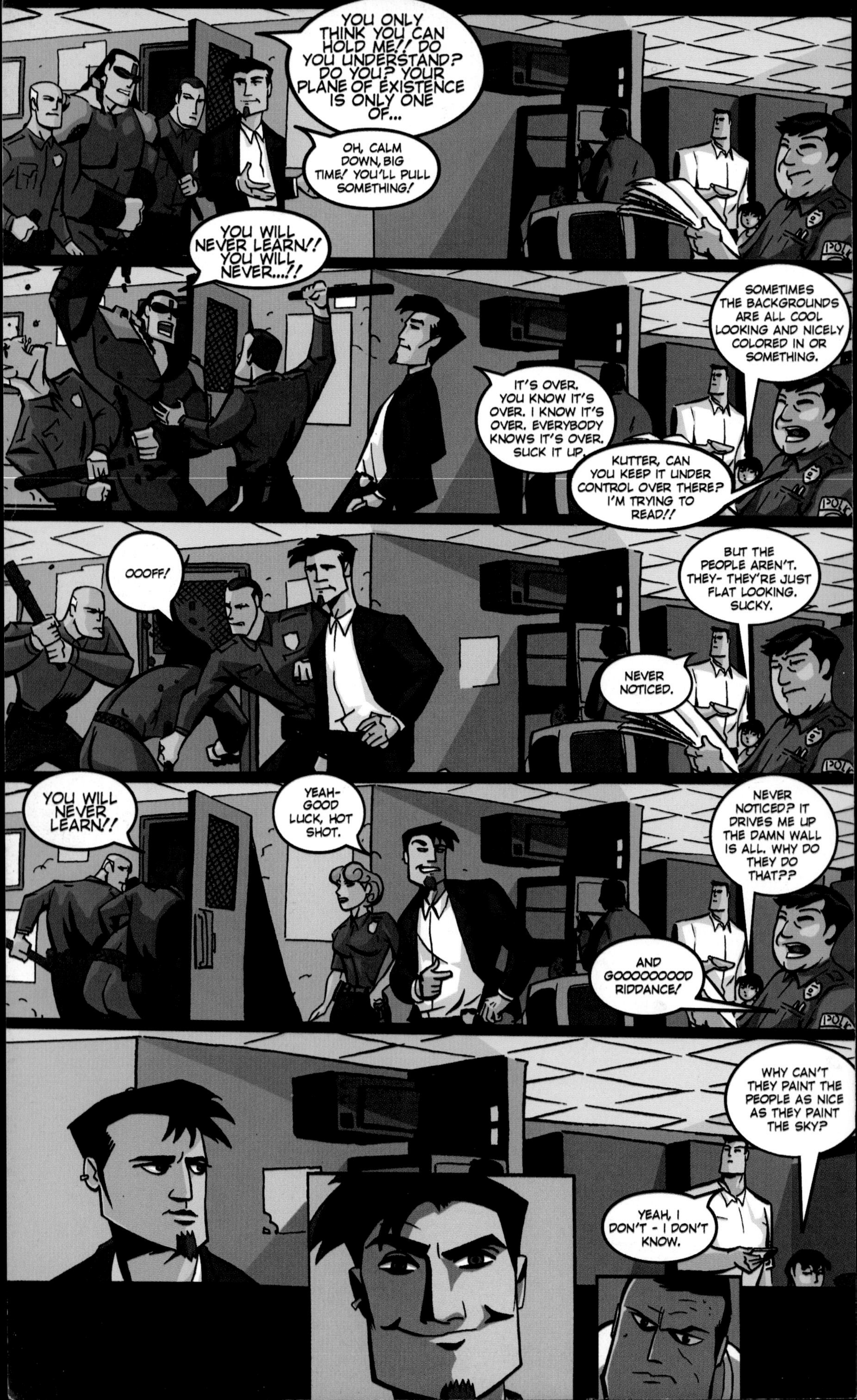
YOU ONLY THINK YOU CAN HOLD ME!! DO YOU UNDERSTAND? DO YOU? YOUR PLANE OF EXISTENCE IS ONLY ONE OF...
OH, CALM DOWN, BIG TIME! YOU'LL PULL SOMETHING!
YOU WILL NEVER LEARN!! YOU WILL NEVER...!!
IT'S OVER. YOU KNOW IT'S OVER. I KNOW IT'S OVER. EVERYBODY KNOWS IT'S OVER. SUCK IT UP.
SOMETIMES THE BACKGROUNDS ARE ALL COOL LOOKING AND NICELY COLORED IN OR SOMETHING.
KUTTER, CAN YOU KEEP IT UNDER CONTROL OVER THERE? I'M TRYING TO READ!!
OOOFF!
BUT THE PEOPLE AREN'T. THEY- THEY'RE JUST FLAT LOOKING. SUCKY.
NEVER NOTICED.
YOU WILL NEVER LEARN!!
YEAH- GOOD LUCK, HOT SHOT.
NEVER NOTICED? IT DRIVES ME UP THE DAMN WALL IS ALL. WHY DO THEY DO THAT??
AND GOOOOOOOOD RIDDANCE!
WHY CAN'T THEY PAINT THE PEOPLE AS NICE AS THEY PAINT THE SKY?
YEAH, I DON'T - I DON'T KNOW.

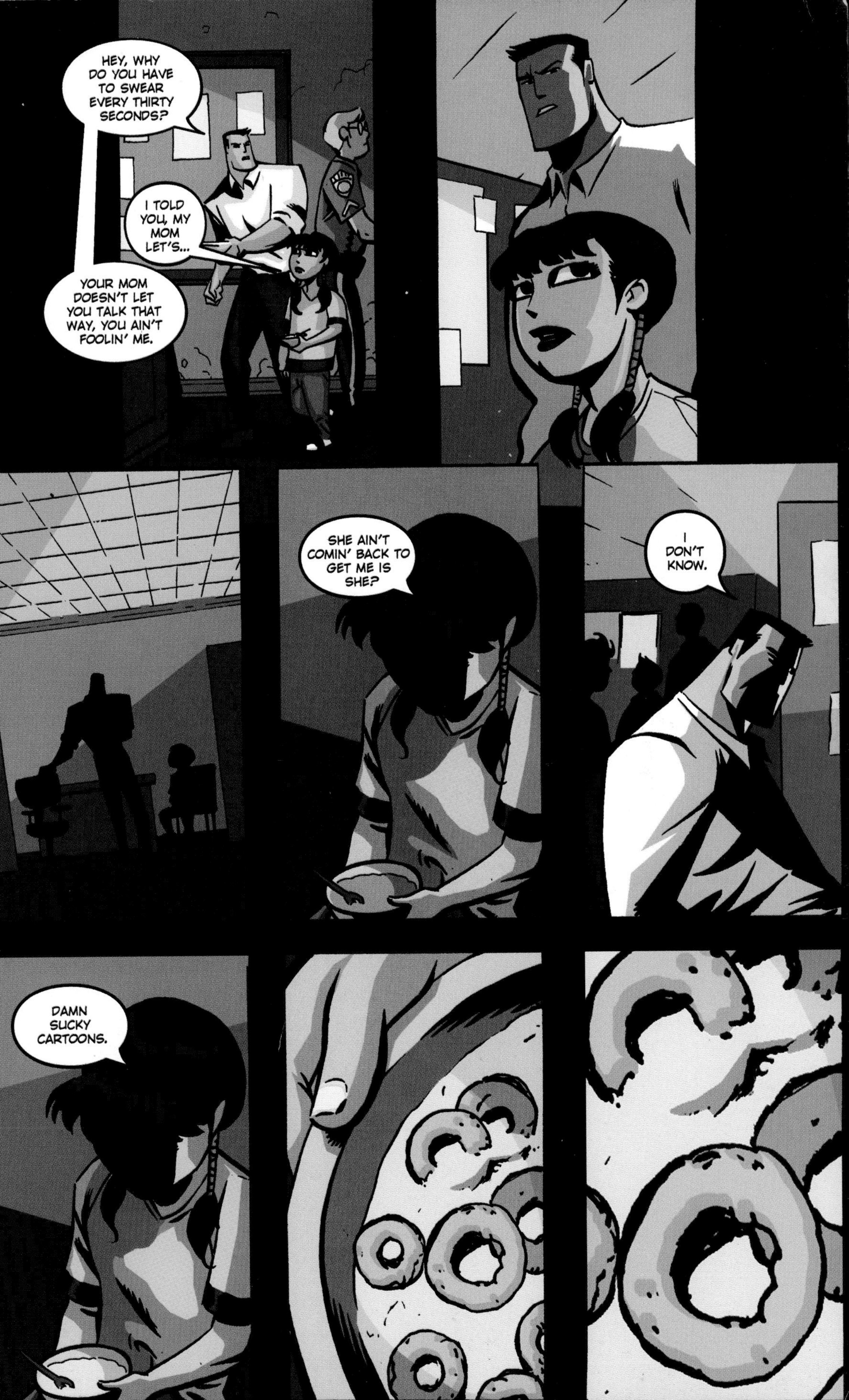
HEY, WHY DO YOU HAVE TO SWEAR EVERY THIRTY SECONDS?
I TOLD YOU, MY MOM LET'S...
YOUR MOM DOESN'T LET YOU TALK THAT WAY, YOU AIN'T FOOLIN' ME.
SHE AIN'T COMIN' BACK TO GET ME IS SHE?
I DON'T KNOW.
DAMN SUCKY CARTOONS.

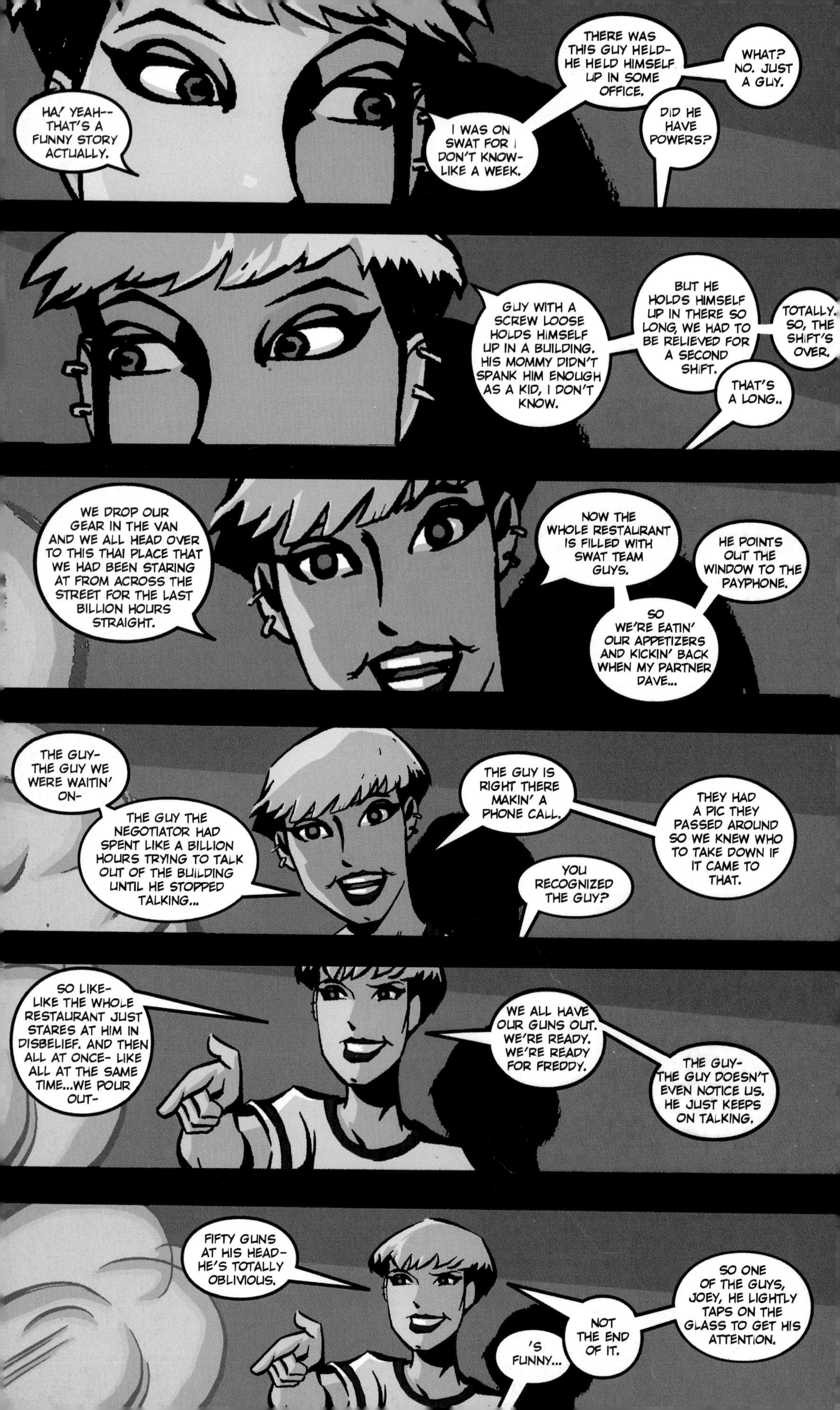
HA! YEAH--
THAT'S A FUNNY STORY ACTUALLY.
I WAS ON SWAT FOR I DON'T KNOW- LIKE A WEEK.
THERE WAS THIS GUY HELD- HE HELD HIMSELF UP IN SOME OFFICE.
WHAT? NO. JUST A GUY.
DID HE HAVE POWERS?
GUY WITH A SCREW LOOSE HOLDS HIMSELF UP IN A BUILDING. HIS MOMMY DIDN'T SPANK HIM ENOUGH AS A KID, I DON'T KNOW.
BUT HE HOLDS HIMSELF UP IN THERE SO LONG, WE HAD TO BE RELIEVED FOR A SECOND SHIFT.
TOTALLY. SO, THE SHIFT'S OVER.
THAT'S A LONG..
WE DROP OUR GEAR IN THE VAN AND WE ALL HEAD OVER TO THIS THAI PLACE THAT WE HAD BEEN STARING AT FROM ACROSS THE STREET FOR THE LAST BILLION HOURS STRAIGHT.
NOW THE WHOLE RESTAURANT IS FILLED WITH SWAT TEAM GUYS.
SO WE'RE EATIN' OUR APPETIZERS AND KICKIN' BACK WHEN MY PARTNER DAVE...
HE POINTS OUT THE WINDOW TO THE PAYPHONE.
THE GUY- THE GUY WE WERE WAITIN' ON-
THE GUY THE NEGOTIATOR HAD SPENT LIKE A BILLION HOURS TRYING TO TALK OUT OF THE BUILDING UNTIL HE STOPPED TALKING...
THE GUY IS RIGHT THERE MAKIN' A PHONE CALL.
YOU RECOGNIZED THE GUY?
THEY HAD A PIC THEY PASSED AROUND SO WE KNEW WHO TO TAKE DOWN IF IT CAME TO THAT.
SO LIKE- LIKE THE WHOLE RESTAURANT JUST STARES AT HIM IN DISBELIEF. AND THEN ALL AT ONCE- LIKE ALL AT THE SAME TIME...WE POUR OUT-
WE ALL HAVE OUR GUNS OUT. WE'RE READY. WE'RE READY FOR FREDDY.
THE GUY- THE GUY DOESN'T EVEN NOTICE US. HE JUST KEEPS ON TALKING.
FIFTY GUNS AT HIS HEAD- HE'S TOTALLY OBLIVIOUS.
'S FUNNY...
NOT THE END OF IT.
SO ONE OF THE GUYS, JOEY, HE LIGHTLY TAPS ON THE GLASS TO GET HIS ATTENTION.

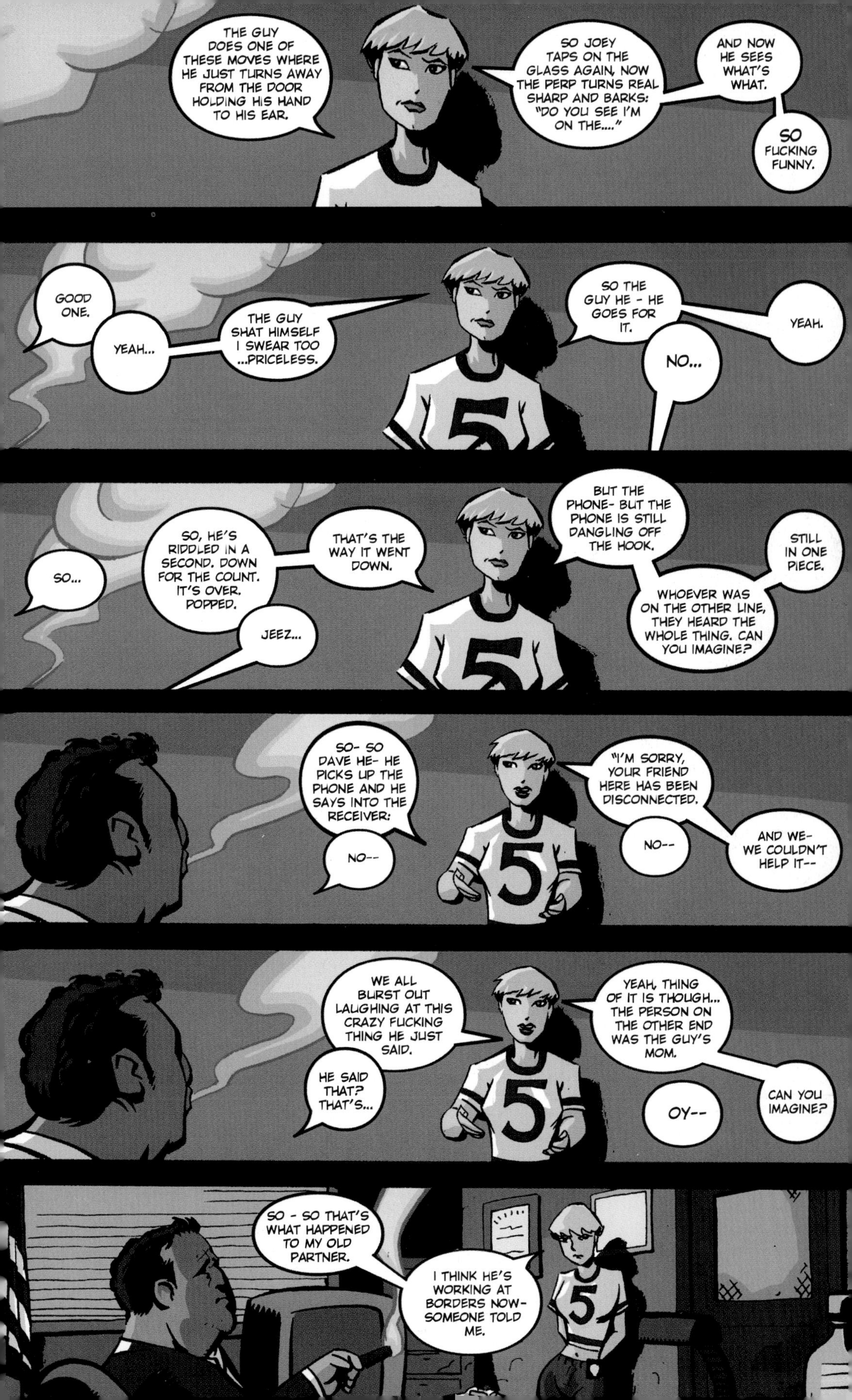
THE GUY DOES ONE OF THESE MOVES WHERE HE JUST TURNS AWAY FROM THE DOOR HOLDING HIS HAND TO HIS EAR.
SO JOEY TAPS ON THE GLASS AGAIN, NOW THE PERP TURNS REAL SHARP AND BARKS: "DO YOU SEE I'M ON THE...."
AND NOW HE SEES WHAT'S WHAT.
SO FUCKING FUNNY.
GOOD ONE.
YEAH...
THE GUY SHAT HIMSELF I SWEAR TOO ...PRICELESS.
SO THE GUY HE - HE GOES FOR IT.
YEAH.
NO...
SO...
SO, HE'S RIDDLED IN A SECOND. DOWN FOR THE COUNT. IT'S OVER. POPPED.
THAT'S THE WAY IT WENT DOWN.
JEEZ...
BUT THE PHONE- BUT THE PHONE IS STILL DANGLING OFF THE HOOK.
STILL IN ONE PIECE.
WHOEVER WAS ON THE OTHER LINE, THEY HEARD THE WHOLE THING. CAN YOU IMAGINE?
SO- SO DAVE HE- HE PICKS UP THE PHONE AND HE SAYS INTO THE RECEIVER:
NO--
"I'M SORRY, YOUR FRIEND HERE HAS BEEN DISCONNECTED.
NO--
AND WE- WE COULDN'T HELP IT--
WE ALL BURST OUT LAUGHING AT THIS CRAZY FUCKING THING HE JUST SAID.
HE SAID THAT? THAT'S...
YEAH, THING OF IT IS THOUGH... THE PERSON ON THE OTHER END WAS THE GUY'S MOM.
OY--
CAN YOU IMAGINE?
SO - SO THAT'S WHAT HAPPENED TO MY OLD PARTNER.
I THINK HE'S WORKING AT BORDERS NOW- SOMEONE TOLD ME.

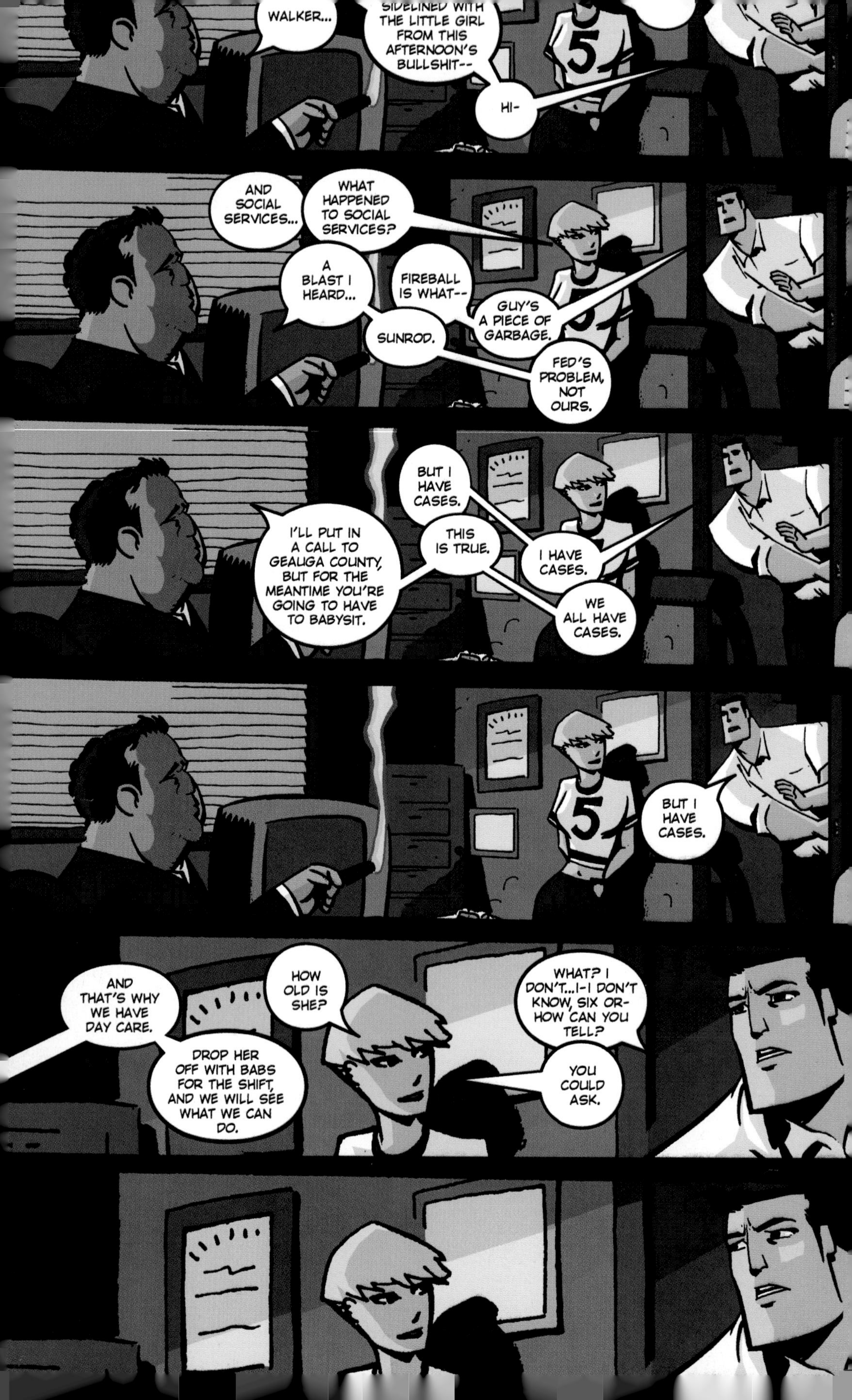
WALKER...
SIDELINED WITH THE LITTLE GIRL FROM THIS AFTERNOON'S BULLSHIT--
HI-
AND SOCIAL SERVICES...
WHAT HAPPENED TO SOCIAL SERVICES?
A BLAST I HEARD...
FIREBALL IS WHAT--
SUNROD.
GUY'S A PIECE OF GARBAGE.
FED'S PROBLEM, NOT OURS.
I'LL PUT IN A CALL TO GEAUGA COUNTY, BUT FOR THE MEANTIME YOU'RE GOING TO HAVE TO BABYSIT.
BUT I HAVE CASES.
THIS IS TRUE.
I HAVE CASES.
WE ALL HAVE CASES.
BUT I HAVE CASES.
AND THAT'S WHY WE HAVE DAY CARE.
DROP HER OFF WITH BABS FOR THE SHIFT, AND WE WILL SEE WHAT WE CAN DO.
HOW OLD IS SHE?
WHAT? I DON'T...I-I DON'T KNOW, SIX OR- HOW CAN YOU TELL?
YOU COULD ASK.

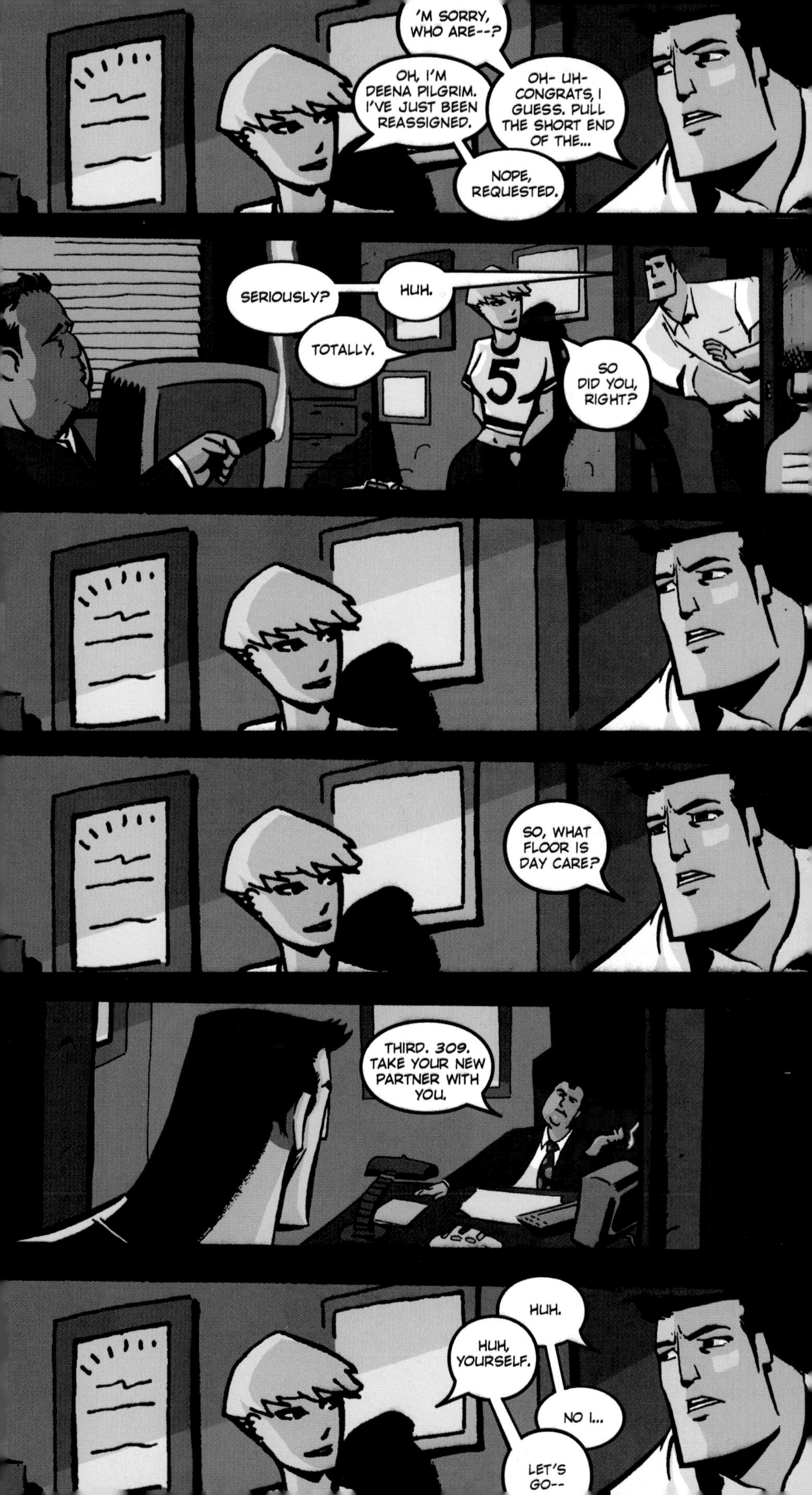
'M SORRY, WHO ARE--?
OH, I'M DEENA PILGRIM. I'VE JUST BEEN REASSIGNED.
OH- UH- CONGRATS, I GUESS. PULL THE SHORT END OF THE...
NOPE, REQUESTED.
HUH.
SERIOUSLY?
TOTALLY.
SO DID YOU, RIGHT?
SO, WHAT FLOOR IS DAY CARE?
THIRD. 309. TAKE YOUR NEW PARTNER WITH YOU.
HUH.
HUH, YOURSELF.
NO I...
LET'S GO--

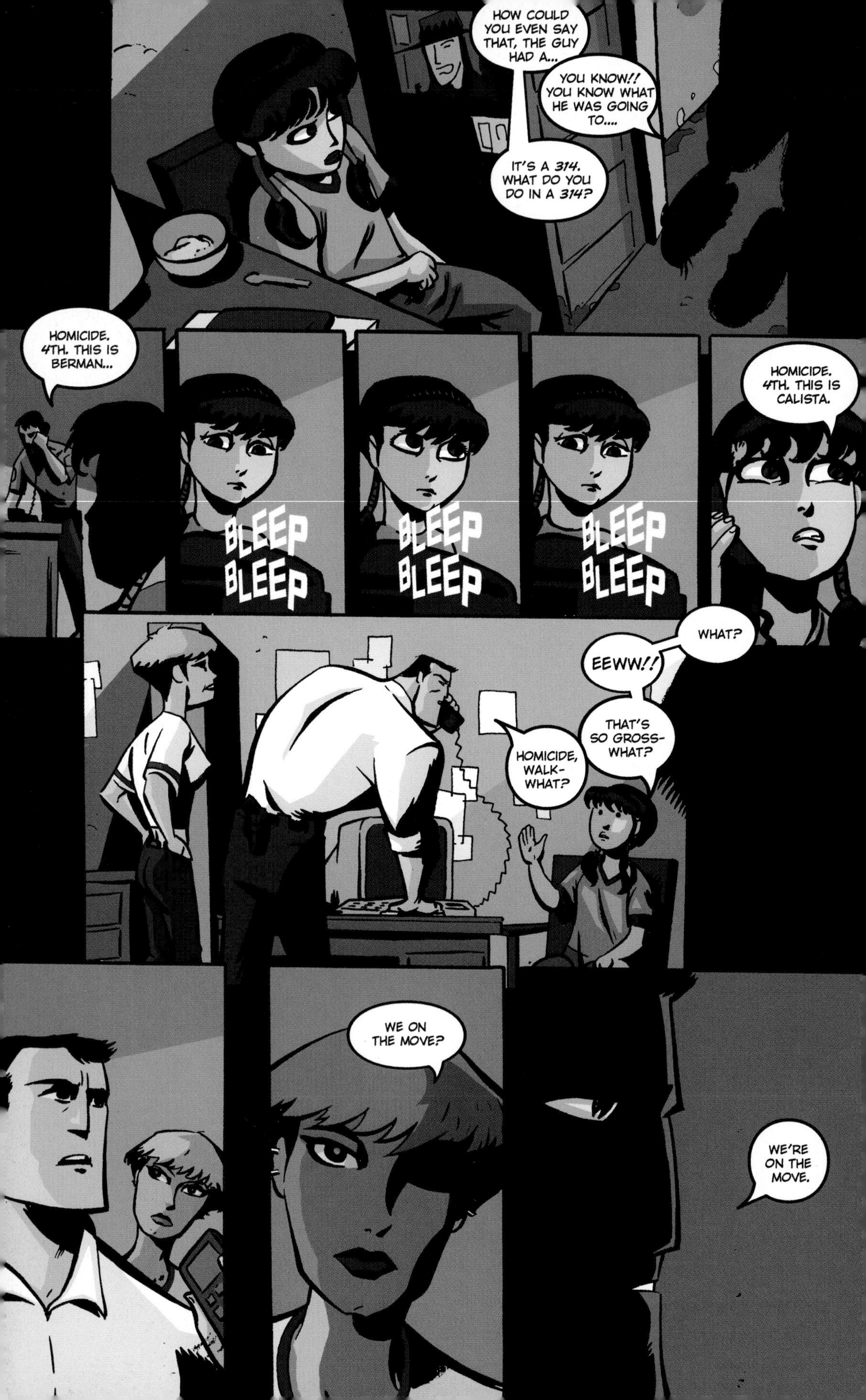
HOW COULD YOU EVEN SAY THAT, THE GUY HAD A...
YOU KNOW!! YOU KNOW WHAT HE WAS GOING TO....
IT'S A 314. WHAT DO YOU DO IN A 314?
HOMICIDE. 4TH. THIS IS BERMAN...
BLEEP BLEEP
BLEEP BLEEP
BLEEP BLEEP
HOMICIDE. 4TH. THIS IS CALISTA.
WHAT?
EEWW!!
THAT'S SO GROSS-WHAT?
HOMICIDE, WALK-WHAT?
WE ON THE MOVE?
WE'RE ON THE MOVE.

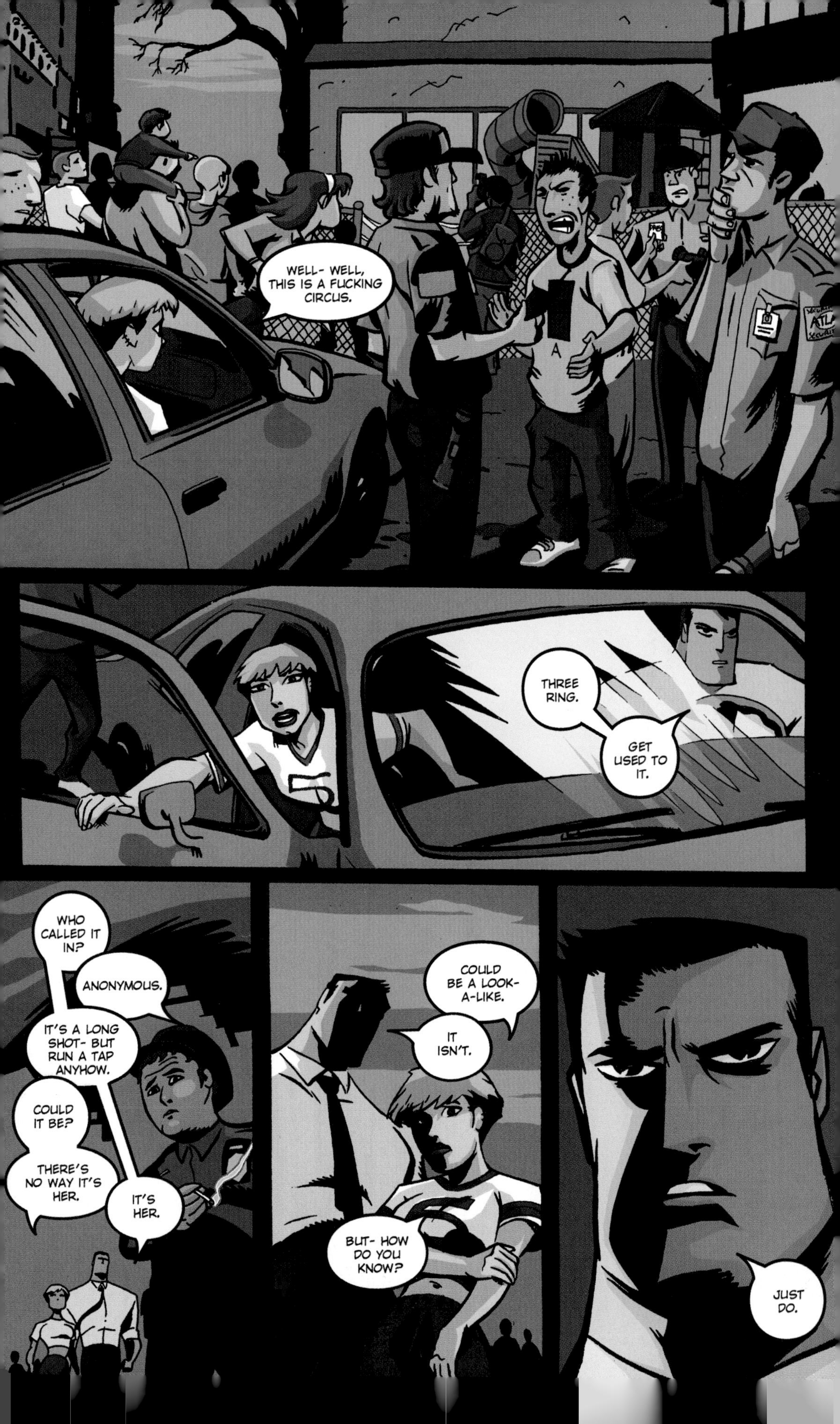
WELL- WELL, THIS IS A FUCKING CIRCUS.
THREE RING.
GET USED TO IT.
WHO CALLED IT IN?
ANONYMOUS.
IT'S A LONG SHOT- BUT RUN A TAP ANYHOW.
COULD IT BE?
THERE'S NO WAY IT'S HER.
IT'S HER.
COULD BE A LOOK-A-LIKE.
IT ISN'T.
BUT- HOW DO YOU KNOW?
JUST DO.

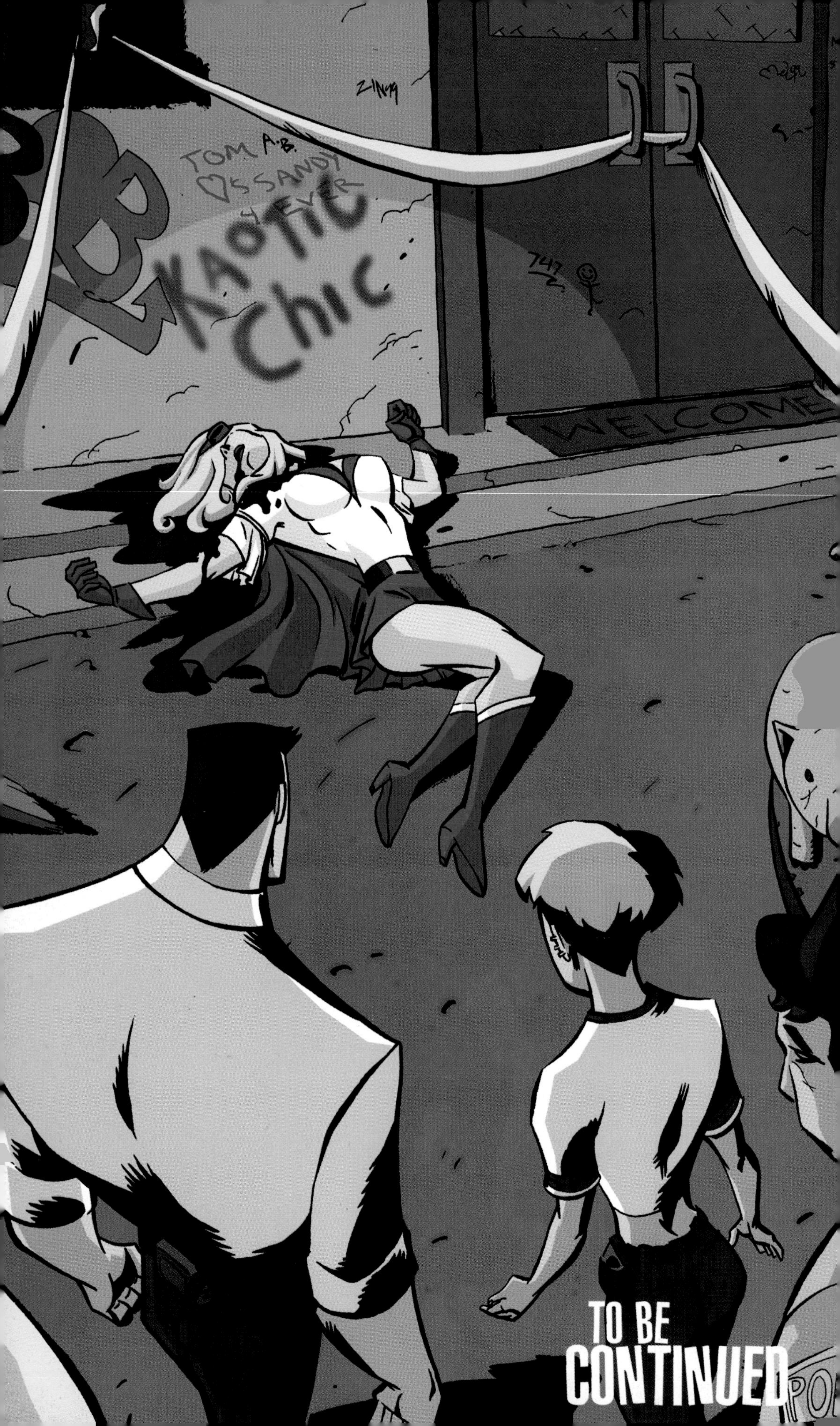
TOM A.B.
♥S SANDY 4 EVER
KAOTIC CHIC
747
WELCOME
TO BE CONTINUED

A PAIR OF RED LEATHER BOOTS. SIZE FOUR.

ITEM 476-99.

WHAT IS THIS? I GUESS IT'S HER CAPE.

ITEM 476-003.

IT'S HER CAPE.

HAD TO REMOVE THESE WITH A HACK SAW AND A BLOW TORCH.

HAD TO GET THEM OFF.

TWO STEEL ARM BANDS.

ITEM 476-000

A BLOW TORCH?

HER TUNIC...

OR COSTUME OR WHATEVER--

SIGH...

THAT'S SO- SO SAD.

ITEM NUMBER 476-006

YEAH--

CAN YOU TELL US HOW YOU'RE FEELING?

SNIFF
I FEEL BA

SHE- SH
WAS SO BEAUTIFUL

AS YOU CAN IMAGINE, DAVID, THE MOOD AT MORRISON ELEMENTARY IS GRIM INDEED.

IT IS HERE AND AT SCHOOLS ALL OVER THE WORLD THAT THIS TERRIBLE LOSS IS BEING FELT THE MOST.

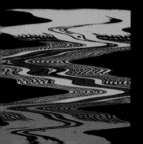

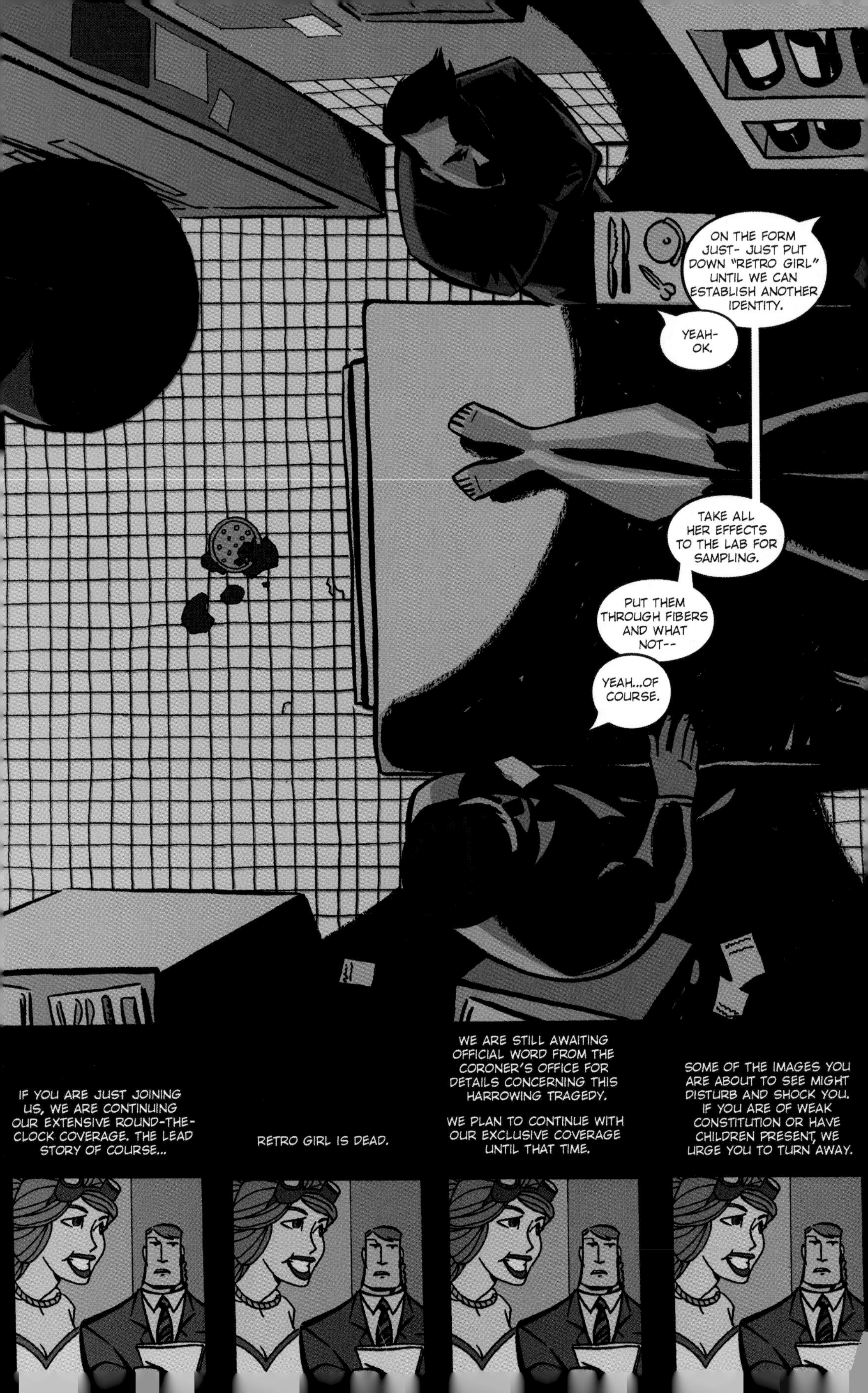
ON THE FORM JUST- JUST PUT DOWN "RETRO GIRL" UNTIL WE CAN ESTABLISH ANOTHER IDENTITY.
YEAH- OK.
TAKE ALL HER EFFECTS TO THE LAB FOR SAMPLING.
PUT THEM THROUGH FIBERS AND WHAT NOT--
YEAH...OF COURSE.
IF YOU ARE JUST JOINING US, WE ARE CONTINUING OUR EXTENSIVE ROUND-THE-CLOCK COVERAGE. THE LEAD STORY OF COURSE...
RETRO GIRL IS DEAD.
WE ARE STILL AWAITING OFFICIAL WORD FROM THE CORONER'S OFFICE FOR DETAILS CONCERNING THIS HARROWING TRAGEDY.
WE PLAN TO CONTINUE WITH OUR EXCLUSIVE COVERAGE UNTIL THAT TIME.
SOME OF THE IMAGES YOU ARE ABOUT TO SEE MIGHT DISTURB AND SHOCK YOU. IF YOU ARE OF WEAK CONSTITUTION OR HAVE CHILDREN PRESENT, WE URGE YOU TO TURN AWAY.

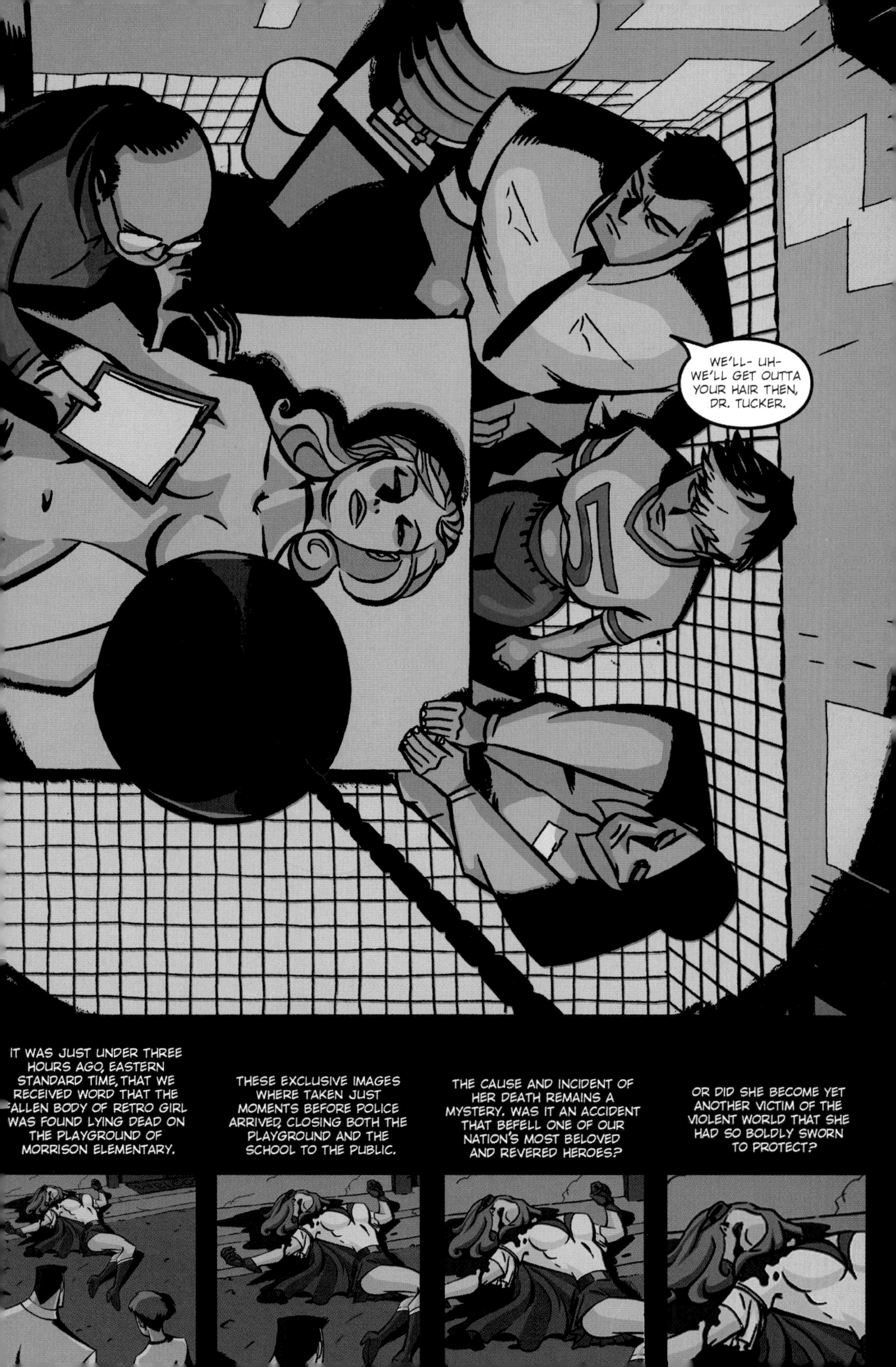
WE'LL- UH- WE'LL GET OUTTA YOUR HAIR THEN, DR. TUCKER.
IT WAS JUST UNDER THREE HOURS AGO, EASTERN STANDARD TIME, THAT WE RECEIVED WORD THAT THE ALLEN BODY OF RETRO GIRL WAS FOUND LYING DEAD ON THE PLAYGROUND OF MORRISON ELEMENTARY.
THESE EXCLUSIVE IMAGES WHERE TAKEN JUST MOMENTS BEFORE POLICE ARRIVED, CLOSING BOTH THE PLAYGROUND AND THE SCHOOL TO THE PUBLIC.
THE CAUSE AND INCIDENT OF HER DEATH REMAINS A MYSTERY. WAS IT AN ACCIDENT THAT BEFELL ONE OF OUR NATION'S MOST BELOVED AND REVERED HEROES?
OR DID SHE BECOME YET ANOTHER VICTIM OF THE VIOLENT WORLD THAT SHE HAD SO BOLDLY SWORN TO PROTECT?

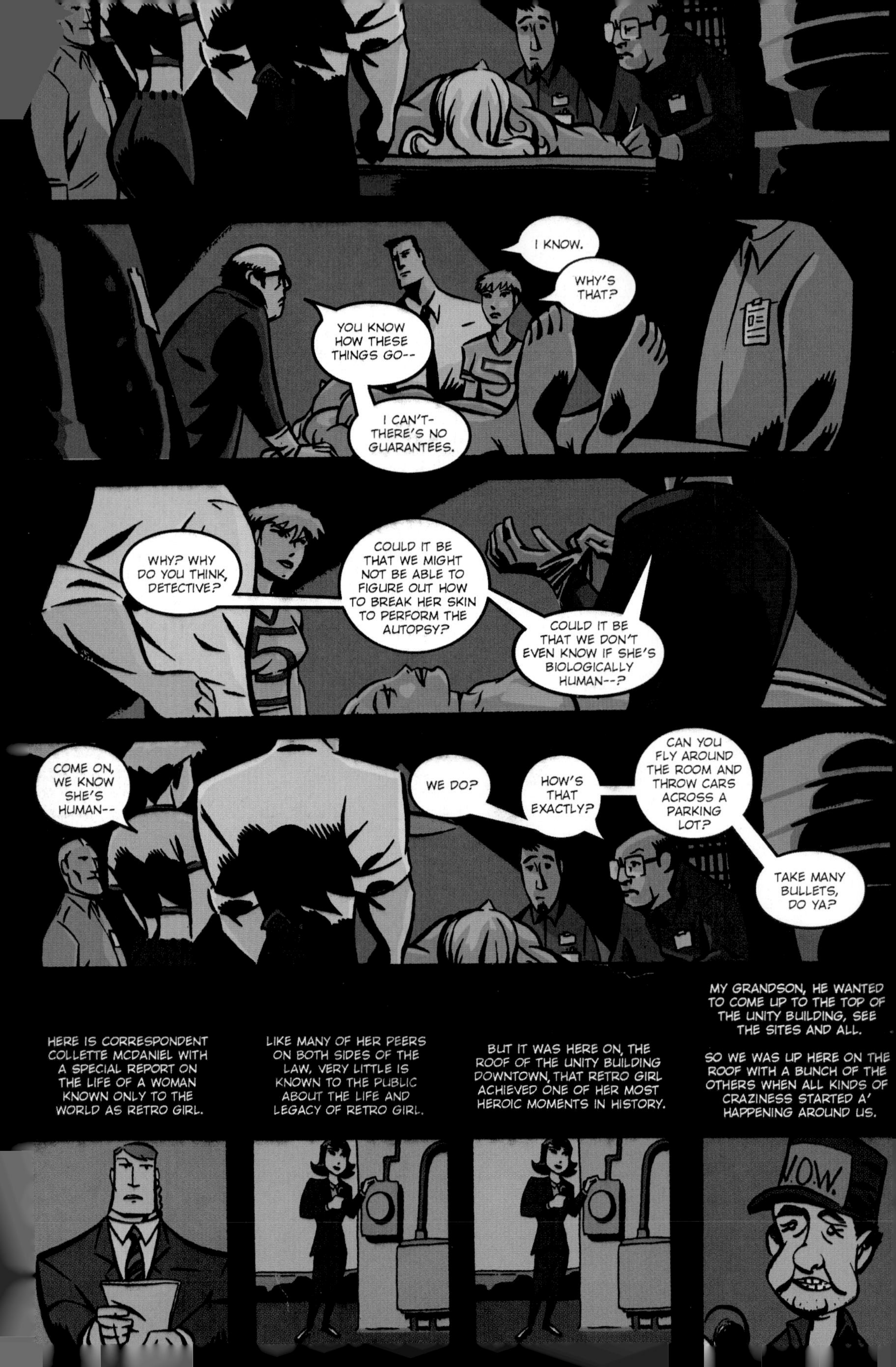

I KNOW.
WHY'S THAT?
YOU KNOW HOW THESE THINGS GO--
I CAN'T- THERE'S NO GUARANTEES.
WHY? WHY DO YOU THINK, DETECTIVE?
COULD IT BE THAT WE MIGHT NOT BE ABLE TO FIGURE OUT HOW TO BREAK HER SKIN TO PERFORM THE AUTOPSY?
COULD IT BE THAT WE DON'T EVEN KNOW IF SHE'S BIOLOGICALLY HUMAN--?
COME ON, WE KNOW SHE'S HUMAN--
WE DO?
HOW'S THAT EXACTLY?
CAN YOU FLY AROUND THE ROOM AND THROW CARS ACROSS A PARKING LOT?
TAKE MANY BULLETS, DO YA?
HERE IS CORRESPONDENT COLLETTE MCDANIEL WITH A SPECIAL REPORT ON THE LIFE OF A WOMAN KNOWN ONLY TO THE WORLD AS RETRO GIRL.
LIKE MANY OF HER PEERS ON BOTH SIDES OF THE LAW, VERY LITTLE IS KNOWN TO THE PUBLIC ABOUT THE LIFE AND LEGACY OF RETRO GIRL.
BUT IT WAS HERE ON, THE ROOF OF THE UNITY BUILDING DOWNTOWN, THAT RETRO GIRL ACHIEVED ONE OF HER MOST HEROIC MOMENTS IN HISTORY.
MY GRANDSON, HE WANTED TO COME UP TO THE TOP OF THE UNITY BUILDING, SEE THE SITES AND ALL.
SO WE WAS UP HERE ON THE ROOF WITH A BUNCH OF THE OTHERS WHEN ALL KINDS OF CRAZINESS STARTED A' HAPPENING AROUND US.
V.O.W.

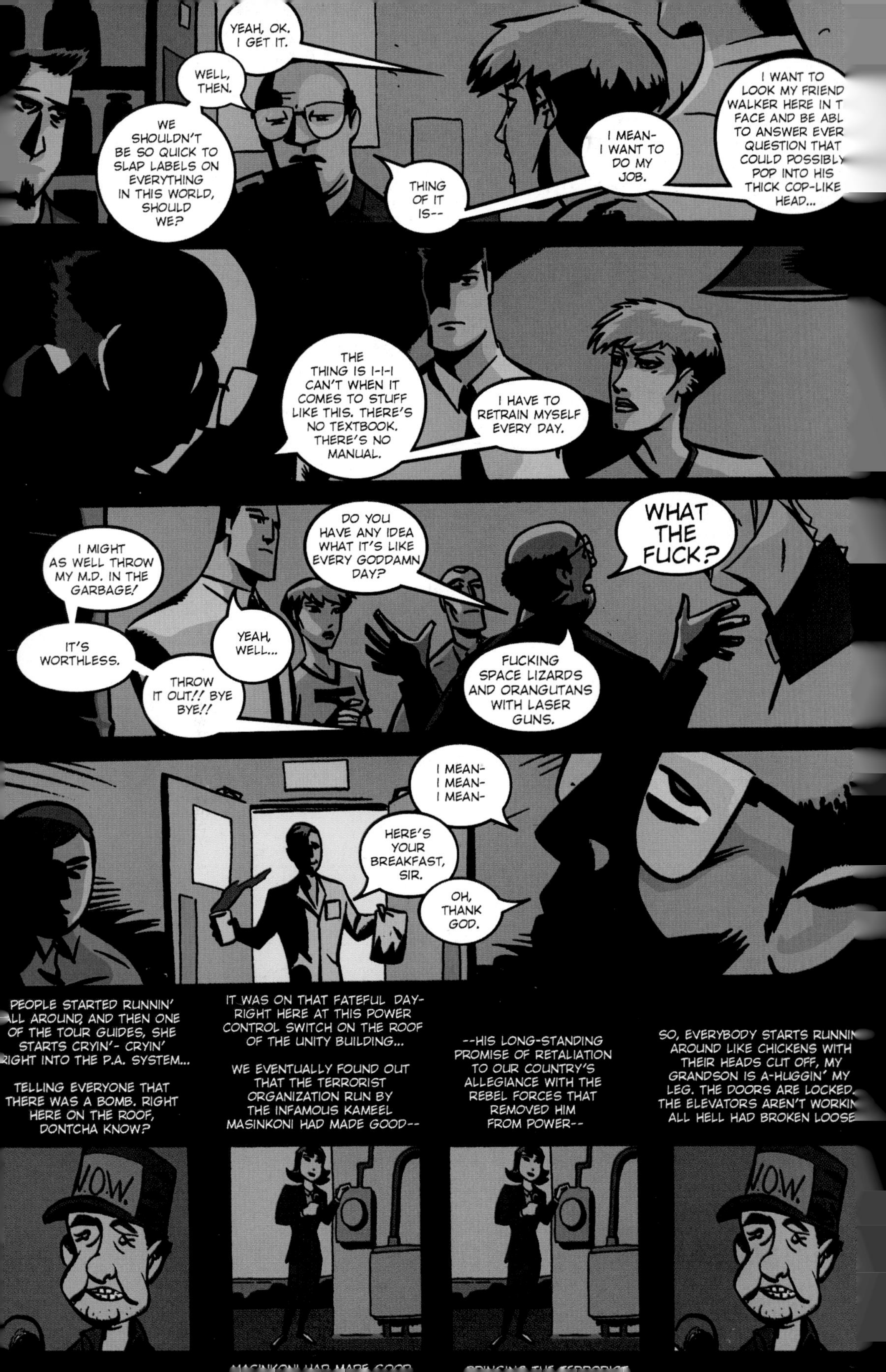
WE SHOULDN'T BE SO QUICK TO SLAP LABELS ON EVERYTHING IN THIS WORLD, SHOULD WE?
WELL, THEN.
YEAH, OK. I GET IT.
THING OF IT IS--
I MEAN- I WANT TO DO MY JOB.
I WANT TO LOOK MY FRIEND WALKER HERE IN T FACE AND BE ABL TO ANSWER EVER QUESTION THAT COULD POSSIBLY POP INTO HIS THICK COP-LIKE HEAD...
THE THING IS I-I-I CAN'T WHEN IT COMES TO STUFF LIKE THIS. THERE'S NO TEXTBOOK. THERE'S NO MANUAL.
I HAVE TO RETRAIN MYSELF EVERY DAY.
I MIGHT AS WELL THROW MY M.D. IN THE GARBAGE!
IT'S WORTHLESS.
YEAH, WELL...
THROW IT OUT!! BYE BYE!!
DO YOU HAVE ANY IDEA WHAT IT'S LIKE EVERY GODDAMN DAY?
WHAT THE FUCK?
FUCKING SPACE LIZARDS AND ORANGUTANS WITH LASER GUNS.
I MEAN- I MEAN- I MEAN-
HERE'S YOUR BREAKFAST, SIR.
OH, THANK GOD.
PEOPLE STARTED RUNNIN' ALL AROUND, AND THEN ONE OF THE TOUR GUIDES, SHE STARTS CRYIN'- CRYIN' RIGHT INTO THE P.A. SYSTEM...
TELLING EVERYONE THAT THERE WAS A BOMB. RIGHT HERE ON THE ROOF, DONTCHA KNOW?
IT WAS ON THAT FATEFUL DAY- RIGHT HERE AT THIS POWER CONTROL SWITCH ON THE ROOF OF THE UNITY BUILDING...
WE EVENTUALLY FOUND OUT THAT THE TERRORIST ORGANIZATION RUN BY THE INFAMOUS KAMEEL MASINKONI HAD MADE GOOD--
--HIS LONG-STANDING PROMISE OF RETALIATION TO OUR COUNTRY'S ALLEGIANCE WITH THE REBEL FORCES THAT REMOVED HIM FROM POWER--
SO, EVERYBODY STARTS RUNNIN AROUND LIKE CHICKENS WITH THEIR HEADS CUT OFF, MY GRANDSON IS A-HUGGIN' MY LEG. THE DOORS ARE LOCKED. THE ELEVATORS AREN'T WORKIN ALL HELL HAD BROKEN LOOSE
N.O.W.
N.O.W.

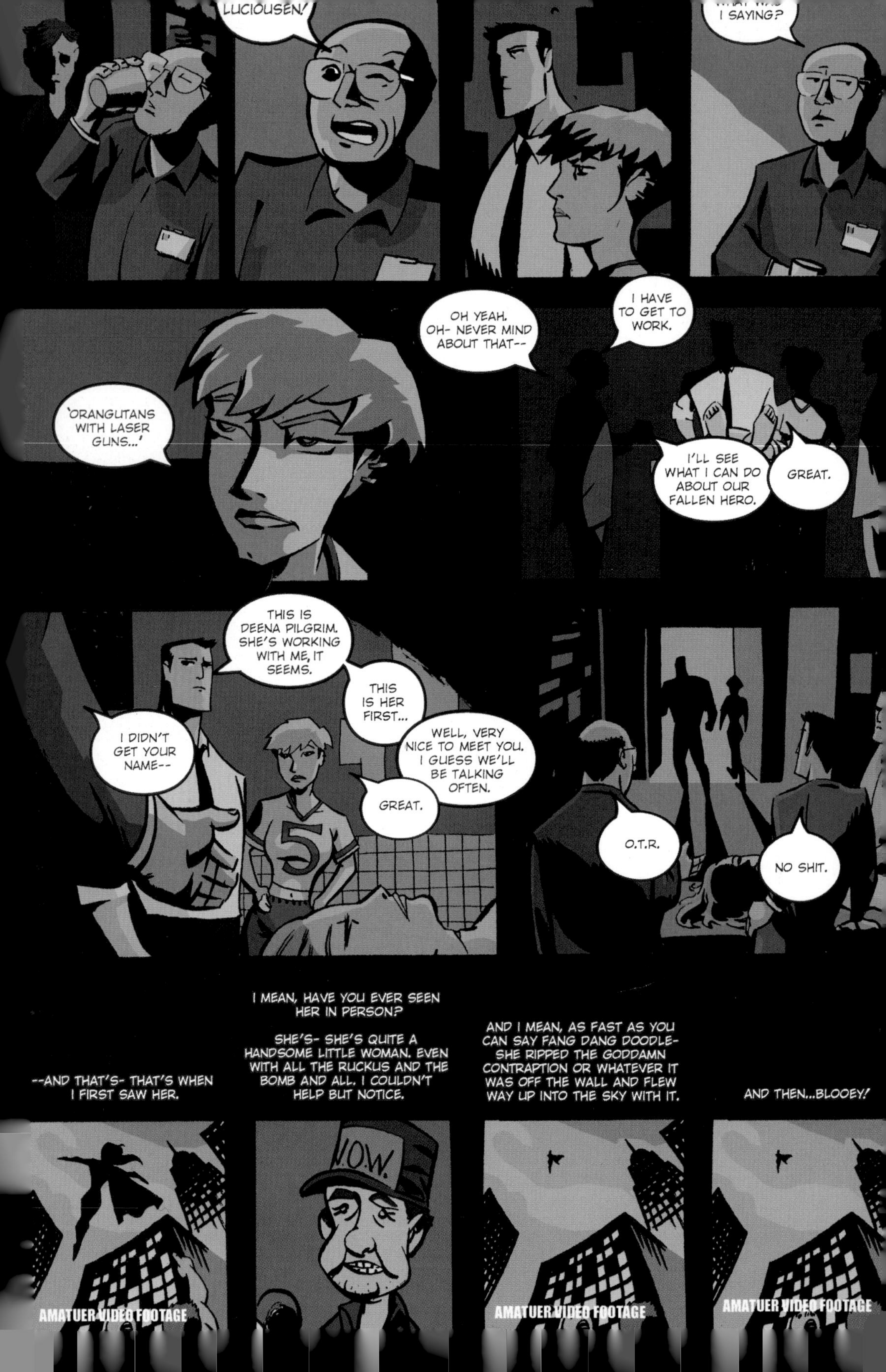
LUCIOUSEN!
I SAYING?
'ORANGUTANS WITH LASER GUNS...'
OH YEAH. OH- NEVER MIND ABOUT THAT--
I HAVE TO GET TO WORK.
I'LL SEE WHAT I CAN DO ABOUT OUR FALLEN HERO.
GREAT.
THIS IS DEENA PILGRIM. SHE'S WORKING WITH ME, IT SEEMS.
THIS IS HER FIRST...
I DIDN'T GET YOUR NAME--
WELL, VERY NICE TO MEET YOU. I GUESS WE'LL BE TALKING OFTEN.
GREAT.
O.T.R.
NO SHIT.
--AND THAT'S- THAT'S WHEN I FIRST SAW HER.
I MEAN, HAVE YOU EVER SEEN HER IN PERSON?
SHE'S- SHE'S QUITE A HANDSOME LITTLE WOMAN. EVEN WITH ALL THE RUCKUS AND THE BOMB AND ALL. I COULDN'T HELP BUT NOTICE.
AND I MEAN, AS FAST AS YOU CAN SAY FANG DANG DOODLE- SHE RIPPED THE GODDAMN CONTRAPTION OR WHATEVER IT WAS OFF THE WALL AND FLEW WAY UP INTO THE SKY WITH IT.
AND THEN...BLOOEY!
AMATUER VIDEO FOOTAGE
V.O.W.
AMATUER VIDEO FOOTAGE
AMATUER VIDEO FOOTAGE

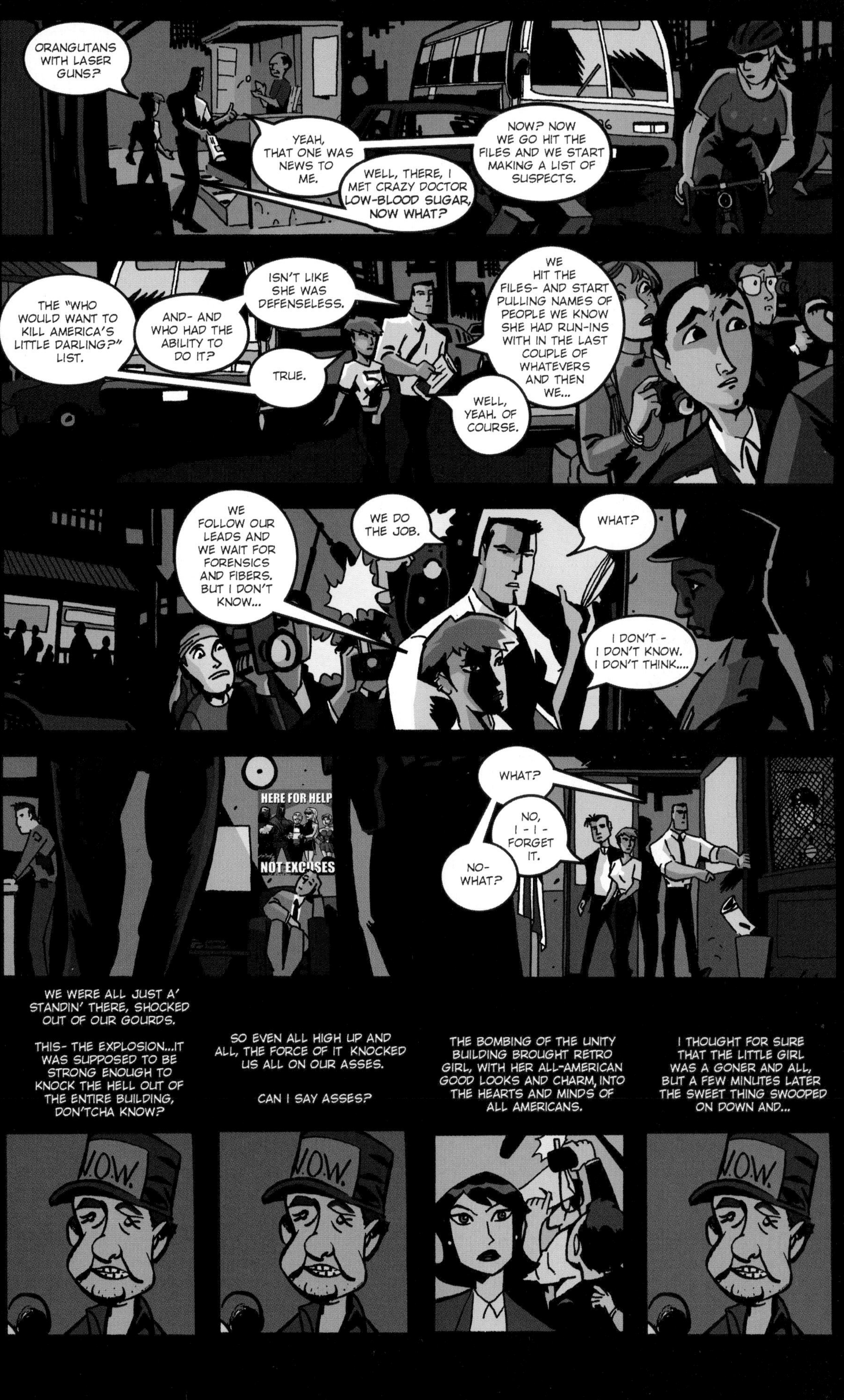
ORANGUTANS WITH LASER GUNS?
YEAH, THAT ONE WAS NEWS TO ME.
WELL, THERE, I MET CRAZY DOCTOR LOW-BLOOD SUGAR, NOW WHAT?
NOW? NOW WE GO HIT THE FILES AND WE START MAKING A LIST OF SUSPECTS.
THE "WHO WOULD WANT TO KILL AMERICA'S LITTLE DARLING?" LIST.
AND- AND WHO HAD THE ABILITY TO DO IT?
ISN'T LIKE SHE WAS DEFENSELESS.
TRUE.
WE HIT THE FILES- AND START PULLING NAMES OF PEOPLE WE KNOW SHE HAD RUN-INS WITH IN THE LAST COUPLE OF WHATEVERS AND THEN WE...
WELL, YEAH. OF COURSE.
WE FOLLOW OUR LEADS AND WE WAIT FOR FORENSICS AND FIBERS. BUT I DON'T KNOW...
WE DO THE JOB.
WHAT?
I DON'T - I DON'T KNOW. I DON'T THINK....
HERE FOR HELP
NOT EXCUSES
WHAT?
NO, I - I - FORGET IT.
NO- WHAT?
WE WERE ALL JUST A' STANDIN' THERE, SHOCKED OUT OF OUR GOURDS.
THIS- THE EXPLOSION...IT WAS SUPPOSED TO BE STRONG ENOUGH TO KNOCK THE HELL OUT OF THE ENTIRE BUILDING, DON'TCHA KNOW?
SO EVEN ALL HIGH UP AND ALL, THE FORCE OF IT KNOCKED US ALL ON OUR ASSES.
CAN I SAY ASSES?
THE BOMBING OF THE UNITY BUILDING BROUGHT RETRO GIRL, WITH HER ALL-AMERICAN GOOD LOOKS AND CHARM, INTO THE HEARTS AND MINDS OF ALL AMERICANS.
I THOUGHT FOR SURE THAT THE LITTLE GIRL WAS A GONER AND ALL, BUT A FEW MINUTES LATER THE SWEET THING SWOOPED ON DOWN AND...
V.O.W.
V.O.W.
V.O.W.

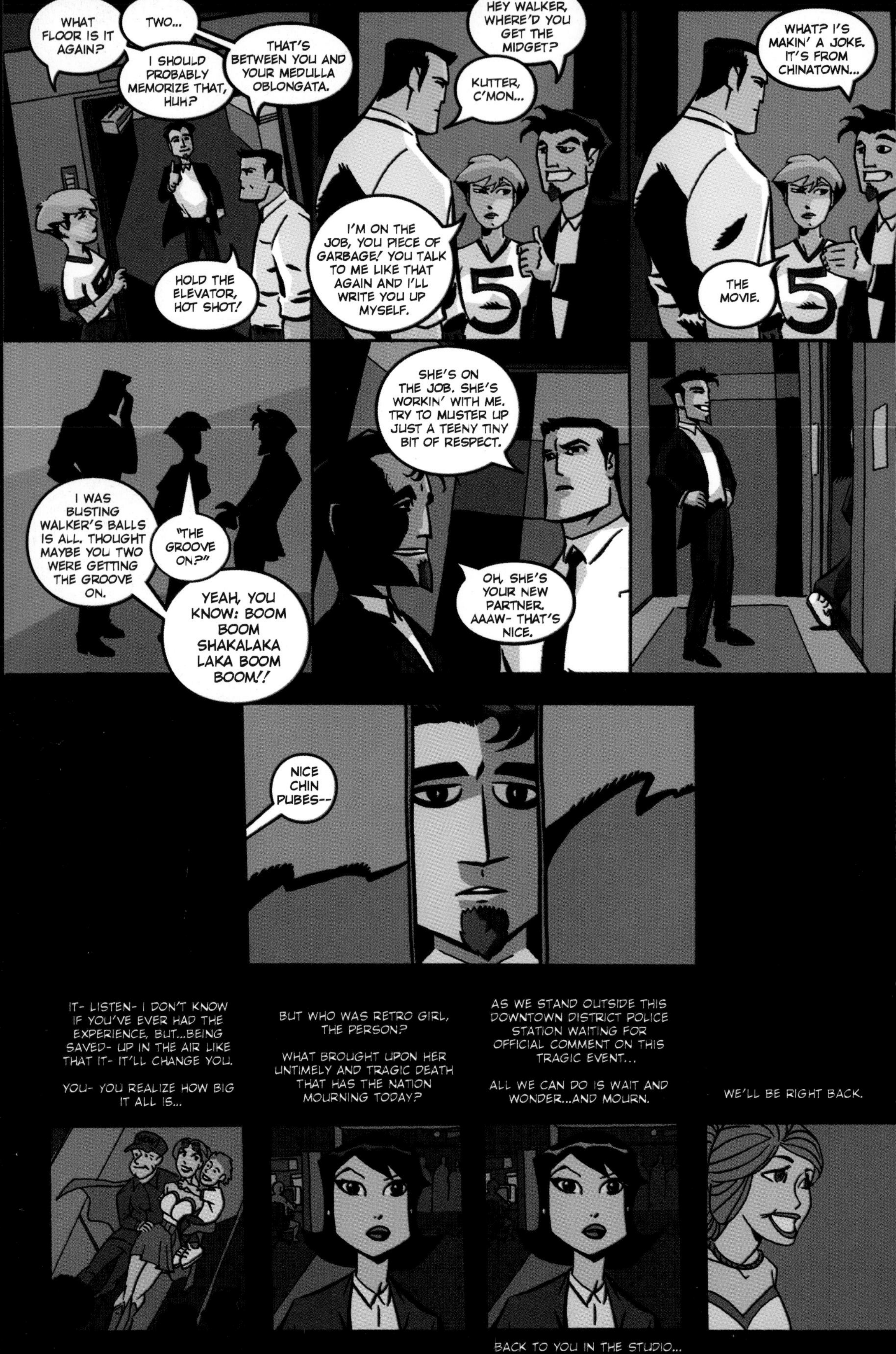
WHAT FLOOR IS IT AGAIN?
TWO...
I SHOULD PROBABLY MEMORIZE THAT, HUH?
THAT'S BETWEEN YOU AND YOUR MEDULLA OBLONGATA.
HOLD THE ELEVATOR, HOT SHOT!
HEY WALKER, WHERE'D YOU GET THE MIDGET?
KUTTER, C'MON...
I'M ON THE JOB, YOU PIECE OF GARBAGE! YOU TALK TO ME LIKE THAT AGAIN AND I'LL WRITE YOU UP MYSELF.
WHAT? I'S MAKIN' A JOKE. IT'S FROM CHINATOWN...
THE MOVIE.
I WAS BUSTING WALKER'S BALLS IS ALL. THOUGHT MAYBE YOU TWO WERE GETTING THE GROOVE ON.
"THE GROOVE ON?"
YEAH, YOU KNOW: BOOM BOOM SHAKALAKA LAKA BOOM BOOM!!
SHE'S ON THE JOB. SHE'S WORKIN' WITH ME. TRY TO MUSTER UP JUST A TEENY TINY BIT OF RESPECT.
OH, SHE'S YOUR NEW PARTNER. AAAW- THAT'S NICE.
NICE CHIN PUBES--
IT- LISTEN- I DON'T KNOW IF YOU'VE EVER HAD THE EXPERIENCE, BUT...BEING SAVED- UP IN THE AIR LIKE THAT IT- IT'LL CHANGE YOU.
YOU- YOU REALIZE HOW BIG IT ALL IS...
BUT WHO WAS RETRO GIRL, THE PERSON?
WHAT BROUGHT UPON HER UNTIMELY AND TRAGIC DEATH THAT HAS THE NATION MOURNING TODAY?
AS WE STAND OUTSIDE THIS DOWNTOWN DISTRICT POLICE STATION WAITING FOR OFFICIAL COMMENT ON THIS TRAGIC EVENT...
ALL WE CAN DO IS WAIT AND WONDER...AND MOURN.
BACK TO YOU IN THE STUDIO...
WE'LL BE RIGHT BACK.

WELL, YOU CAUGHT A DOOZY, DIDN'T YOU?

WHAT AM I SUPPOSED TO DO? NOT PICK UP THE PHONE?

I JUST- I CAME HOME FOR LUNCH.

ABOUT THIS?

MY GIRL- MY EIGHT-YEAR-OLD WAS CRYING HER EYES OUT...

I HAD TO SPEND MY LUNCH HAVING "THE TALK." THE LIFE-AND-DEATH TALK...

LISTEN, KEEP YOUR NOSE OUT OF THE PRESS UNTIL THE CASE IS DOWN.

IF YOU NEED SOMETHING, ASK FOR IT.

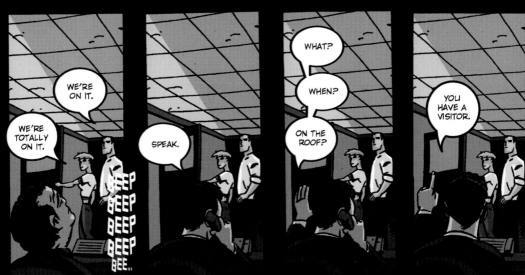

WE'RE ON IT.

WE'RE TOTALLY ON IT.

BEEP BEEP BEEP BEEP BEE...

SPEAK.

WHAT?

WHEN?

ON THE ROOF?

YOU HAVE A VISITOR.

IF YOU'RE JUST JOINING US, WE ARE CONTINUING OUR ROUND-THE-CLOCK COVERAGE OF THIS TRUE AMERICAN TRAGEDY.

THE YOUNG PIXIE KNOWN ONLY TO HER PUBLIC AS RETRO GIRL HAS BEEN FOUND DEAD ON THE PLAYGROUND OF MORRISON ELEMENTARY.

THE CAUSE OF HER DEATH IS STILL UNKNOWN, BUT NUMEROUS REPORTS BELIEVE THAT SHE WAS FOUND WITH A FATAL WOUND TO THE NECK AND THROAT AREA...

WE HAVE COLLEEN MCBRIDE OUTSIDE THE JUSTICE CENTER WAITING FOR OFFICIAL WORD FROM POLICE AND AUTHORITIES.

BUT IN THE MEANWHILE, HERE IS ROGER SANDERS WITH A LOOK BACK AT THE POWERFUL LEGACY OF RETRO GIRL.

LIKE MANY OF THE COLORFUL CHARACTERS THAT SURROUND OUR CITY, REALLY VERY LITTLE IS KNOWN ABOUT RETRO GIRL.

MOST OF WHAT WE KNOW IS WHAT SHE HAS LET US KNOW.

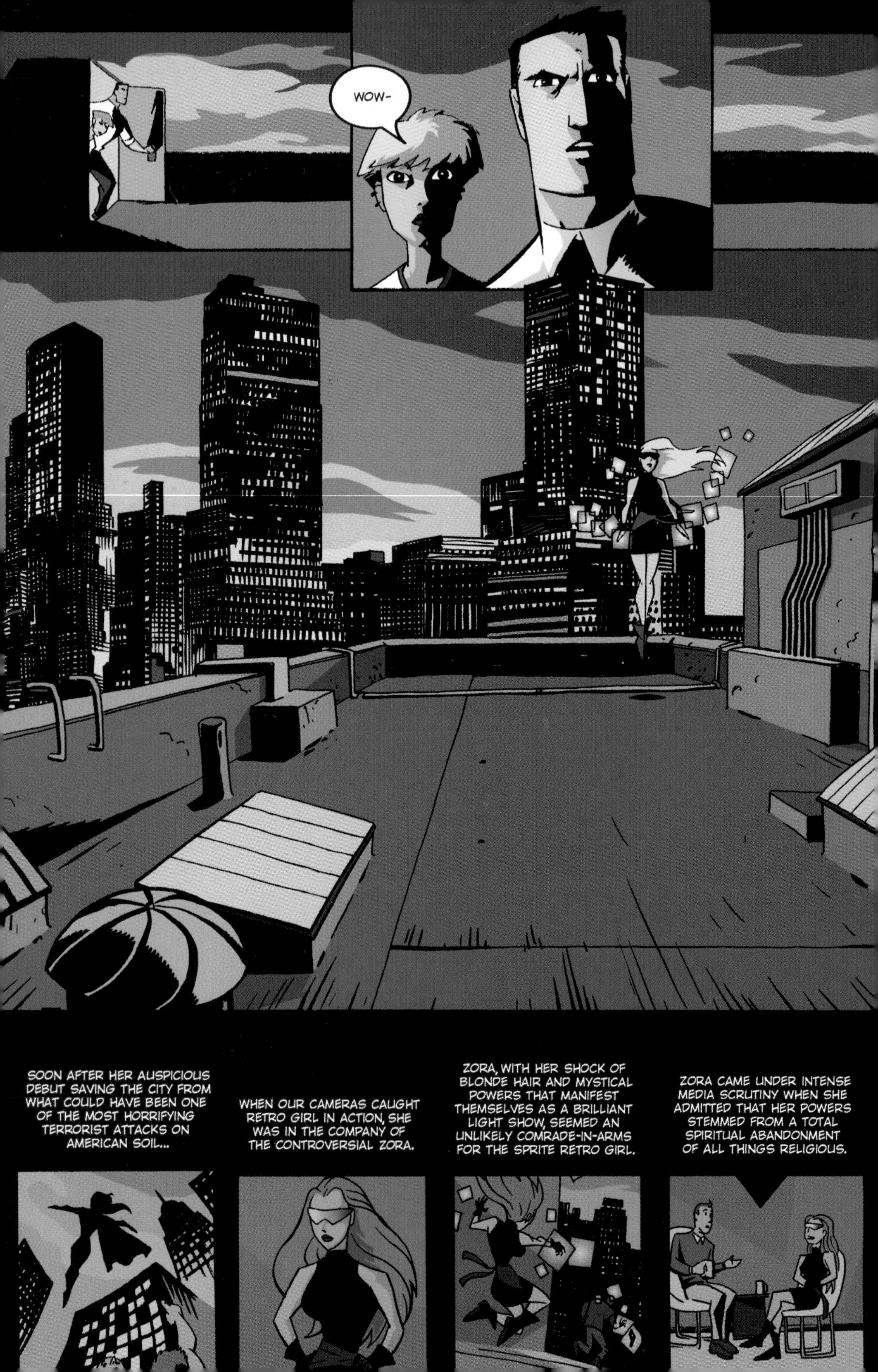
WOW-
SOON AFTER HER AUSPICIOUS DEBUT SAVING THE CITY FROM WHAT COULD HAVE BEEN ONE OF THE MOST HORRIFYING TERRORIST ATTACKS ON AMERICAN SOIL...
WHEN OUR CAMERAS CAUGHT RETRO GIRL IN ACTION, SHE WAS IN THE COMPANY OF THE CONTROVERSIAL ZORA.
ZORA, WITH HER SHOCK OF BLONDE HAIR AND MYSTICAL POWERS THAT MANIFEST THEMSELVES AS A BRILLIANT LIGHT SHOW, SEEMED AN UNLIKELY COMRADE-IN-ARMS FOR THE SPRITE RETRO GIRL.
ZORA CAME UNDER INTENSE MEDIA SCRUTINY WHEN SHE ADMITTED THAT HER POWERS STEMMED FROM A TOTAL SPIRITUAL ABANDONMENT OF ALL THINGS RELIGIOUS.

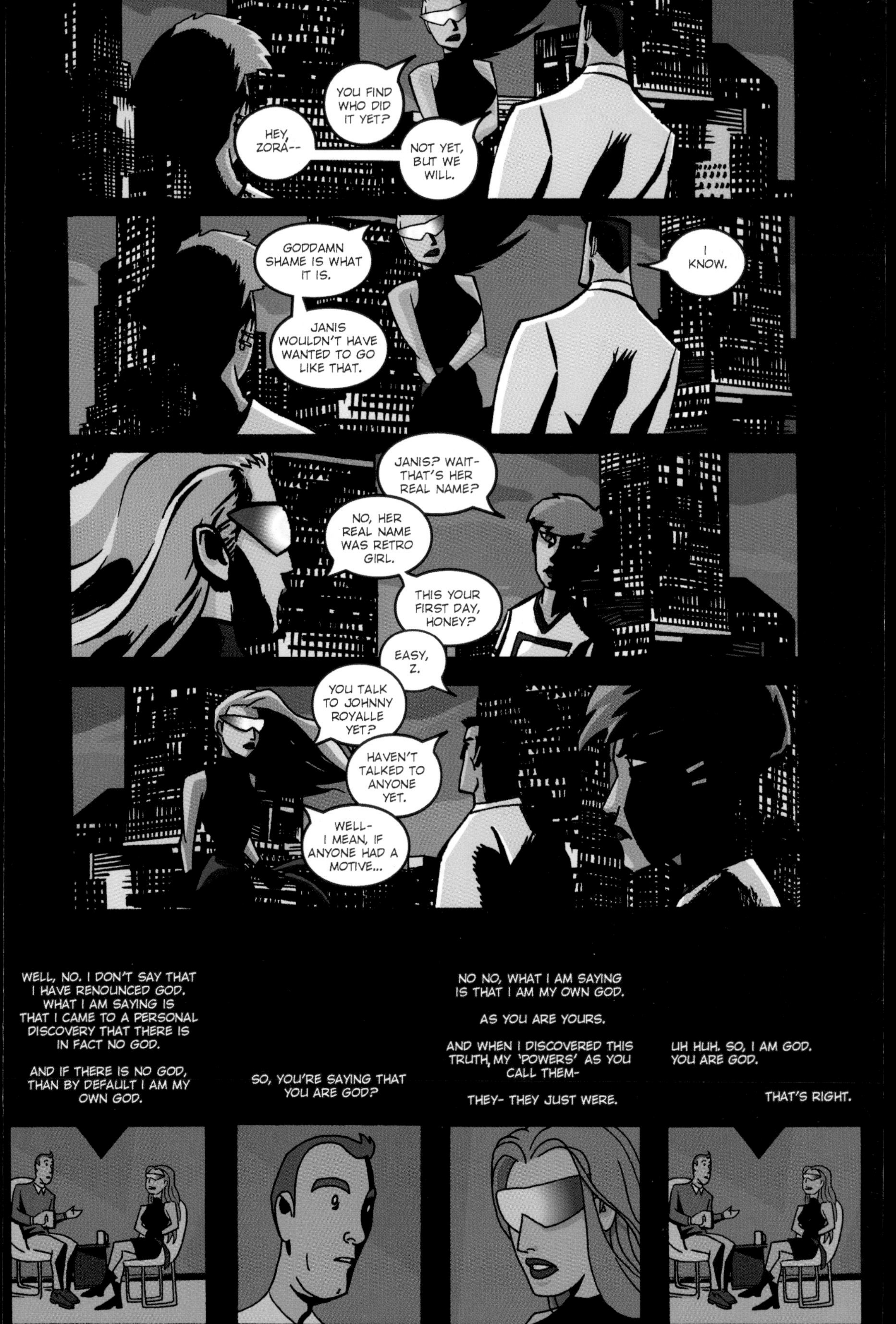
HEY, ZORA--
YOU FIND WHO DID IT YET?
NOT YET, BUT WE WILL.
GODDAMN SHAME IS WHAT IT IS.
JANIS WOULDN'T HAVE WANTED TO GO LIKE THAT.
I KNOW.
JANIS? WAIT- THAT'S HER REAL NAME?
NO, HER REAL NAME WAS RETRO GIRL.
THIS YOUR FIRST DAY, HONEY?
EASY, Z.
YOU TALK TO JOHNNY ROYALLE YET?
HAVEN'T TALKED TO ANYONE YET.
WELL- I MEAN, IF ANYONE HAD A MOTIVE...
WELL, NO. I DON'T SAY THAT I HAVE RENOUNCED GOD. WHAT I AM SAYING IS THAT I CAME TO A PERSONAL DISCOVERY THAT THERE IS IN FACT NO GOD.
AND IF THERE IS NO GOD, THAN BY DEFAULT I AM MY OWN GOD.
SO, YOU'RE SAYING THAT YOU ARE GOD?
NO NO, WHAT I AM SAYING IS THAT I AM MY OWN GOD.
AS YOU ARE YOURS.
AND WHEN I DISCOVERED THIS TRUTH, MY 'POWERS' AS YOU CALL THEM-
THEY- THEY JUST WERE.
UH HUH. SO, I AM GOD. YOU ARE GOD.
THAT'S RIGHT.

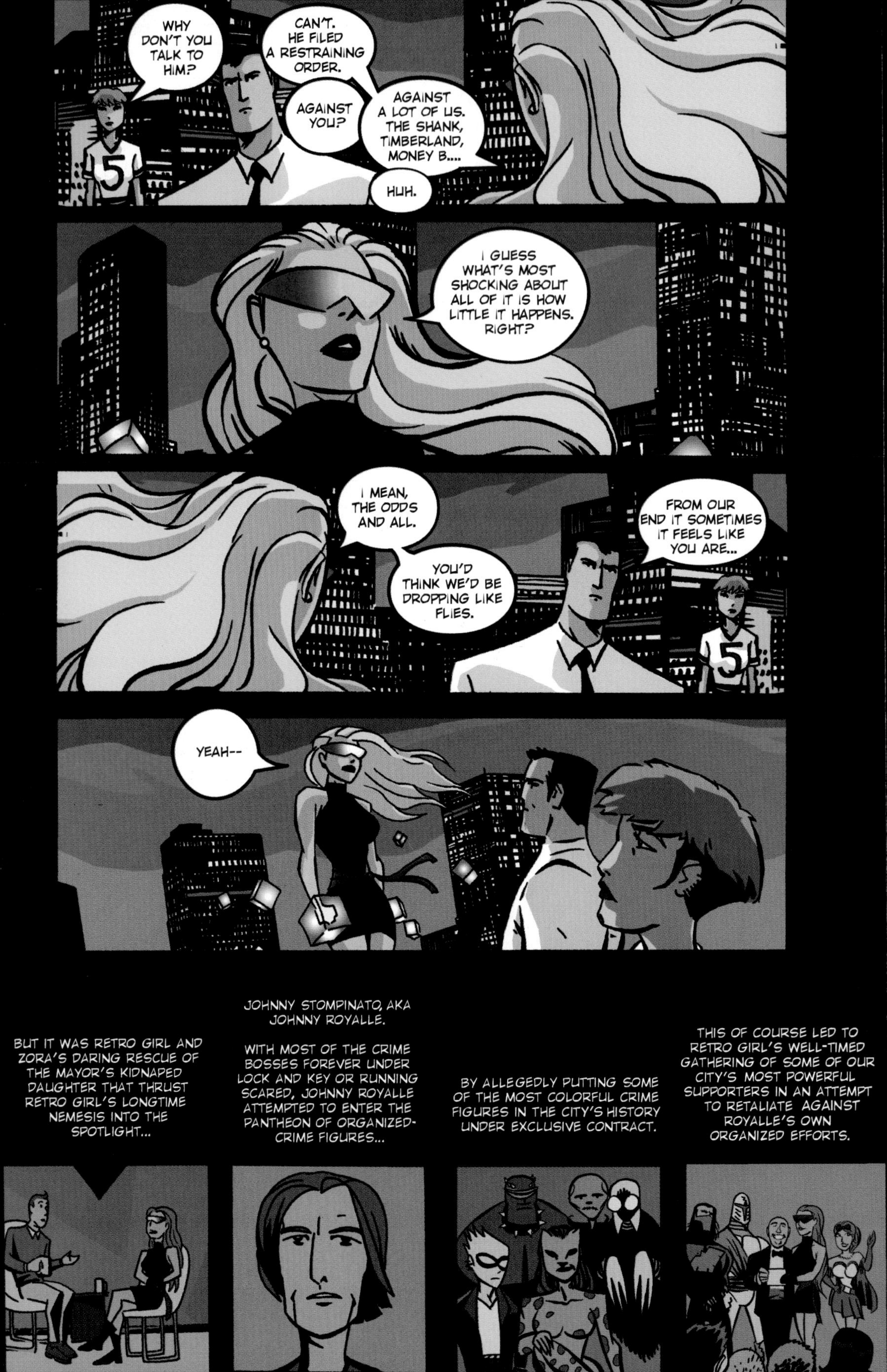
WHY DON'T YOU TALK TO HIM?
CAN'T. HE FILED A RESTRAINING ORDER.
AGAINST YOU?
AGAINST A LOT OF US. THE SHANK, TIMBERLAND, MONEY B....
HUH.
I GUESS WHAT'S MOST SHOCKING ABOUT ALL OF IT IS HOW LITTLE IT HAPPENS. RIGHT?
I MEAN, THE ODDS AND ALL.
YOU'D THINK WE'D BE DROPPING LIKE FLIES.
FROM OUR END IT SOMETIMES IT FEELS LIKE YOU ARE...
YEAH--
BUT IT WAS RETRO GIRL AND ZORA'S DARING RESCUE OF THE MAYOR'S KIDNAPED DAUGHTER THAT THRUST RETRO GIRL'S LONGTIME NEMESIS INTO THE SPOTLIGHT...
JOHNNY STOMPINATO, AKA JOHNNY ROYALLE.
WITH MOST OF THE CRIME BOSSES FOREVER UNDER LOCK AND KEY OR RUNNING SCARED, JOHNNY ROYALLE ATTEMPTED TO ENTER THE PANTHEON OF ORGANIZED-CRIME FIGURES...
BY ALLEGEDLY PUTTING SOME OF THE MOST COLORFUL CRIME FIGURES IN THE CITY'S HISTORY UNDER EXCLUSIVE CONTRACT.
THIS OF COURSE LED TO RETRO GIRL'S WELL-TIMED GATHERING OF SOME OF OUR CITY'S MOST POWERFUL SUPPORTERS IN AN ATTEMPT TO RETALIATE AGAINST ROYALLE'S OWN ORGANIZED EFFORTS.

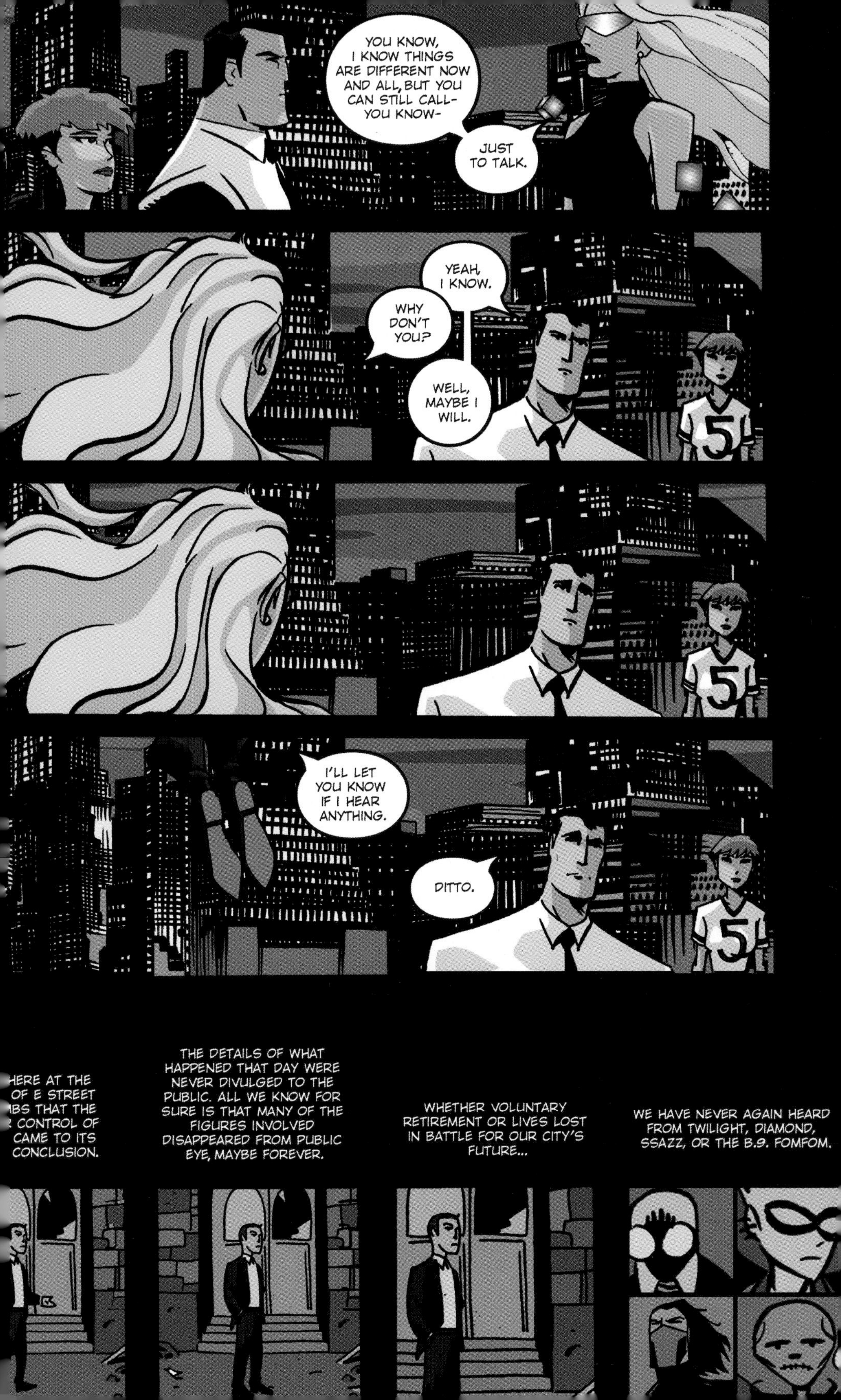

YOU KNOW, I KNOW THINGS ARE DIFFERENT NOW AND ALL, BUT YOU CAN STILL CALL- YOU KNOW-
JUST TO TALK.
YEAH, I KNOW.
WHY DON'T YOU?
WELL, MAYBE I WILL.
I'LL LET YOU KNOW IF I HEAR ANYTHING.
DITTO.
HERE AT THE
OF E STREET
BS THAT THE
CONTROL OF
CAME TO ITS
CONCLUSION.
THE DETAILS OF WHAT HAPPENED THAT DAY WERE NEVER DIVULGED TO THE PUBLIC. ALL WE KNOW FOR SURE IS THAT MANY OF THE FIGURES INVOLVED DISAPPEARED FROM PUBLIC EYE, MAYBE FOREVER.
WHETHER VOLUNTARY RETIREMENT OR LIVES LOST IN BATTLE FOR OUR CITY'S FUTURE...
WE HAVE NEVER AGAIN HEARD FROM TWILIGHT, DIAMOND, SSAZZ, OR THE B.9. FOMFOM.

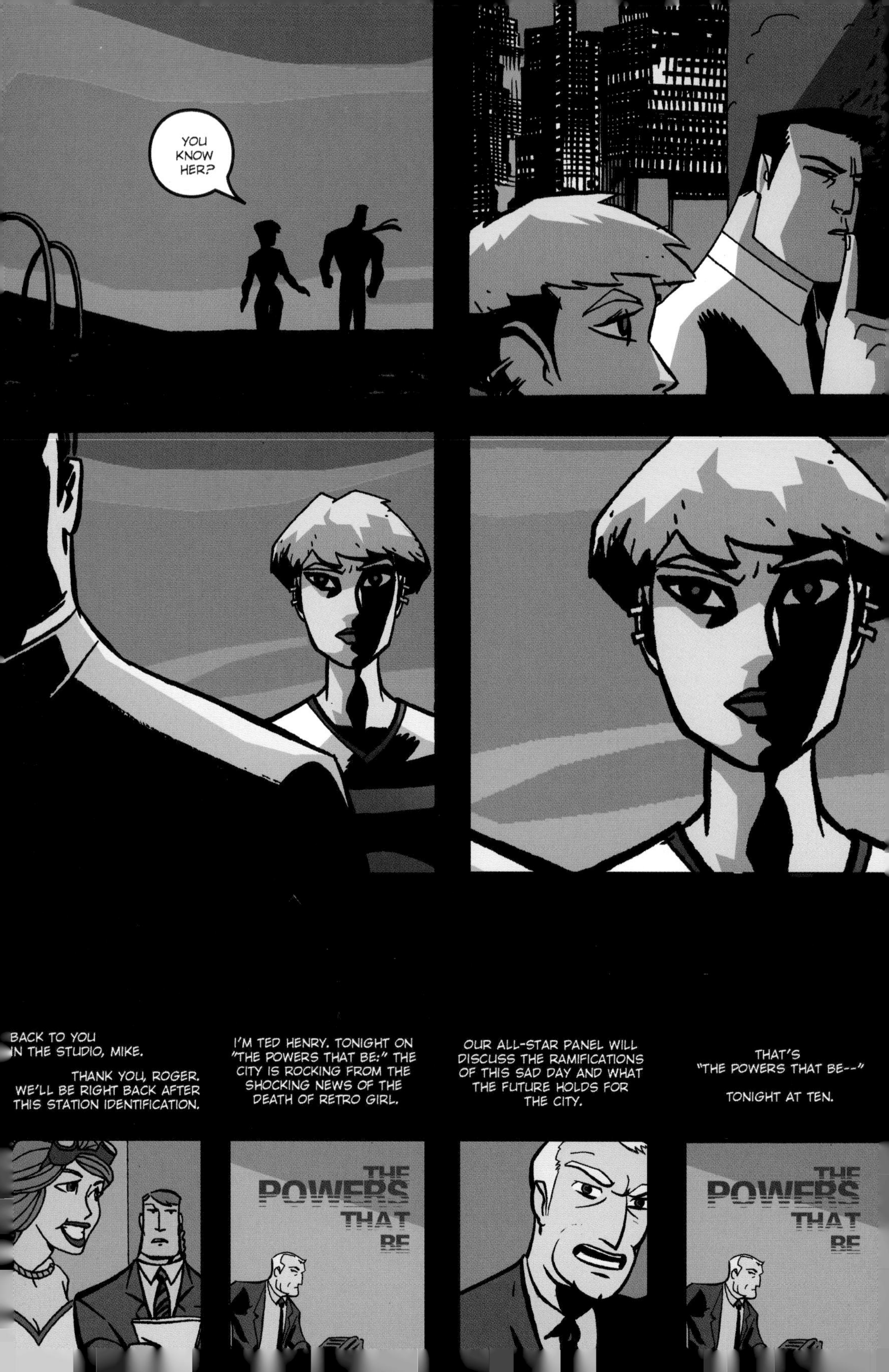
YOU KNOW HER?
BACK TO YOU IN THE STUDIO, MIKE.
THANK YOU, ROGER. WE'LL BE RIGHT BACK AFTER THIS STATION IDENTIFICATION.
I'M TED HENRY. TONIGHT ON "THE POWERS THAT BE:" THE CITY IS ROCKING FROM THE SHOCKING NEWS OF THE DEATH OF RETRO GIRL.
OUR ALL-STAR PANEL WILL DISCUSS THE RAMIFICATIONS OF THIS SAD DAY AND WHAT THE FUTURE HOLDS FOR THE CITY.
THAT'S "THE POWERS THAT BE--"
TONIGHT AT TEN.
THE POWERS THAT BE
THE POWERS THAT BE

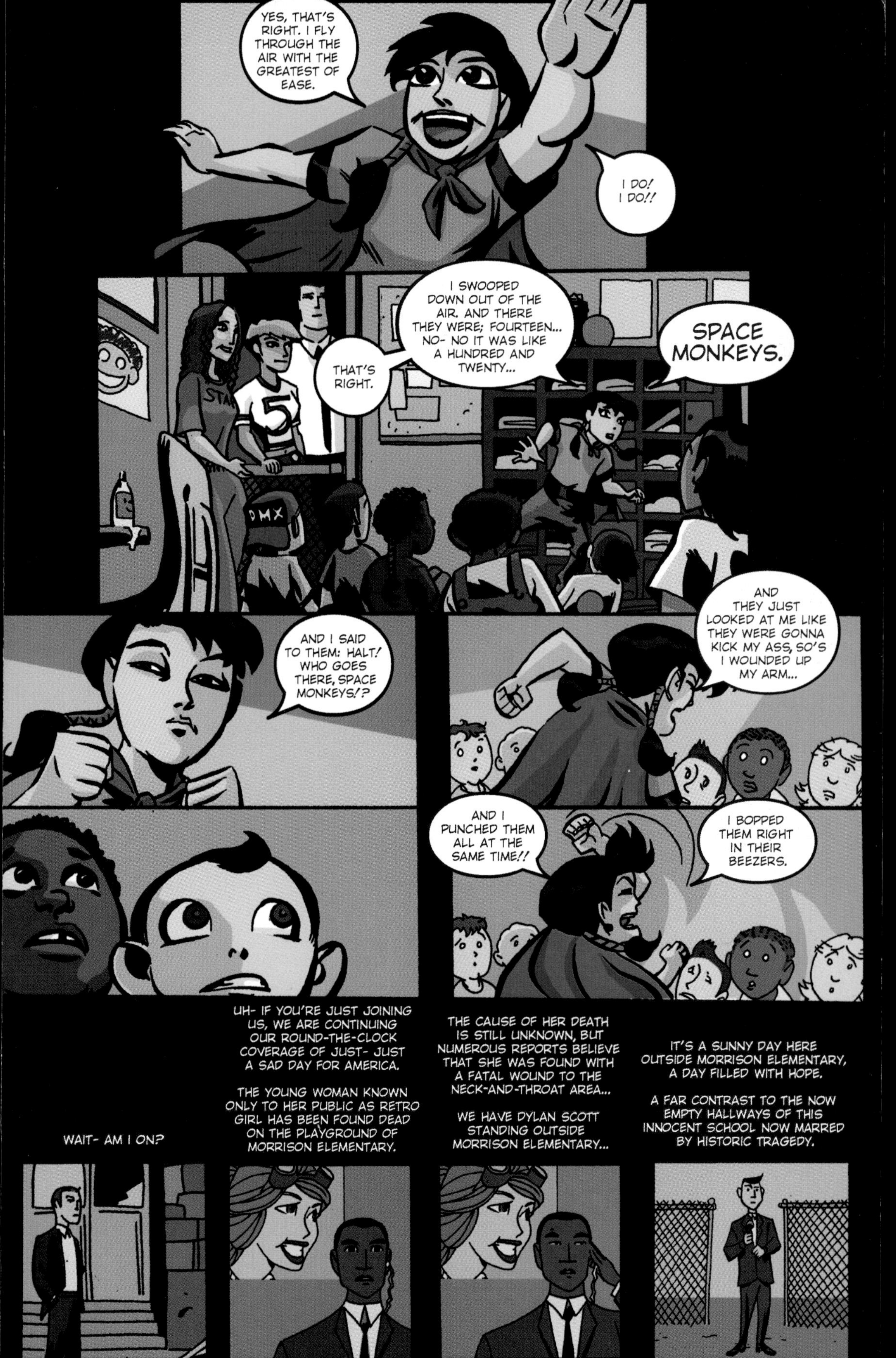

YES, THAT'S RIGHT. I FLY THROUGH THE AIR WITH THE GREATEST OF EASE.
I DO! I DO!!
I SWOOPED DOWN OUT OF THE AIR. AND THERE THEY WERE; FOURTEEN... NO- NO IT WAS LIKE A HUNDRED AND TWENTY...
THAT'S RIGHT.
SPACE MONKEYS.
AND I SAID TO THEM: HALT! WHO GOES THERE, SPACE MONKEYS!?
AND THEY JUST LOOKED AT ME LIKE THEY WERE GONNA KICK MY ASS, SO'S I WOUNDED UP MY ARM...
AND I PUNCHED THEM ALL AT THE SAME TIME!!
I BOPPED THEM RIGHT IN THEIR BEEZERS.
WAIT- AM I ON?
UH- IF YOU'RE JUST JOINING US, WE ARE CONTINUING OUR ROUND-THE-CLOCK COVERAGE OF JUST- JUST A SAD DAY FOR AMERICA.
THE YOUNG WOMAN KNOWN ONLY TO HER PUBLIC AS RETRO GIRL HAS BEEN FOUND DEAD ON THE PLAYGROUND OF MORRISON ELEMENTARY.
THE CAUSE OF HER DEATH IS STILL UNKNOWN, BUT NUMEROUS REPORTS BELIEVE THAT SHE WAS FOUND WITH A FATAL WOUND TO THE NECK-AND-THROAT AREA...
WE HAVE DYLAN SCOTT STANDING OUTSIDE MORRISON ELEMENTARY...
IT'S A SUNNY DAY HERE OUTSIDE MORRISON ELEMENTARY, A DAY FILLED WITH HOPE.
A FAR CONTRAST TO THE NOW EMPTY HALLWAYS OF THIS INNOCENT SCHOOL NOW MARRED BY HISTORIC TRAGEDY.

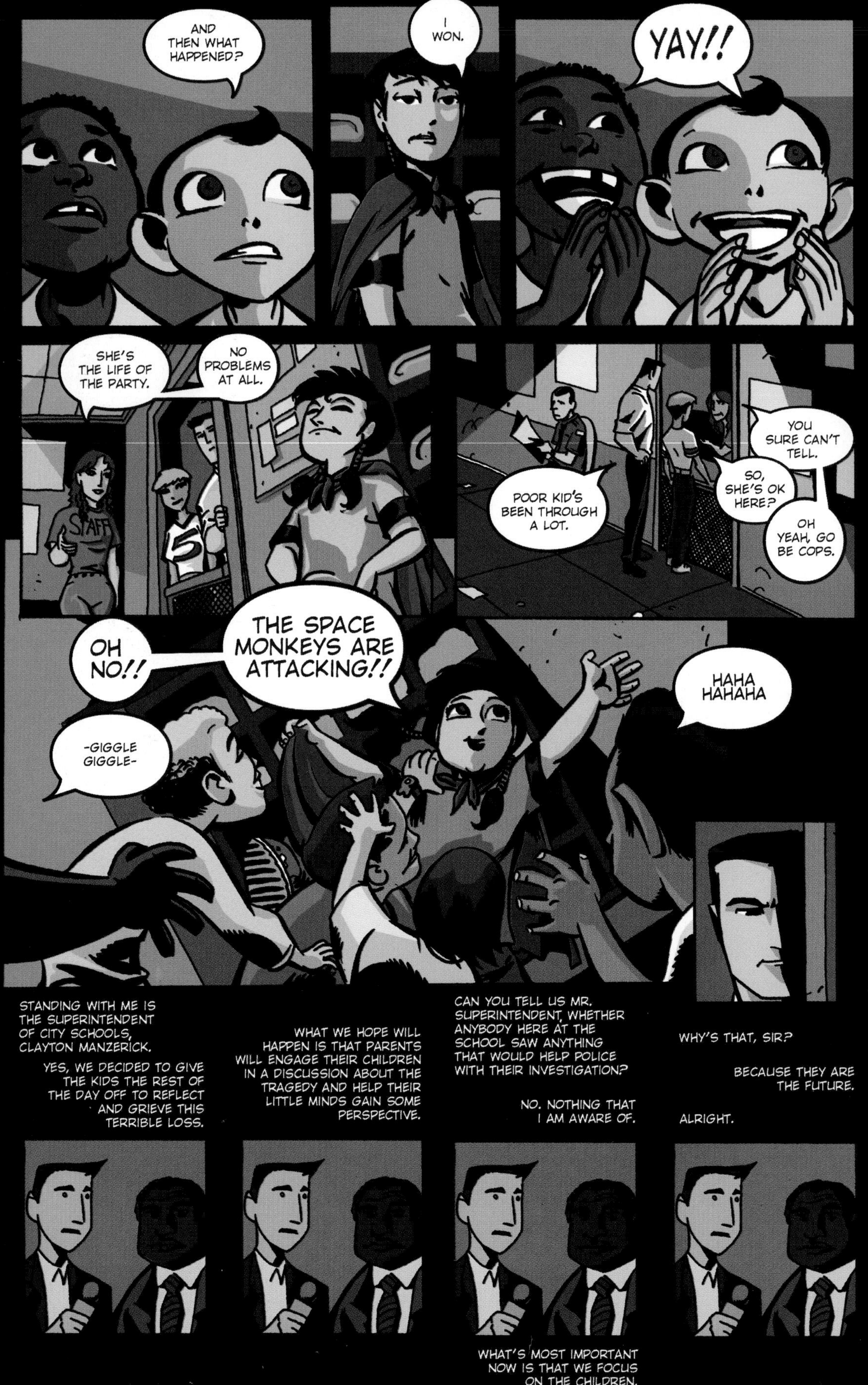
AND THEN WHAT HAPPENED?
I WON.
YAY!!
SHE'S THE LIFE OF THE PARTY.
NO PROBLEMS AT ALL.
POOR KID'S BEEN THROUGH A LOT.
YOU SURE CAN'T TELL.
SO, SHE'S OK HERE?
OH YEAH, GO BE COPS.
OH NO!!
THE SPACE MONKEYS ARE ATTACKING!!
-GIGGLE GIGGLE-
HAHA HAHAHA
STANDING WITH ME IS THE SUPERINTENDENT OF CITY SCHOOLS, CLAYTON MANZERICK.
YES, WE DECIDED TO GIVE THE KIDS THE REST OF THE DAY OFF TO REFLECT AND GRIEVE THIS TERRIBLE LOSS.
WHAT WE HOPE WILL HAPPEN IS THAT PARENTS WILL ENGAGE THEIR CHILDREN IN A DISCUSSION ABOUT THE TRAGEDY AND HELP THEIR LITTLE MINDS GAIN SOME PERSPECTIVE.
CAN YOU TELL US MR. SUPERINTENDENT, WHETHER ANYBODY HERE AT THE SCHOOL SAW ANYTHING THAT WOULD HELP POLICE WITH THEIR INVESTIGATION?
NO. NOTHING THAT I AM AWARE OF.
WHAT'S MOST IMPORTANT NOW IS THAT WE FOCUS ON THE CHILDREN.
WHY'S THAT, SIR?
BECAUSE THEY ARE THE FUTURE.
ALRIGHT.

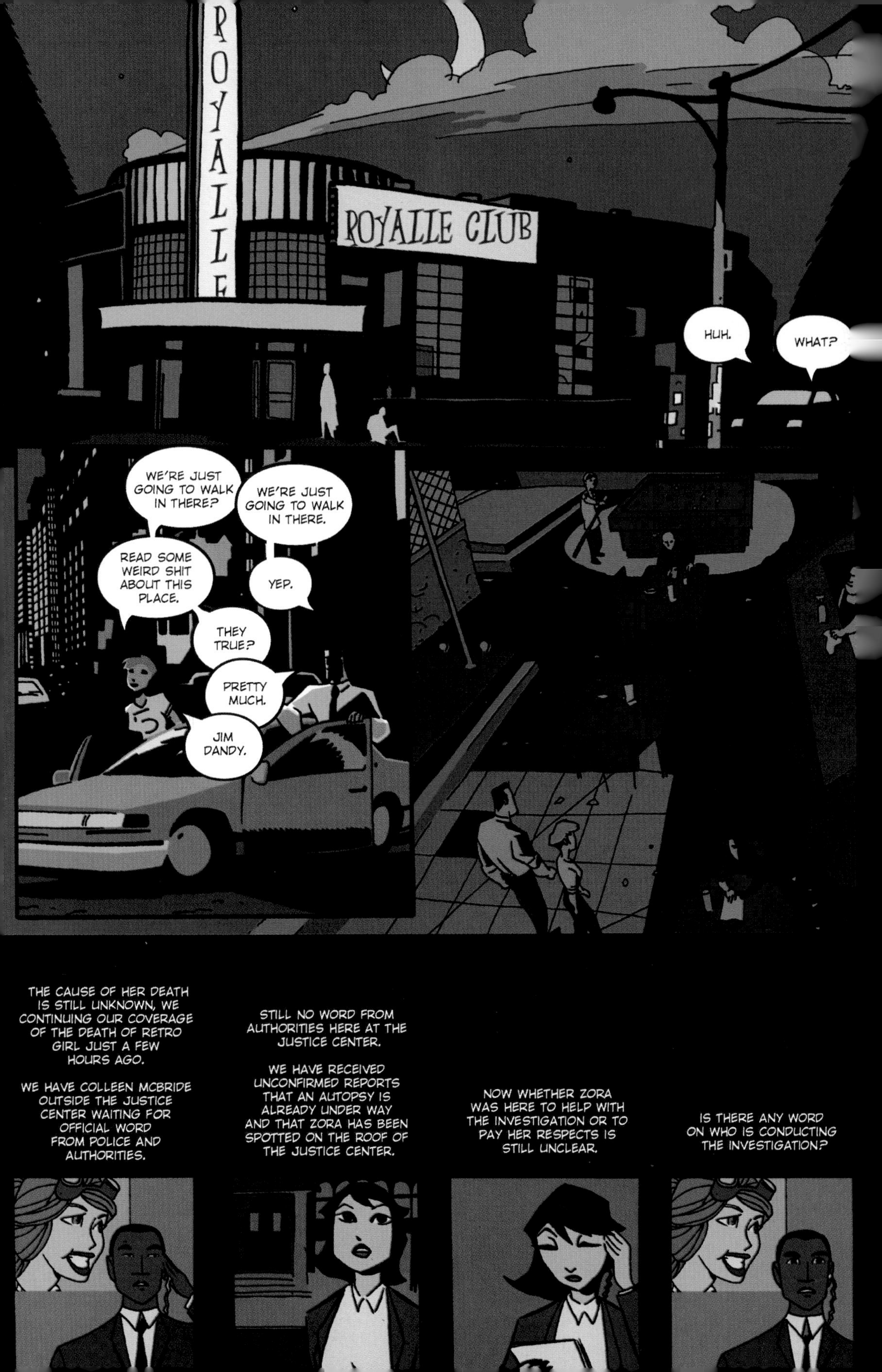
ROYALLE
ROYALLE CLUB
HUH.
WHAT?
WE'RE JUST GOING TO WALK IN THERE?
WE'RE JUST GOING TO WALK IN THERE.
READ SOME WEIRD SHIT ABOUT THIS PLACE.
YEP.
THEY TRUE?
PRETTY MUCH.
JIM DANDY.
THE CAUSE OF HER DEATH IS STILL UNKNOWN, WE CONTINUING OUR COVERAGE OF THE DEATH OF RETRO GIRL JUST A FEW HOURS AGO.
WE HAVE COLLEEN MCBRIDE OUTSIDE THE JUSTICE CENTER WAITING FOR OFFICIAL WORD FROM POLICE AND AUTHORITIES.
STILL NO WORD FROM AUTHORITIES HERE AT THE JUSTICE CENTER.
WE HAVE RECEIVED UNCONFIRMED REPORTS THAT AN AUTOPSY IS ALREADY UNDER WAY AND THAT ZORA HAS BEEN SPOTTED ON THE ROOF OF THE JUSTICE CENTER.
NOW WHETHER ZORA WAS HERE TO HELP WITH THE INVESTIGATION OR TO PAY HER RESPECTS IS STILL UNCLEAR.
IS THERE ANY WORD ON WHO IS CONDUCTING THE INVESTIGATION?

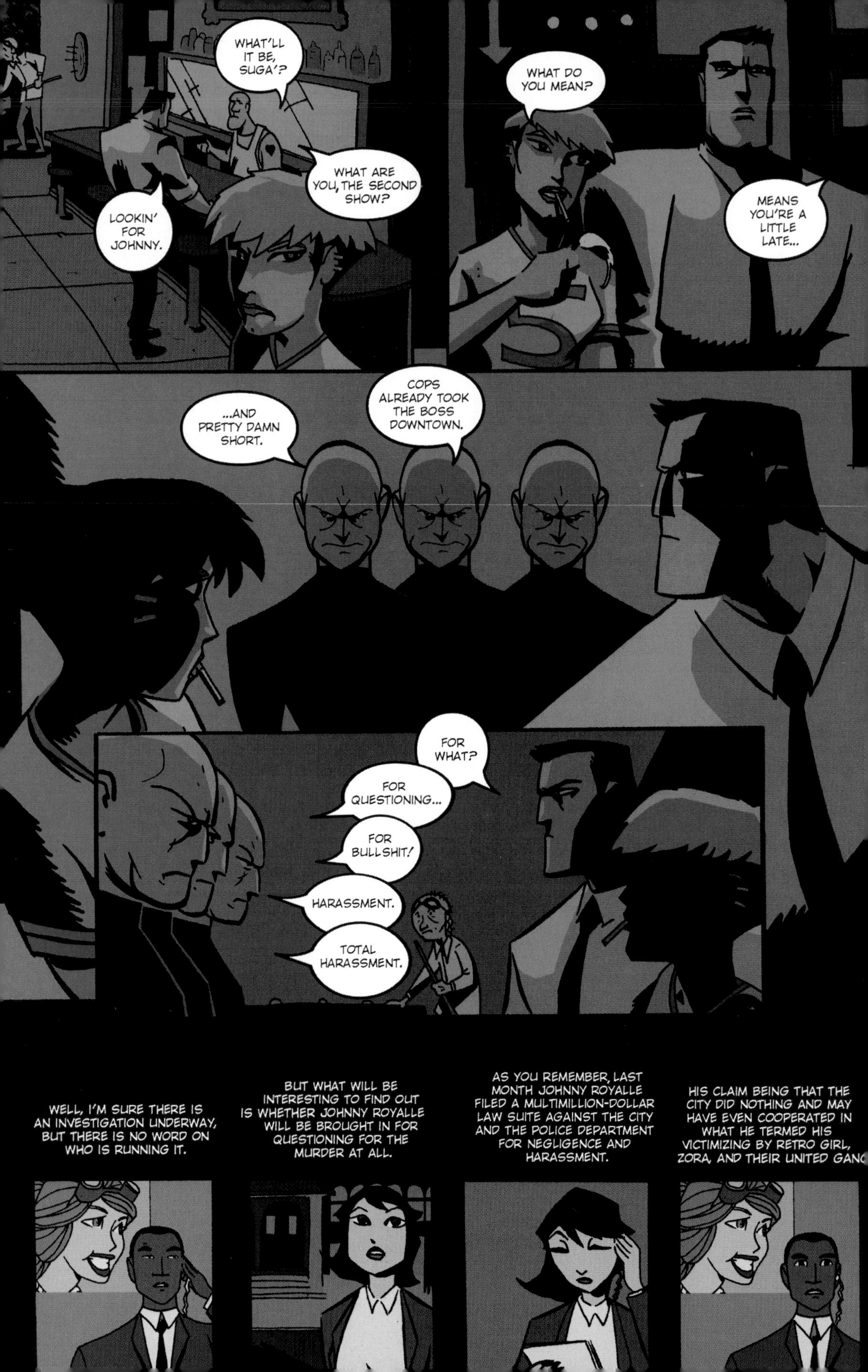
WHAT'LL IT BE, SUGA'?
LOOKIN' FOR JOHNNY.
WHAT ARE YOU, THE SECOND SHOW?
WHAT DO YOU MEAN?
MEANS YOU'RE A LITTLE LATE...
...AND PRETTY DAMN SHORT.
COPS ALREADY TOOK THE BOSS DOWNTOWN.
FOR WHAT?
FOR QUESTIONING...
FOR BULLSHIT!
HARASSMENT.
TOTAL HARASSMENT.
WELL, I'M SURE THERE IS AN INVESTIGATION UNDERWAY, BUT THERE IS NO WORD ON WHO IS RUNNING IT.
BUT WHAT WILL BE INTERESTING TO FIND OUT IS WHETHER JOHNNY ROYALLE WILL BE BROUGHT IN FOR QUESTIONING FOR THE MURDER AT ALL.
AS YOU REMEMBER, LAST MONTH JOHNNY ROYALLE FILED A MULTIMILLION-DOLLAR LAW SUITE AGAINST THE CITY AND THE POLICE DEPARTMENT FOR NEGLIGENCE AND HARASSMENT.
HIS CLAIM BEING THAT THE CITY DID NOTHING AND MAY HAVE EVEN COOPERATED IN WHAT HE TERMED HIS VICTIMIZING BY RETRO GIRL, ZORA, AND THEIR UNITED GANG

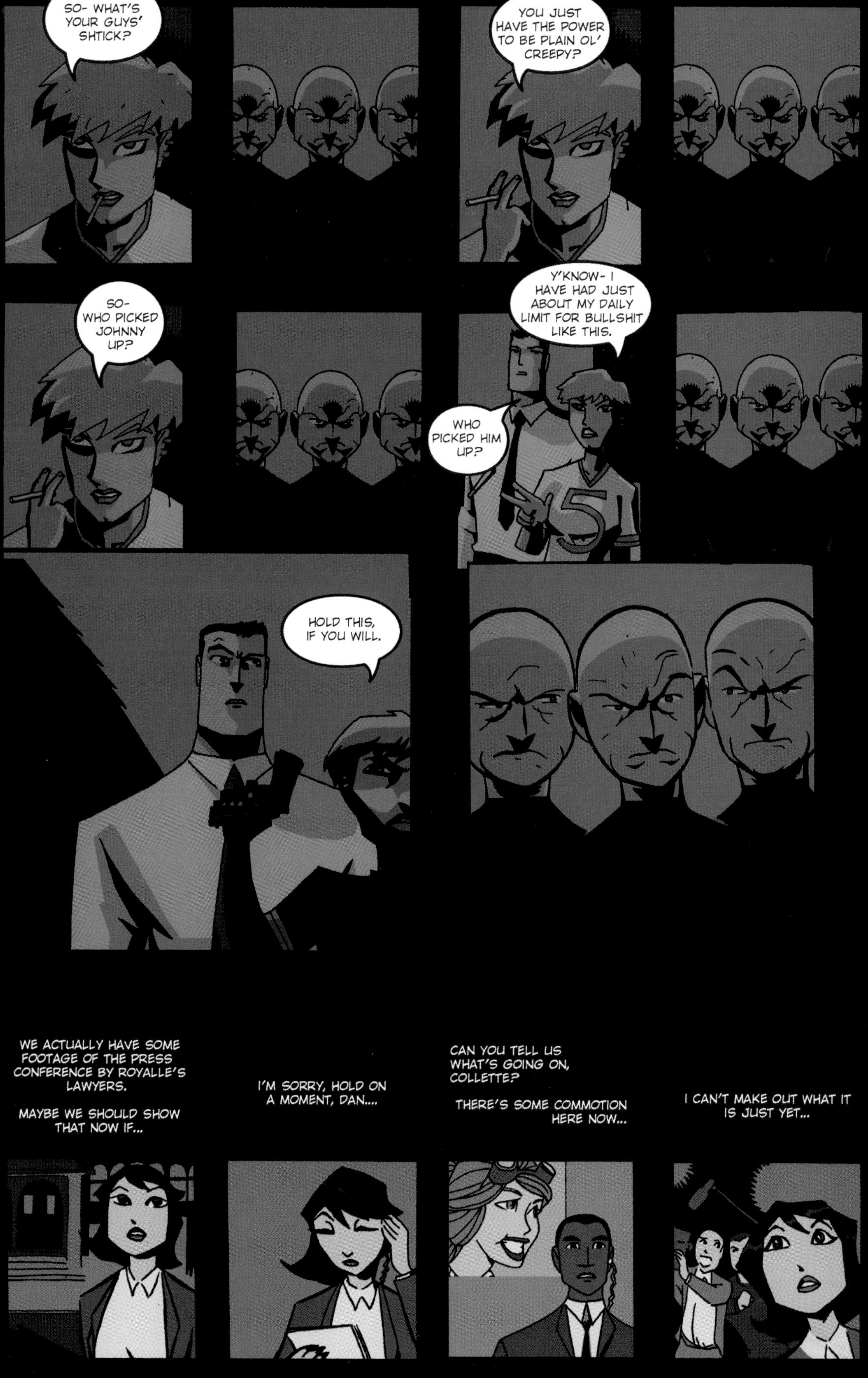
SO- WHAT'S YOUR GUYS' SHTICK?
YOU JUST HAVE THE POWER TO BE PLAIN OL' CREEPY?
SO- WHO PICKED JOHNNY UP?
Y'KNOW- I HAVE HAD JUST ABOUT MY DAILY LIMIT FOR BULLSHIT LIKE THIS.
WHO PICKED HIM UP?
HOLD THIS, IF YOU WILL.
WE ACTUALLY HAVE SOME FOOTAGE OF THE PRESS CONFERENCE BY ROYALLE'S LAWYERS.
MAYBE WE SHOULD SHOW THAT NOW IF...
I'M SORRY, HOLD ON A MOMENT, DAN....
CAN YOU TELL US WHAT'S GOING ON, COLLETTE?
THERE'S SOME COMMOTION HERE NOW...
I CAN'T MAKE OUT WHAT IT IS JUST YET...

HOLD ON.

BOBBY, TURN THE
CAMERA AROUND.

NOT ON ME, AROUND.

WE'RE- WE'RE TRYING TO-
TO GET IN HERE--

   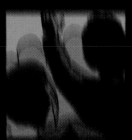

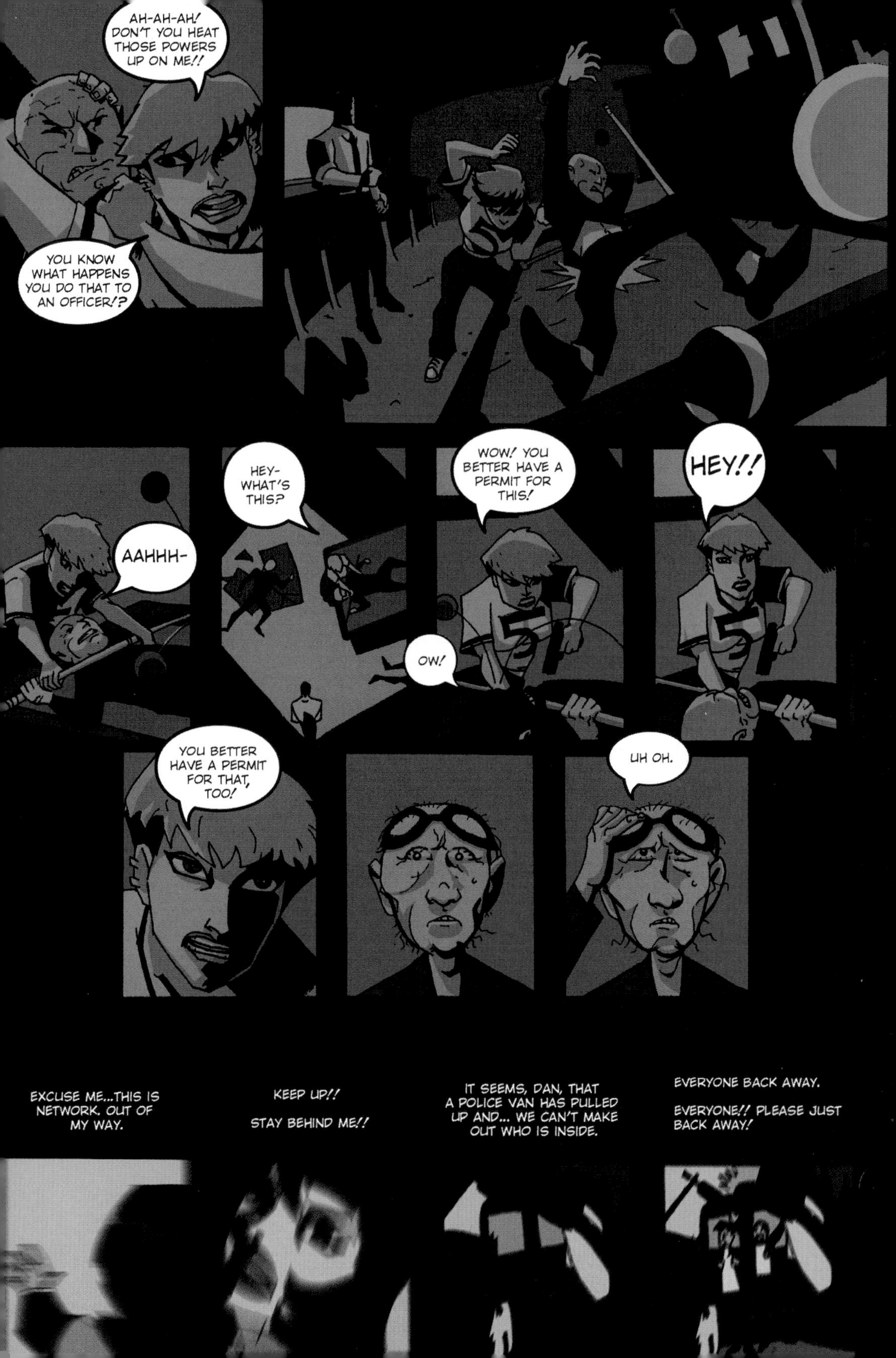
AH-AH-AH! DON'T YOU HEAT THOSE POWERS UP ON ME!!
YOU KNOW WHAT HAPPENS YOU DO THAT TO AN OFFICER!?
AAHHH-
HEY- WHAT'S THIS?
WOW! YOU BETTER HAVE A PERMIT FOR THIS!
OW!
HEY!!
YOU BETTER HAVE A PERMIT FOR THAT, TOO!
UH OH.
EXCUSE ME...THIS IS NETWORK. OUT OF MY WAY.
KEEP UP!!
STAY BEHIND ME!!
IT SEEMS, DAN, THAT A POLICE VAN HAS PULLED UP AND... WE CAN'T MAKE OUT WHO IS INSIDE.
EVERYONE BACK AWAY.
EVERYONE!! PLEASE JUST BACK AWAY!

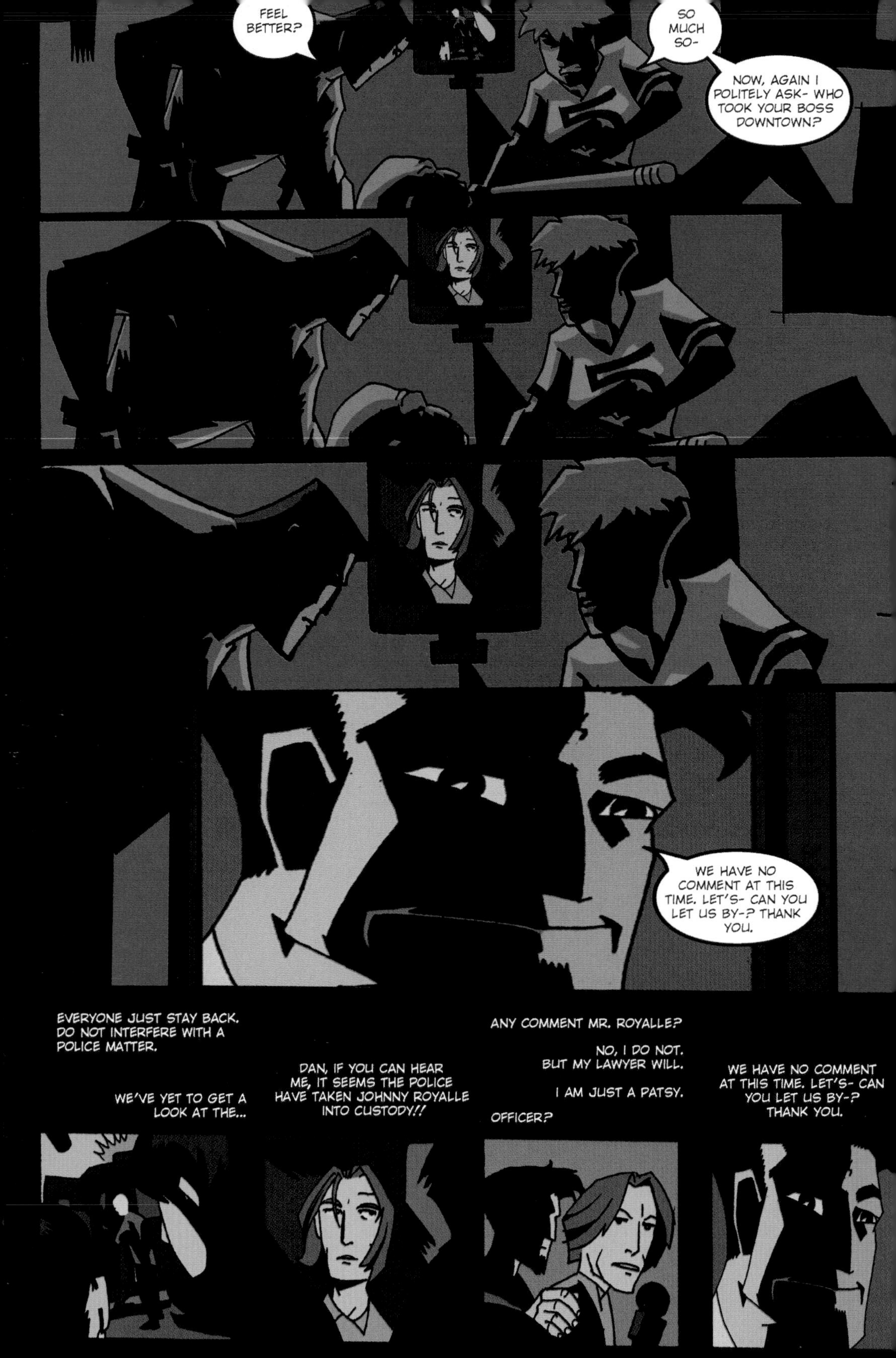
FEEL BETTER?
SO MUCH SO-
NOW, AGAIN I POLITELY ASK- WHO TOOK YOUR BOSS DOWNTOWN?
WE HAVE NO COMMENT AT THIS TIME. LET'S- CAN YOU LET US BY-? THANK YOU.
EVERYONE JUST STAY BACK. DO NOT INTERFERE WITH A POLICE MATTER.
WE'VE YET TO GET A LOOK AT THE...
DAN, IF YOU CAN HEAR ME, IT SEEMS THE POLICE HAVE TAKEN JOHNNY ROYALLE INTO CUSTODY!!
ANY COMMENT MR. ROYALLE?
NO, I DO NOT. BUT MY LAWYER WILL.
I AM JUST A PATSY.
OFFICER?
WE HAVE NO COMMENT AT THIS TIME. LET'S- CAN YOU LET US BY-? THANK YOU.

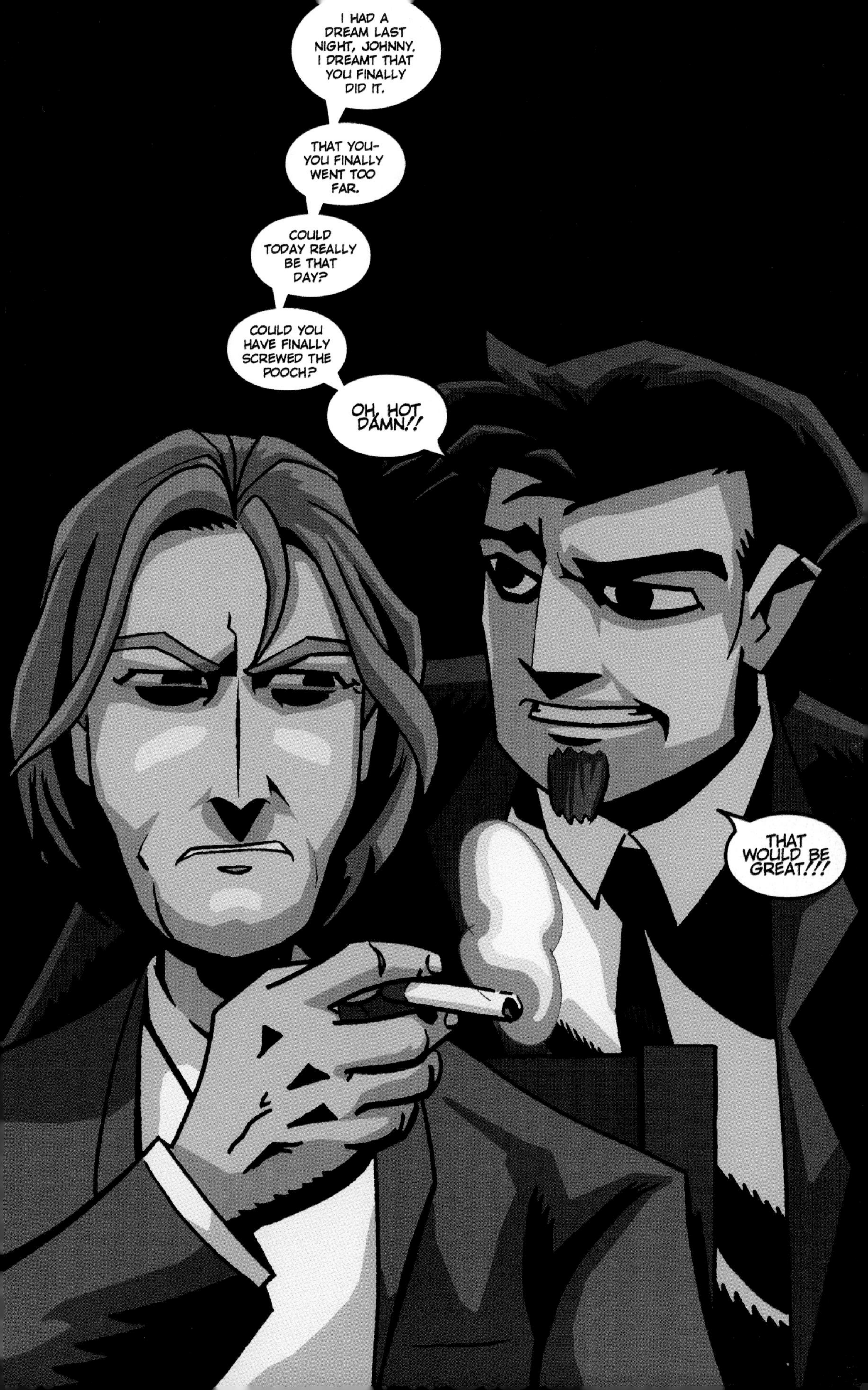
I HAD A DREAM LAST NIGHT, JOHNNY. I DREAMT THAT YOU FINALLY DID IT.
THAT YOU- YOU FINALLY WENT TOO FAR.
COULD TODAY REALLY BE THAT DAY?
COULD YOU HAVE FINALLY SCREWED THE POOCH?
OH, HOT DAMN!!
THAT WOULD BE GREAT!!!

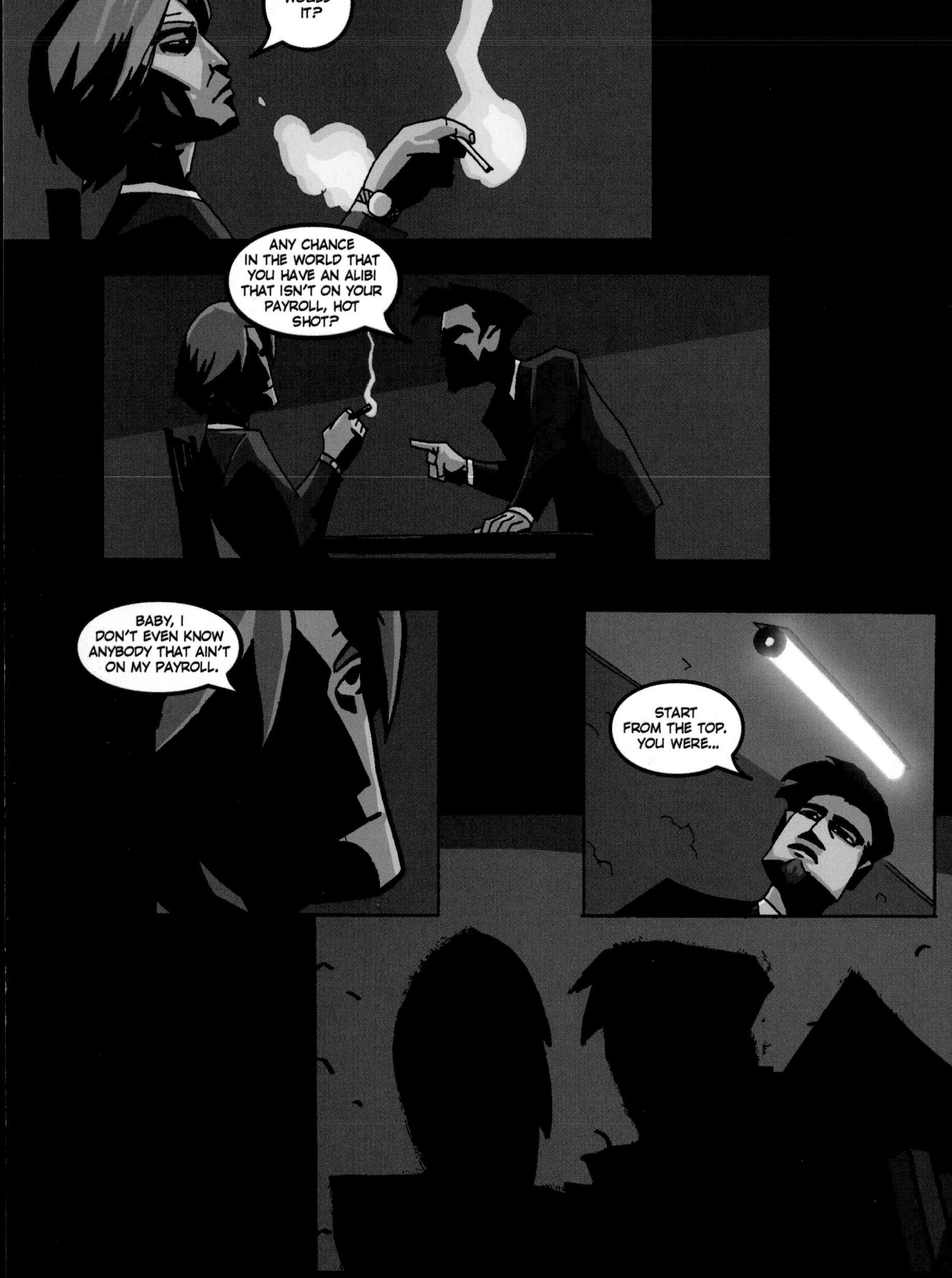
IT?
ANY CHANCE IN THE WORLD THAT YOU HAVE AN ALIBI THAT ISN'T ON YOUR PAYROLL, HOT SHOT?
BABY, I DON'T EVEN KNOW ANYBODY THAT AIN'T ON MY PAYROLL.
START FROM THE TOP. YOU WERE...

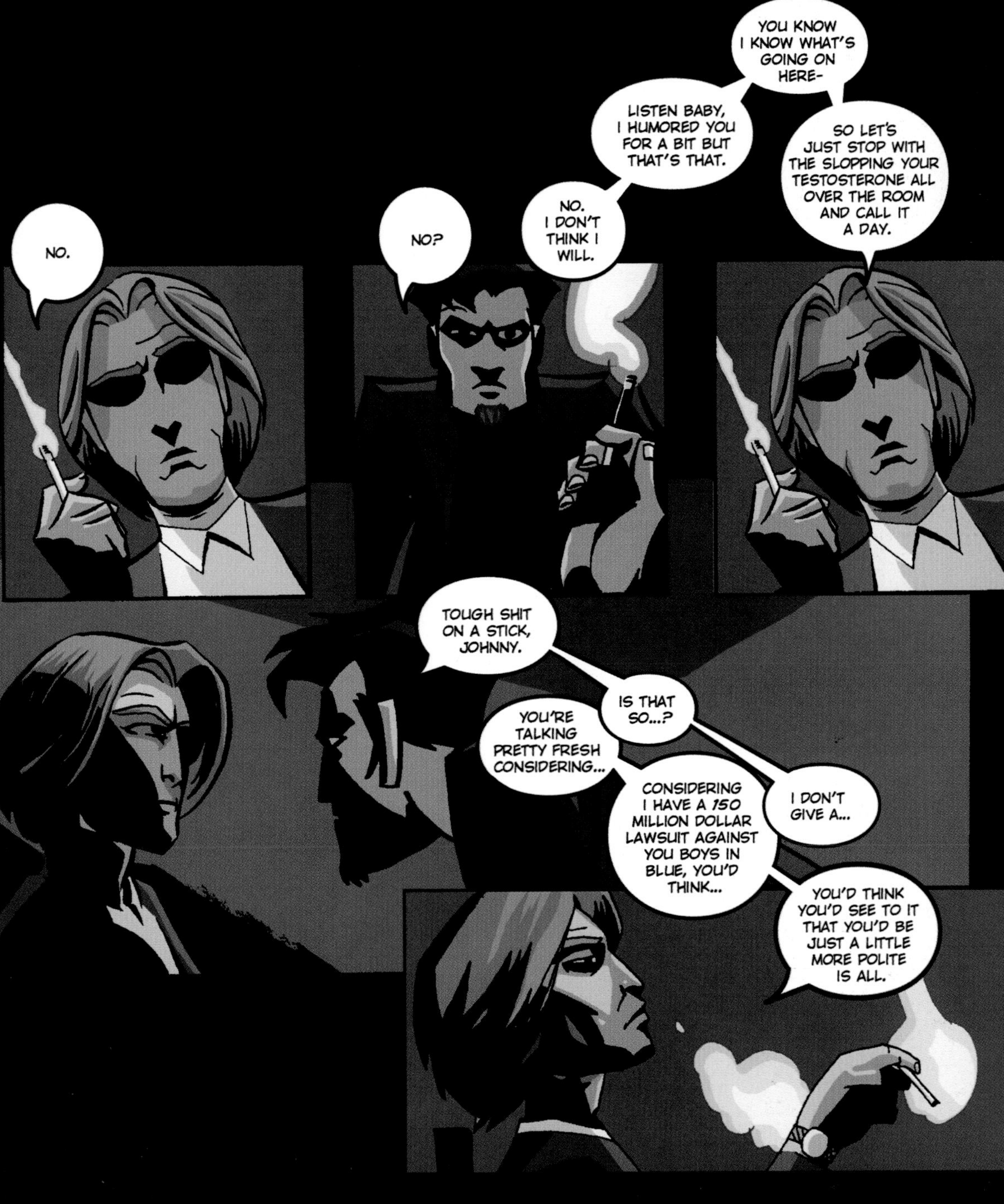
NO.
NO?
NO. I DON'T THINK I WILL.
LISTEN BABY, I HUMORED YOU FOR A BIT BUT THAT'S THAT.
YOU KNOW I KNOW WHAT'S GOING ON HERE-
SO LET'S JUST STOP WITH THE SLOPPING YOUR TESTOSTERONE ALL OVER THE ROOM AND CALL IT A DAY.
TOUGH SHIT ON A STICK, JOHNNY.
IS THAT SO...?
YOU'RE TALKING PRETTY FRESH CONSIDERING...
CONSIDERING I HAVE A *150* MILLION DOLLAR LAWSUIT AGAINST YOU BOYS IN BLUE, YOU'D THINK...
I DON'T GIVE A...
YOU'D THINK YOU'D SEE TO IT THAT YOU'D BE JUST A LITTLE MORE POLITE IS ALL.

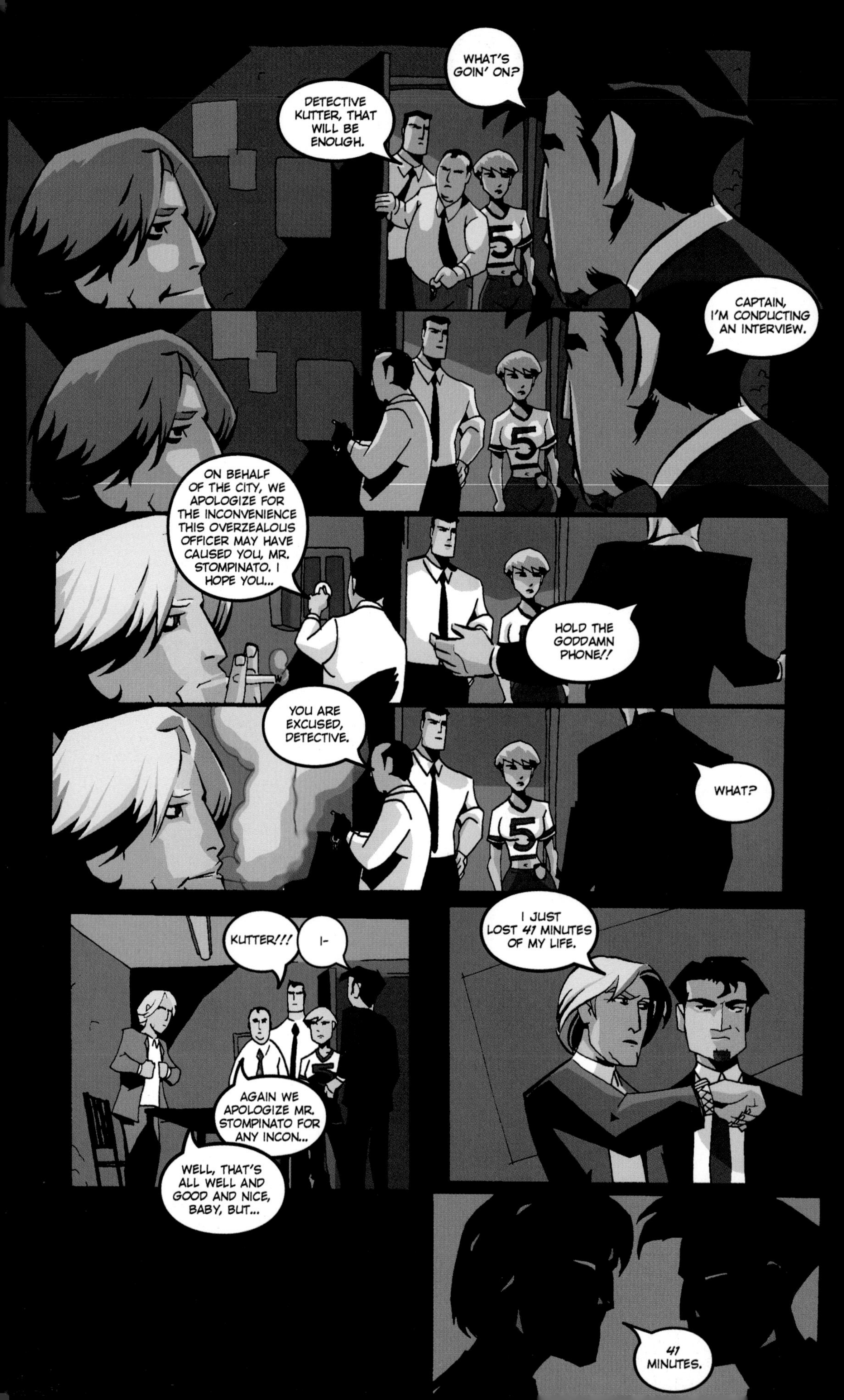
WHAT'S GOIN' ON?
DETECTIVE KUTTER, THAT WILL BE ENOUGH.
CAPTAIN, I'M CONDUCTING AN INTERVIEW.
ON BEHALF OF THE CITY, WE APOLOGIZE FOR THE INCONVENIENCE THIS OVERZEALOUS OFFICER MAY HAVE CAUSED YOU, MR. STOMPINATO. I HOPE YOU...
HOLD THE GODDAMN PHONE!!
YOU ARE EXCUSED, DETECTIVE.
WHAT?
KUTTER!!!
I-
AGAIN WE APOLOGIZE MR. STOMPINATO FOR ANY INCON...
WELL, THAT'S ALL WELL AND GOOD AND NICE, BABY, BUT...
I JUST LOST 41 MINUTES OF MY LIFE.
41 MINUTES.

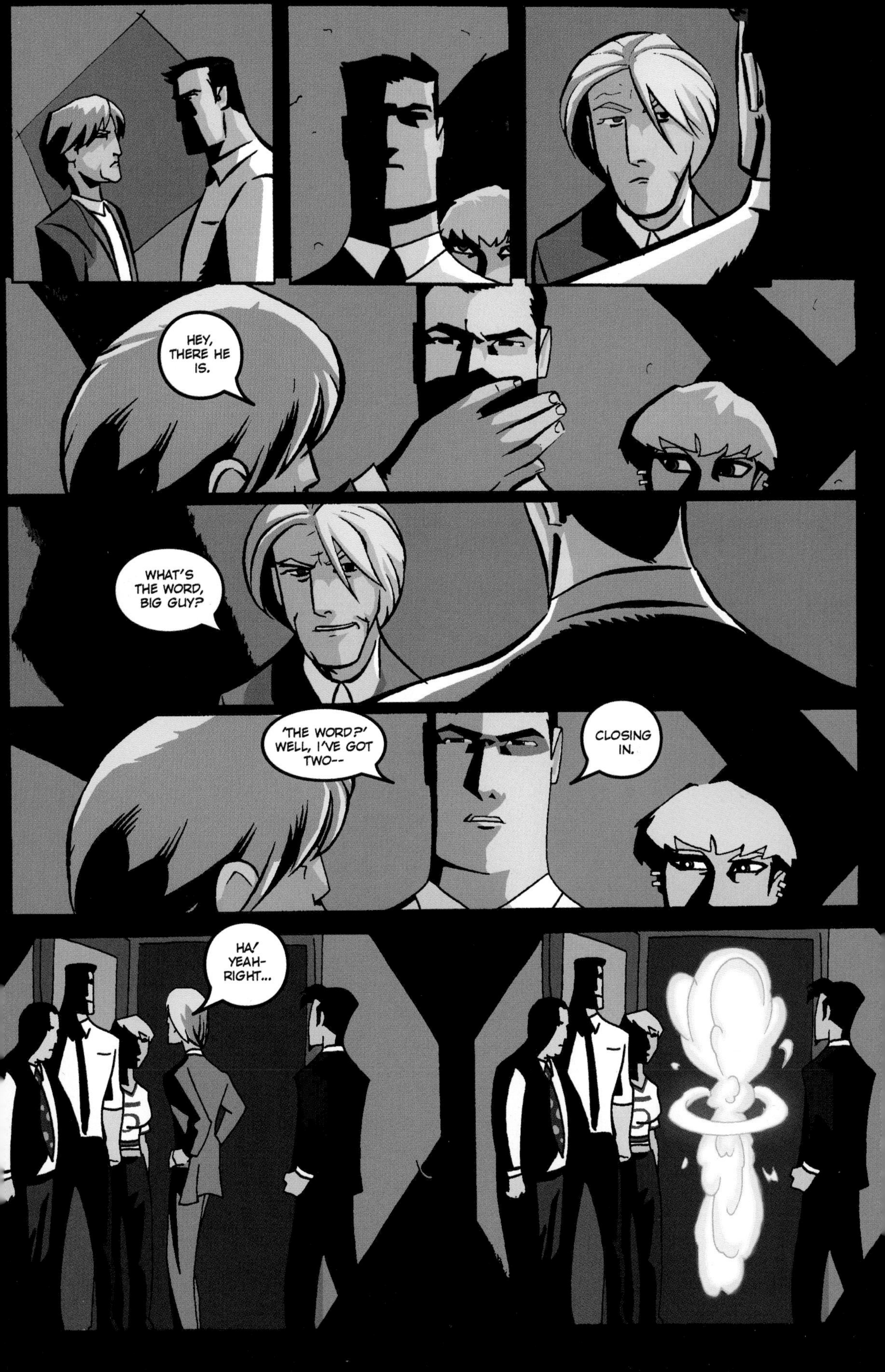

HEY, THERE HE IS.
WHAT'S THE WORD, BIG GUY?
'THE WORD?' WELL, I'VE GOT TWO--
CLOSING IN.
HA! YEAH-RIGHT...

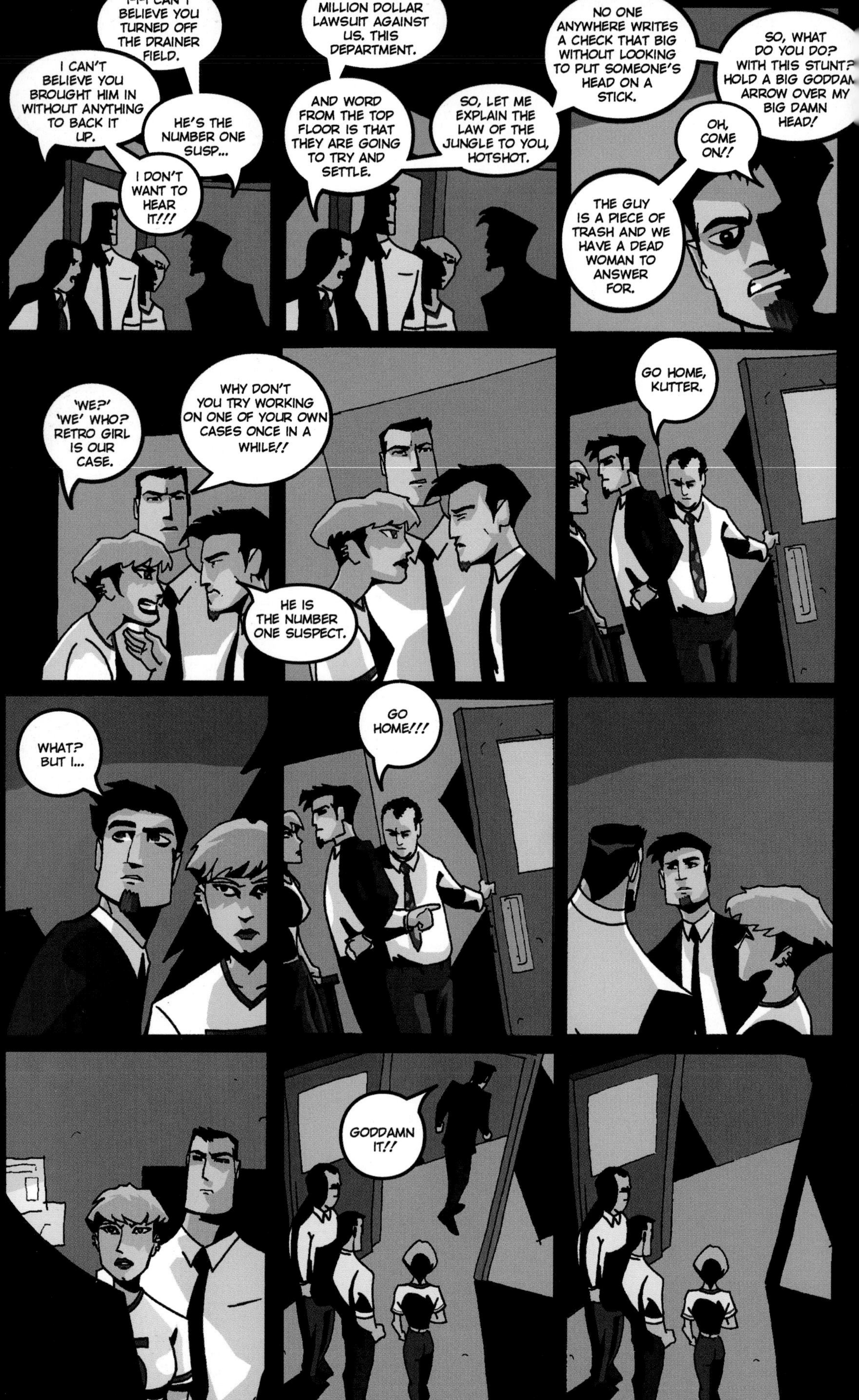

I-I-I CAN'T BELIEVE YOU TURNED OFF THE DRAINER FIELD.
I CAN'T BELIEVE YOU BROUGHT HIM IN WITHOUT ANYTHING TO BACK IT UP.
HE'S THE NUMBER ONE SUSP...
I DON'T WANT TO HEAR IT!!!
IT'S A 150 MILLION DOLLAR LAWSUIT AGAINST US. THIS DEPARTMENT.
AND WORD FROM THE TOP FLOOR IS THAT THEY ARE GOING TO TRY AND SETTLE.
SO, LET ME EXPLAIN THE LAW OF THE JUNGLE TO YOU, HOTSHOT.
NO ONE ANYWHERE WRITES A CHECK THAT BIG WITHOUT LOOKING TO PUT SOMEONE'S HEAD ON A STICK.
SO, WHAT DO YOU DO? WITH THIS STUNT? HOLD A BIG GODDAM ARROW OVER MY BIG DAMN HEAD!
OH, COME ON!!
THE GUY IS A PIECE OF TRASH AND WE HAVE A DEAD WOMAN TO ANSWER FOR.
'WE?' 'WE' WHO? RETRO GIRL IS OUR CASE.
WHY DON'T YOU TRY WORKING ON ONE OF YOUR OWN CASES ONCE IN A WHILE!!
HE IS THE NUMBER ONE SUSPECT.
GO HOME, KUTTER.
WHAT? BUT I...
GO HOME!!!
GODDAMN IT!!

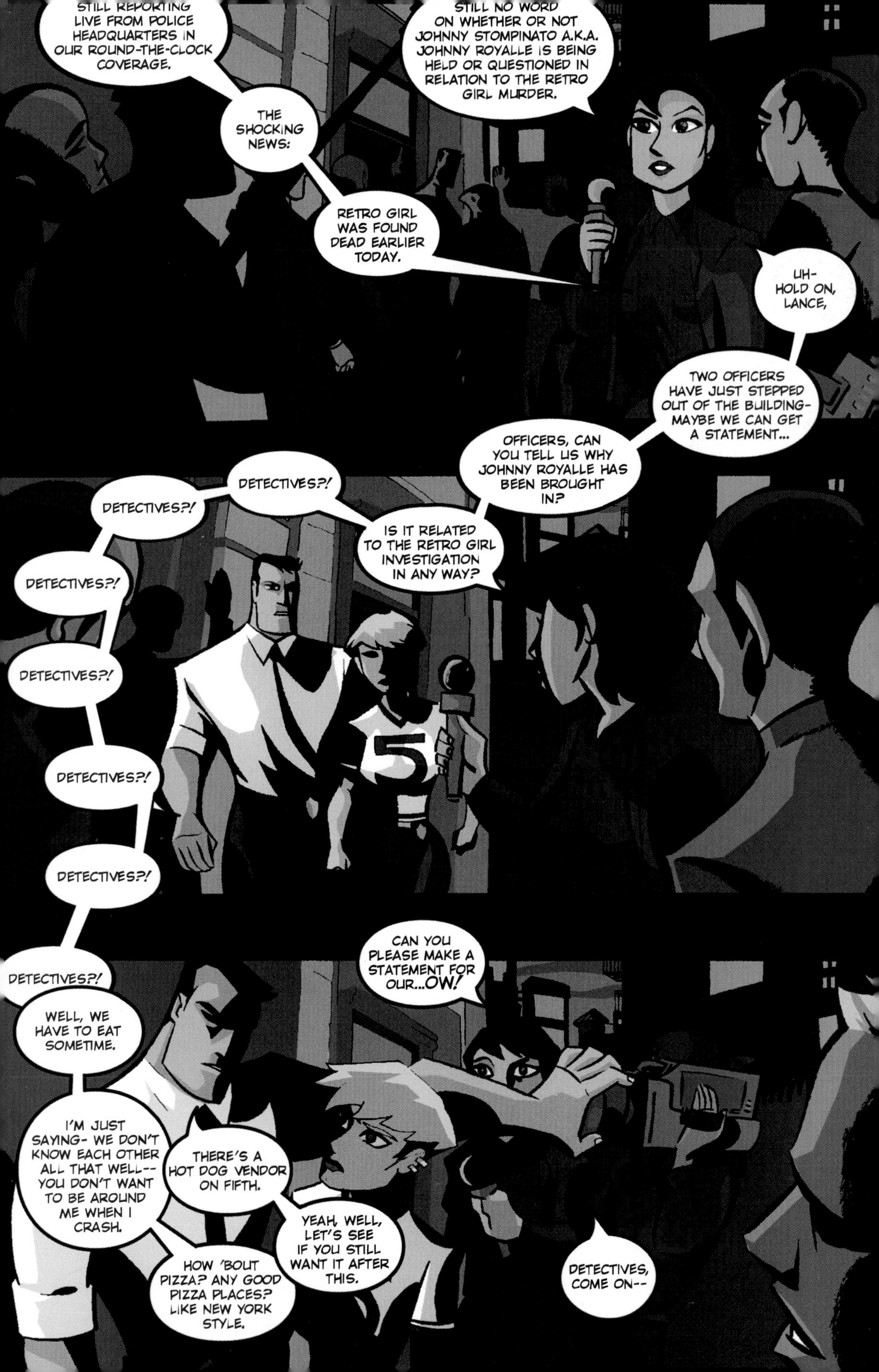
STILL REPORTING LIVE FROM POLICE HEADQUARTERS IN OUR ROUND-THE-CLOCK COVERAGE.
THE SHOCKING NEWS:
RETRO GIRL WAS FOUND DEAD EARLIER TODAY.
STILL NO WORD ON WHETHER OR NOT JOHNNY STOMPINATO A.K.A. JOHNNY ROYALLE IS BEING HELD OR QUESTIONED IN RELATION TO THE RETRO GIRL MURDER.
UH- HOLD ON, LANCE,
TWO OFFICERS HAVE JUST STEPPED OUT OF THE BUILDING- MAYBE WE CAN GET A STATEMENT...
OFFICERS, CAN YOU TELL US WHY JOHNNY ROYALLE HAS BEEN BROUGHT IN?
IS IT RELATED TO THE RETRO GIRL INVESTIGATION IN ANY WAY?
DETECTIVES?!
DETECTIVES?!
DETECTIVES?!
DETECTIVES?!
DETECTIVES?!
DETECTIVES?!
DETECTIVES?!
CAN YOU PLEASE MAKE A STATEMENT FOR OUR...OW!
WELL, WE HAVE TO EAT SOMETIME.
I'M JUST SAYING- WE DON'T KNOW EACH OTHER ALL THAT WELL-- YOU DON'T WANT TO BE AROUND ME WHEN I CRASH.
THERE'S A HOT DOG VENDOR ON FIFTH.
HOW 'BOUT PIZZA? ANY GOOD PIZZA PLACES? LIKE NEW YORK STYLE.
YEAH, WELL, LET'S SEE IF YOU STILL WANT IT AFTER THIS.
DETECTIVES, COME ON--

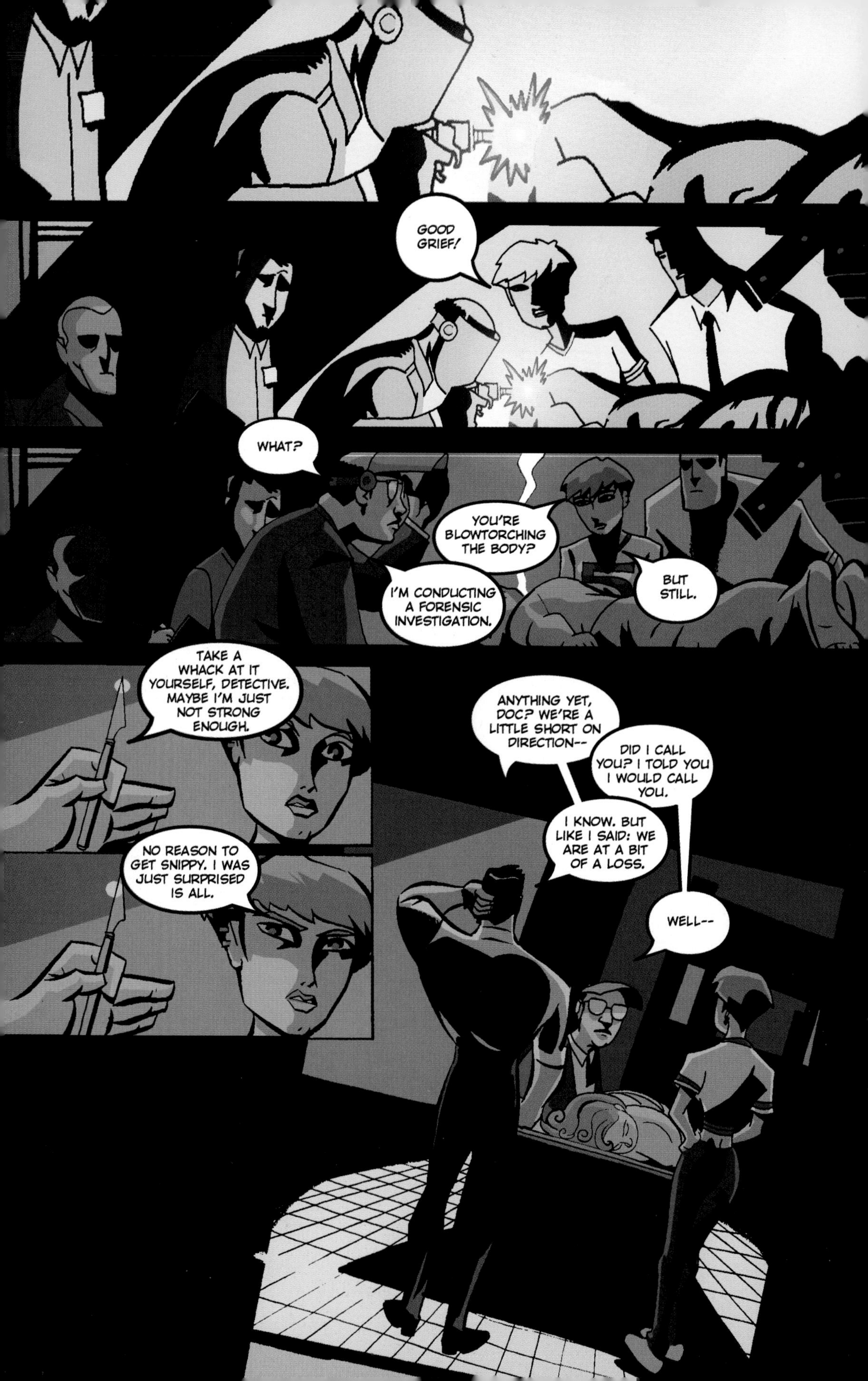
GOOD GRIEF!
WHAT?
YOU'RE BLOWTORCHING THE BODY?
I'M CONDUCTING A FORENSIC INVESTIGATION.
BUT STILL.
TAKE A WHACK AT IT YOURSELF, DETECTIVE. MAYBE I'M JUST NOT STRONG ENOUGH.
NO REASON TO GET SNIPPY. I WAS JUST SURPRISED IS ALL.
ANYTHING YET, DOC? WE'RE A LITTLE SHORT ON DIRECTION--
DID I CALL YOU? I TOLD YOU I WOULD CALL YOU.
I KNOW. BUT LIKE I SAID: WE ARE AT A BIT OF A LOSS.
WELL--

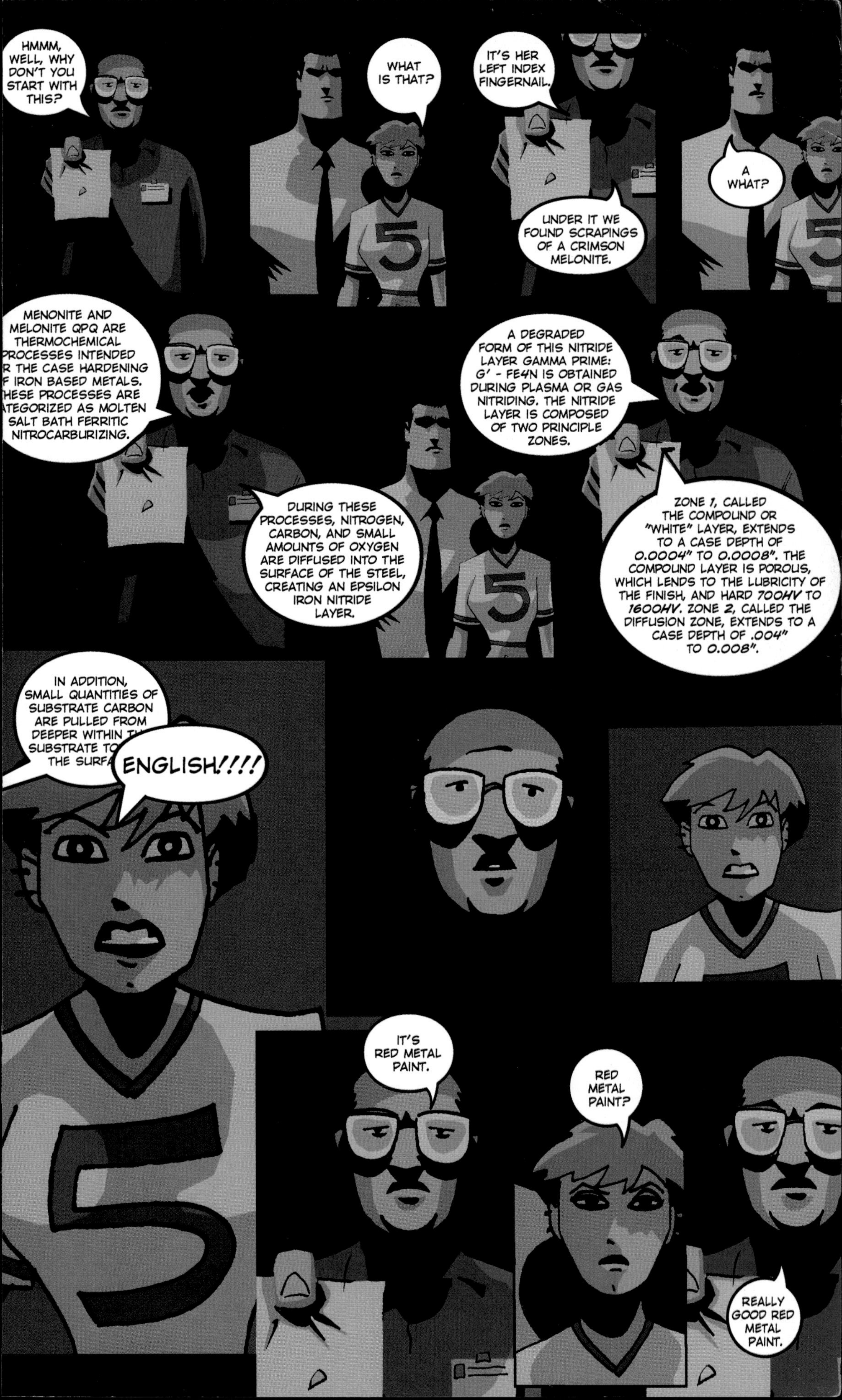
HMMM, WELL, WHY DON'T YOU START WITH THIS?
WHAT IS THAT?
IT'S HER LEFT INDEX FINGERNAIL.
UNDER IT WE FOUND SCRAPINGS OF A CRIMSON MELONITE.
A WHAT?
MENONITE AND MELONITE QPQ ARE THERMOCHEMICAL PROCESSES INTENDED R THE CASE HARDENING F IRON BASED METALS. HESE PROCESSES ARE ATEGORIZED AS MOLTEN SALT BATH FERRITIC NITROCARBURIZING.
DURING THESE PROCESSES, NITROGEN, CARBON, AND SMALL AMOUNTS OF OXYGEN ARE DIFFUSED INTO THE SURFACE OF THE STEEL, CREATING AN EPSILON IRON NITRIDE LAYER.
A DEGRADED FORM OF THIS NITRIDE LAYER GAMMA PRIME: G' - FE4N IS OBTAINED DURING PLASMA OR GAS NITRIDING. THE NITRIDE LAYER IS COMPOSED OF TWO PRINCIPLE ZONES.
ZONE 1, CALLED THE COMPOUND OR "WHITE" LAYER, EXTENDS TO A CASE DEPTH OF 0.0004" TO 0.0008". THE COMPOUND LAYER IS POROUS, WHICH LENDS TO THE LUBRICITY OF THE FINISH, AND HARD 700HV TO 1600HV. ZONE 2, CALLED THE DIFFUSION ZONE, EXTENDS TO A CASE DEPTH OF .004" TO 0.008".
IN ADDITION, SMALL QUANTITIES OF SUBSTRATE CARBON ARE PULLED FROM DEEPER WITHIN TH SUBSTRATE TO THE SURFA
ENGLISH!!!!
IT'S RED METAL PAINT.
RED METAL PAINT?
REALLY GOOD RED METAL PAINT.

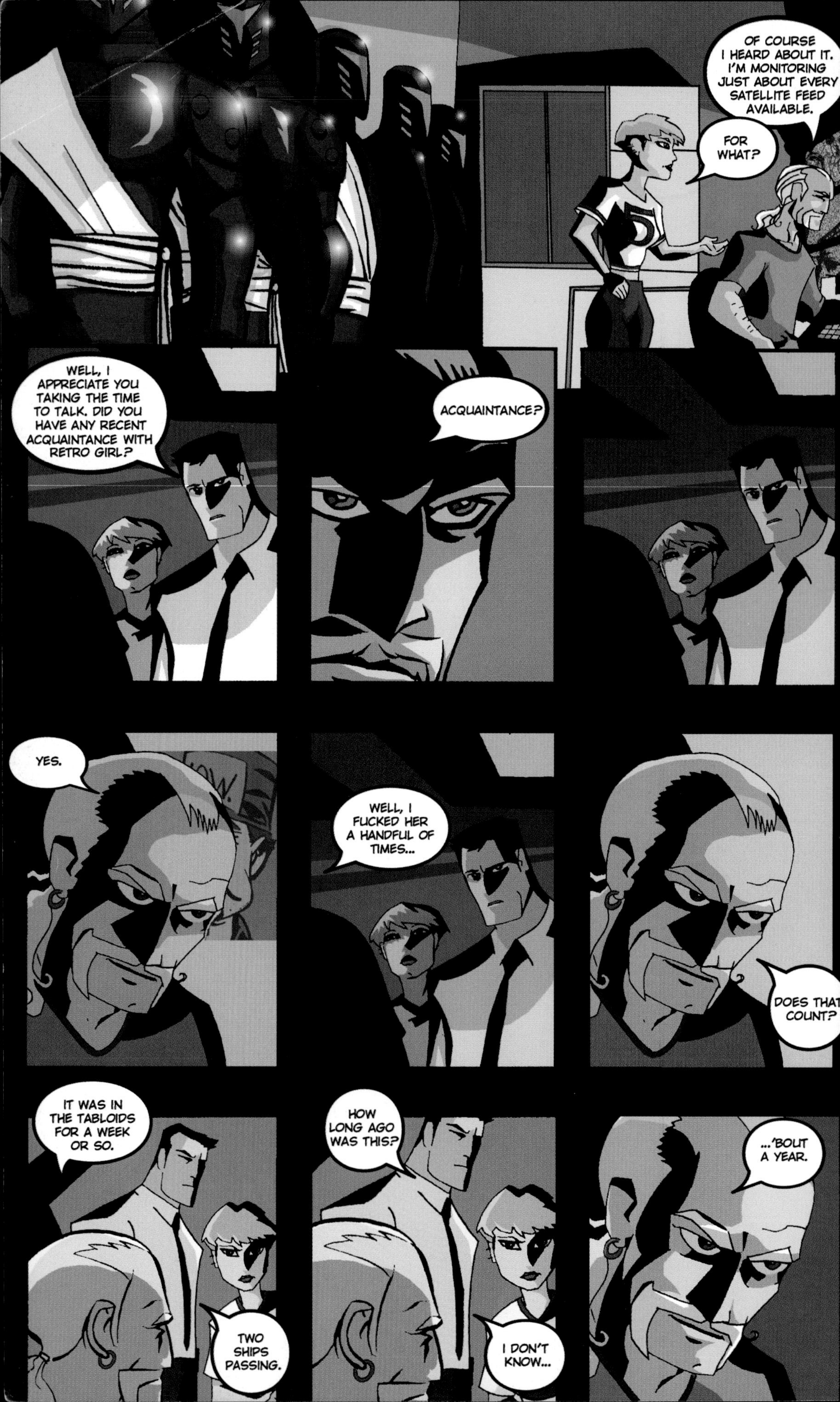
OF COURSE I HEARD ABOUT IT. I'M MONITORING JUST ABOUT EVERY SATELLITE FEED AVAILABLE.
FOR WHAT?
WELL, I APPRECIATE YOU TAKING THE TIME TO TALK. DID YOU HAVE ANY RECENT ACQUAINTANCE WITH RETRO GIRL?
ACQUAINTANCE?
YES.
WELL, I FUCKED HER A HANDFUL OF TIMES...
DOES THAT COUNT?
IT WAS IN THE TABLOIDS FOR A WEEK OR SO.
TWO SHIPS PASSING.
HOW LONG AGO WAS THIS?
I DON'T KNOW...
...'BOUT A YEAR.

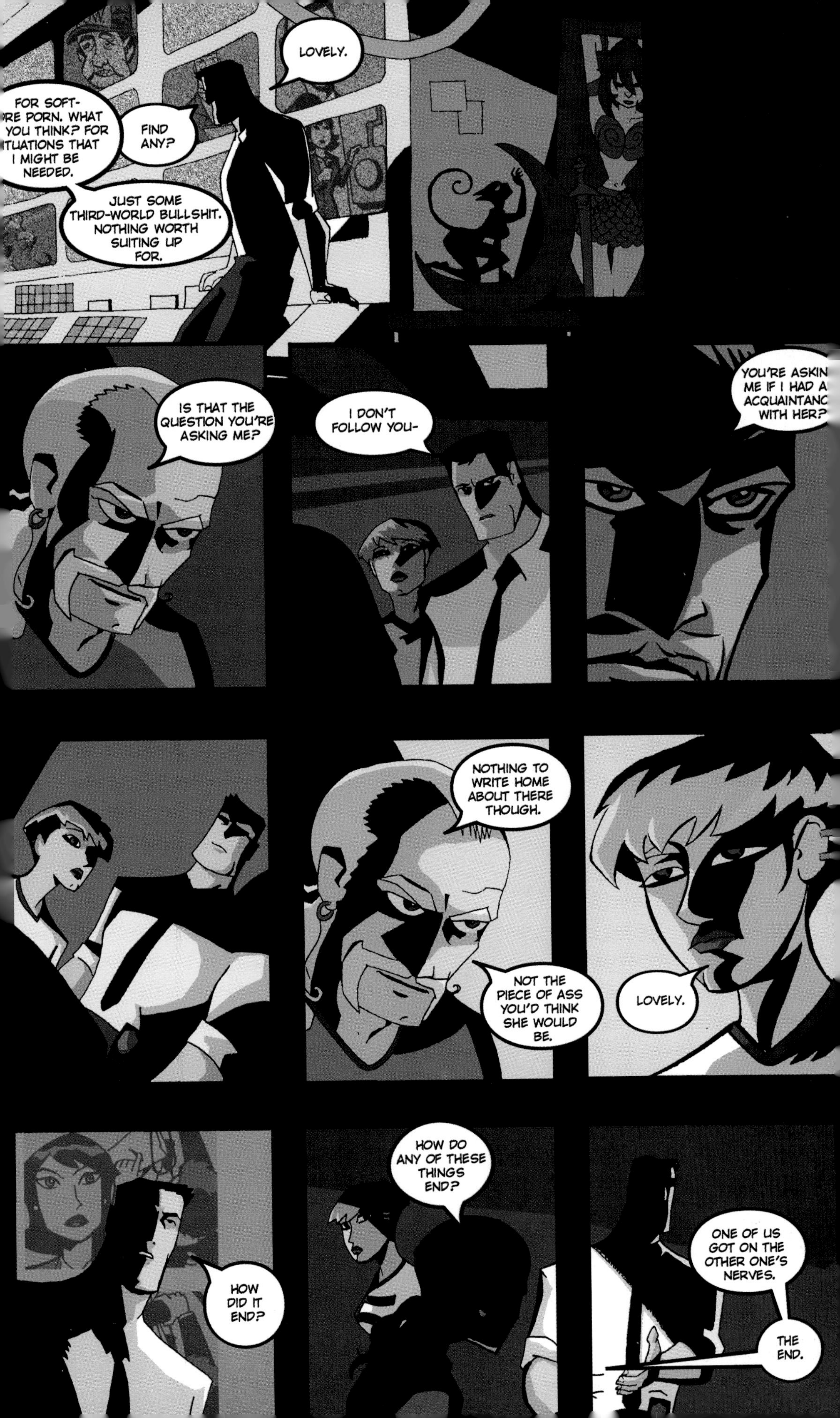
LOVELY.
FOR SOFT-
RE PORN. WHAT YOU THINK? FOR
TUATIONS THAT I MIGHT BE NEEDED.
FIND ANY?
JUST SOME THIRD-WORLD BULLSHIT. NOTHING WORTH SUITING UP FOR.
IS THAT THE QUESTION YOU'RE ASKING ME?
I DON'T FOLLOW YOU-
YOU'RE ASKIN ME IF I HAD A ACQUAINTANC WITH HER?
NOTHING TO WRITE HOME ABOUT THERE THOUGH.
NOT THE PIECE OF ASS YOU'D THINK SHE WOULD BE.
LOVELY.
HOW DID IT END?
HOW DO ANY OF THESE THINGS END?
ONE OF US GOT ON THE OTHER ONE'S NERVES.
THE END.

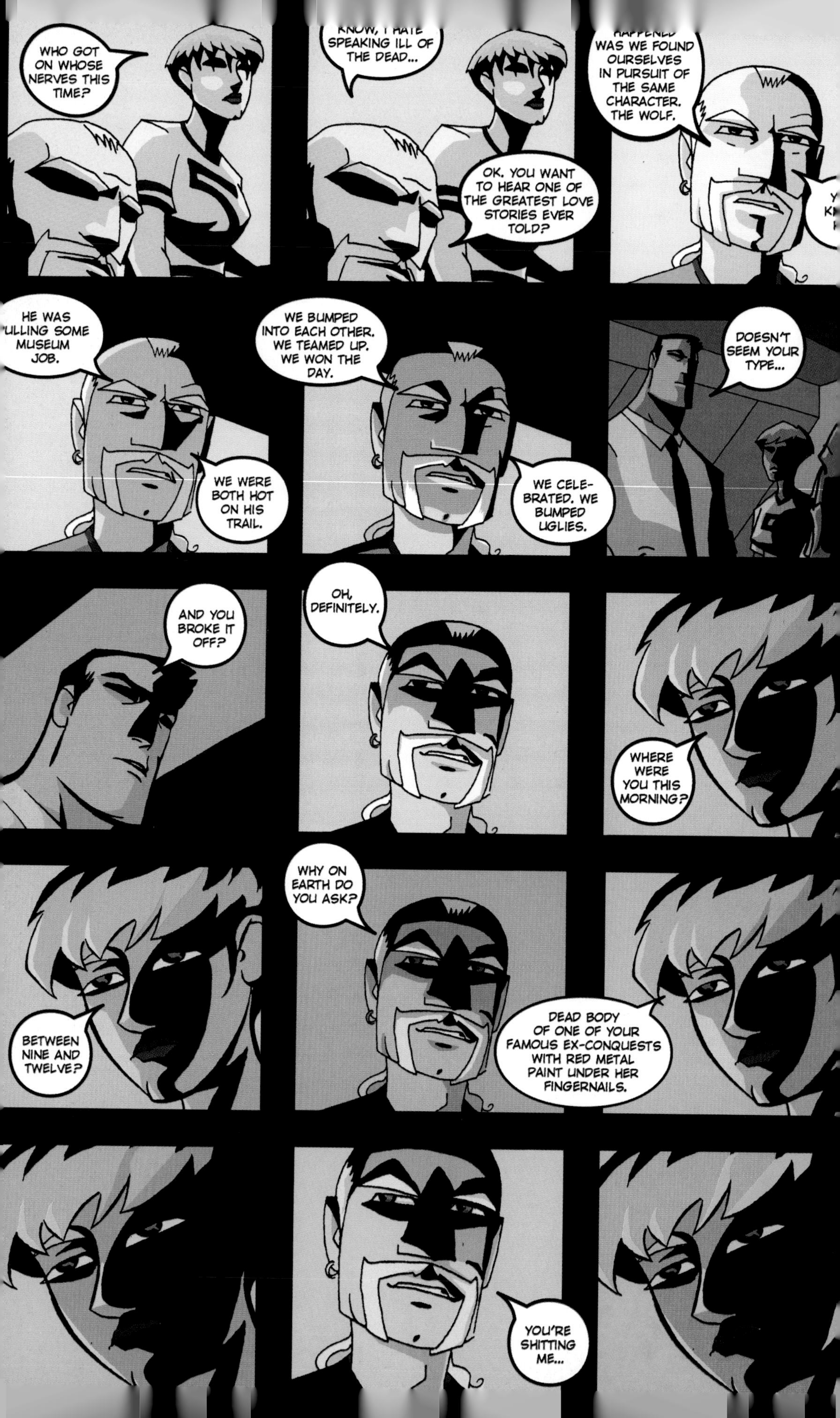

WHO GOT ON WHOSE NERVES THIS TIME?
KNOW, I HATE SPEAKING ILL OF THE DEAD...
OK. YOU WANT TO HEAR ONE OF THE GREATEST LOVE STORIES EVER TOLD?
WAS WE FOUND OURSELVES IN PURSUIT OF THE SAME CHARACTER. THE WOLF.
HE WAS ULLING SOME MUSEUM JOB.
WE WERE BOTH HOT ON HIS TRAIL.
WE BUMPED INTO EACH OTHER. WE TEAMED UP. WE WON THE DAY.
WE CELE-BRATED. WE BUMPED UGLIES.
DOESN'T SEEM YOUR TYPE...
AND YOU BROKE IT OFF?
OH, DEFINITELY.
WHERE WERE YOU THIS MORNING?
BETWEEN NINE AND TWELVE?
WHY ON EARTH DO YOU ASK?
DEAD BODY OF ONE OF YOUR FAMOUS EX-CONQUESTS WITH RED METAL PAINT UNDER HER FINGERNAILS.
YOU'RE SHITTING ME...

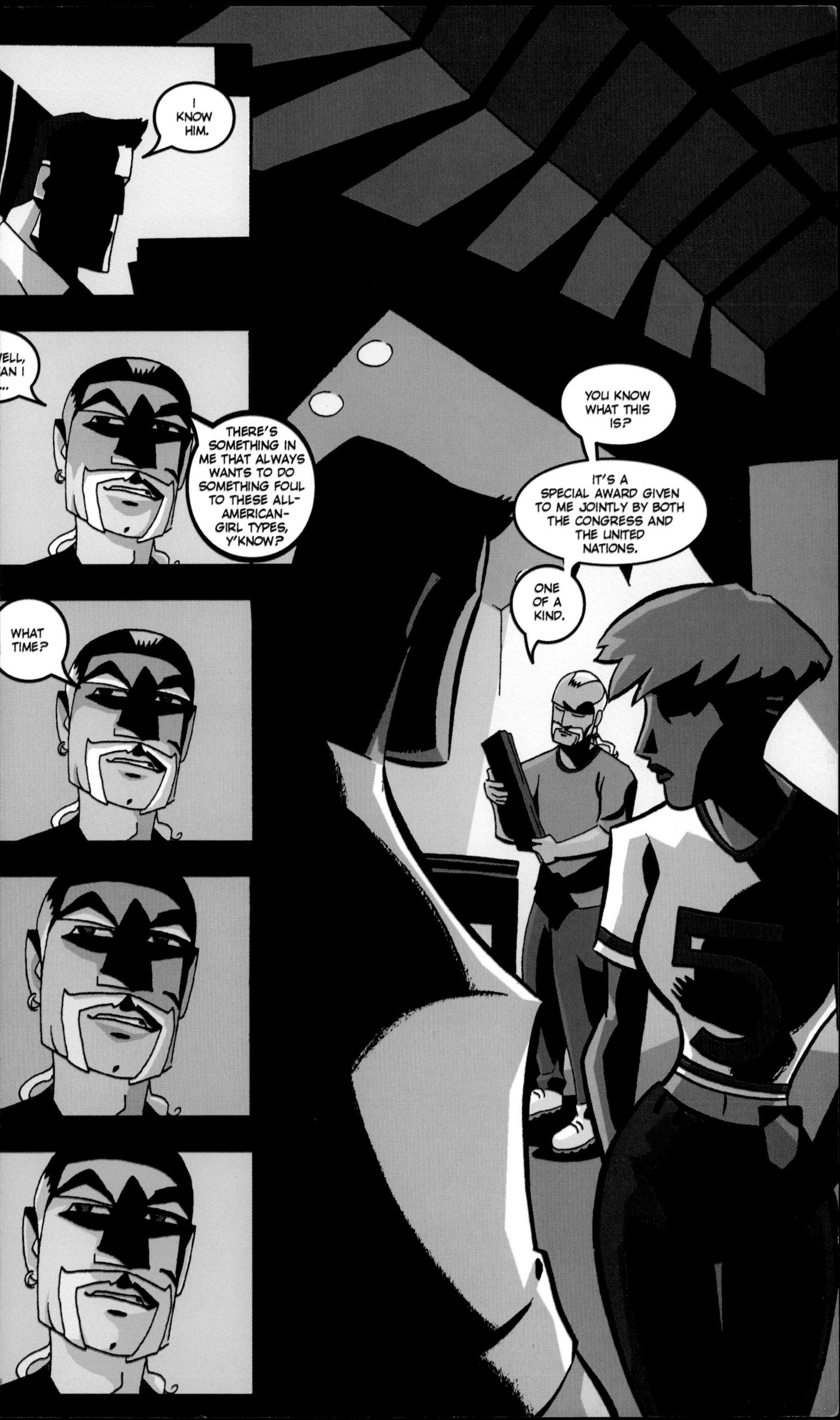
I KNOW HIM.
ELL, AN I ...
THERE'S SOMETHING IN ME THAT ALWAYS WANTS TO DO SOMETHING FOUL TO THESE ALL-AMERICAN-GIRL TYPES, Y'KNOW?
WHAT TIME?
YOU KNOW WHAT THIS IS?
IT'S A SPECIAL AWARD GIVEN TO ME JOINTLY BY BOTH THE CONGRESS AND THE UNITED NATIONS.
ONE OF A KIND.

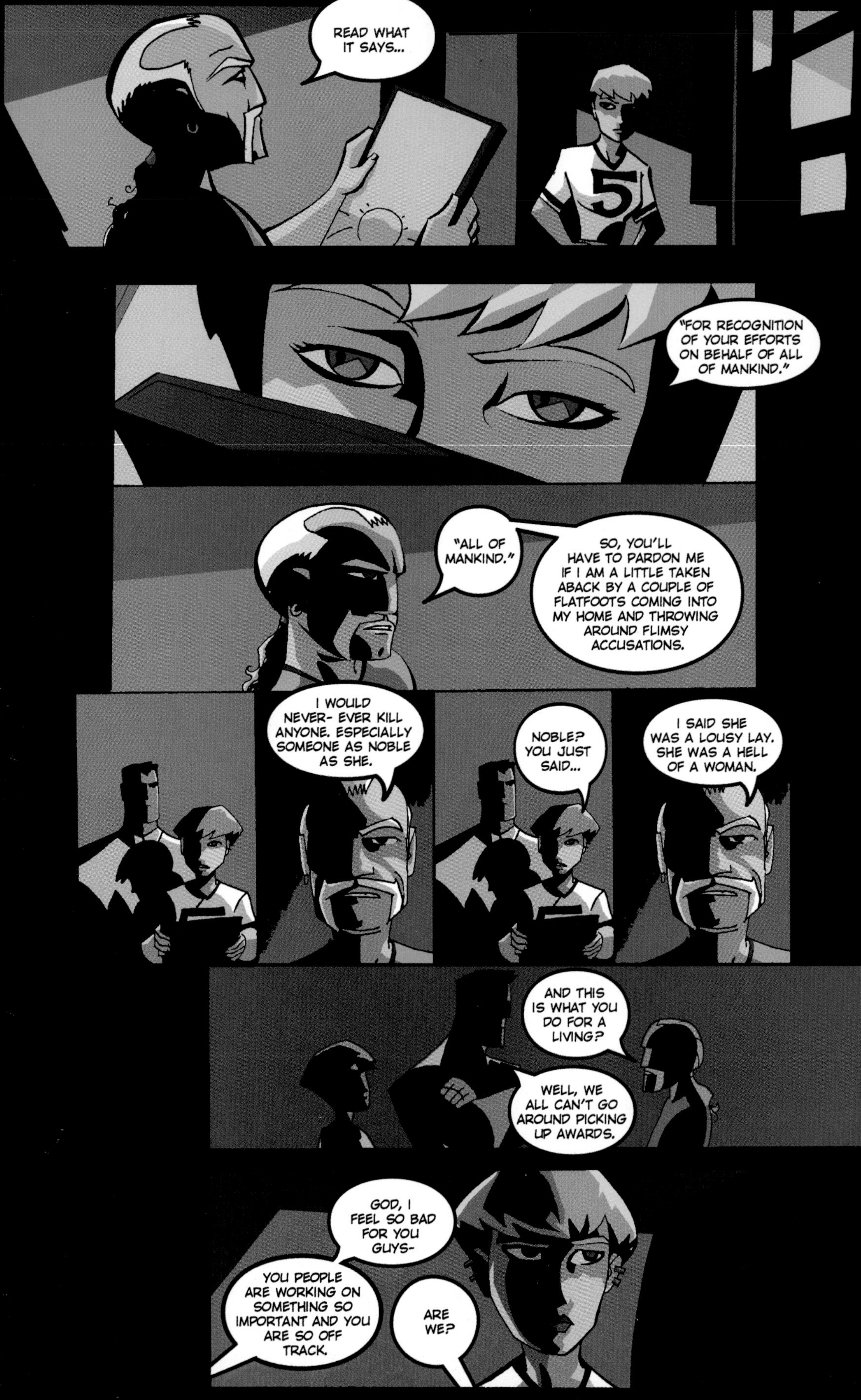
READ WHAT IT SAYS...
"FOR RECOGNITION OF YOUR EFFORTS ON BEHALF OF ALL OF MANKIND."
"ALL OF MANKIND."
SO, YOU'LL HAVE TO PARDON ME IF I AM A LITTLE TAKEN ABACK BY A COUPLE OF FLATFOOTS COMING INTO MY HOME AND THROWING AROUND FLIMSY ACCUSATIONS.
I WOULD NEVER- EVER KILL ANYONE. ESPECIALLY SOMEONE AS NOBLE AS SHE.
NOBLE? YOU JUST SAID...
I SAID SHE WAS A LOUSY LAY. SHE WAS A HELL OF A WOMAN.
AND THIS IS WHAT YOU DO FOR A LIVING?
WELL, WE ALL CAN'T GO AROUND PICKING UP AWARDS.
GOD, I FEEL SO BAD FOR YOU GUYS-
YOU PEOPLE ARE WORKING ON SOMETHING SO IMPORTANT AND YOU ARE SO OFF TRACK.
ARE WE?

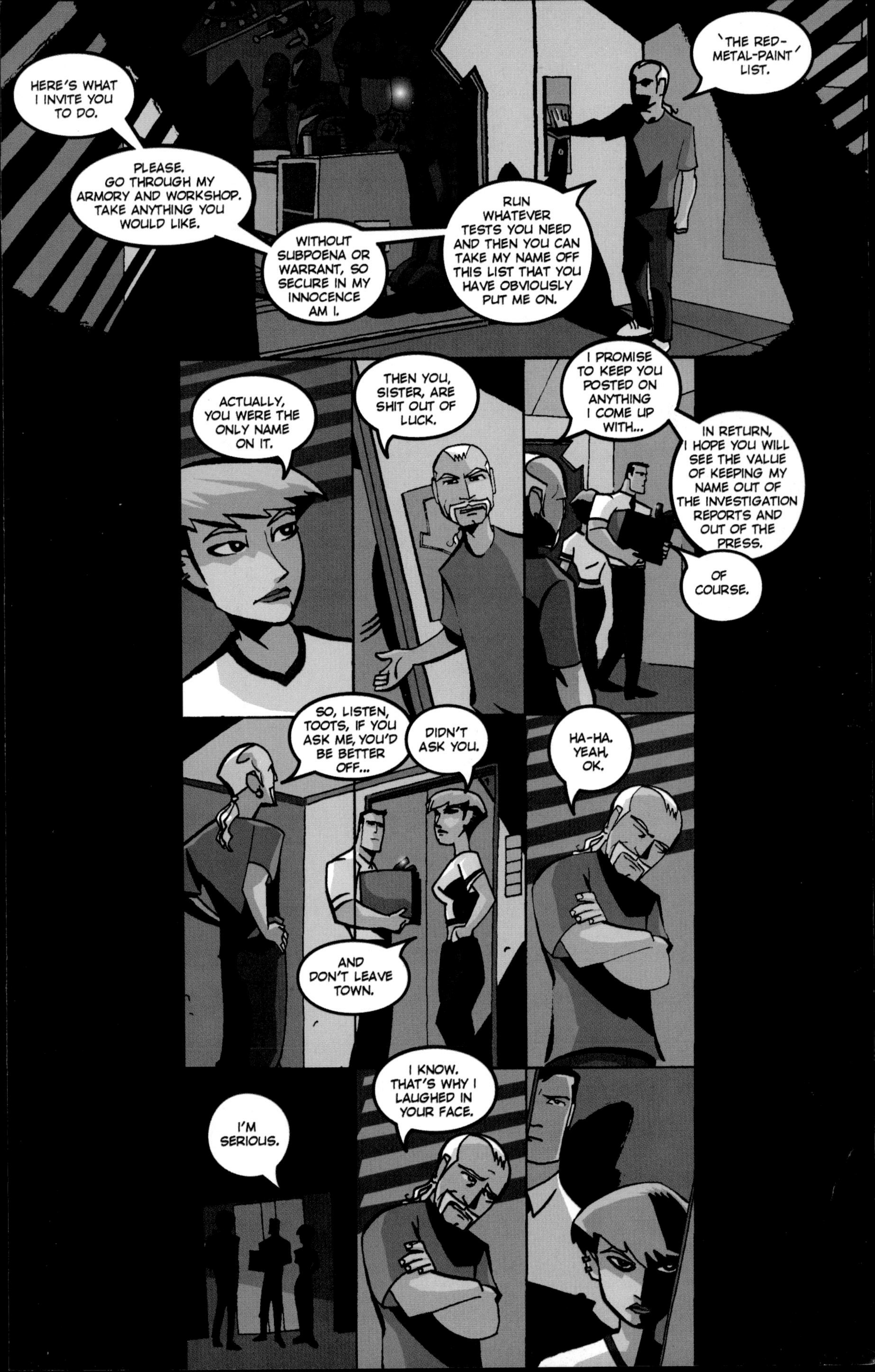
HERE'S WHAT I INVITE YOU TO DO.
PLEASE. GO THROUGH MY ARMORY AND WORKSHOP. TAKE ANYTHING YOU WOULD LIKE.
WITHOUT SUBPOENA OR WARRANT, SO SECURE IN MY INNOCENCE AM I.
RUN WHATEVER TESTS YOU NEED AND THEN YOU CAN TAKE MY NAME OFF THIS LIST THAT YOU HAVE OBVIOUSLY PUT ME ON.
`THE RED-METAL-PAINT' LIST.
ACTUALLY, YOU WERE THE ONLY NAME ON IT.
THEN YOU, SISTER, ARE SHIT OUT OF LUCK.
I PROMISE TO KEEP YOU POSTED ON ANYTHING I COME UP WITH...
IN RETURN, I HOPE YOU WILL SEE THE VALUE OF KEEPING MY NAME OUT OF THE INVESTIGATION REPORTS AND OUT OF THE PRESS.
OF COURSE.
SO, LISTEN, TOOTS, IF YOU ASK ME, YOU'D BE BETTER OFF...
DIDN'T ASK YOU.
AND DON'T LEAVE TOWN.
HA-HA. YEAH, OK.
I'M SERIOUS.
I KNOW. THAT'S WHY I LAUGHED IN YOUR FACE.

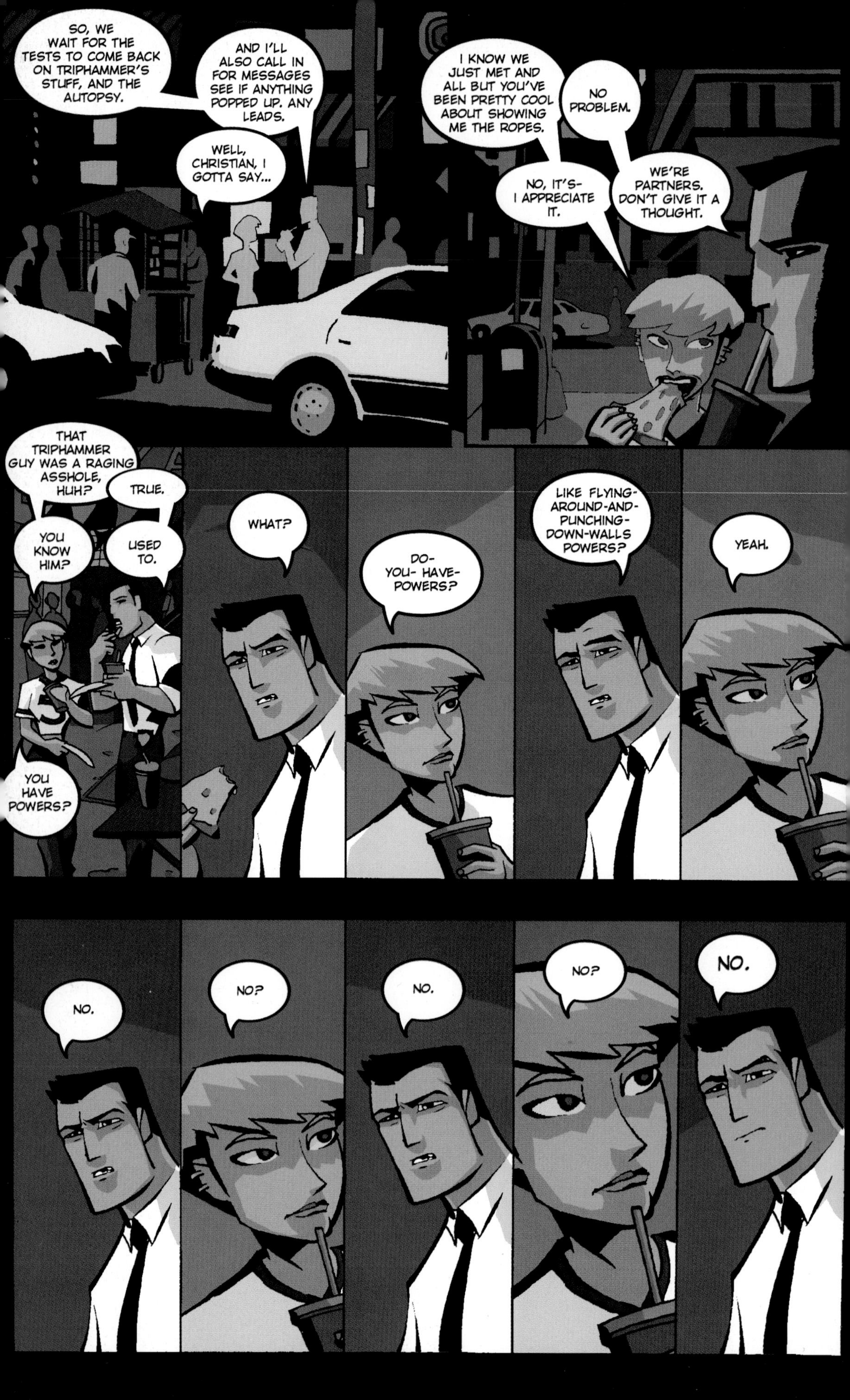
SO, WE WAIT FOR THE TESTS TO COME BACK ON TRIPHAMMER'S STUFF, AND THE AUTOPSY.
AND I'LL ALSO CALL IN FOR MESSAGES SEE IF ANYTHING POPPED UP. ANY LEADS.
WELL, CHRISTIAN, I GOTTA SAY...
I KNOW WE JUST MET AND ALL BUT YOU'VE BEEN PRETTY COOL ABOUT SHOWING ME THE ROPES.
NO PROBLEM.
NO, IT'S- I APPRECIATE IT.
WE'RE PARTNERS. DON'T GIVE IT A THOUGHT.
THAT TRIPHAMMER GUY WAS A RAGING ASSHOLE, HUH?
TRUE.
YOU KNOW HIM?
USED TO.
YOU HAVE POWERS?
WHAT?
DO- YOU- HAVE- POWERS?
LIKE FLYING- AROUND-AND- PUNCHING- DOWN-WALLS POWERS?
YEAH.
NO.
NO?
NO.
NO?
NO.

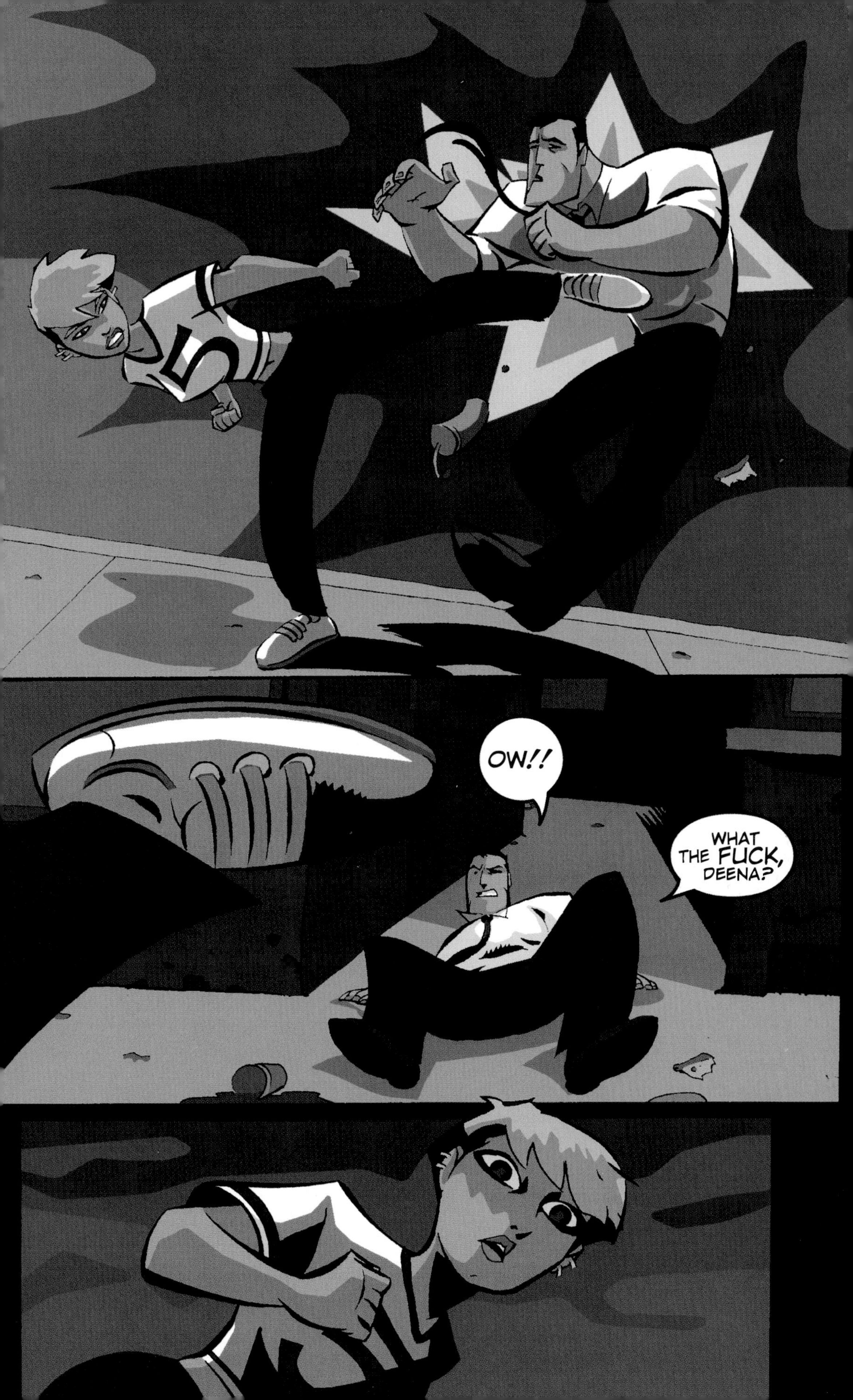
OW!!
WHAT THE FUCK, DEENA?

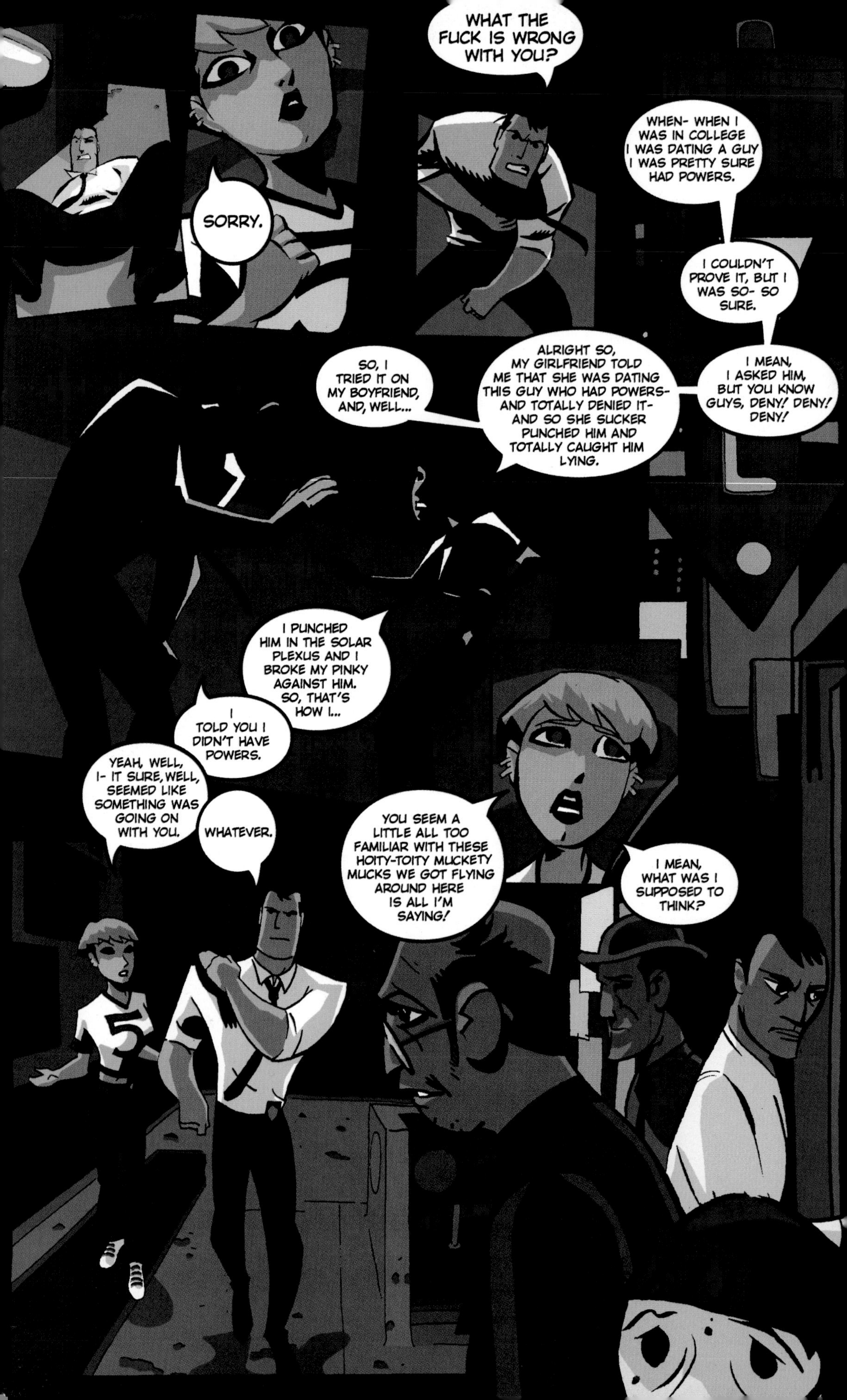
SORRY.
WHAT THE FUCK IS WRONG WITH YOU?
WHEN- WHEN I WAS IN COLLEGE I WAS DATING A GUY I WAS PRETTY SURE HAD POWERS.
I COULDN'T PROVE IT, BUT I WAS SO- SO SURE.
I MEAN, I ASKED HIM, BUT YOU KNOW GUYS, DENY! DENY! DENY!
ALRIGHT SO, MY GIRLFRIEND TOLD ME THAT SHE WAS DATING THIS GUY WHO HAD POWERS- AND TOTALLY DENIED IT- AND SO SHE SUCKER PUNCHED HIM AND TOTALLY CAUGHT HIM LYING.
SO, I TRIED IT ON MY BOYFRIEND, AND, WELL...
I PUNCHED HIM IN THE SOLAR PLEXUS AND I BROKE MY PINKY AGAINST HIM. SO, THAT'S HOW I...
I TOLD YOU I DIDN'T HAVE POWERS.
YEAH, WELL, I- IT SURE, WELL, SEEMED LIKE SOMETHING WAS GOING ON WITH YOU.
WHATEVER.
YOU SEEM A LITTLE ALL TOO FAMILIAR WITH THESE HOITY-TOITY MUCKETY MUCKS WE GOT FLYING AROUND HERE IS ALL I'M SAYING!
I MEAN, WHAT WAS I SUPPOSED TO THINK?

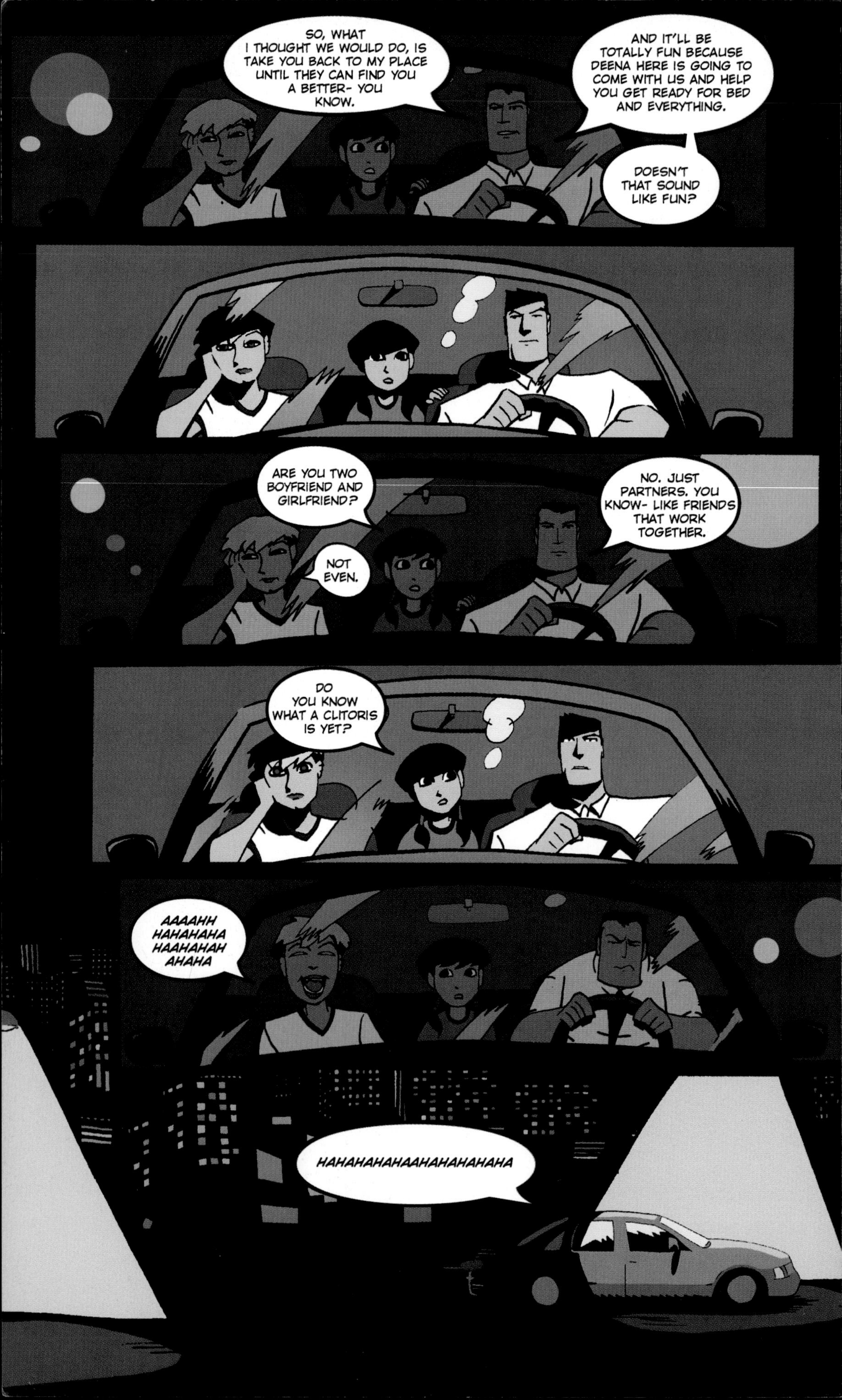

SO, WHAT I THOUGHT WE WOULD DO, IS TAKE YOU BACK TO MY PLACE UNTIL THEY CAN FIND YOU A BETTER- YOU KNOW.
AND IT'LL BE TOTALLY FUN BECAUSE DEENA HERE IS GOING TO COME WITH US AND HELP YOU GET READY FOR BED AND EVERYTHING.
DOESN'T THAT SOUND LIKE FUN?
ARE YOU TWO BOYFRIEND AND GIRLFRIEND?
NOT EVEN.
NO. JUST PARTNERS. YOU KNOW- LIKE FRIENDS THAT WORK TOGETHER.
DO YOU KNOW WHAT A CLITORIS IS YET?
AAAAHH HAHAHAHA HAAHAHAH AHAHA
HAHAHAHAHAAHAHAHAHAHA

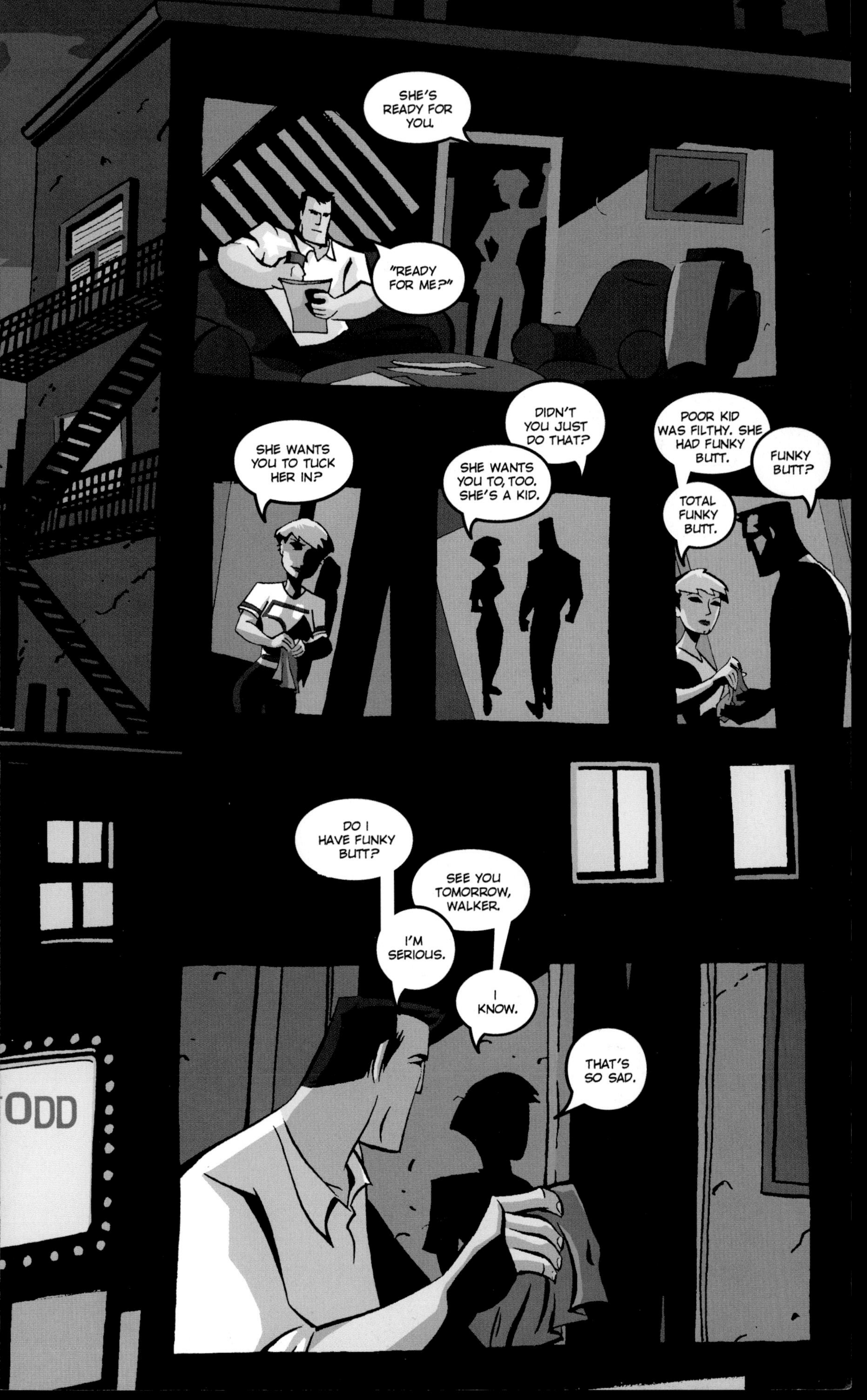
SHE'S READY FOR YOU.
"READY FOR ME?"
SHE WANTS YOU TO TUCK HER IN?
DIDN'T YOU JUST DO THAT?
SHE WANTS YOU TO, TOO. SHE'S A KID.
POOR KID WAS FILTHY. SHE HAD FUNKY BUTT.
FUNKY BUTT?
TOTAL FUNKY BUTT.
DO I HAVE FUNKY BUTT?
I'M SERIOUS.
SEE YOU TOMORROW, WALKER.
I KNOW.
THAT'S SO SAD.
ODD

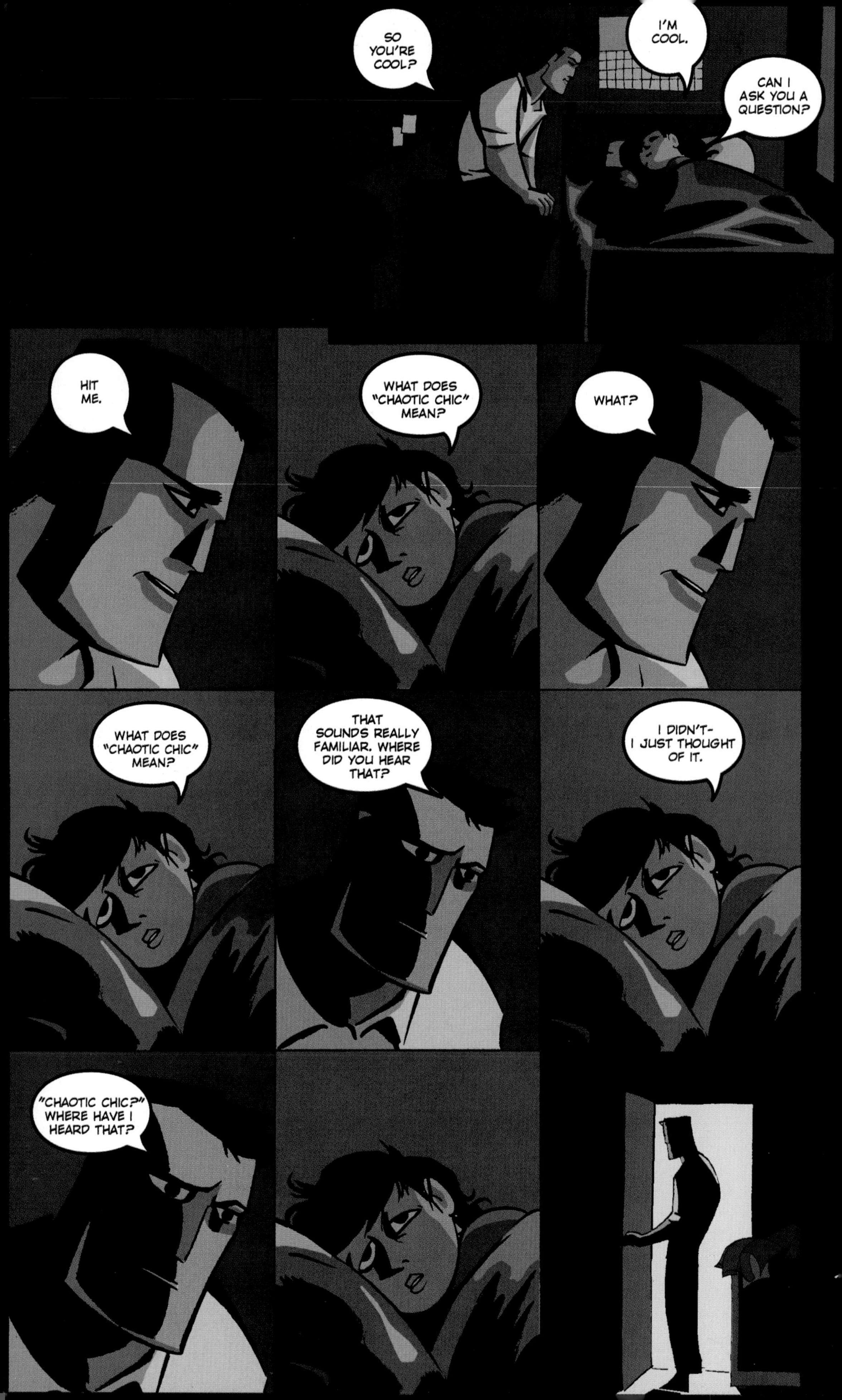
SO YOU'RE COOL?
I'M COOL.
CAN I ASK YOU A QUESTION?
HIT ME.
WHAT DOES "CHAOTIC CHIC" MEAN?
WHAT?
WHAT DOES "CHAOTIC CHIC" MEAN?
THAT SOUNDS REALLY FAMILIAR. WHERE DID YOU HEAR THAT?
I DIDN'T- I JUST THOUGHT OF IT.
"CHAOTIC CHIC?" WHERE HAVE I HEARD THAT?

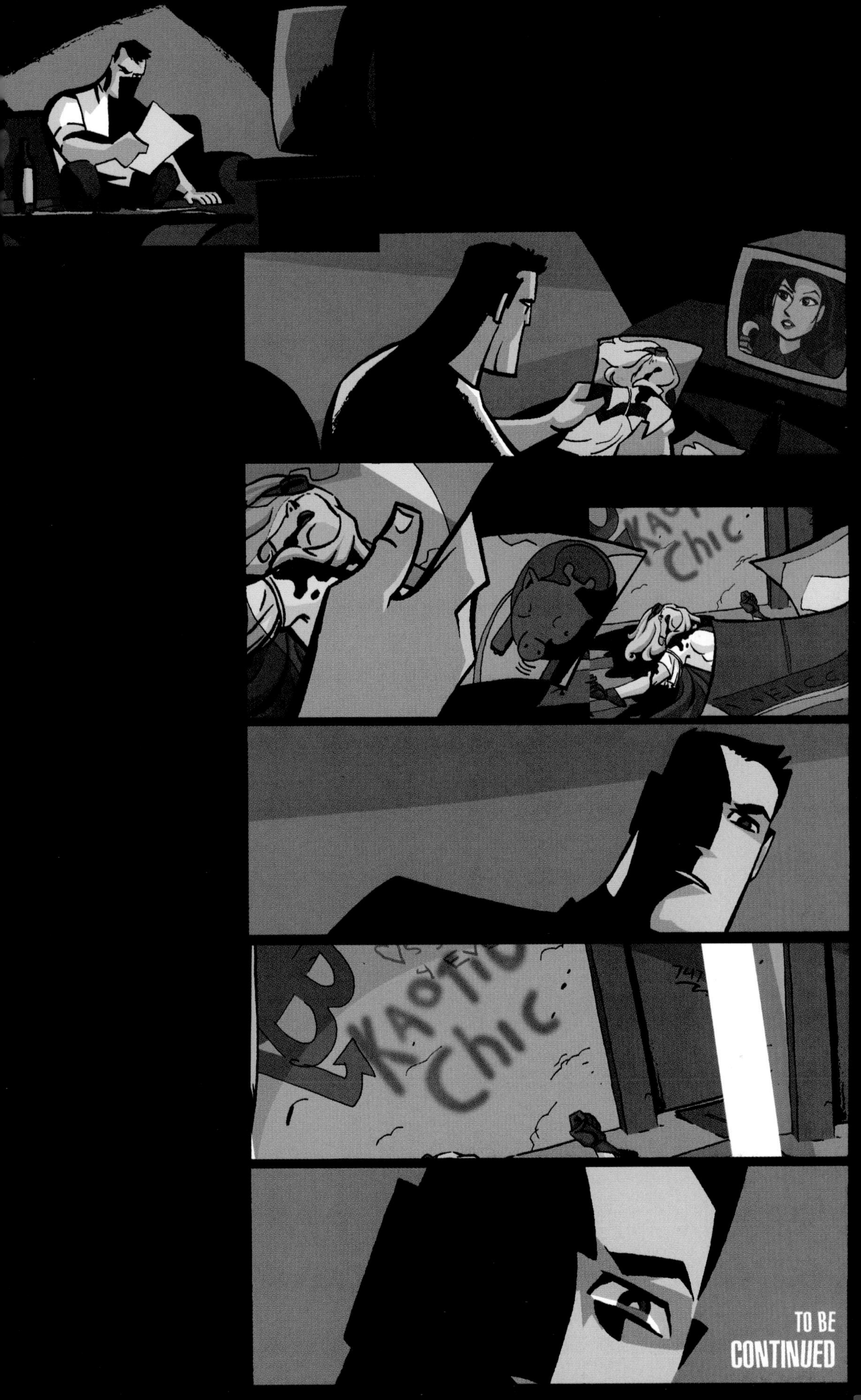
TO BE
CONTINUED

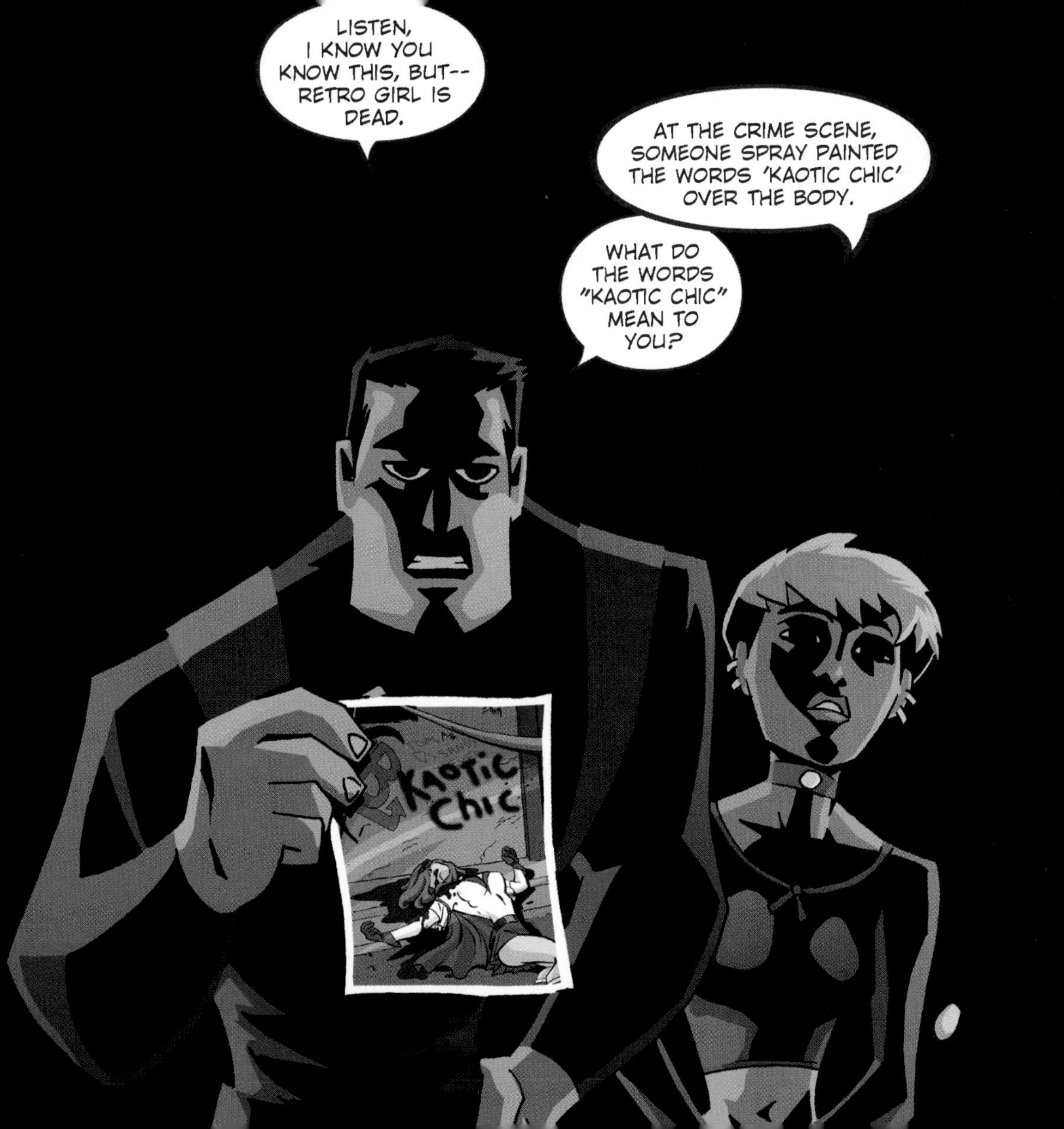
LISTEN, I KNOW YOU KNOW THIS, BUT-- RETRO GIRL IS DEAD.
AT THE CRIME SCENE, SOMEONE SPRAY PAINTED THE WORDS 'KAOTIC CHIC' OVER THE BODY.
WHAT DO THE WORDS "KAOTIC CHIC" MEAN TO YOU?
KAOTIC CHIC

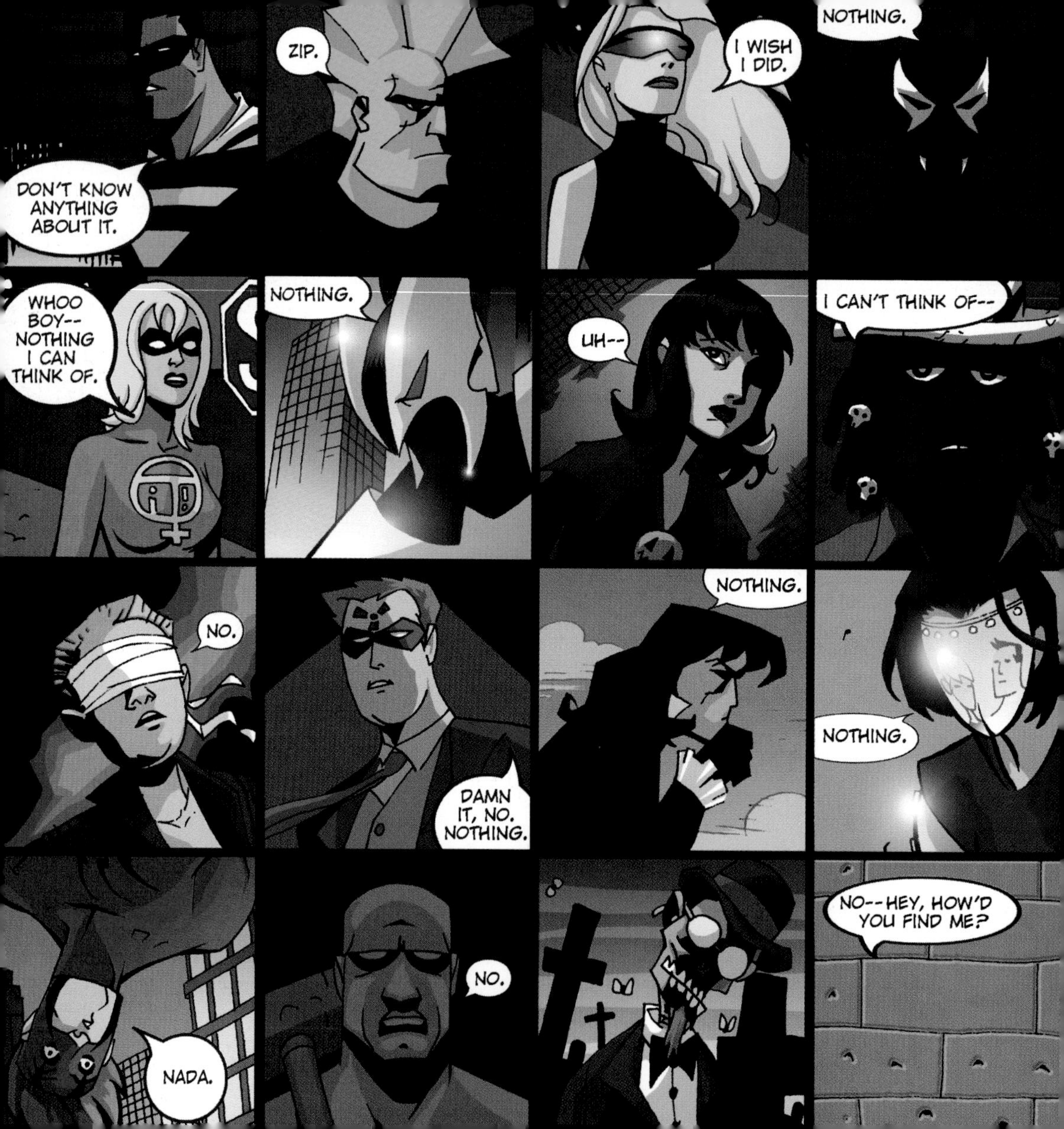
DON'T KNOW ANYTHING ABOUT IT.
ZIP.
I WISH I DID.
NOTHING.
WHOO BOY-- NOTHING I CAN THINK OF.
NOTHING.
UH--
I CAN'T THINK OF--
NO.
DAMN IT, NO. NOTHING.
NOTHING.
NOTHING.
NADA.
NO.
NO--HEY, HOW'D YOU FIND ME?

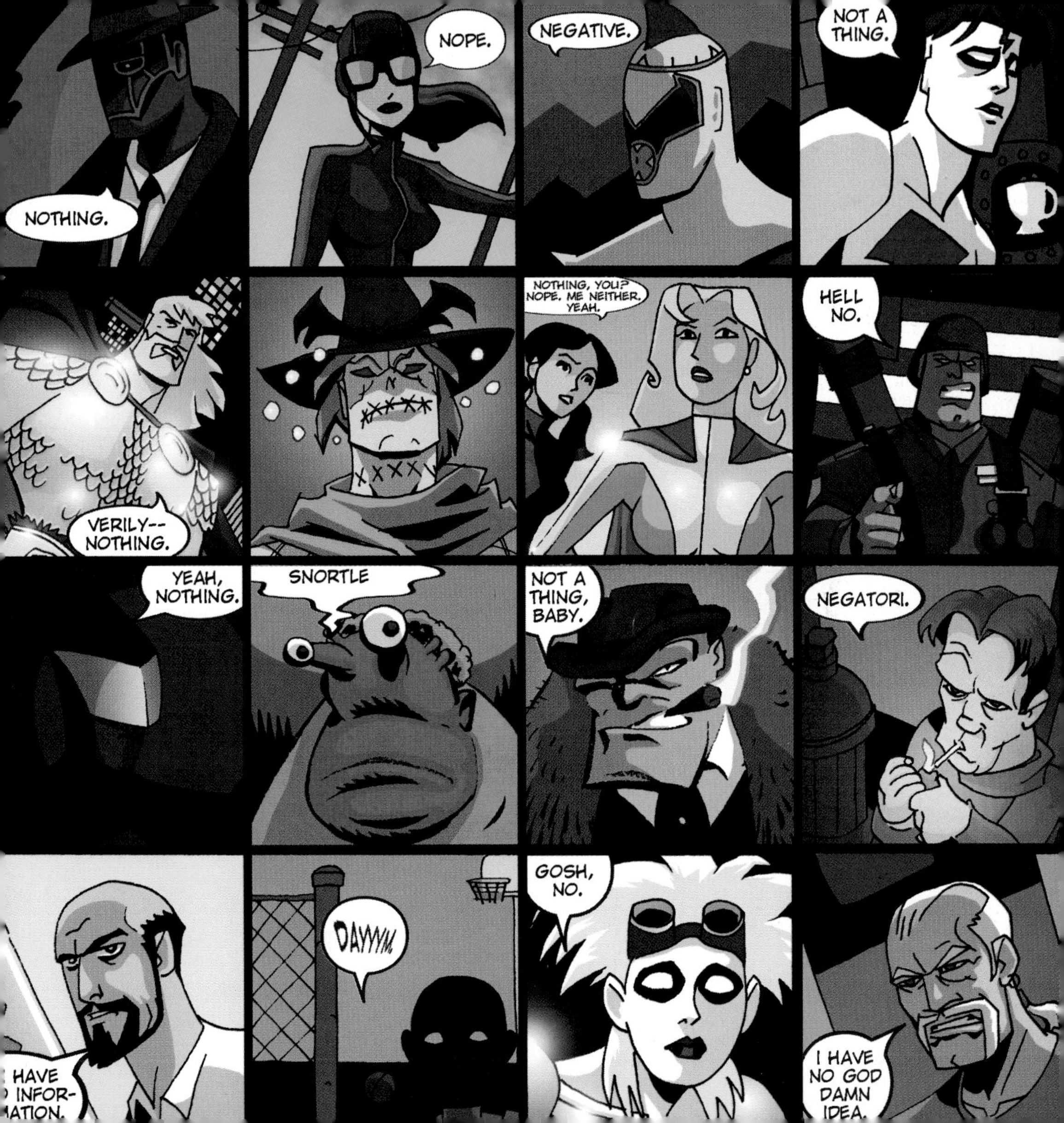
NOTHING.
NOPE.
NEGATIVE.
NOT A THING.
VERILY-- NOTHING.
NOTHING, YOU? NOPE. ME NEITHER. YEAH.
HELL NO.
YEAH, NOTHING.
SNORTLE
NOT A THING, BABY.
NEGATORI.
HAVE INFOR- ATION.
DAYYYM.
GOSH, NO.
I HAVE NO GOD DAMN IDEA.

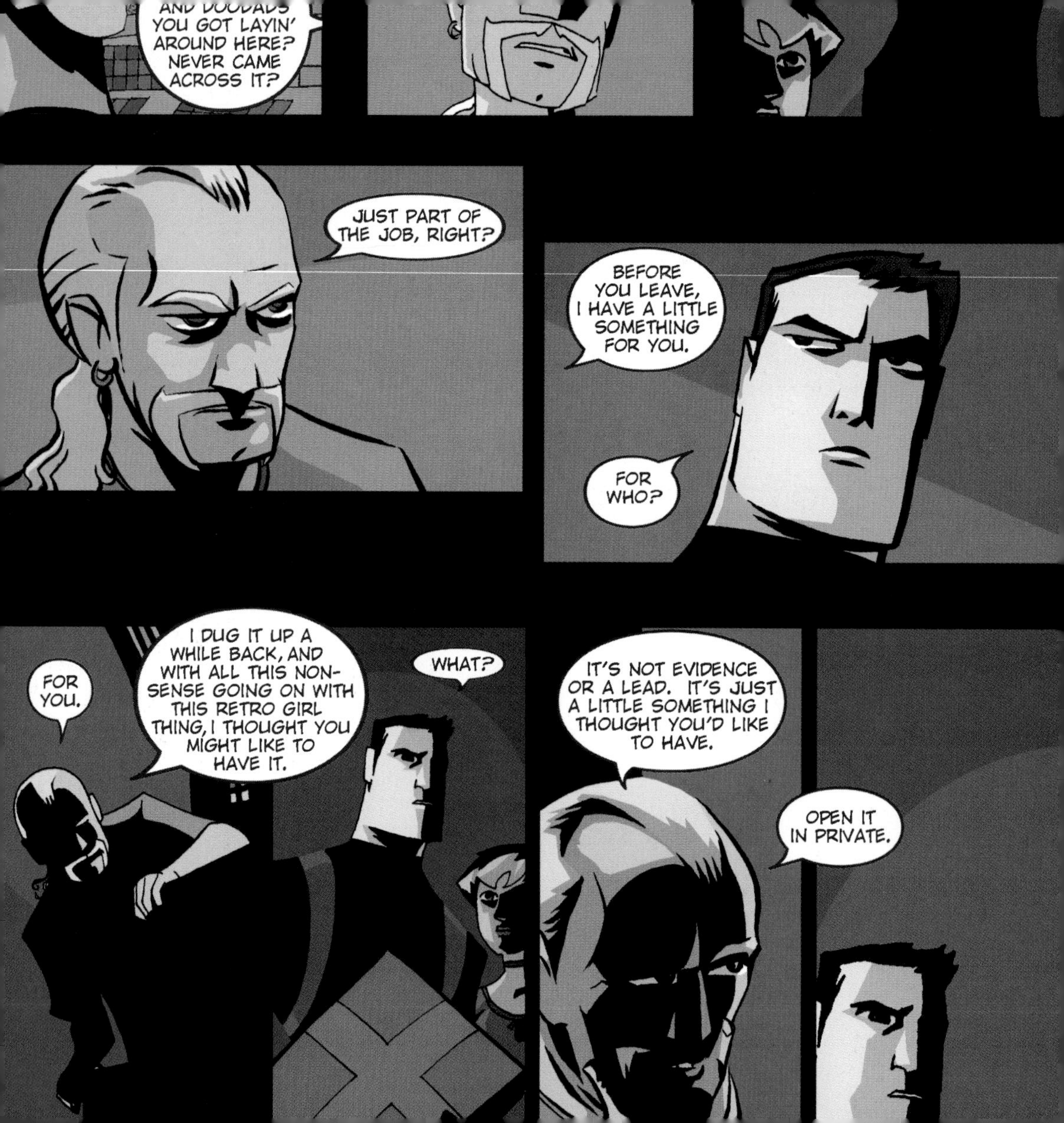
AND DOODADS YOU GOT LAYIN' AROUND HERE? NEVER CAME ACROSS IT?
JUST PART OF THE JOB, RIGHT?
BEFORE YOU LEAVE, I HAVE A LITTLE SOMETHING FOR YOU.
FOR WHO?
FOR YOU.
I DUG IT UP A WHILE BACK, AND WITH ALL THIS NON-SENSE GOING ON WITH THIS RETRO GIRL THING, I THOUGHT YOU MIGHT LIKE TO HAVE IT.
WHAT?
IT'S NOT EVIDENCE OR A LEAD. IT'S JUST A LITTLE SOMETHING I THOUGHT YOU'D LIKE TO HAVE.
OPEN IT IN PRIVATE.

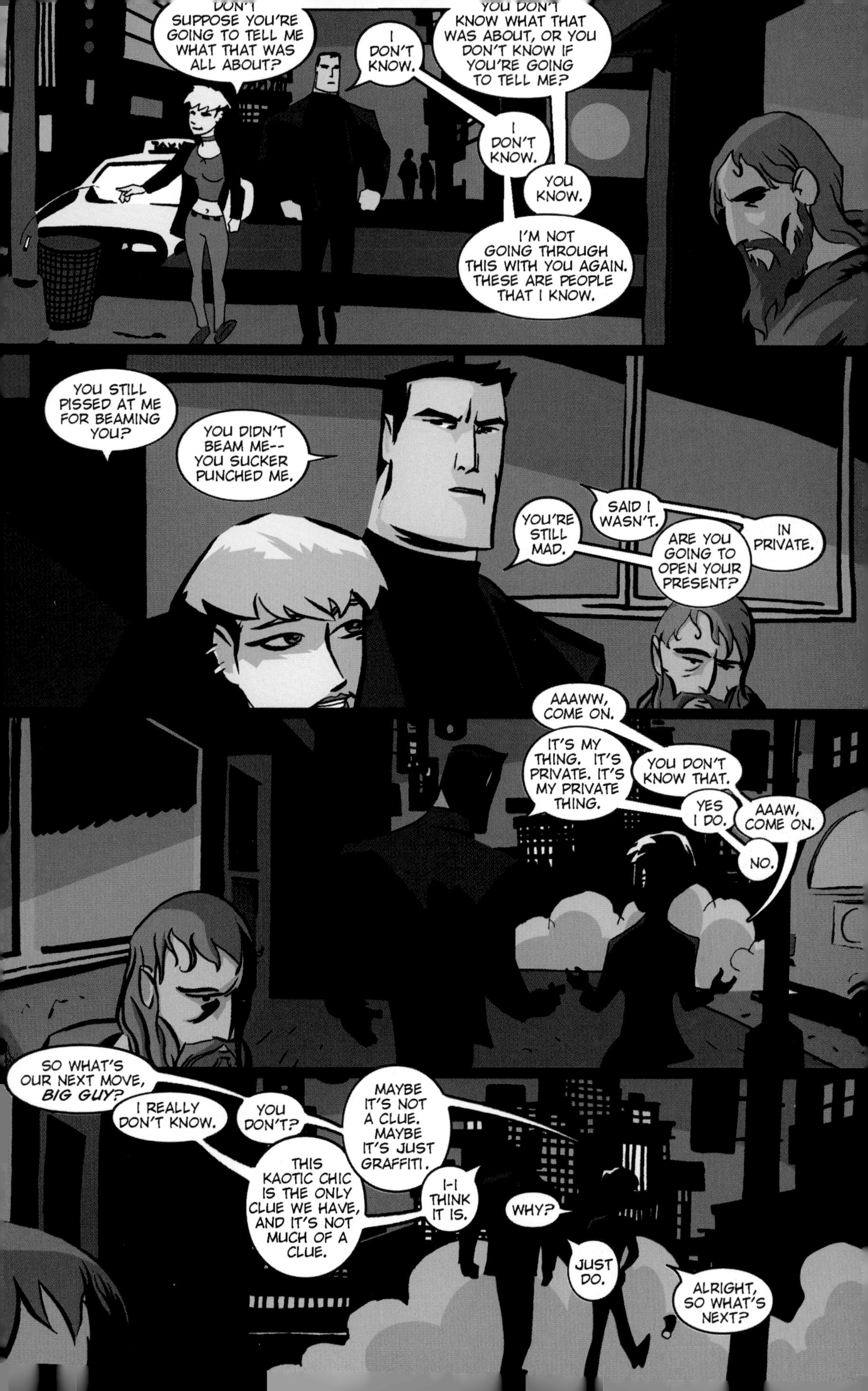
DON'T SUPPOSE YOU'RE GOING TO TELL ME WHAT THAT WAS ALL ABOUT?
I DON'T KNOW.
YOU DON'T KNOW WHAT THAT WAS ABOUT, OR YOU DON'T KNOW IF YOU'RE GOING TO TELL ME?
I DON'T KNOW.
YOU KNOW.
I'M NOT GOING THROUGH THIS WITH YOU AGAIN. THESE ARE PEOPLE THAT I KNOW.
YOU STILL PISSED AT ME FOR BEAMING YOU?
YOU DIDN'T BEAM ME-- YOU SUCKER PUNCHED ME.
YOU'RE STILL MAD.
SAID I WASN'T.
IN PRIVATE.
ARE YOU GOING TO OPEN YOUR PRESENT?
AAAWW, COME ON.
IT'S MY THING. IT'S PRIVATE. IT'S MY PRIVATE THING.
YOU DON'T KNOW THAT.
YES I DO.
AAAW, COME ON.
NO.
SO WHAT'S OUR NEXT MOVE, *BIG GUY?*
I REALLY DON'T KNOW.
YOU DON'T?
THIS KAOTIC CHIC IS THE ONLY CLUE WE HAVE, AND IT'S NOT MUCH OF A CLUE.
MAYBE IT'S NOT A CLUE. MAYBE IT'S JUST GRAFFITI.
I-I THINK IT IS.
WHY?
JUST DO.
ALRIGHT, SO WHAT'S NEXT?

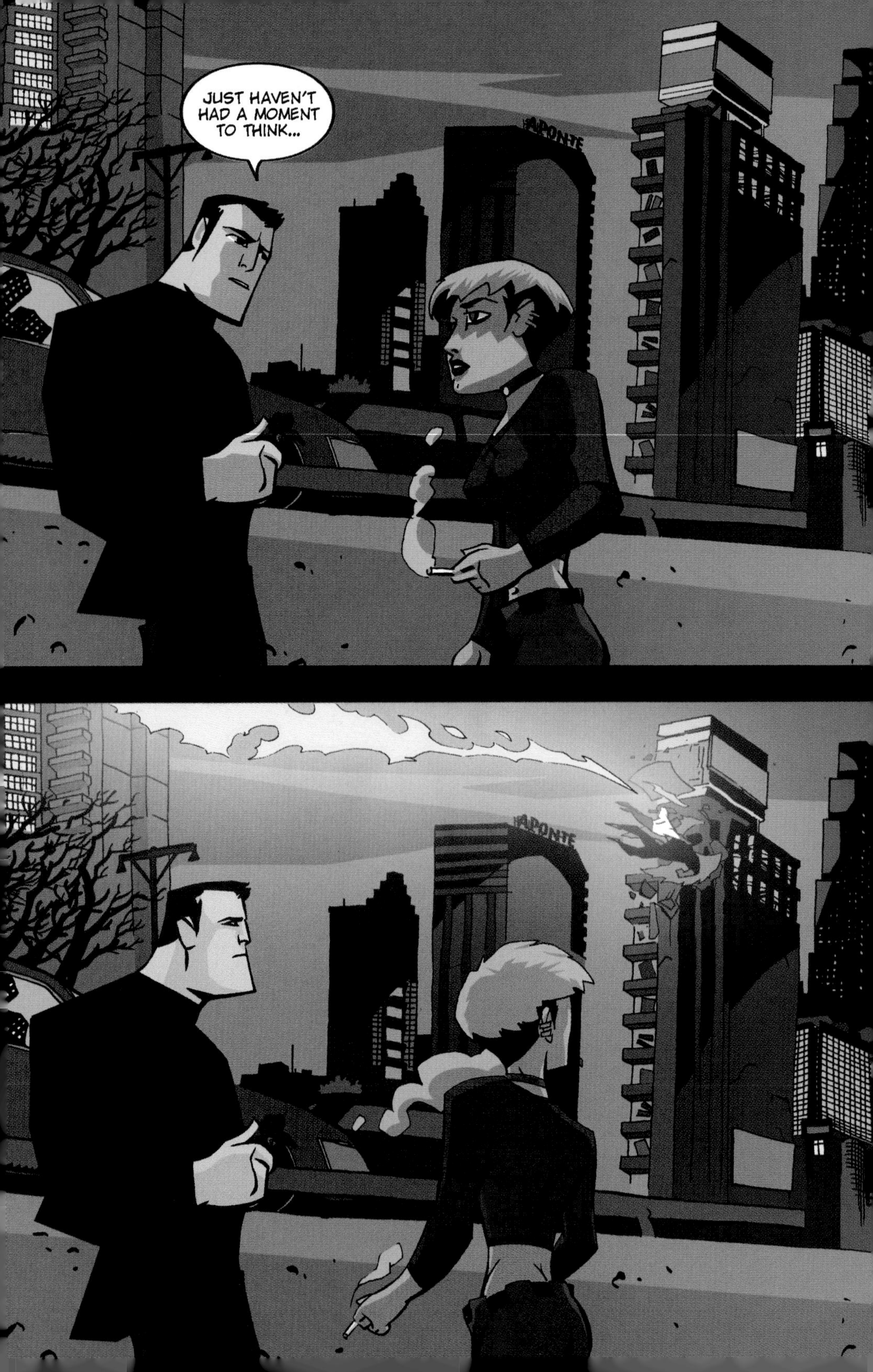
JUST HAVEN'T HAD A MOMENT TO THINK...

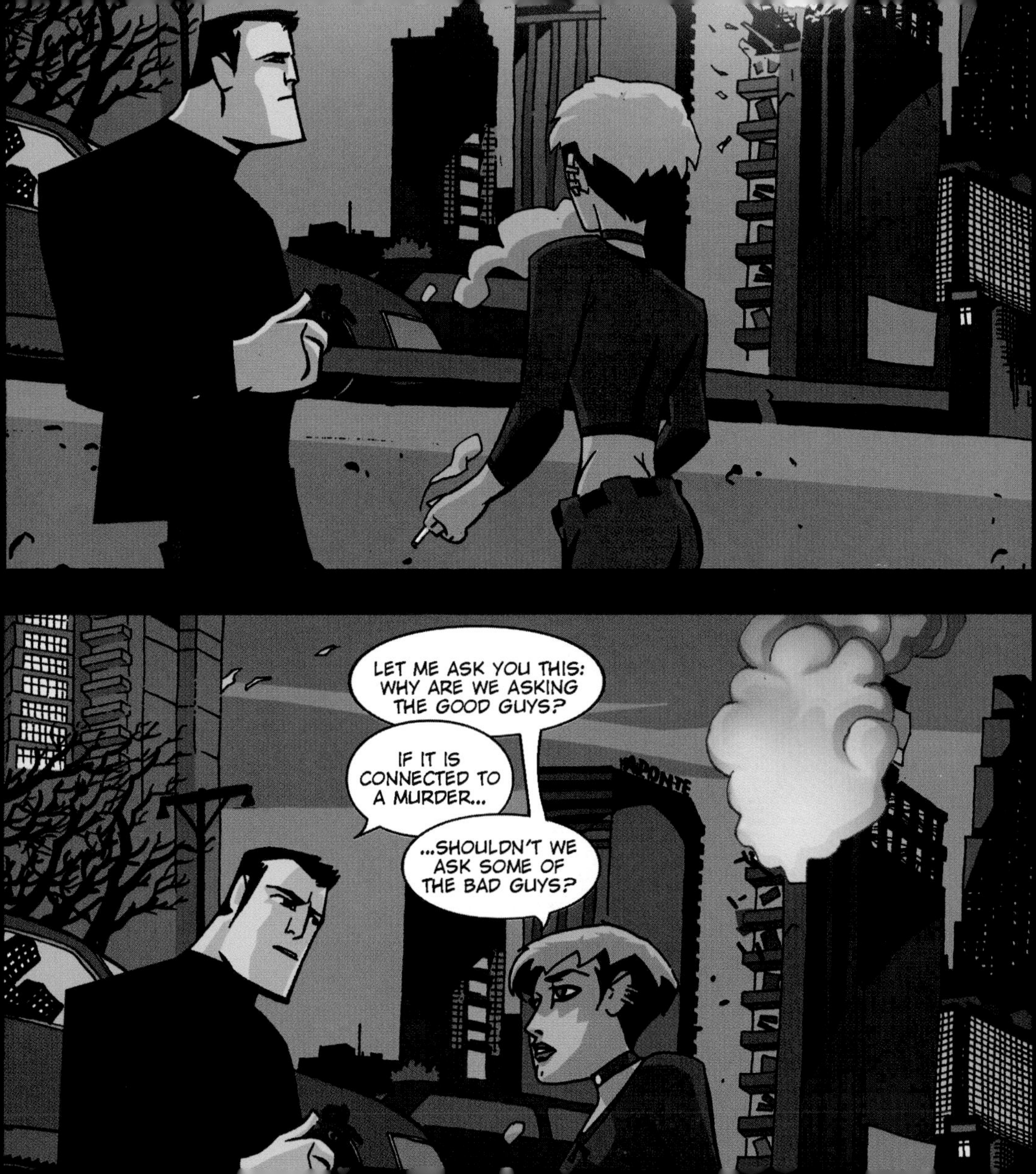
LET ME ASK YOU THIS: WHY ARE WE ASKING THE GOOD GUYS?
IF IT IS CONNECTED TO A MURDER...
...SHOULDN'T WE ASK SOME OF THE BAD GUYS?

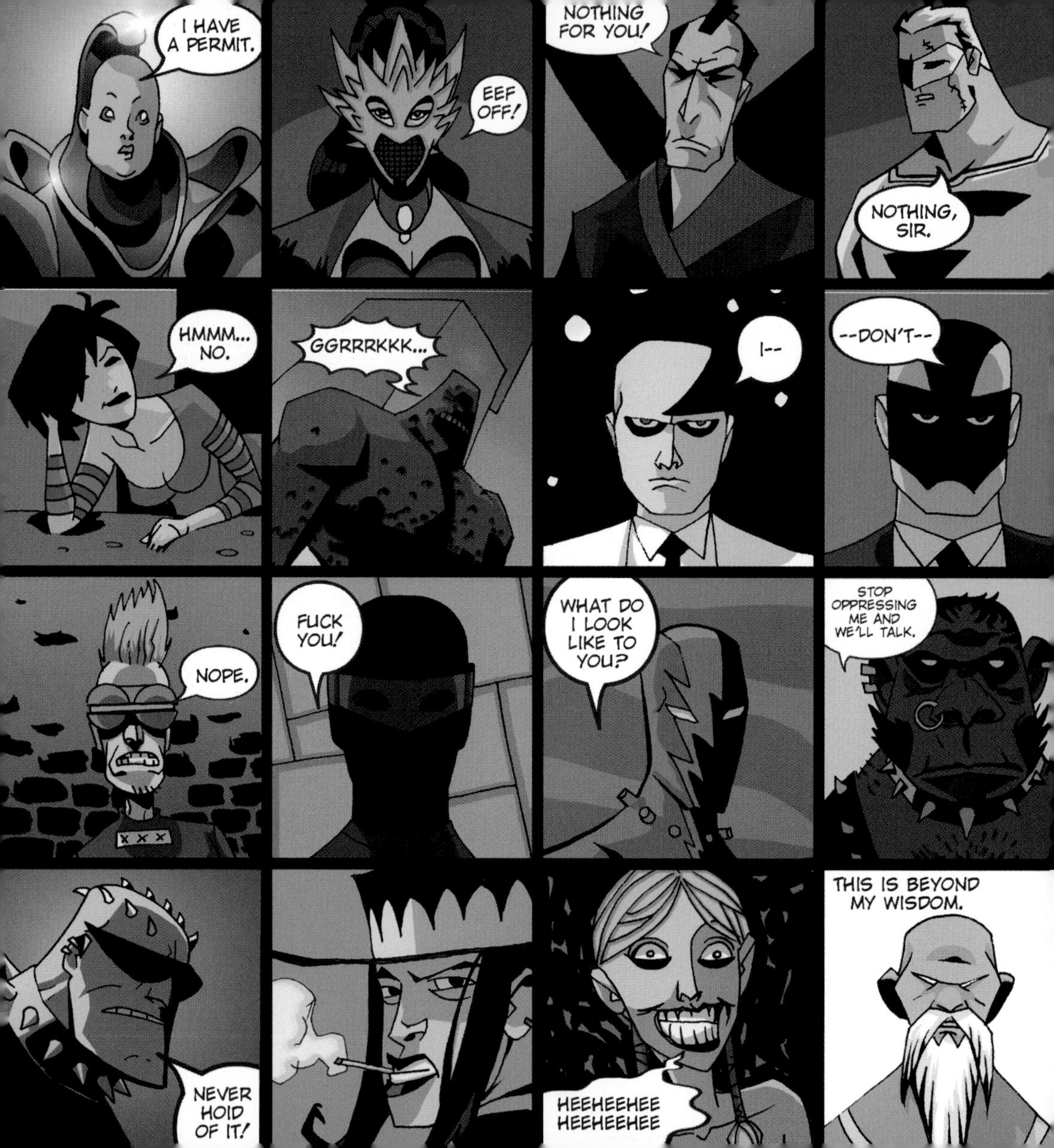
I HAVE A PERMIT.
EEF OFF!
NOTHING FOR YOU!
NOTHING, SIR.
HMMM... NO.
GGRRRKKK...
I--
--DON'T--
NOPE.
FUCK YOU!
WHAT DO I LOOK LIKE TO YOU?
STOP OPPRESSING ME AND WE'LL TALK.
NEVER HOID OF IT!
HEEHEEHEE HEEHEEHEE
THIS IS BEYOND MY WISDOM.

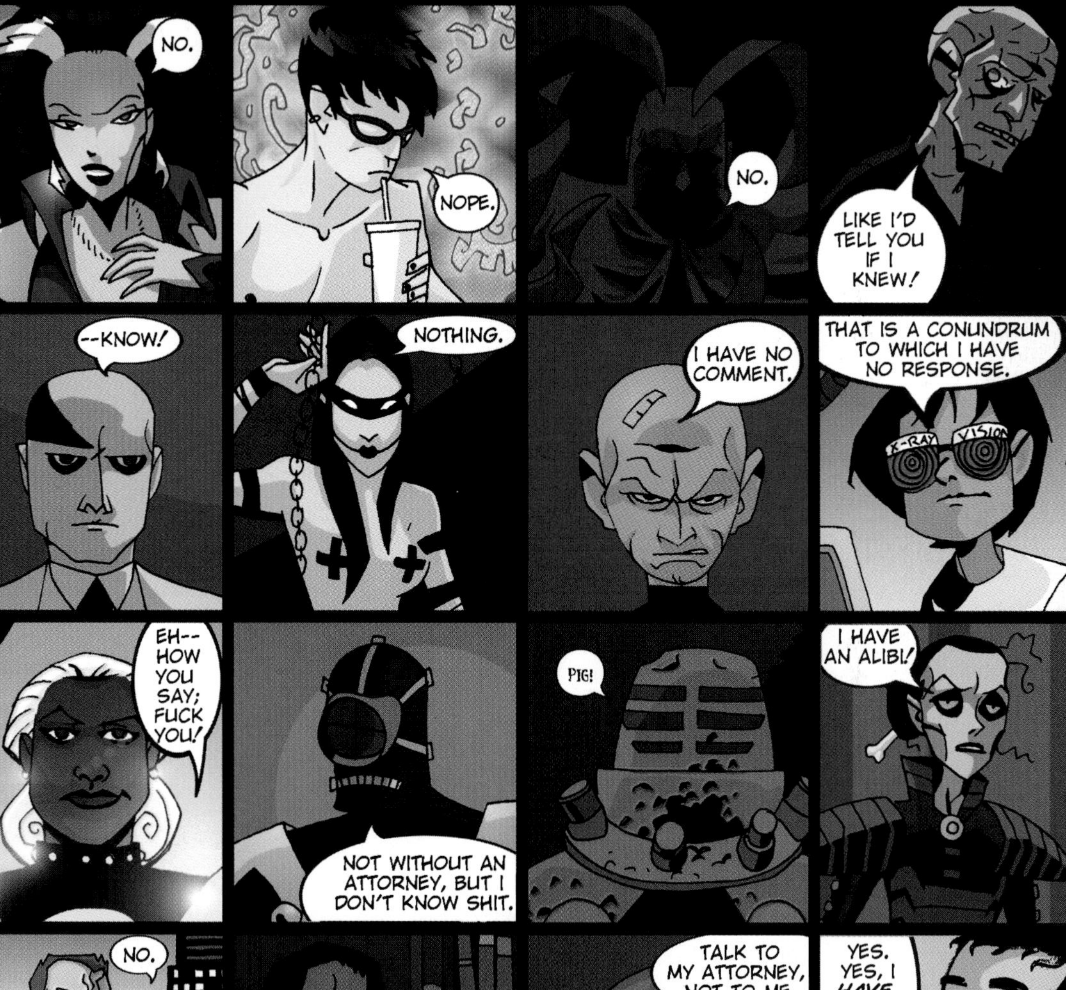
NO.
NOPE.
NO.
LIKE I'D TELL YOU IF I KNEW!
--KNOW!
NOTHING.
I HAVE NO COMMENT.
THAT IS A CONUNDRUM TO WHICH I HAVE NO RESPONSE.
X-RAY VISION
EH--HOW YOU SAY; FUCK YOU!
NOT WITHOUT AN ATTORNEY, BUT I DON'T KNOW SHIT.
PIG!
I HAVE AN ALIBI!
NO.
NOTHING.
TALK TO MY ATTORNEY, NOT TO ME.
YES. YES, I *HAVE* SEEN THAT BEFORE.

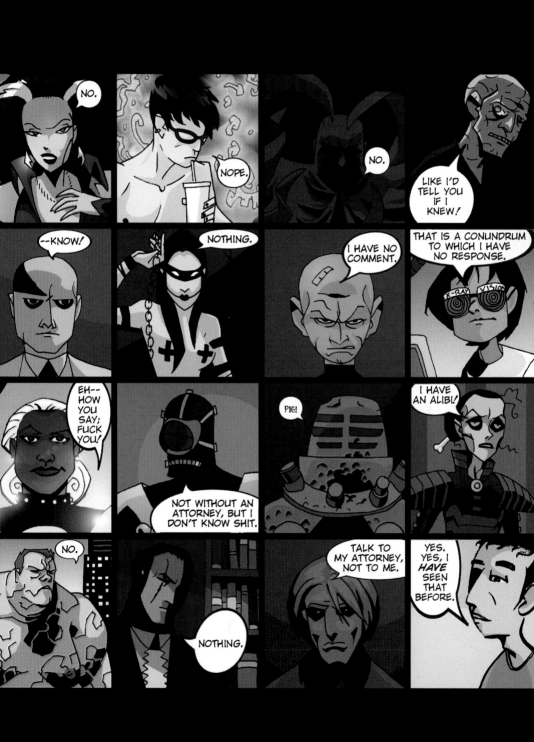

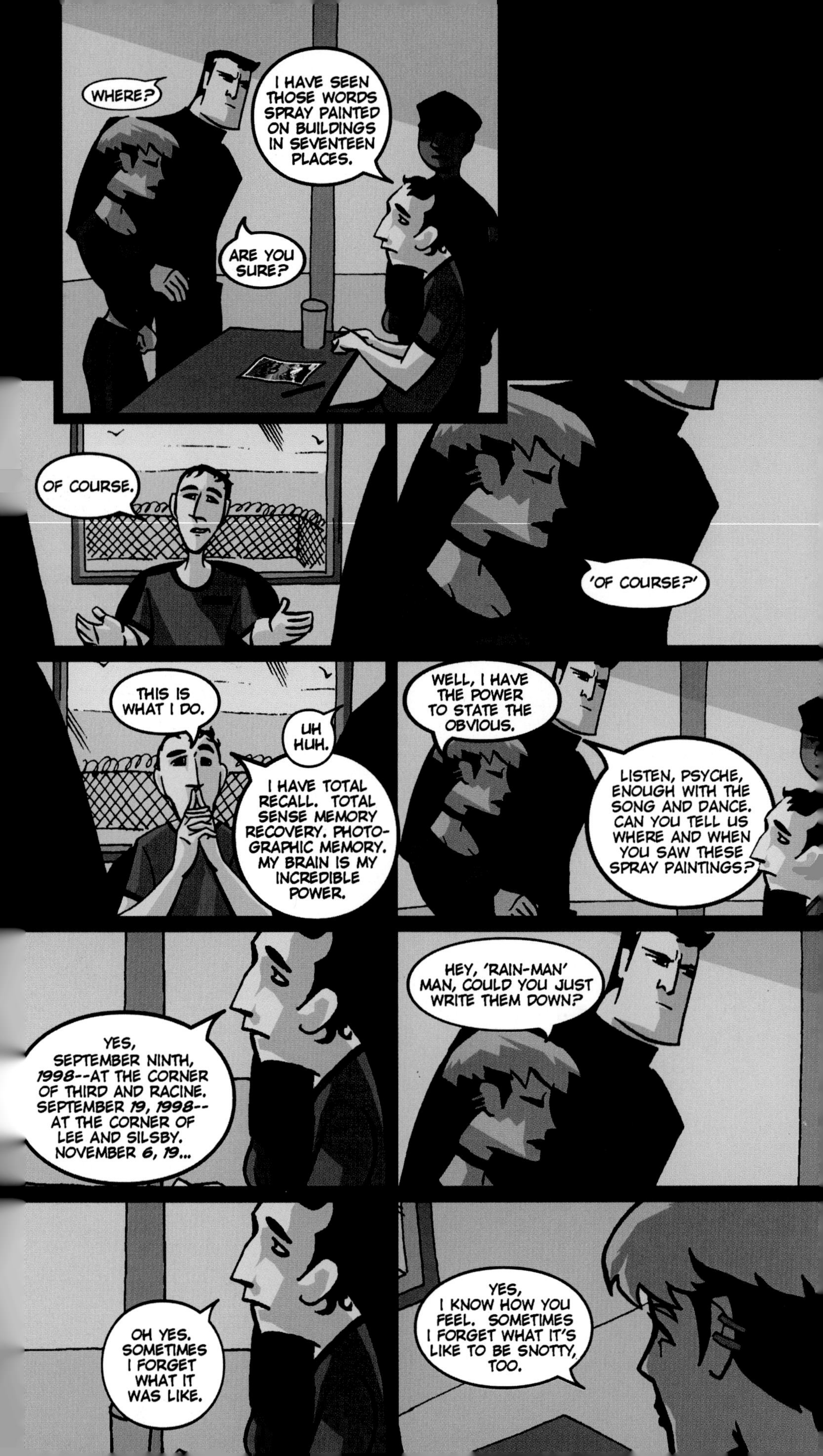
WHERE?
I HAVE SEEN THOSE WORDS SPRAY PAINTED ON BUILDINGS IN SEVENTEEN PLACES.
ARE YOU SURE?
OF COURSE.
'OF COURSE?'
THIS IS WHAT I DO.
UH HUH.
I HAVE TOTAL RECALL. TOTAL SENSE MEMORY RECOVERY. PHOTO-GRAPHIC MEMORY. MY BRAIN IS MY INCREDIBLE POWER.
WELL, I HAVE THE POWER TO STATE THE OBVIOUS.
LISTEN, PSYCHE, ENOUGH WITH THE SONG AND DANCE. CAN YOU TELL US WHERE AND WHEN YOU SAW THESE SPRAY PAINTINGS?
YES, SEPTEMBER NINTH, 1998--AT THE CORNER OF THIRD AND RACINE. SEPTEMBER 19, 1998--AT THE CORNER OF LEE AND SILSBY. NOVEMBER 6, 19...
HEY, 'RAIN-MAN' MAN, COULD YOU JUST WRITE THEM DOWN?
OH YES. SOMETIMES I FORGET WHAT IT WAS LIKE.
YES, I KNOW HOW YOU FEEL. SOMETIMES I FORGET WHAT IT'S LIKE TO BE SNOTTY, TOO.

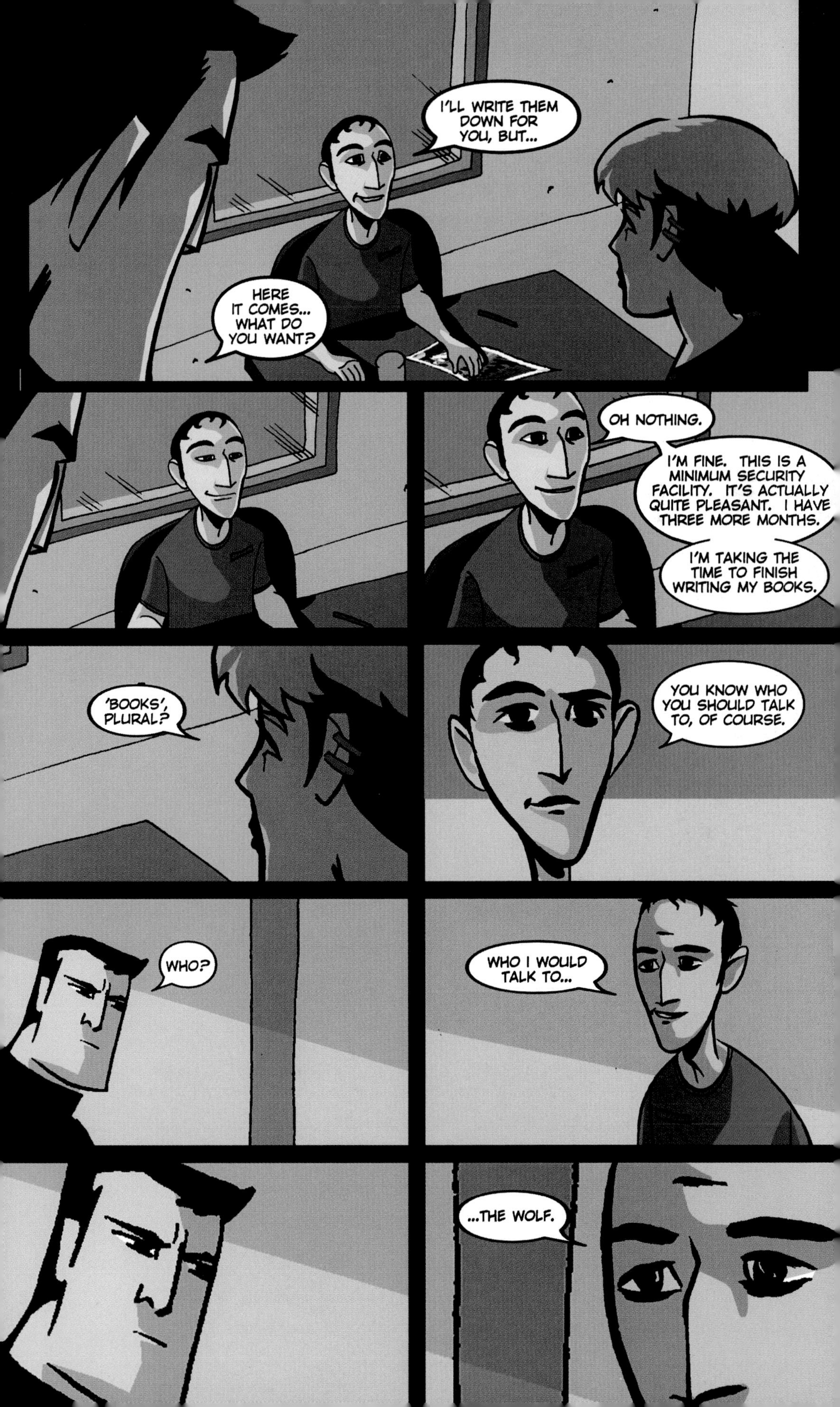
I'LL WRITE THEM DOWN FOR YOU, BUT...
HERE IT COMES... WHAT DO YOU WANT?
OH NOTHING.
I'M FINE. THIS IS A MINIMUM SECURITY FACILITY. IT'S ACTUALLY QUITE PLEASANT. I HAVE THREE MORE MONTHS.
I'M TAKING THE TIME TO FINISH WRITING MY BOOKS.
'BOOKS', PLURAL?
YOU KNOW WHO YOU SHOULD TALK TO, OF COURSE.
WHO?
WHO I WOULD TALK TO...
...THE WOLF.

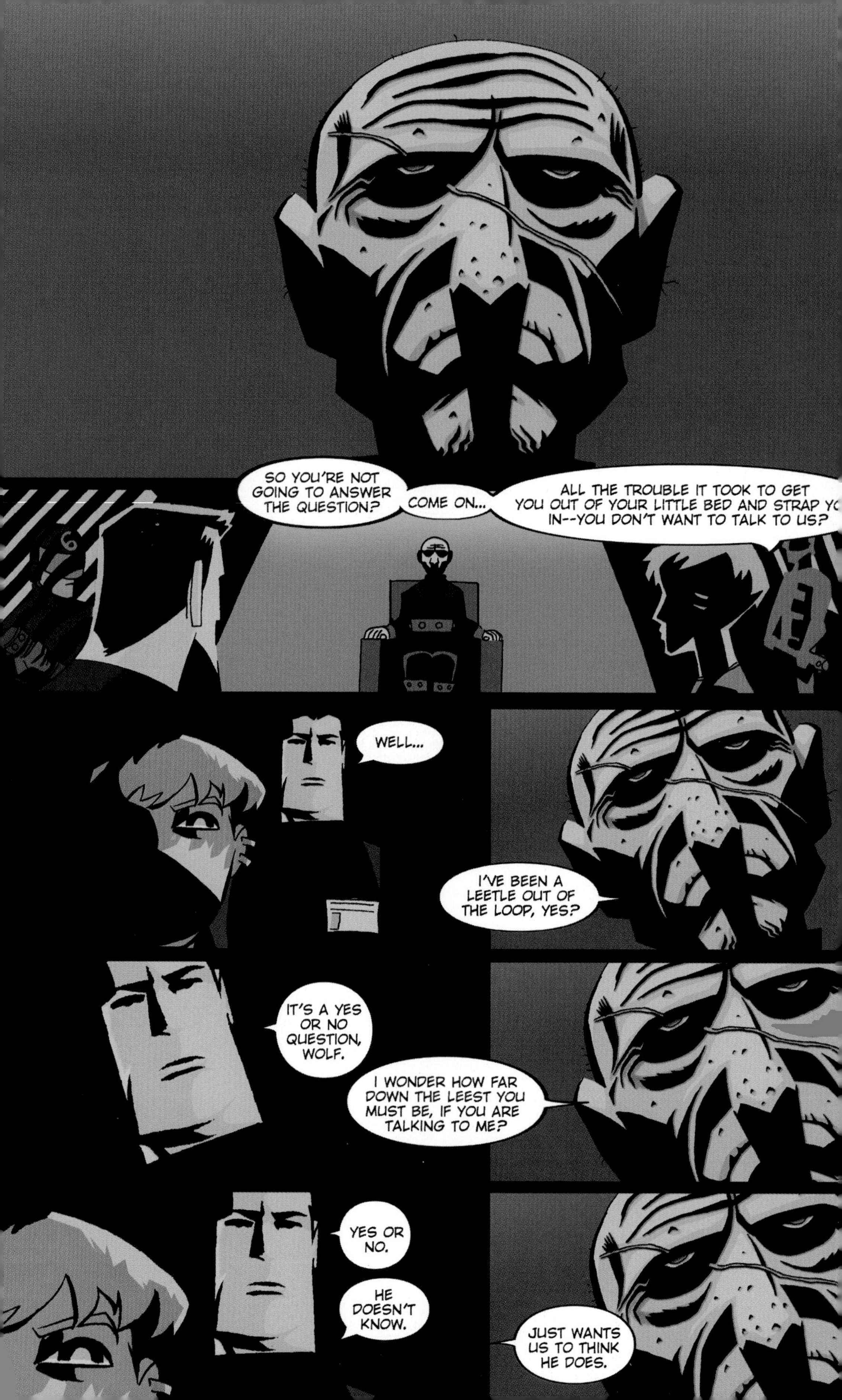
SO YOU'RE NOT GOING TO ANSWER THE QUESTION?
COME ON...
ALL THE TROUBLE IT TOOK TO GET YOU OUT OF YOUR LITTLE BED AND STRAP YO IN--YOU DON'T WANT TO TALK TO US?
WELL...
I'VE BEEN A LEETLE OUT OF THE LOOP, YES?
IT'S A YES OR NO QUESTION, WOLF.
I WONDER HOW FAR DOWN THE LEEST YOU MUST BE, IF YOU ARE TALKING TO ME?
YES OR NO.
HE DOESN'T KNOW.
JUST WANTS US TO THINK HE DOES.

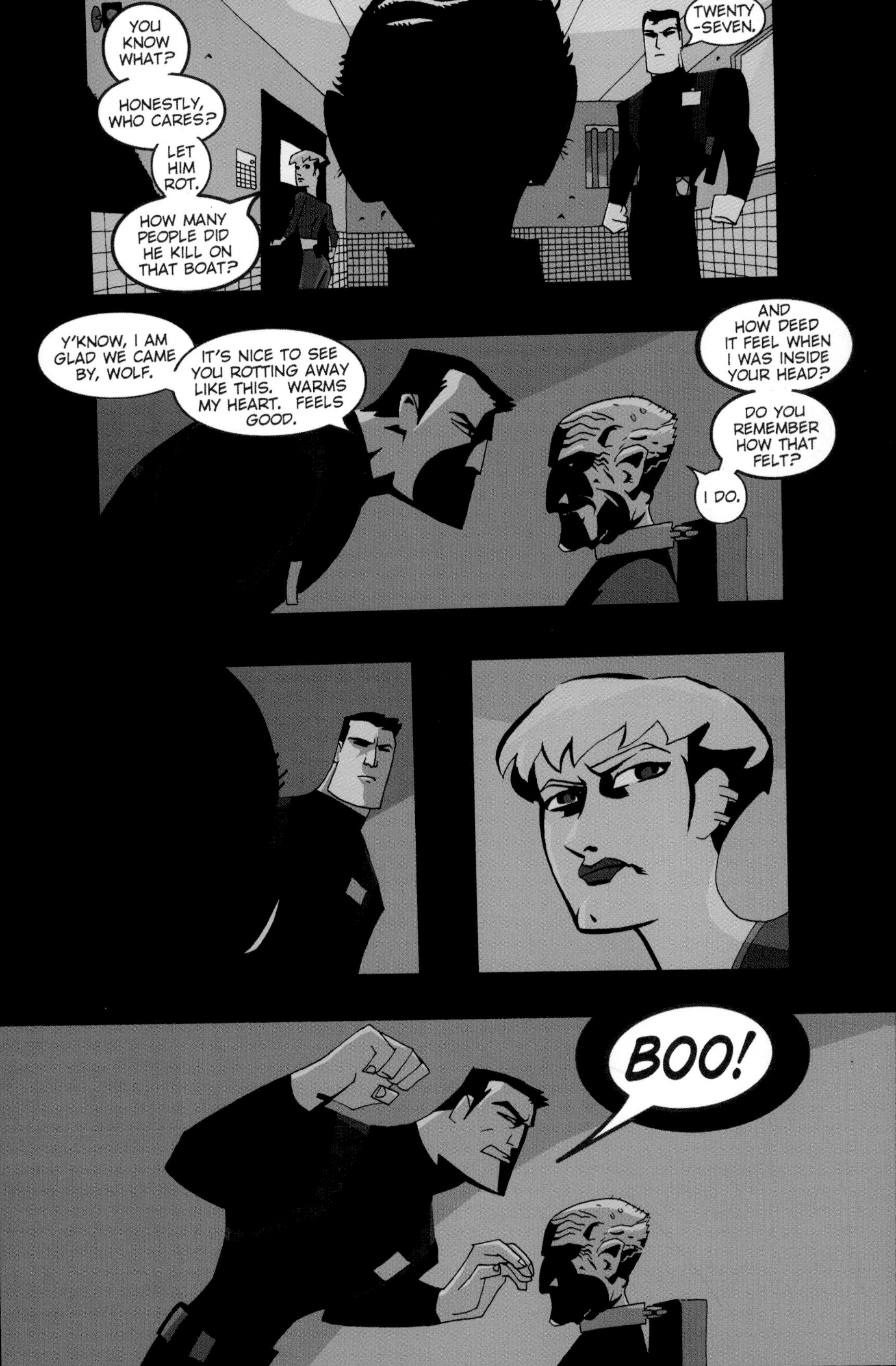
YOU KNOW WHAT?
HONESTLY, WHO CARES?
LET HIM ROT.
TWENTY-SEVEN.
HOW MANY PEOPLE DID HE KILL ON THAT BOAT?
Y'KNOW, I AM GLAD WE CAME BY, WOLF.
IT'S NICE TO SEE YOU ROTTING AWAY LIKE THIS. WARMS MY HEART. FEELS GOOD.
AND HOW DEED IT FEEL WHEN I WAS INSIDE YOUR HEAD?
DO YOU REMEMBER HOW THAT FELT?
I DO.
BOO!

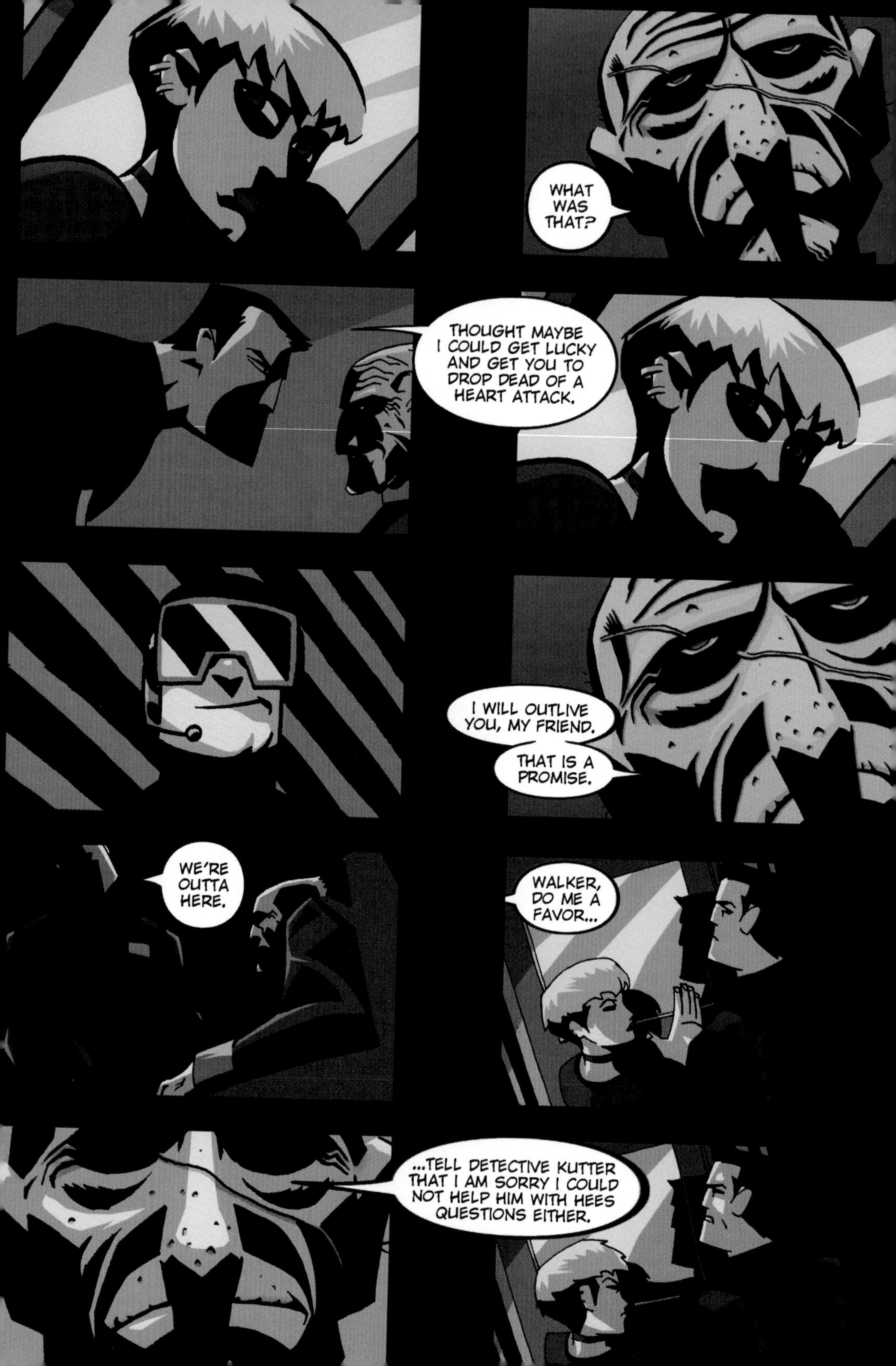
WHAT WAS THAT?
THOUGHT MAYBE I COULD GET LUCKY AND GET YOU TO DROP DEAD OF A HEART ATTACK.
I WILL OUTLIVE YOU, MY FRIEND.
THAT IS A PROMISE.
WE'RE OUTTA HERE.
WALKER, DO ME A FAVOR...
...TELL DETECTIVE KUTTER THAT I AM SORRY I COULD NOT HELP HIM WITH HEES QUESTIONS EITHER.

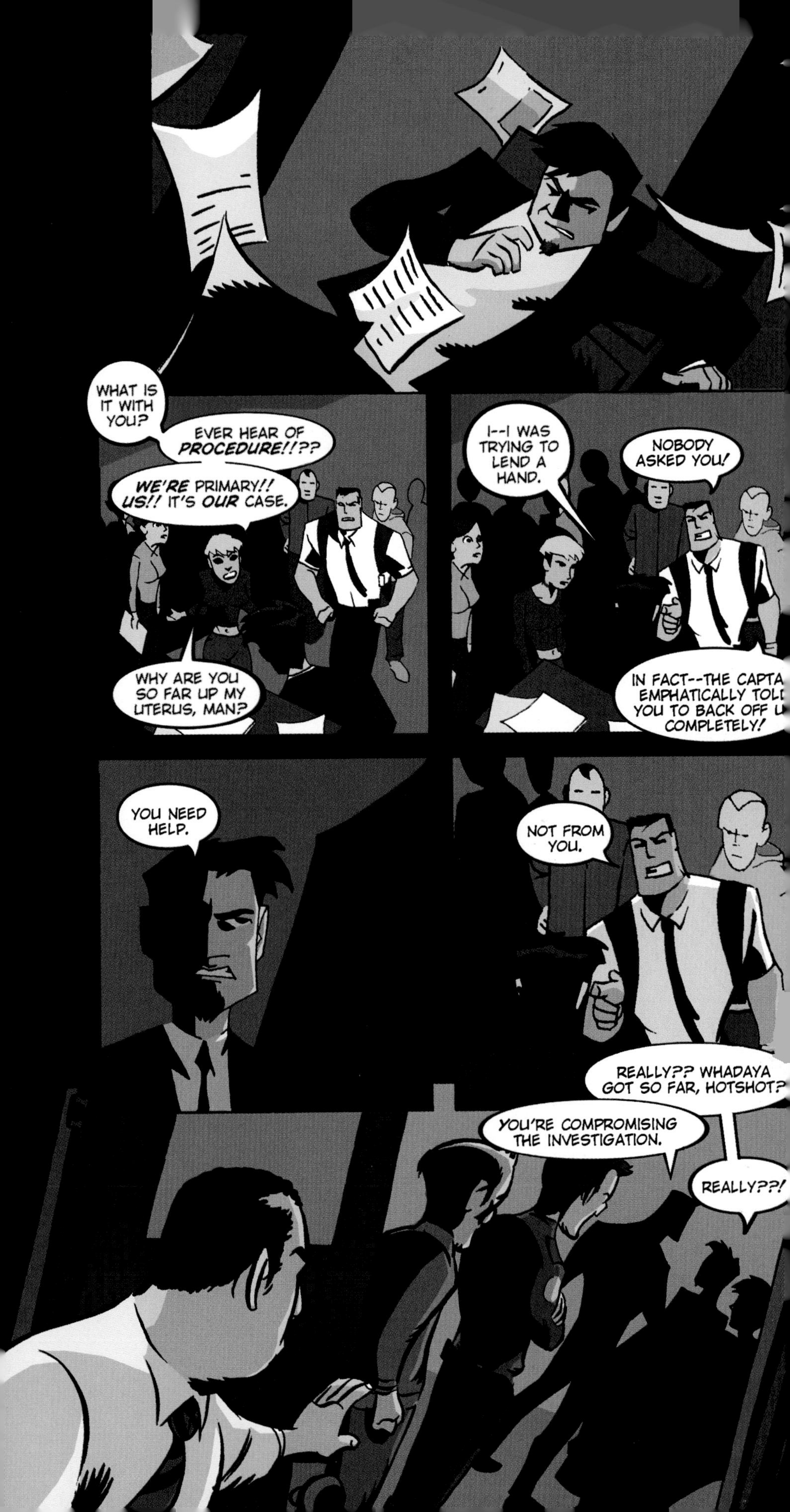
WHAT IS IT WITH YOU?
EVER HEAR OF PROCEDURE!!??
WE'RE PRIMARY!! US!! IT'S OUR CASE.
WHY ARE YOU SO FAR UP MY UTERUS, MAN?
I--I WAS TRYING TO LEND A HAND.
NOBODY ASKED YOU!
IN FACT--THE CAPTA EMPHATICALLY TOLD YOU TO BACK OFF U COMPLETELY!
YOU NEED HELP.
NOT FROM YOU.
REALLY?? WHADAYA GOT SO FAR, HOTSHOT?
YOU'RE COMPROMISING THE INVESTIGATION.
REALLY??!

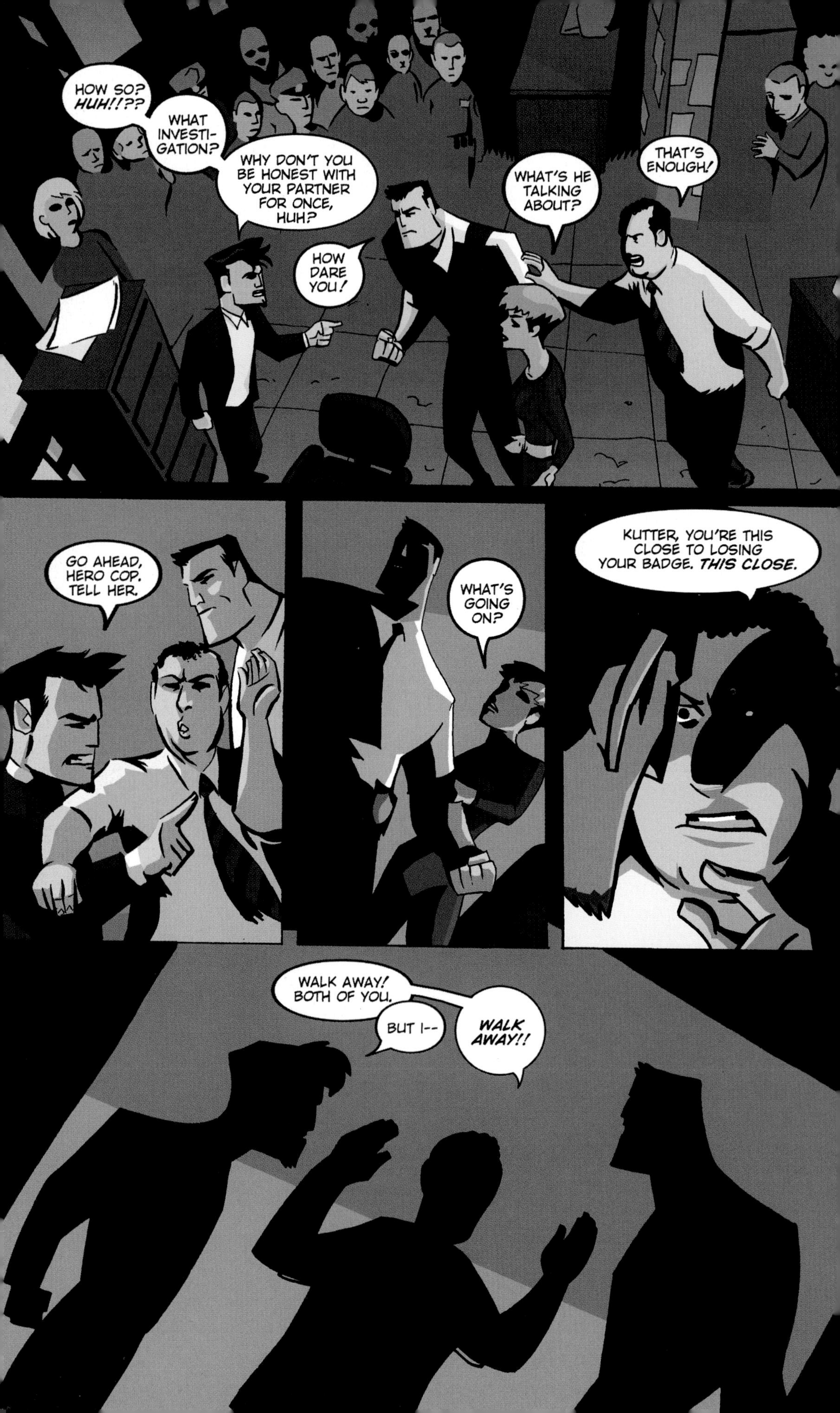
HOW SO? HUH!!??
WHAT INVESTI-GATION?
WHY DON'T YOU BE HONEST WITH YOUR PARTNER FOR ONCE, HUH?
HOW DARE YOU!
WHAT'S HE TALKING ABOUT?
THAT'S ENOUGH!
GO AHEAD, HERO COP. TELL HER.
WHAT'S GOING ON?
KUTTER, YOU'RE THIS CLOSE TO LOSING YOUR BADGE. THIS CLOSE.
WALK AWAY! BOTH OF YOU.
BUT I--
WALK AWAY!!

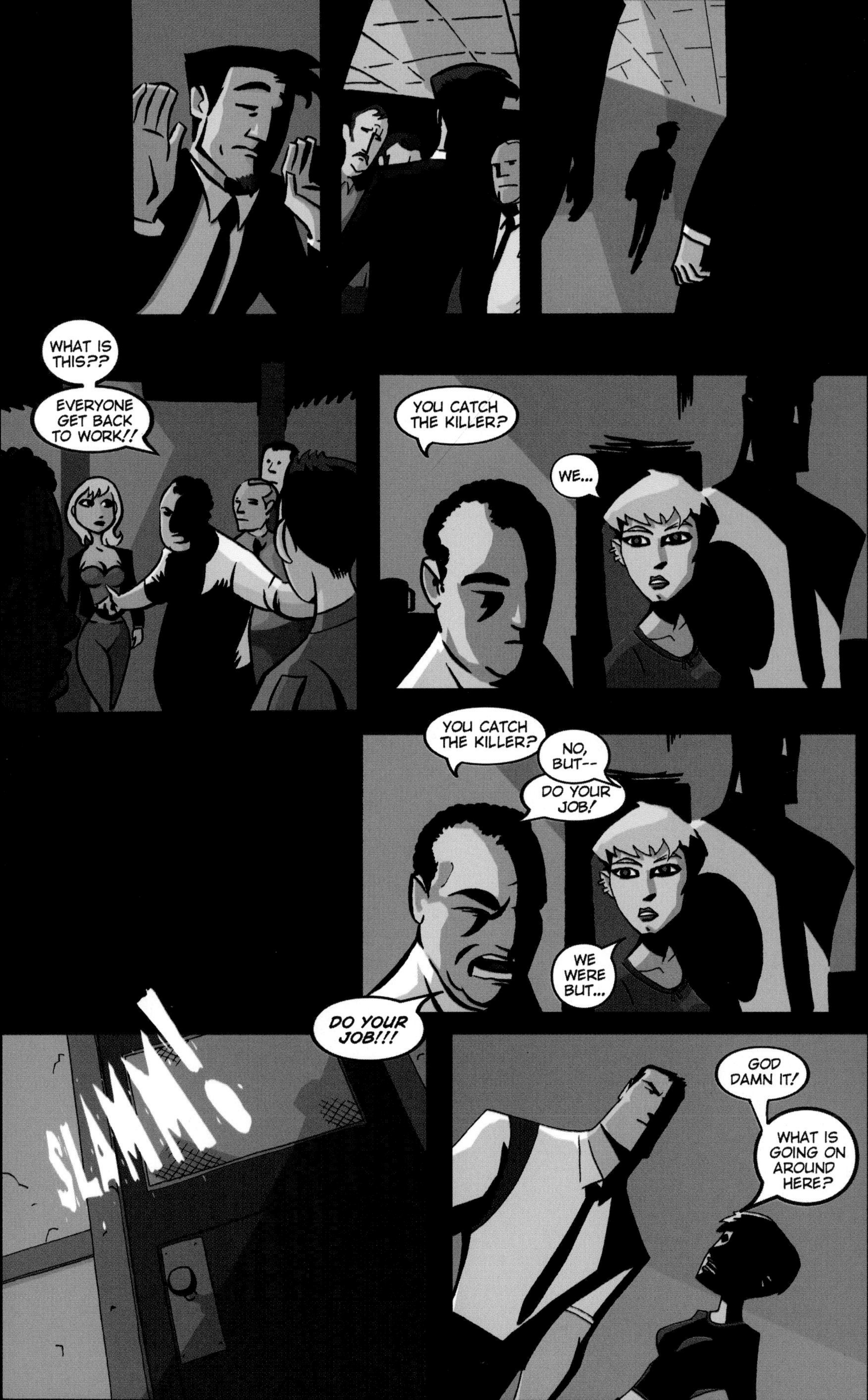
WHAT IS THIS??
EVERYONE GET BACK TO WORK!!
YOU CATCH THE KILLER?
WE...
YOU CATCH THE KILLER?
NO, BUT--
DO YOUR JOB!
WE WERE BUT...
DO YOUR JOB!!!
SLAMM!
GOD DAMN IT!
WHAT IS GOING ON AROUND HERE?

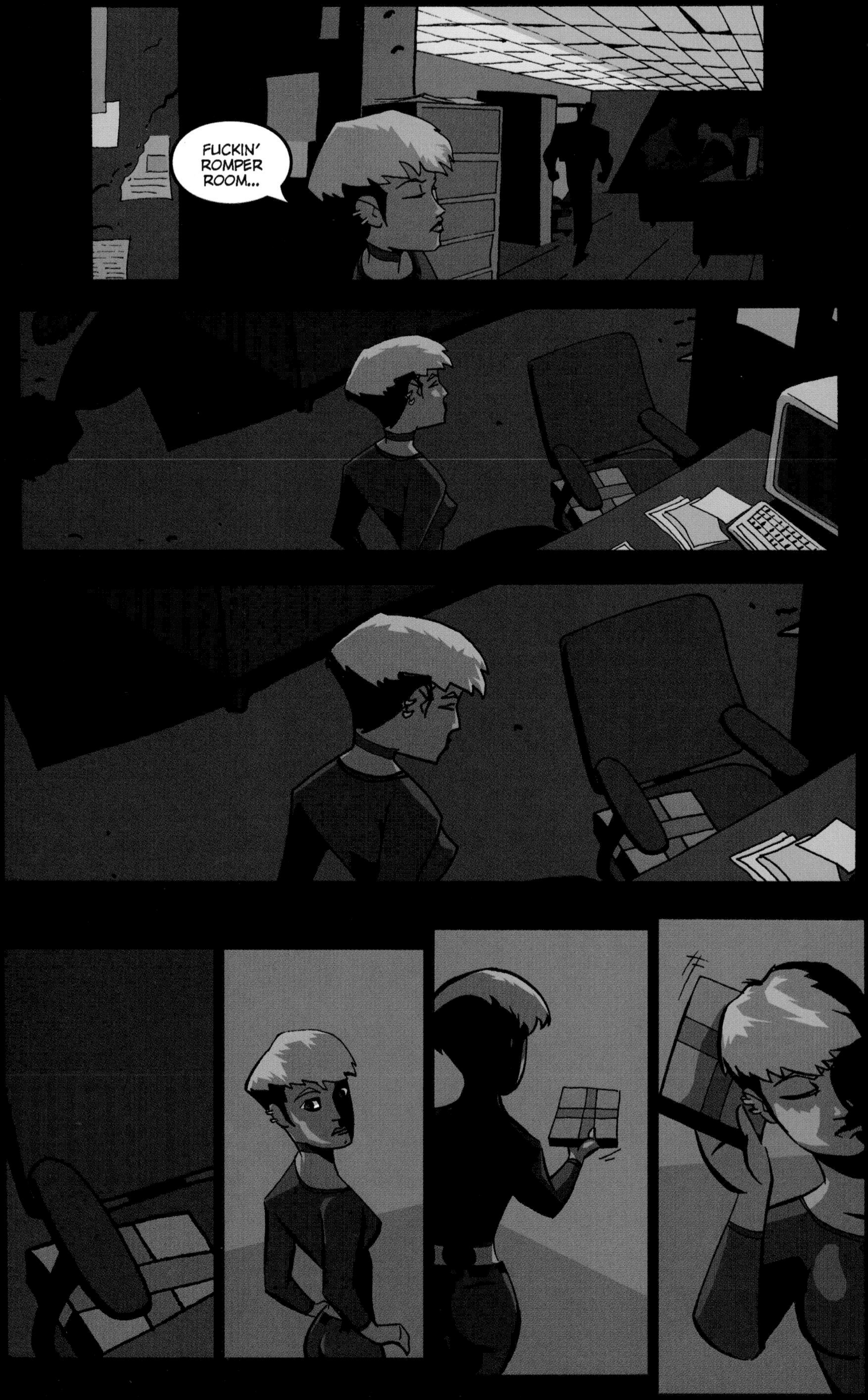
FUCKIN' ROMPER ROOM...

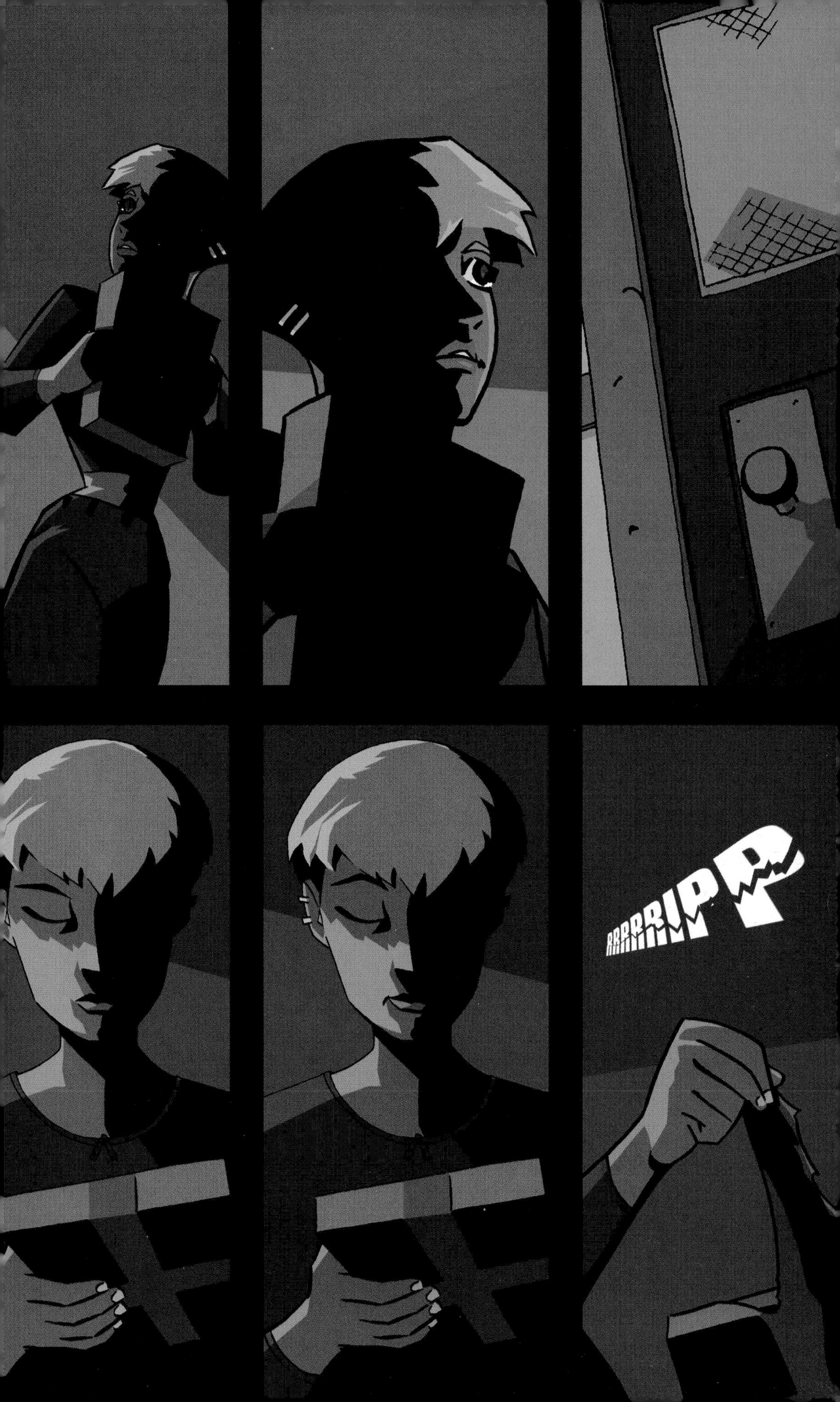
RRRRRIPP

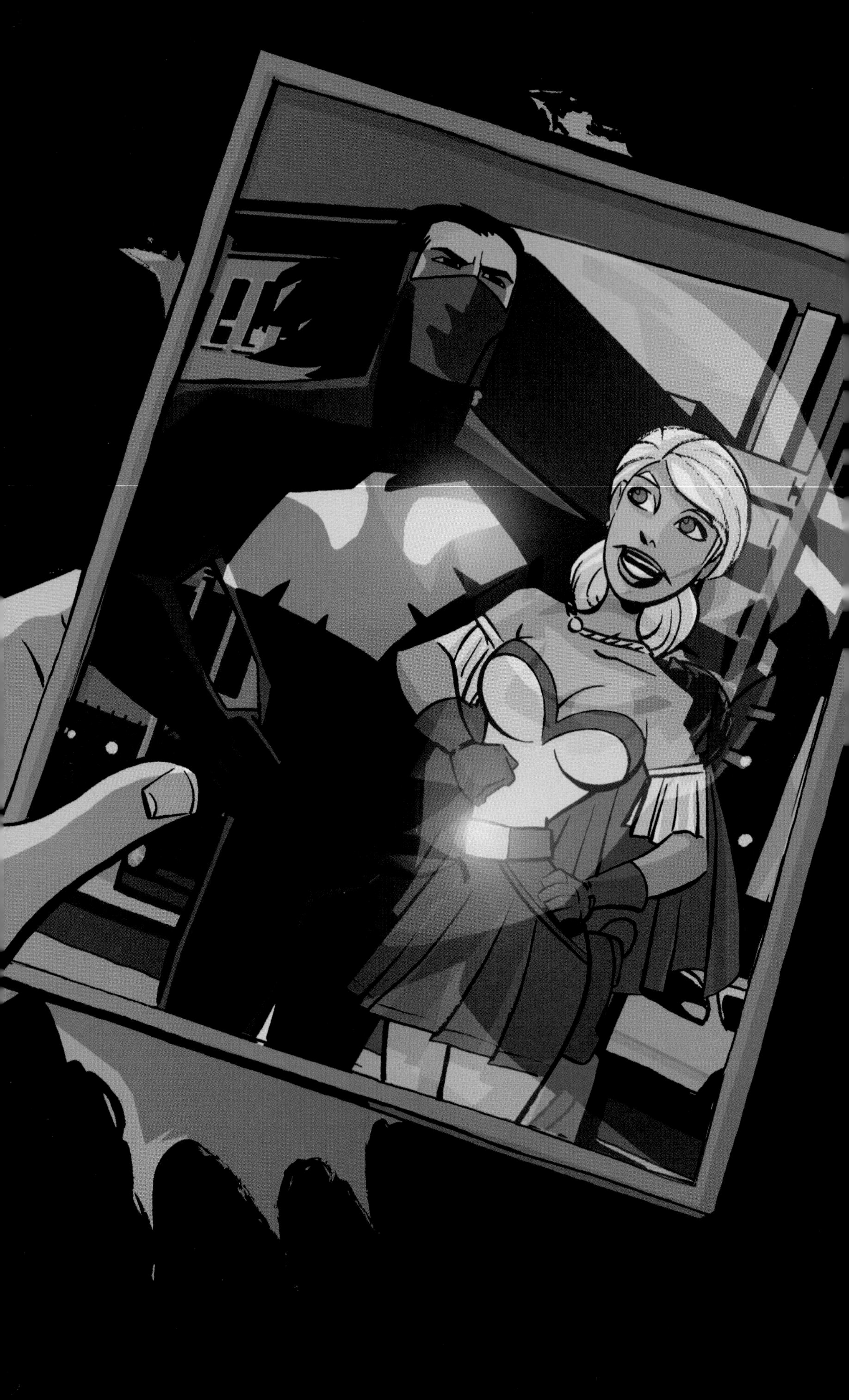

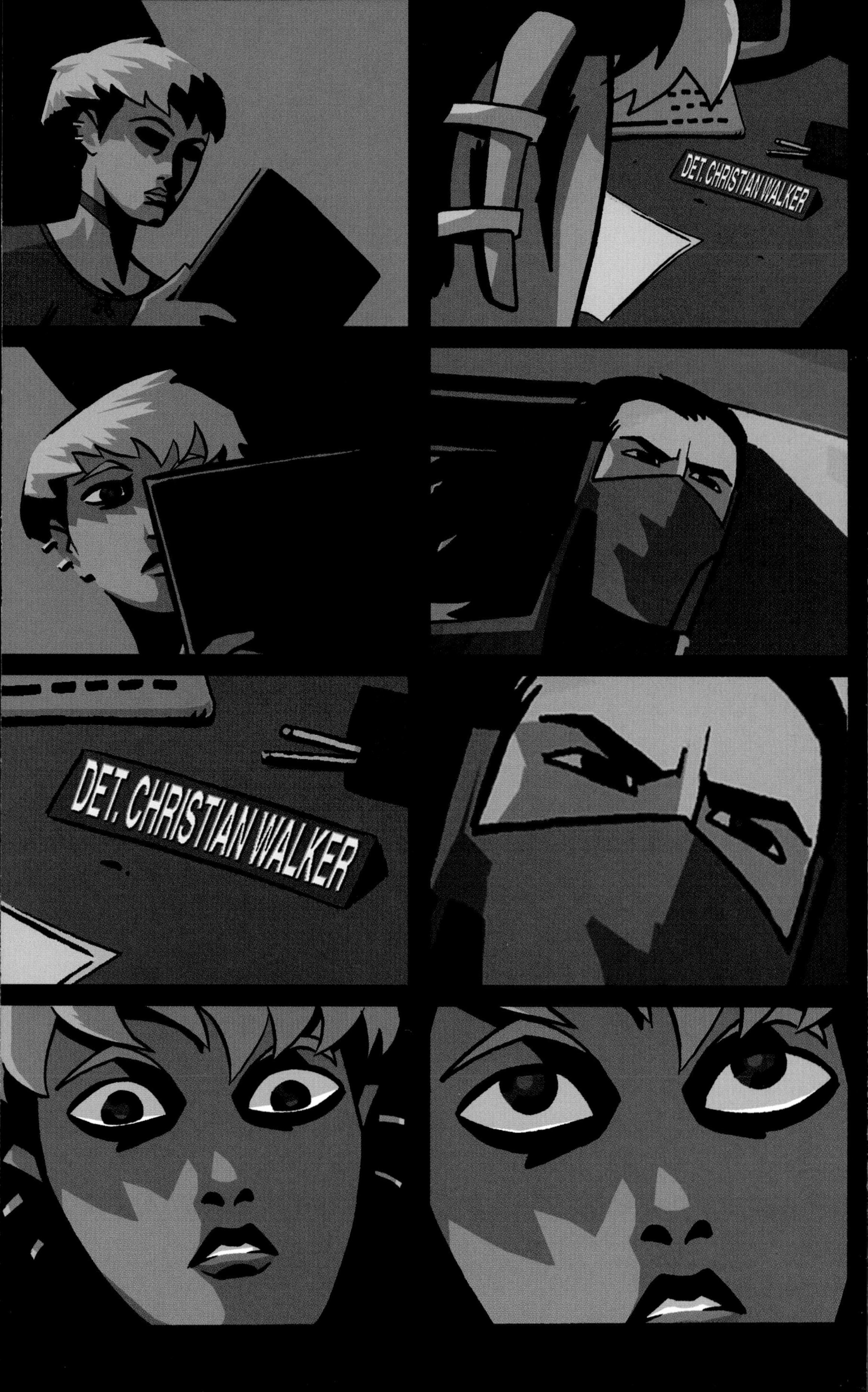
DET. CHRISTIAN WALKER
DET. CHRISTIAN WALKER

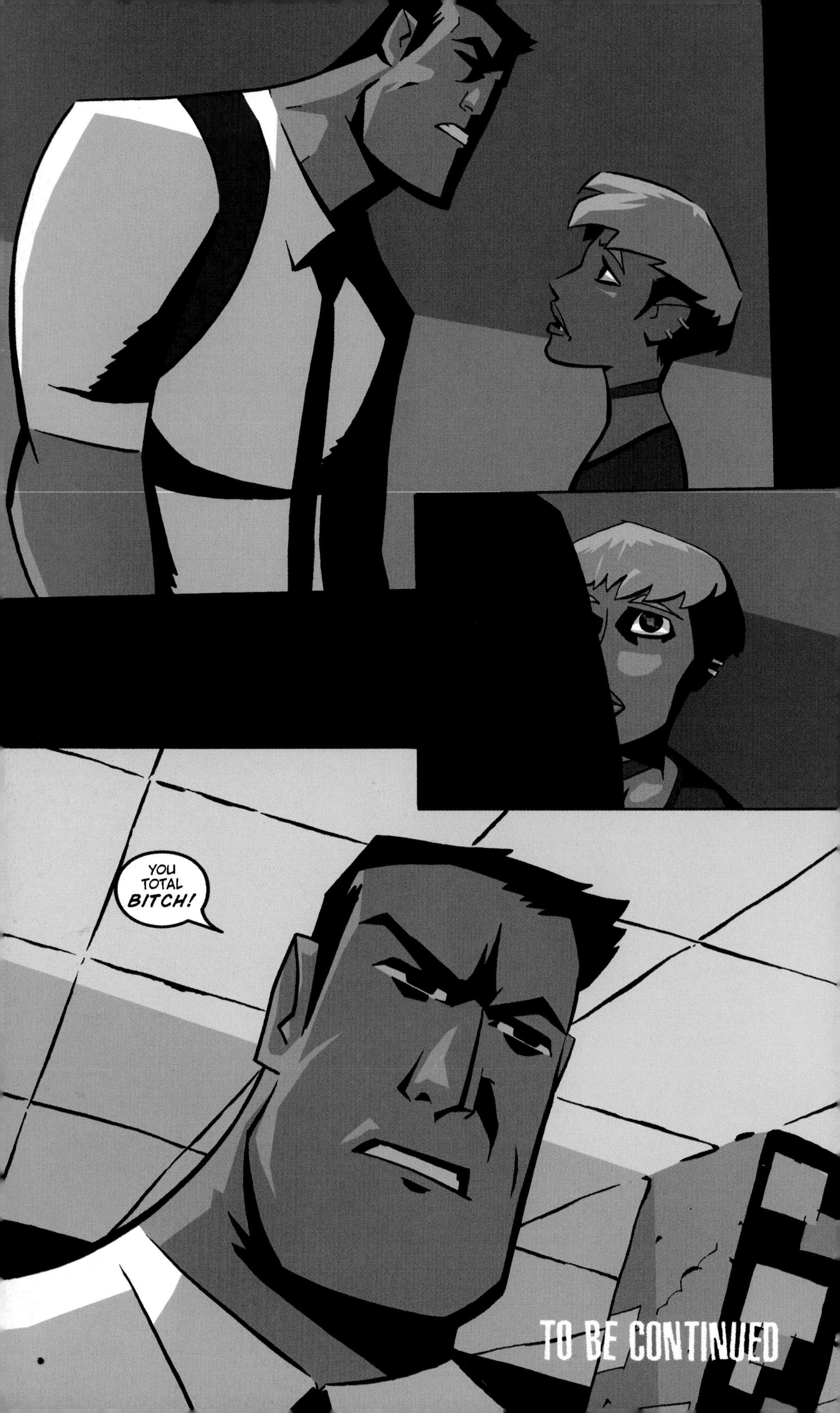
YOU TOTAL BITCH!
TO BE CONTINUED

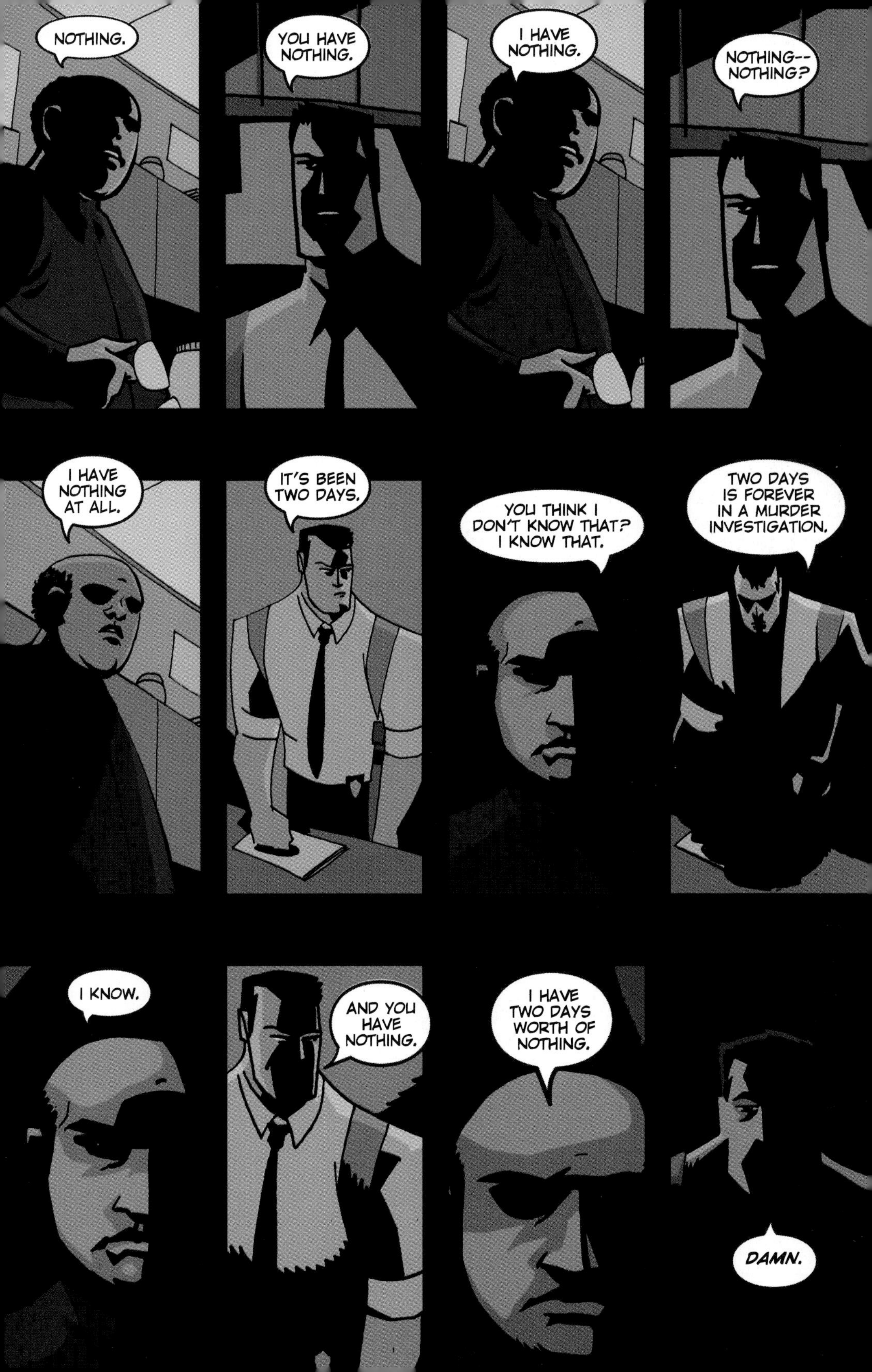
NOTHING.
YOU HAVE NOTHING.
I HAVE NOTHING.
NOTHING-- NOTHING?
I HAVE NOTHING AT ALL.
IT'S BEEN TWO DAYS.
YOU THINK I DON'T KNOW THAT? I KNOW THAT.
TWO DAYS IS FOREVER IN A MURDER INVESTIGATION.
I KNOW.
AND YOU HAVE NOTHING.
I HAVE TWO DAYS WORTH OF NOTHING.
DAMN.

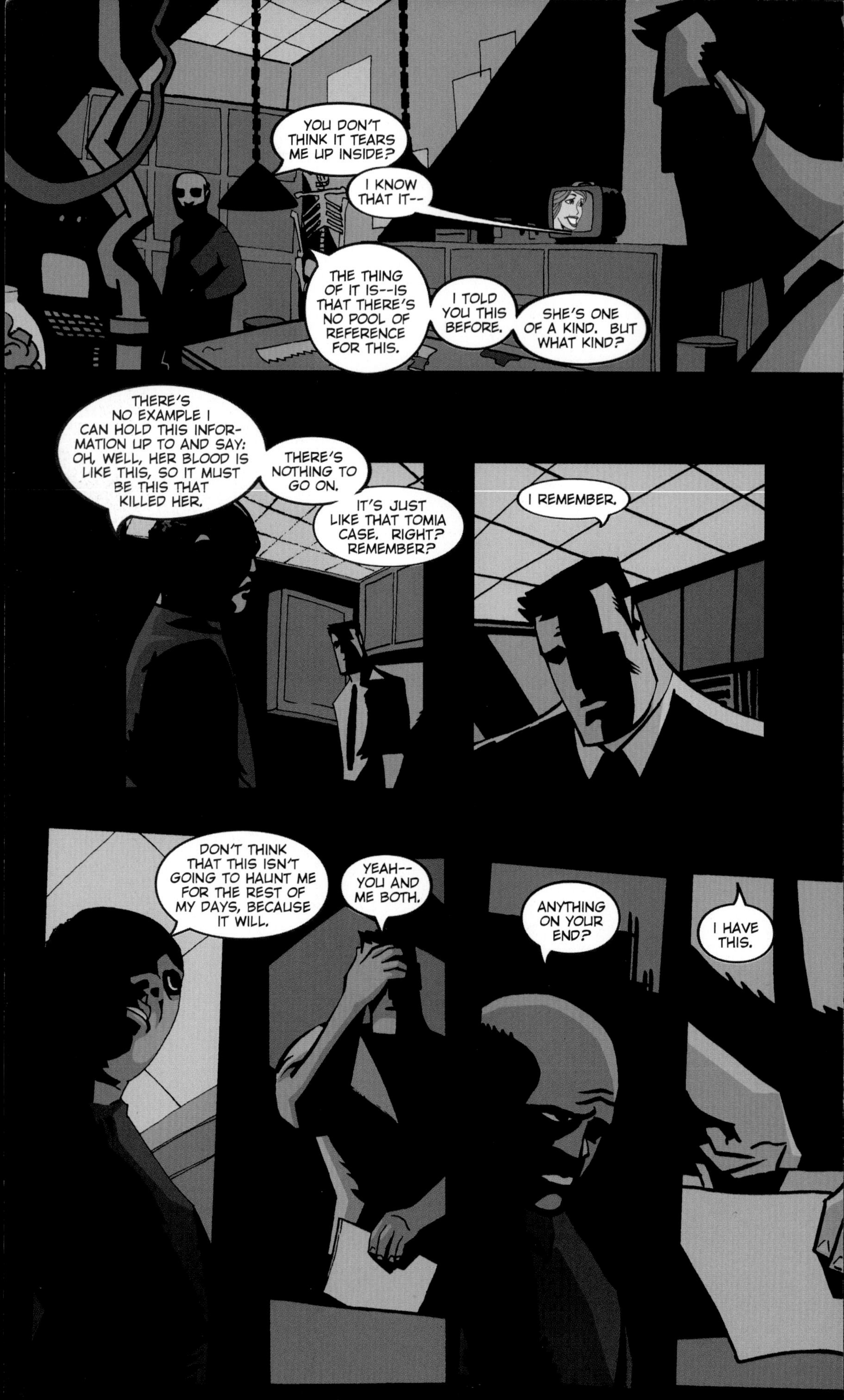
YOU DON'T THINK IT TEARS ME UP INSIDE?
I KNOW THAT IT--
THE THING OF IT IS--IS THAT THERE'S NO POOL OF REFERENCE FOR THIS.
I TOLD YOU THIS BEFORE.
SHE'S ONE OF A KIND. BUT WHAT KIND?
THERE'S NO EXAMPLE I CAN HOLD THIS INFORMATION UP TO AND SAY: OH, WELL, HER BLOOD IS LIKE THIS, SO IT MUST BE THIS THAT KILLED HER.
THERE'S NOTHING TO GO ON.
IT'S JUST LIKE THAT TOMIA CASE. RIGHT? REMEMBER?
I REMEMBER.
DON'T THINK THAT THIS ISN'T GOING TO HAUNT ME FOR THE REST OF MY DAYS, BECAUSE IT WILL.
YEAH--YOU AND ME BOTH.
ANYTHING ON YOUR END?
I HAVE THIS.

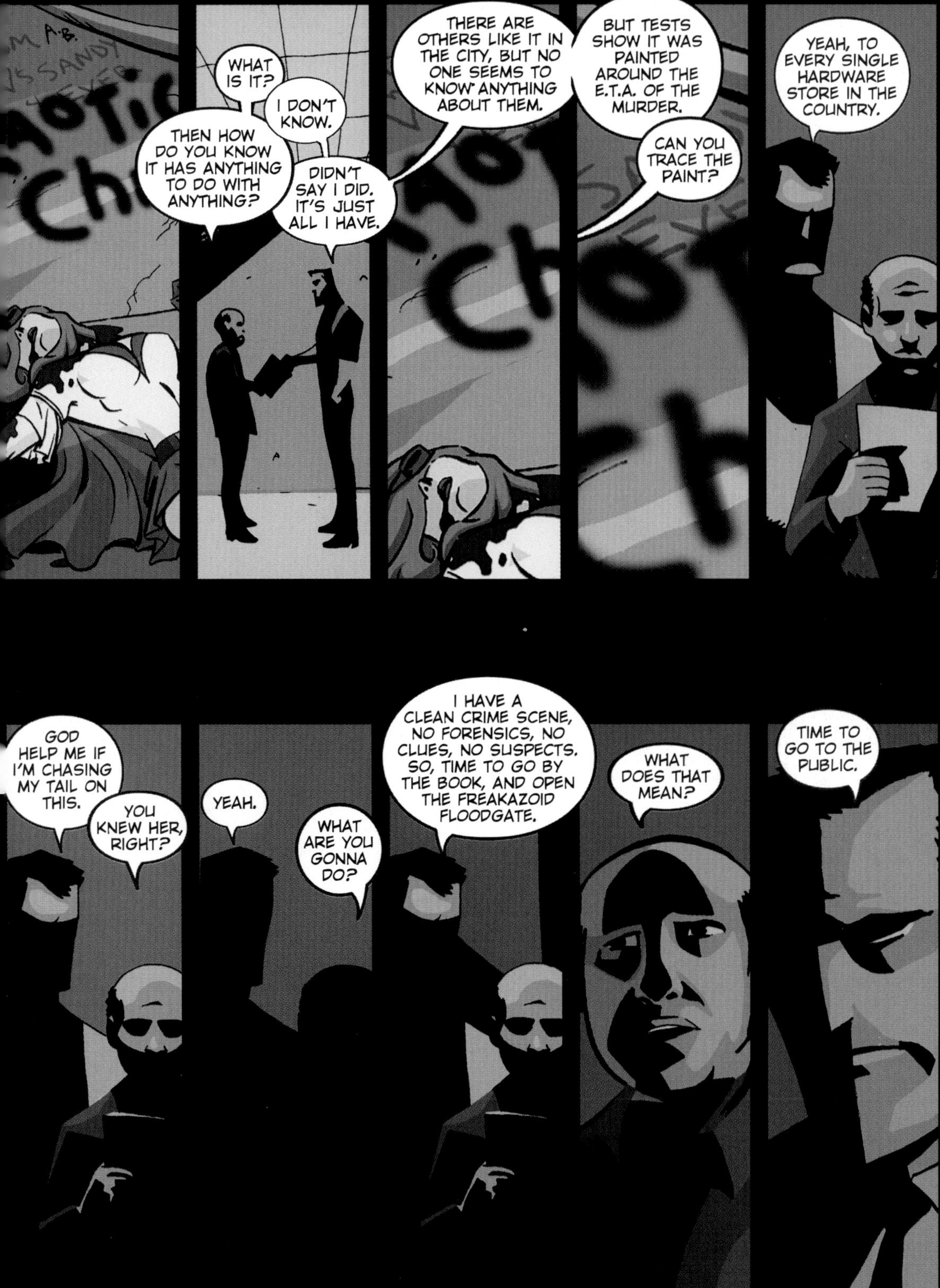
WHAT IS IT?
I DON'T KNOW.
THEN HOW DO YOU KNOW IT HAS ANYTHING TO DO WITH ANYTHING?
DIDN'T SAY I DID. IT'S JUST ALL I HAVE.
THERE ARE OTHERS LIKE IT IN THE CITY, BUT NO ONE SEEMS TO KNOW ANYTHING ABOUT THEM.
BUT TESTS SHOW IT WAS PAINTED AROUND THE E.T.A. OF THE MURDER.
CAN YOU TRACE THE PAINT?
YEAH, TO EVERY SINGLE HARDWARE STORE IN THE COUNTRY.
GOD HELP ME IF I'M CHASING MY TAIL ON THIS.
YOU KNEW HER, RIGHT?
YEAH.
WHAT ARE YOU GONNA DO?
I HAVE A CLEAN CRIME SCENE, NO FORENSICS, NO CLUES, NO SUSPECTS. SO, TIME TO GO BY THE BOOK, AND OPEN THE FREAKAZOID FLOODGATE.
WHAT DOES THAT MEAN?
TIME TO GO TO THE PUBLIC.

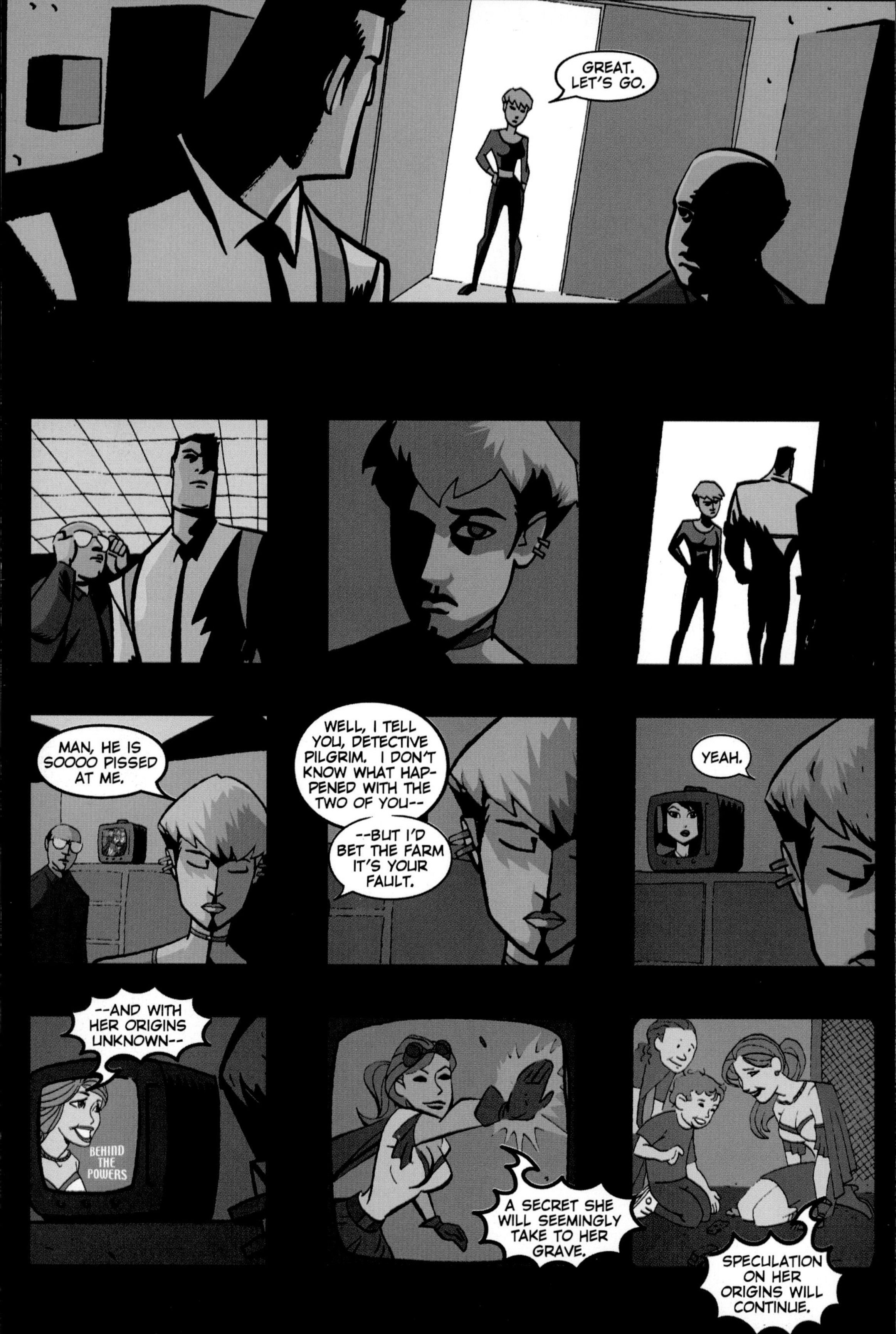
GREAT. LET'S GO.
MAN, HE IS SOOOO PISSED AT ME.
WELL, I TELL YOU, DETECTIVE PILGRIM. I DON'T KNOW WHAT HAPPENED WITH THE TWO OF YOU--
--BUT I'D BET THE FARM IT'S YOUR FAULT.
YEAH.
--AND WITH HER ORIGINS UNKNOWN--
BEHIND THE POWERS
A SECRET SHE WILL SEEMINGLY TAKE TO HER GRAVE.
SPECULATION ON HER ORIGINS WILL CONTINUE.

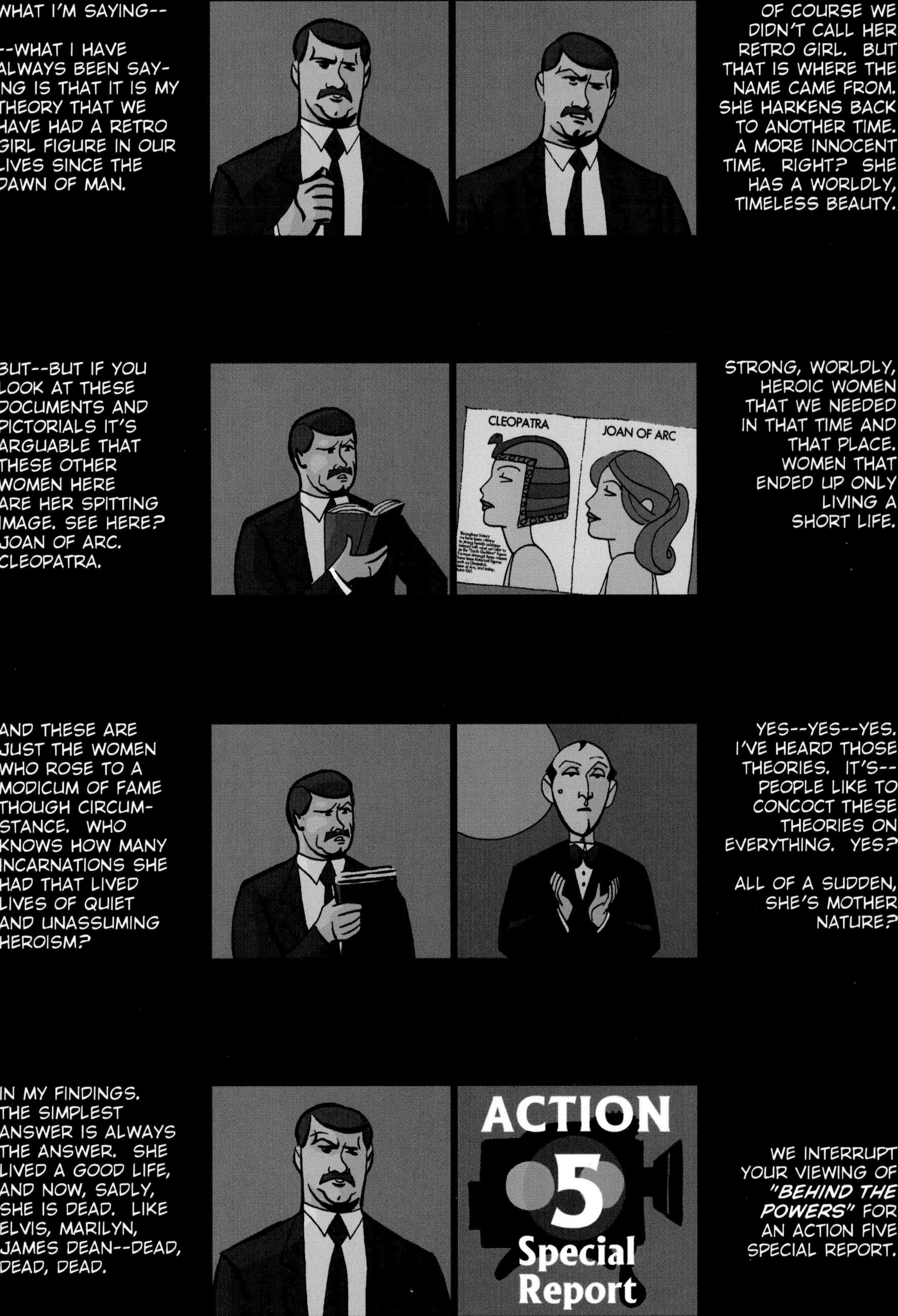
WHAT I'M SAYING--
--WHAT I HAVE ALWAYS BEEN SAYING IS THAT IT IS MY THEORY THAT WE HAVE HAD A RETRO GIRL FIGURE IN OUR LIVES SINCE THE DAWN OF MAN.
OF COURSE WE DIDN'T CALL HER RETRO GIRL. BUT THAT IS WHERE THE NAME CAME FROM. SHE HARKENS BACK TO ANOTHER TIME. A MORE INNOCENT TIME. RIGHT? SHE HAS A WORLDLY, TIMELESS BEAUTY.
BUT--BUT IF YOU LOOK AT THESE DOCUMENTS AND PICTORIALS IT'S ARGUABLE THAT THESE OTHER WOMEN HERE ARE HER SPITTING IMAGE. SEE HERE? JOAN OF ARC. CLEOPATRA.
CLEOPATRA
JOAN OF ARC
STRONG, WORLDLY, HEROIC WOMEN THAT WE NEEDED IN THAT TIME AND THAT PLACE. WOMEN THAT ENDED UP ONLY LIVING A SHORT LIFE.
AND THESE ARE JUST THE WOMEN WHO ROSE TO A MODICUM OF FAME THOUGH CIRCUMSTANCE. WHO KNOWS HOW MANY INCARNATIONS SHE HAD THAT LIVED LIVES OF QUIET AND UNASSUMING HEROISM?
YES--YES--YES. I'VE HEARD THOSE THEORIES. IT'S-- PEOPLE LIKE TO CONCOCT THESE THEORIES ON EVERYTHING. YES?
ALL OF A SUDDEN, SHE'S MOTHER NATURE?
IN MY FINDINGS. THE SIMPLEST ANSWER IS ALWAYS THE ANSWER. SHE LIVED A GOOD LIFE, AND NOW, SADLY, SHE IS DEAD. LIKE ELVIS, MARILYN, JAMES DEAN--DEAD, DEAD, DEAD.
ACTION 5 Special Report
WE INTERRUPT YOUR VIEWING OF "BEHIND THE POWERS" FOR AN ACTION FIVE SPECIAL REPORT.

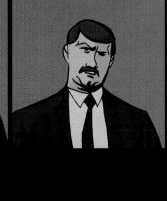

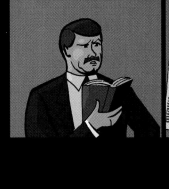

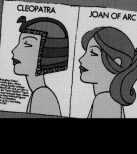

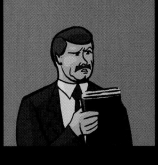

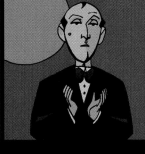

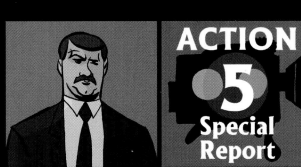

THIS IS AN ACTION FIVE SPECIAL REPORT.

WE NOW BRING YOU LIVE INSIDE THE CITY JUSTICE CENTER WHERE COLLETTE MCDANIEL IS REPORTING LIVE. COLLETTE?

ACTION
5
Special Report

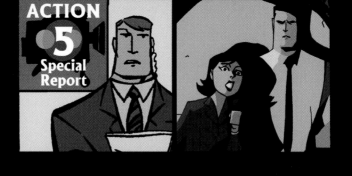

THIS IS COLLETTE MCDANIEL. I AM HERE INSIDE THE HOMICIDE UNIT OF DISTRICT 55.

STANDING WITH ME IS DETECTIVE CHRISTIAN WALKER.

DETECTIVE WALKER IS THE PRIMARY DETECTIVE FOR THE RETRO GIRL MURDER INVESTI-GATION--THE HORRIBLE RETRO GIRL TRADGEDY THAT HAS GRIPPED OUR CITY IN MOURNING.

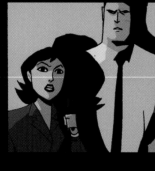

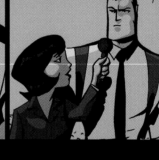

DETECTIVE, WHAT CAN YOU TELL US ABOUT YOUR PROGRESS ON THE INVESTIGATION SO FAR?

WELL, MA'AM, MOST OF THAT INFORMATION IS CLASSIFIED UNTIL THE CASE IS OFFICIALLY CLOSED, WHICH AT THIS TIME IS NOT THE CASE.

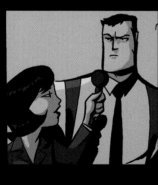

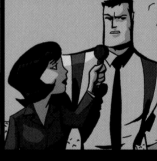

WE ARE ASKING THE PUBLIC'S HELP WITH INFORMATION IN REGARD TO THE MURDER, SPECIFICALLY TO A PIECE OF GRAFFITI THAT WE HAVE AT THE CRIME SCENE. I BELIEVE WE HA--

YES, IT'S UP NOW.

ANY INFORMATION THAT ANYONE HAS ABOUT THIS OR ANYTHING THAT CAN HELP US IN OUR INVESTIGATION --ANY INFORMATION ABOUT THE MEANING OF THE WORDS OF THE PERSON OR PERSONS RESPON-SIBLE FOR THE GRAFFITI-- PLEASE CALL OUR HOTLINE AT *1-888-333-6665.*

KAOTIC CHIC

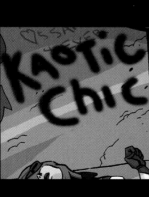

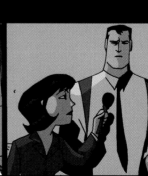

OBVIOUSLY THIS MATTER IS OF THE HIGHEST IMPORT-ANCE--ANYONE CALLING WITH PURPOSELY FALSE OR PRANK INFOR-MATION WILL BE TRACED AND PROSECUTED FOR OBSTRUCTION OF JUSTICE.

DETECTIVE, ANY WORD ON WHY JOHNNY ROYALLE WAS BROUGHT INTO THE STATION YESTERDAY?

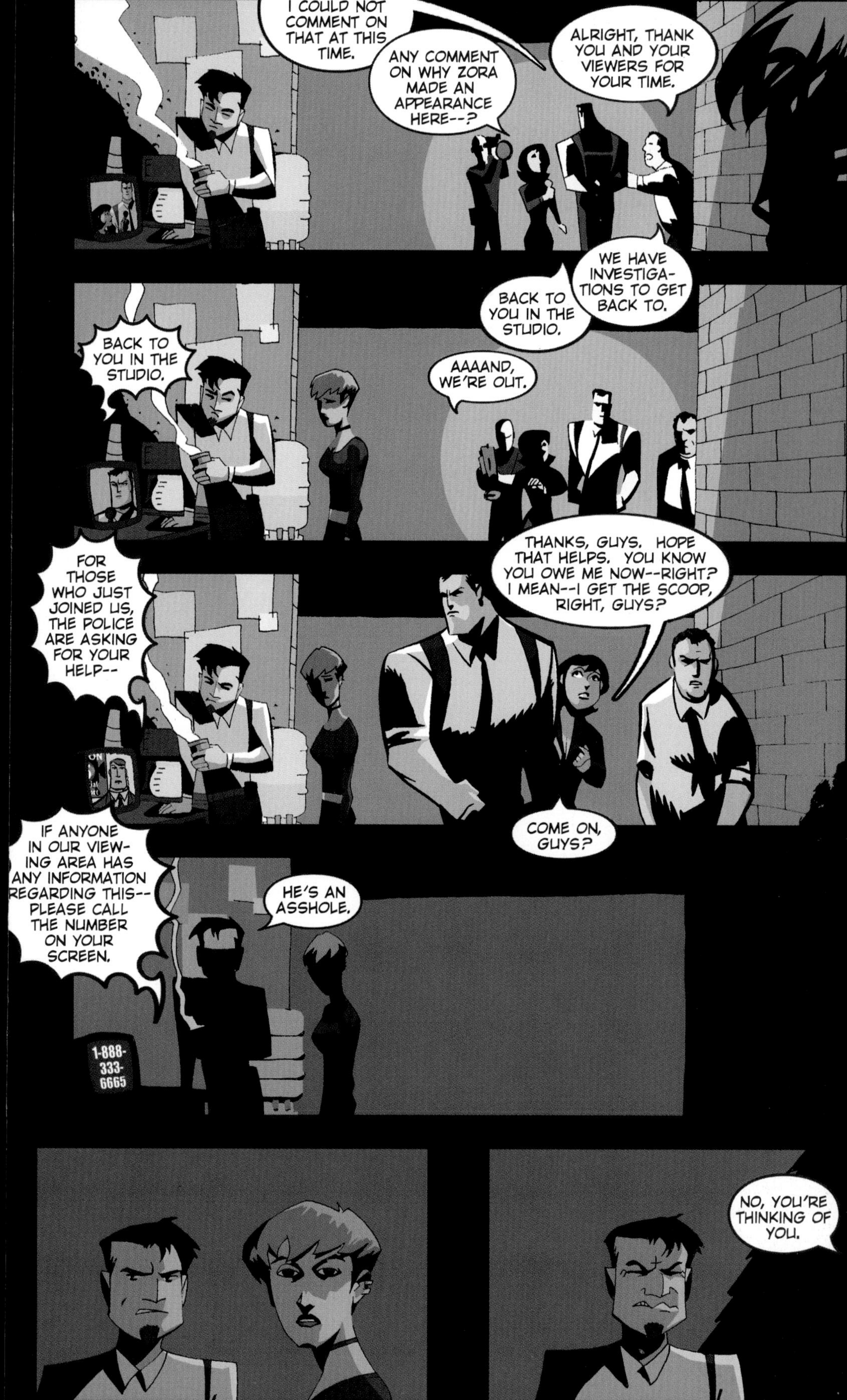
I COULD NOT COMMENT ON THAT AT THIS TIME.
ANY COMMENT ON WHY ZORA MADE AN APPEARANCE HERE--?
ALRIGHT, THANK YOU AND YOUR VIEWERS FOR YOUR TIME.
WE HAVE INVESTIGA-TIONS TO GET BACK TO.
BACK TO YOU IN THE STUDIO.
BACK TO YOU IN THE STUDIO.
AAAAND, WE'RE OUT.
FOR THOSE WHO JUST JOINED US, THE POLICE ARE ASKING FOR YOUR HELP--
THANKS, GUYS. HOPE THAT HELPS. YOU KNOW YOU OWE ME NOW--RIGHT? I MEAN--I GET THE SCOOP, RIGHT, GUYS?
COME ON, GUYS?
IF ANYONE IN OUR VIEW-ING AREA HAS ANY INFORMATION REGARDING THIS--PLEASE CALL THE NUMBER ON YOUR SCREEN.
HE'S AN ASSHOLE.
1-888-333-6665
NO, YOU'RE THINKING OF YOU.

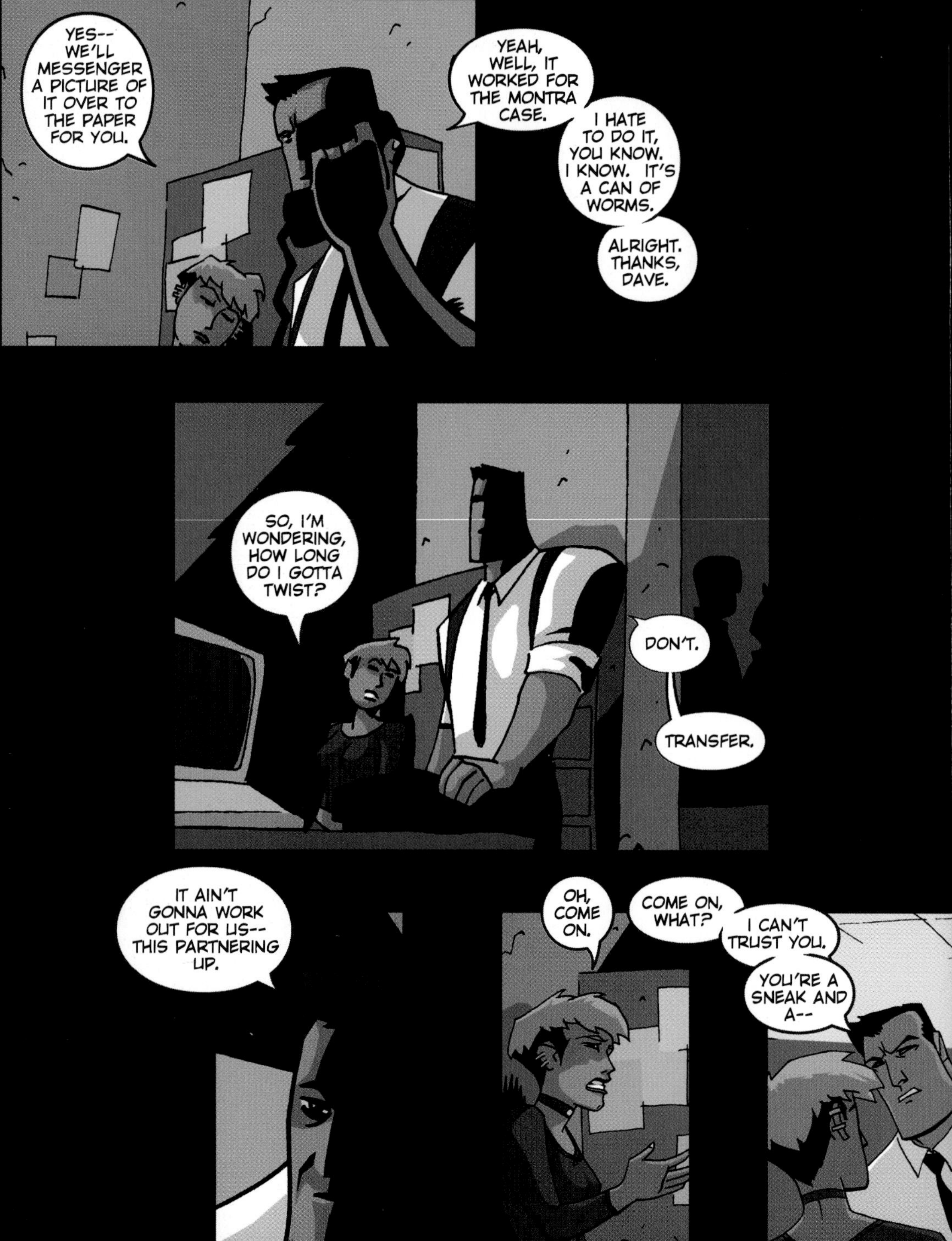

YES-- WE'LL MESSENGER A PICTURE OF IT OVER TO THE PAPER FOR YOU.
YEAH, WELL, IT WORKED FOR THE MONTRA CASE.
I HATE TO DO IT, YOU KNOW. I KNOW. IT'S A CAN OF WORMS.
ALRIGHT. THANKS, DAVE.
SO, I'M WONDERING, HOW LONG DO I GOTTA TWIST?
DON'T.
TRANSFER.
IT AIN'T GONNA WORK OUT FOR US-- THIS PARTNERING UP.
OH, COME ON.
COME ON, WHAT?
I CAN'T TRUST YOU.
YOU'RE A SNEAK AND A--

I'M A SNEAK??
YES.
YOU--
YOU ARE A SNEAK AND I CAN'T--
WELL, WHICH ONE OF US HAS THE SECRET FUCKING IDENTITY?

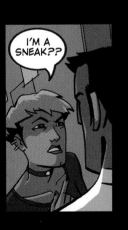

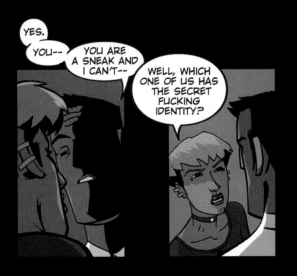

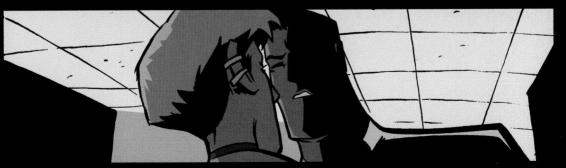

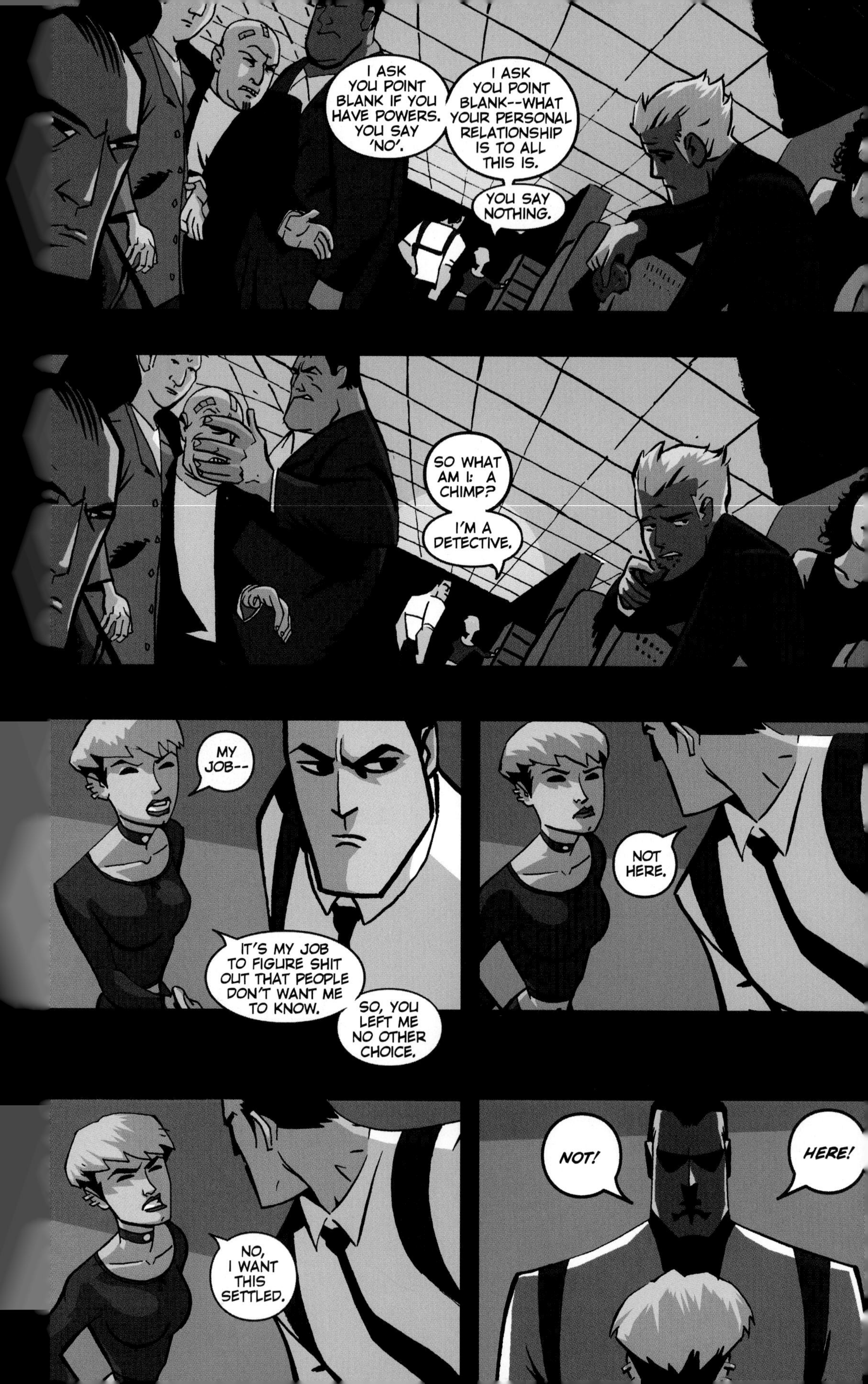
I ASK YOU POINT BLANK IF YOU HAVE POWERS. YOU SAY 'NO'.
I ASK YOU POINT BLANK--WHAT YOUR PERSONAL RELATIONSHIP IS TO ALL THIS IS.
YOU SAY NOTHING.
SO WHAT AM I: A CHIMP?
I'M A DETECTIVE.
MY JOB--
IT'S MY JOB TO FIGURE SHIT OUT THAT PEOPLE DON'T WANT ME TO KNOW.
SO, YOU LEFT ME NO OTHER CHOICE.
NOT HERE.
NO, I WANT THIS SETTLED.
NOT!
HERE!

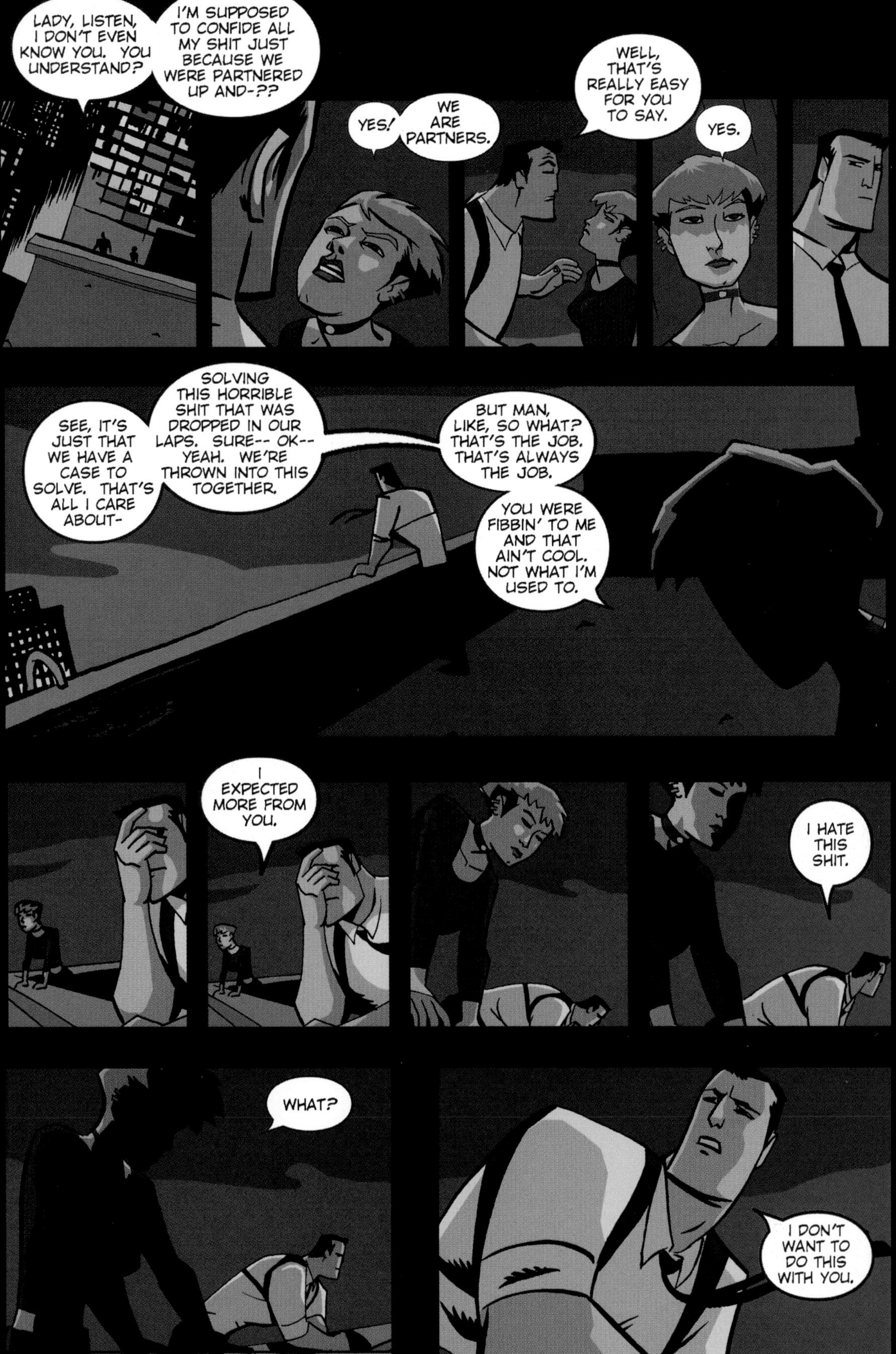
LADY, LISTEN, I DON'T EVEN KNOW YOU. YOU UNDERSTAND?
I'M SUPPOSED TO CONFIDE ALL MY SHIT JUST BECAUSE WE WERE PARTNERED UP AND-??
YES!
WE ARE PARTNERS.
WELL, THAT'S REALLY EASY FOR YOU TO SAY.
YES.
SEE, IT'S JUST THAT WE HAVE A CASE TO SOLVE. THAT'S ALL I CARE ABOUT-
SOLVING THIS HORRIBLE SHIT THAT WAS DROPPED IN OUR LAPS. SURE-- OK-- YEAH. WE'RE THROWN INTO THIS TOGETHER.
BUT MAN, LIKE, SO WHAT? THAT'S THE JOB. THAT'S ALWAYS THE JOB.
YOU WERE FIBBIN' TO ME AND THAT AIN'T COOL. NOT WHAT I'M USED TO.
I EXPECTED MORE FROM YOU.
I HATE THIS SHIT.
WHAT?
I DON'T WANT TO DO THIS WITH YOU.

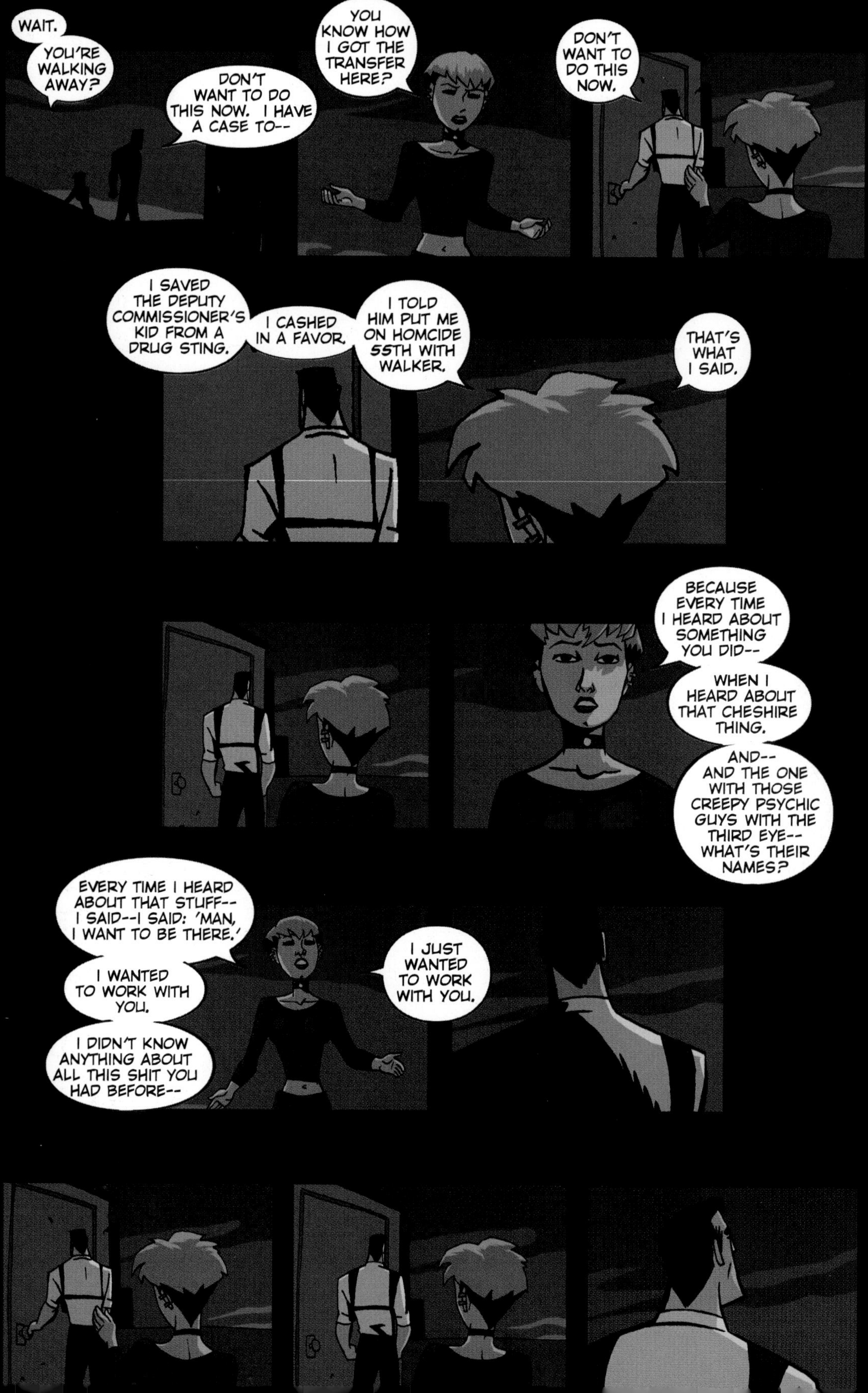
WAIT.
YOU'RE WALKING AWAY?
DON'T WANT TO DO THIS NOW. I HAVE A CASE TO--
YOU KNOW HOW I GOT THE TRANSFER HERE?
DON'T WANT TO DO THIS NOW.
I SAVED THE DEPUTY COMMISSIONER'S KID FROM A DRUG STING.
I CASHED IN A FAVOR.
I TOLD HIM PUT ME ON HOMCIDE 55TH WITH WALKER.
THAT'S WHAT I SAID.
BECAUSE EVERY TIME I HEARD ABOUT SOMETHING YOU DID--
WHEN I HEARD ABOUT THAT CHESHIRE THING.
AND-- AND THE ONE WITH THOSE CREEPY PSYCHIC GUYS WITH THE THIRD EYE-- WHAT'S THEIR NAMES?
EVERY TIME I HEARD ABOUT THAT STUFF-- I SAID--I SAID: 'MAN, I WANT TO BE THERE.'
I WANTED TO WORK WITH YOU.
I DIDN'T KNOW ANYTHING ABOUT ALL THIS SHIT YOU HAD BEFORE--
I JUST WANTED TO WORK WITH YOU.

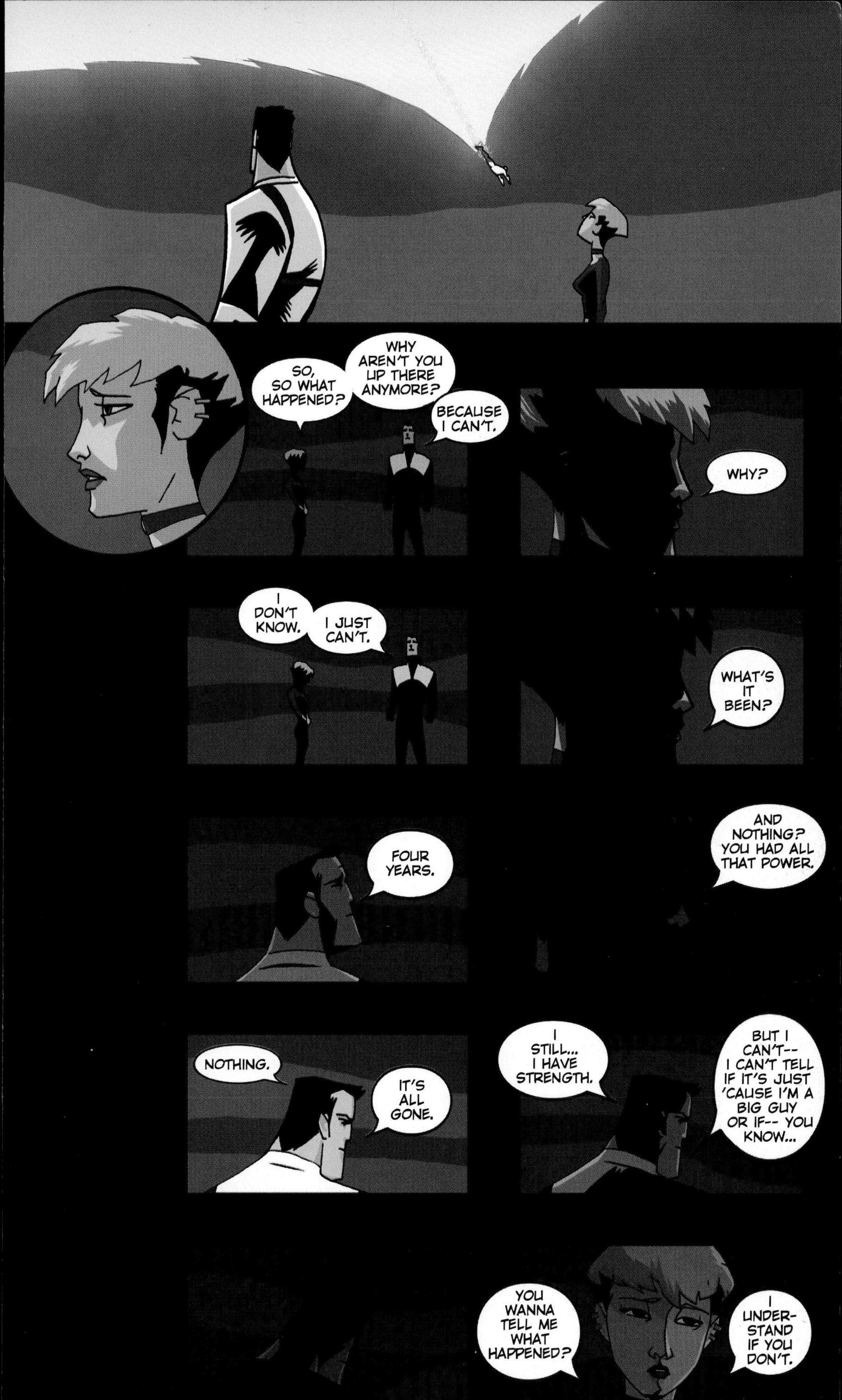
SO, SO WHAT HAPPENED?
WHY AREN'T YOU UP THERE ANYMORE?
BECAUSE I CAN'T.
WHY?
I DON'T KNOW.
I JUST CAN'T.
WHAT'S IT BEEN?
FOUR YEARS.
AND NOTHING? YOU HAD ALL THAT POWER.
NOTHING.
IT'S ALL GONE.
I STILL... I HAVE STRENGTH.
BUT I CAN'T-- I CAN'T TELL IF IT'S JUST 'CAUSE I'M A BIG GUY OR IF-- YOU KNOW...
YOU WANNA TELL ME WHAT HAPPENED?
I UNDER-STAND IF YOU DON'T.

WELL Y'SEE, I--I REALLY HAVE NO DAMN IDEA WHAT HAPPENED. JUST WHEN--IT WAS DURING THE WHOLE TERRIBLE INCIDENT WITH THE JOHNNY ROYALLE GANG.

OH YEAH--THAT'S THE LAST ANYONE EVER SAW OR HEARD FROM YOU--LIKE THAT. AS DIAMOND.

YEAH. WE WERE--WE WERE GOING AT IT PRETTY TOUGH, YOU KNOW. I MEAN--ALL THE FIGHTS ARE TOUGH--BUT THIS ONE--THIS ONE--THERE WAS SOMETHING JUST OFF ABOUT IT. IT WAS VERY CARNAL. VERY ANIMAL-LIKE. IT WAS ME AND TRIPHAMMER, WHO YOU'VE MET, AND ZORA AND RETRO GIRL AGAINST ALL THESE WACKOS. I MEAN, I DON'T EVEN REMEMBER HOW IT STARTED. SOME STUPID SCHEME OR SOMETHING.

SHIT! THAT FREAKY B.9. FOM-FOM DUDE WAS THERE.

YEAH--YEAH THAT'S RIGHT. AND CHESHIRE, AND TWILIGHT, BUT I WAS FIGHTING SSAZZ. AGAIN! HE'S SOME KIND OF MUTATION OR SOMETHING. ONE OF THOSE GENETIC MISHAPS WITH A HARD-ON FOR EVERY-THING. AND HE SMELLS SO--SO BAD. WE HAD FOUGHT BEFORE, Y'SEE, AND OF COURSE I BEAT THE HOLY CRAP OUT OF HIM. BUT THIS TIME HE HAD SOME KIND OF--SOME KIND OF ENHANCEMENT ON HIM OR SOMETHING.

LIKE A POWER ENHANCER?

YEAH.

I READ ABOUT THOSE IN SCIENTIFIC AMERI--

AND--AND I'M DOING EVERY-THING I CAN JUST TO END THE FIGHT. JUST END THE FIGHTING. JUST STOP IT. I GET, LIKE, THIS SUDDEN BURST OF ADRENALINE OR WHATNOT, LIKE A BURST OF ENERGY. NEVER HAPPENED BEFORE. BUT, WHAM!, AND I WAS WINNING THE DAY. AND THEN--AND THEN--***POOF!***

POOF?

POOF.

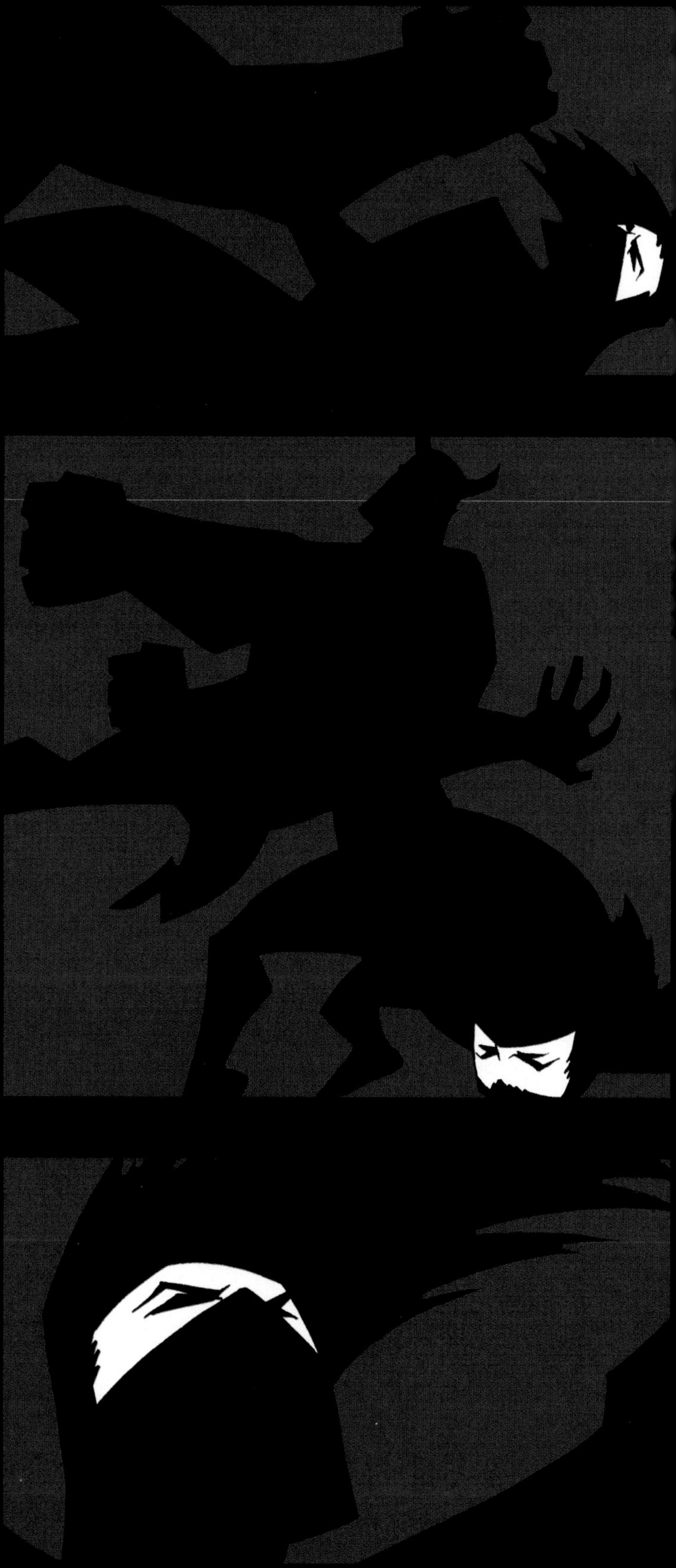

THAT'S IT?

THAT'S IT. BUT I WAS RIGHT
IN THE MIDDLE OF IT. THE
FRAY. Y'SEE? I MEAN. HERE
I AM--AND NOW I'M JUST A
GUY IN AN OUTFIT. AND ON
TOP OF IT, I'M CONFUSED AND
DISORIENTED. AND I HAVE NO
WAY TO DEFEND MYSELF, AND
I DON'T KNOW WHAT THE FUCK
HAS HAPPENED TO ME

DO YOU THINK IT'S
SOMETHING THAT
SSAZZ GUY
DID TO YOU?

NO, ACTUALLY. BECAUSE
WHEN GUYS LIKE THAT DO
SOMETHING LIKE THAT--
THEY NEVER SHUT UP ABOUT
IT. I DON'T THINK HE EVEN
FIGURED IT OUT. JUST
THOUGHT HE WAS PUTTING A
BEATING ON ME

HOW'D YOU GET OUT
OF THERE?

WELL, I WAS GETTING BEATEN
ON PRETTY BAD. AND SSAZZ--
HE WAS ABOUT TO BASICALLY
ELECTROCUTE ME, WHEN--
WHEN JANIS--*RETRO GIRL*--
SHE SAVED MY LIFE. SHE
FLEW ME OUT OF THERE

SHE STOPPED--*HA*--SHE
STOPPED TO KISS THE
BOO BOO I HAD ON MY
FOREHEAD. AND SHE
FLEW BACK TO FINISH THE
FIGHT. THAT'S ACTUALLY THE
LAST TIME I EVER SAW HER

BUT WEREN'T YOU
GUYS FRIENDS?

SEE, YOU KEEP MISSING
THE POINT ON THAT

WERE YOU OR
WEREN'T YOU?

WELL, YES AND NO. WE--
WE WORKED TOGETHER ON
OCCASION IS ALL. WE--WE
DIDN'T MAKE A HABIT OF
GETTING INTO EACH OTHER'S
PERSONAL LIVES. WE DIDN'T
HAVE A CLUB HOUSE. JUST--

WE UNDERSTOOD THIS--IT
WAS AN UNWRITTEN RULE TO
SUPPORT EACH OTHER IN
PUBLIC AND NOT TO GET INTO
EACH OTHER'S BUSINESS

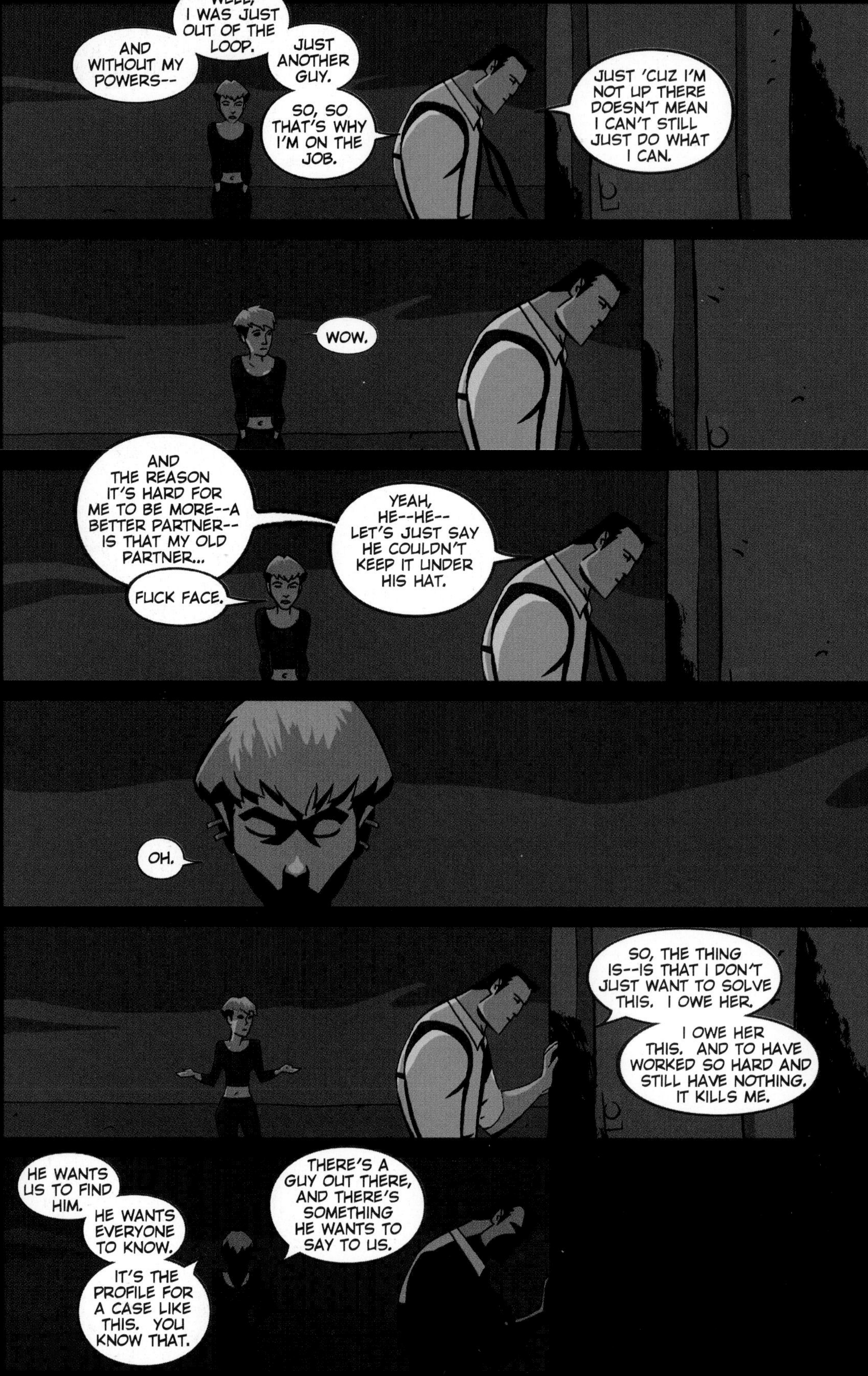
AND WITHOUT MY POWERS--
WELL, I WAS JUST OUT OF THE LOOP.
JUST ANOTHER GUY.
SO, SO THAT'S WHY I'M ON THE JOB.
JUST 'CUZ I'M NOT UP THERE DOESN'T MEAN I CAN'T STILL JUST DO WHAT I CAN.
WOW.
AND THE REASON IT'S HARD FOR ME TO BE MORE--A BETTER PARTNER--IS THAT MY OLD PARTNER...
FUCK FACE.
YEAH, HE--HE--LET'S JUST SAY HE COULDN'T KEEP IT UNDER HIS HAT.
OH.
SO, THE THING IS--IS THAT I DON'T JUST WANT TO SOLVE THIS. I OWE HER.
I OWE HER THIS. AND TO HAVE WORKED SO HARD AND STILL HAVE NOTHING. IT KILLS ME.
HE WANTS US TO FIND HIM.
HE WANTS EVERYONE TO KNOW.
IT'S THE PROFILE FOR A CASE LIKE THIS. YOU KNOW THAT.
THERE'S A GUY OUT THERE, AND THERE'S SOMETHING HE WANTS TO SAY TO US.

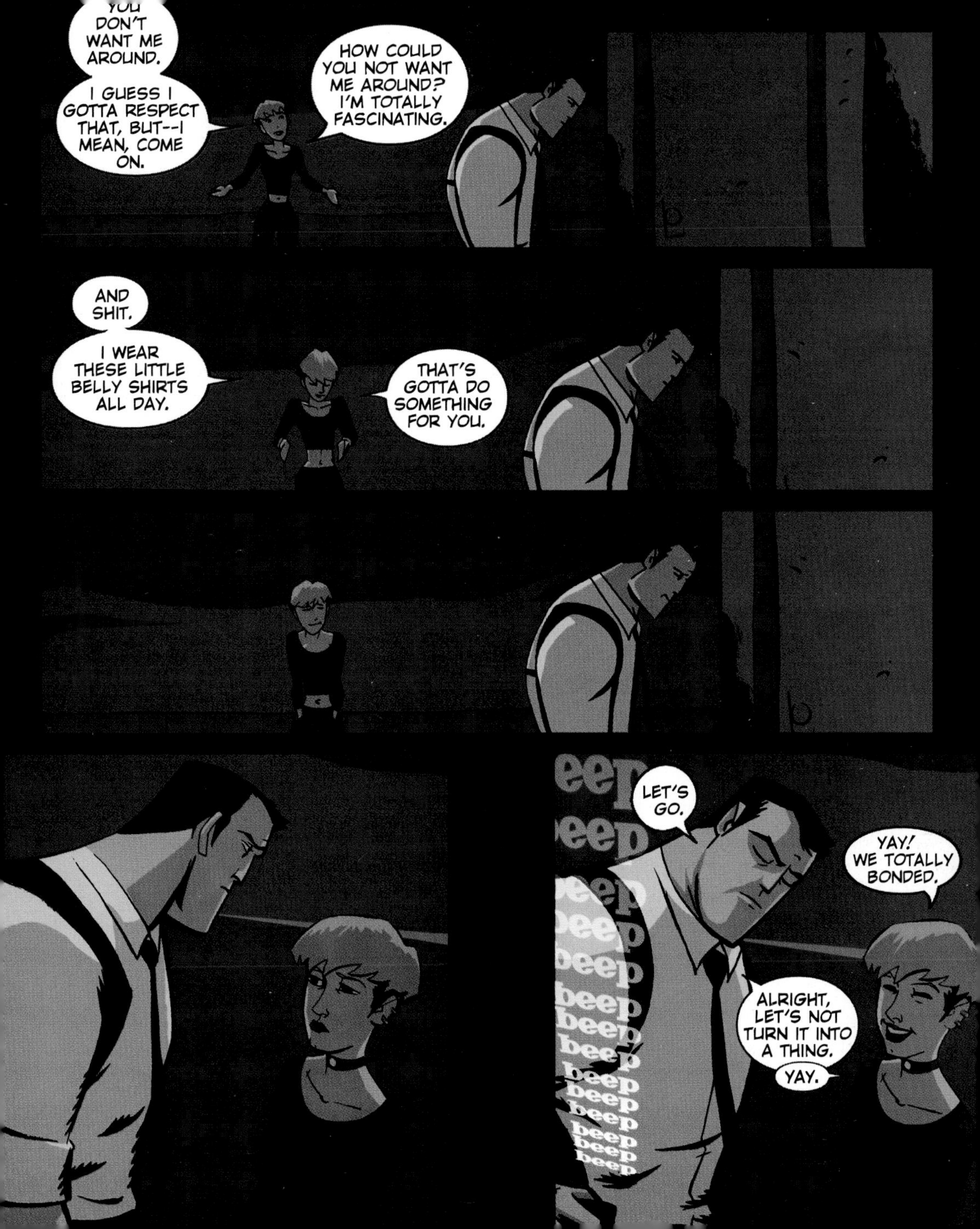
YOU DON'T WANT ME AROUND.
I GUESS I GOTTA RESPECT THAT, BUT--I MEAN, COME ON.
HOW COULD YOU NOT WANT ME AROUND? I'M TOTALLY FASCINATING.
AND SHIT.
I WEAR THESE LITTLE BELLY SHIRTS ALL DAY.
THAT'S GOTTA DO SOMETHING FOR YOU.
beep beep beep beep beep beep beep beep beep beep beep beep beep beep beep
LET'S GO.
YAY! WE TOTALLY BONDED.
ALRIGHT, LET'S NOT TURN IT INTO A THING.
YAY.

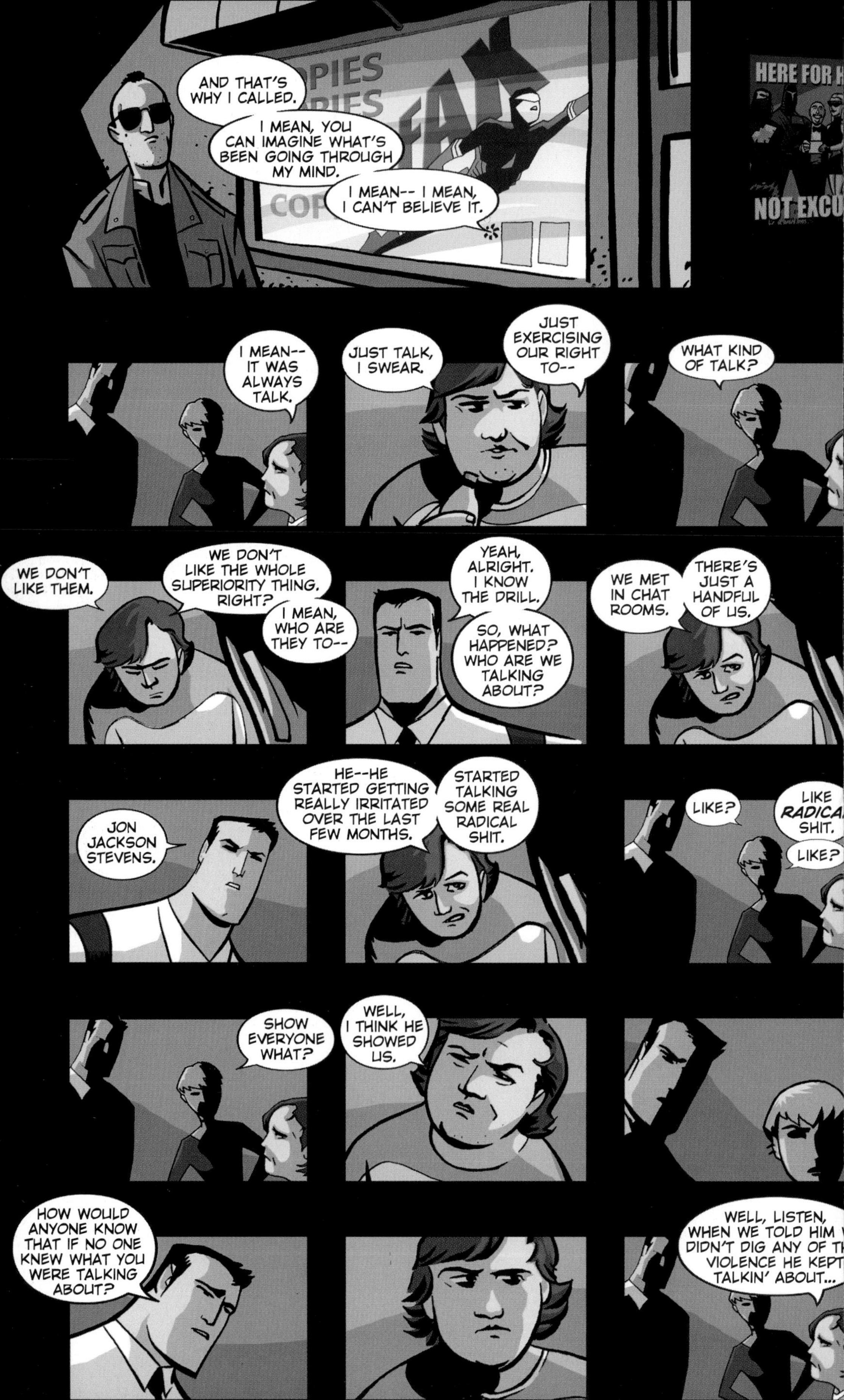
HERE FOR H
NOT EXCU
AND THAT'S WHY I CALLED.
I MEAN, YOU CAN IMAGINE WHAT'S BEEN GOING THROUGH MY MIND.
I MEAN-- I MEAN, I CAN'T BELIEVE IT.
I MEAN-- IT WAS ALWAYS TALK.
JUST TALK, I SWEAR.
JUST EXERCISING OUR RIGHT TO--
WHAT KIND OF TALK?
WE DON'T LIKE THEM.
WE DON'T LIKE THE WHOLE SUPERIORITY THING. RIGHT?
I MEAN, WHO ARE THEY TO--
YEAH, ALRIGHT. I KNOW THE DRILL.
SO, WHAT HAPPENED? WHO ARE WE TALKING ABOUT?
WE MET IN CHAT ROOMS.
THERE'S JUST A HANDFUL OF US.
JON JACKSON STEVENS.
HE--HE STARTED GETTING REALLY IRRITATED OVER THE LAST FEW MONTHS.
STARTED TALKING SOME REAL RADICAL SHIT.
LIKE?
LIKE *RADICA* SHIT.
LIKE?
SHOW EVERYONE WHAT?
WELL, I THINK HE SHOWED US.
HOW WOULD ANYONE KNOW THAT IF NO ONE KNEW WHAT YOU WERE TALKING ABOUT?
WELL, LISTEN, WHEN WE TOLD HIM W DIDN'T DIG ANY OF TH VIOLENCE HE KEPT TALKIN' ABOUT...

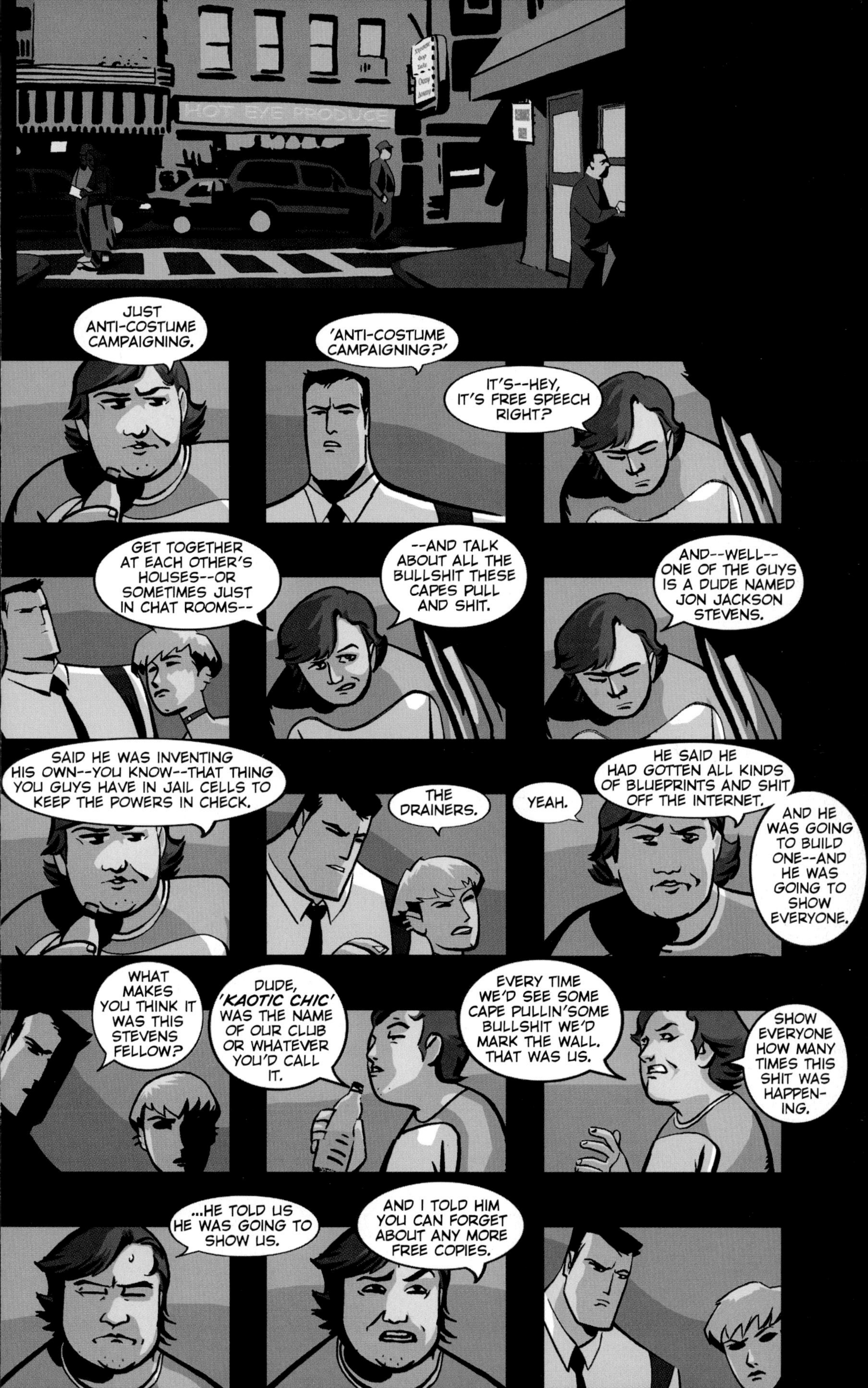
HOT EYE PRODUCE
JUST ANTI-COSTUME CAMPAIGNING.
'ANTI-COSTUME CAMPAIGNING?'
IT'S--HEY, IT'S FREE SPEECH RIGHT?
GET TOGETHER AT EACH OTHER'S HOUSES--OR SOMETIMES JUST IN CHAT ROOMS--
--AND TALK ABOUT ALL THE BULLSHIT THESE CAPES PULL AND SHIT.
AND--WELL--ONE OF THE GUYS IS A DUDE NAMED JON JACKSON STEVENS.
SAID HE WAS INVENTING HIS OWN--YOU KNOW--THAT THING YOU GUYS HAVE IN JAIL CELLS TO KEEP THE POWERS IN CHECK.
THE DRAINERS.
YEAH.
HE SAID HE HAD GOTTEN ALL KINDS OF BLUEPRINTS AND SHIT OFF THE INTERNET.
AND HE WAS GOING TO BUILD ONE--AND HE WAS GOING TO SHOW EVERYONE.
WHAT MAKES YOU THINK IT WAS THIS STEVENS FELLOW?
DUDE, 'KAOTIC CHIC' WAS THE NAME OF OUR CLUB OR WHATEVER YOU'D CALL IT.
EVERY TIME WE'D SEE SOME CAPE PULLIN'SOME BULLSHIT WE'D MARK THE WALL. THAT WAS US.
SHOW EVERYONE HOW MANY TIMES THIS SHIT WAS HAPPEN-ING.
...HE TOLD US HE WAS GOING TO SHOW US.
AND I TOLD HIM YOU CAN FORGET ABOUT ANY MORE FREE COPIES.

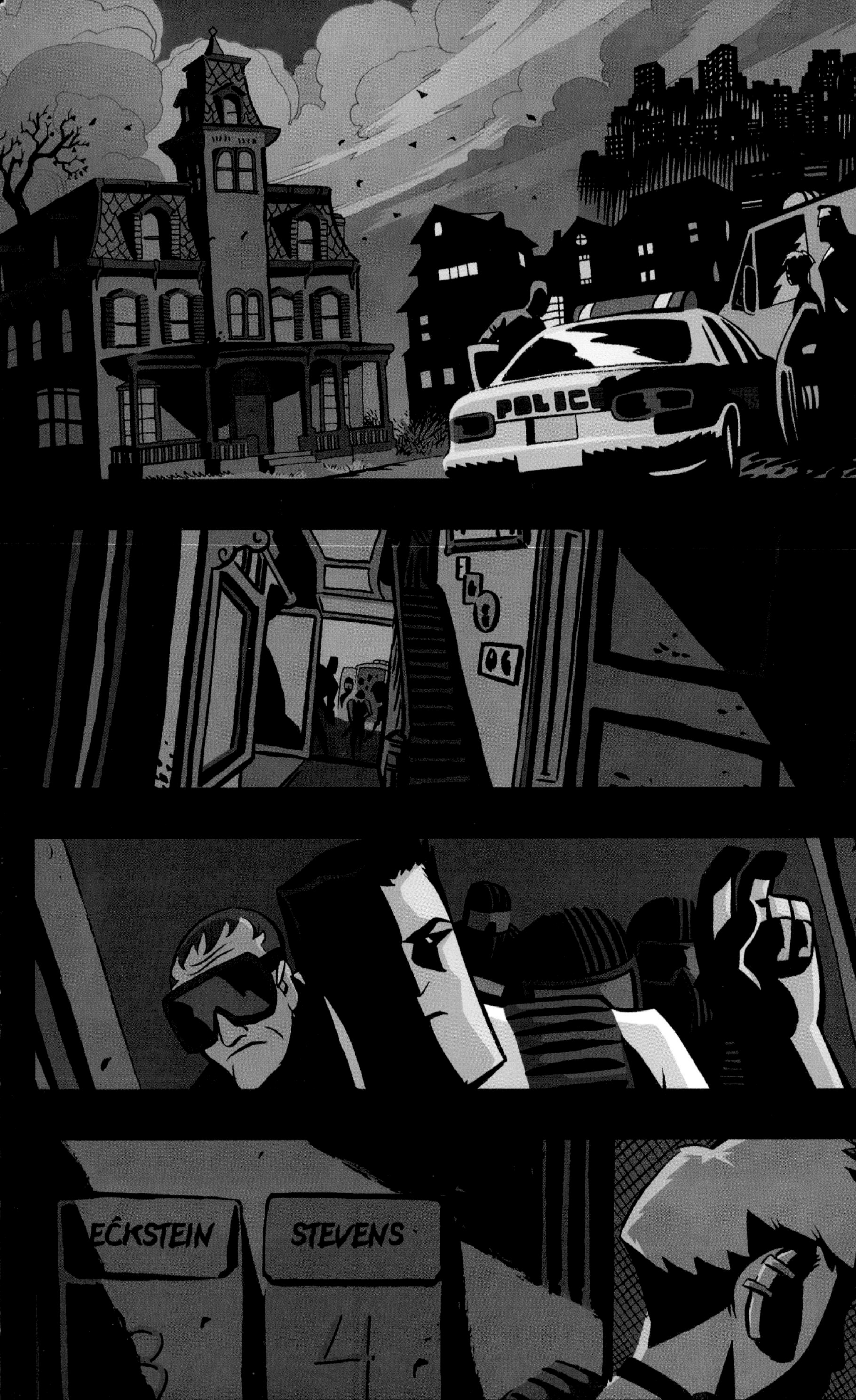
POLICE
06
ECKSTEIN
STEVENS

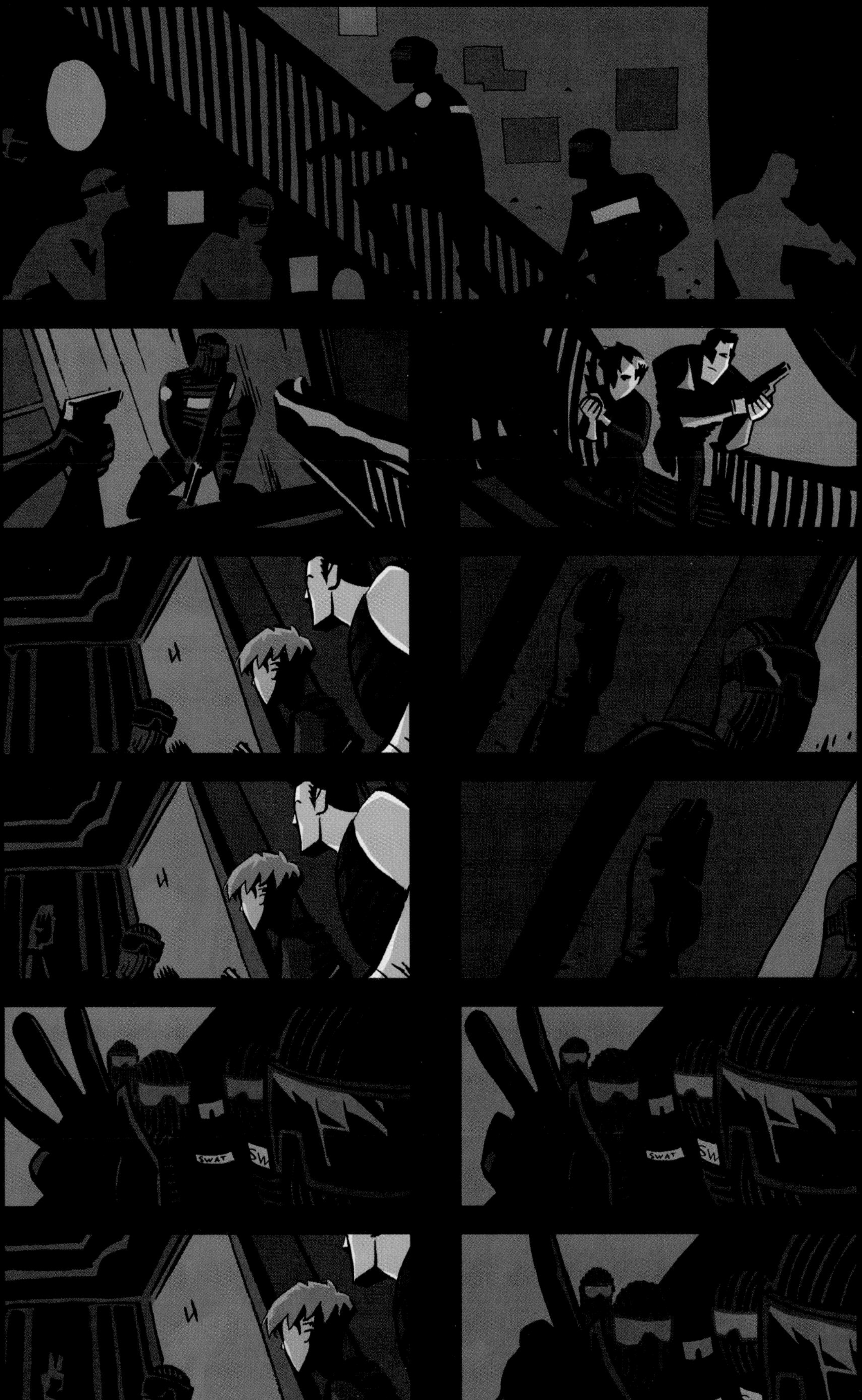
SWAT
SWAT
SWAT

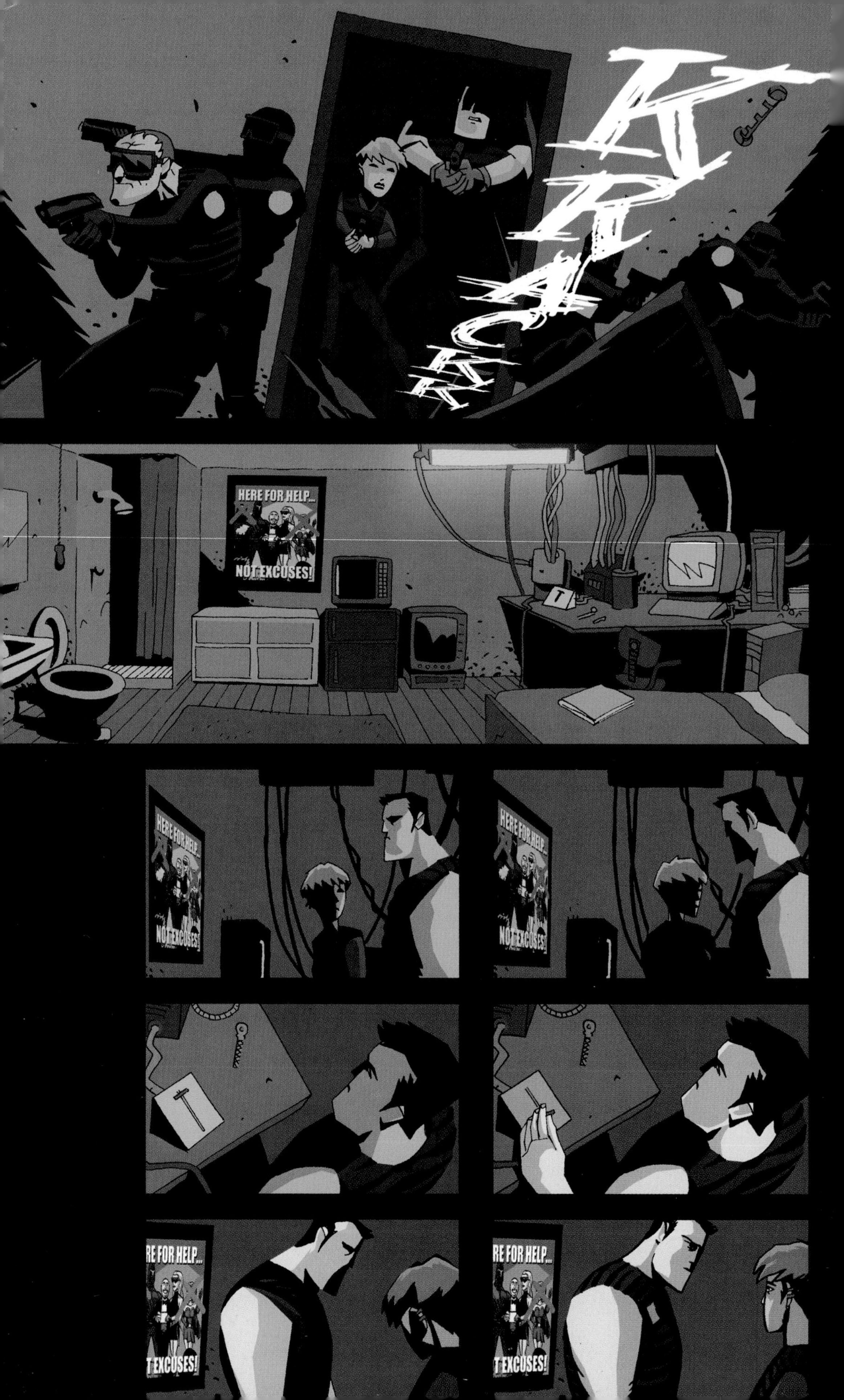
KRACK
HERE FOR HELP...
NOT EXCUSES!

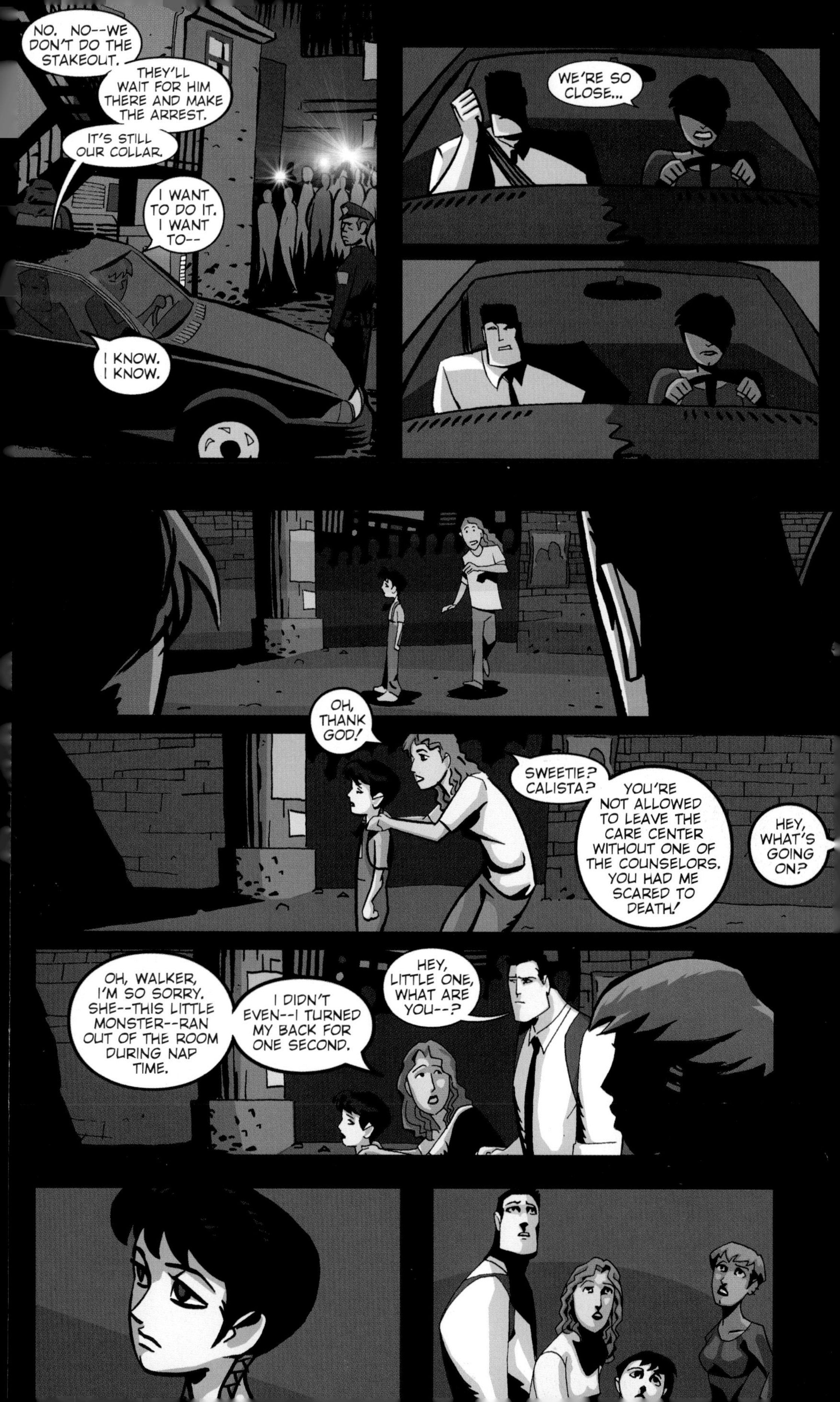
NO. NO--WE DON'T DO THE STAKEOUT.
THEY'LL WAIT FOR HIM THERE AND MAKE THE ARREST.
IT'S STILL OUR COLLAR.
I WANT TO DO IT. I WANT TO--
I KNOW. I KNOW.
WE'RE SO CLOSE...
OH, THANK GOD!
SWEETIE? CALISTA?
YOU'RE NOT ALLOWED TO LEAVE THE CARE CENTER WITHOUT ONE OF THE COUNSELORS. YOU HAD ME SCARED TO DEATH!
HEY, WHAT'S GOING ON?
OH, WALKER, I'M SO SORRY. SHE--THIS LITTLE MONSTER--RAN OUT OF THE ROOM DURING NAP TIME.
I DIDN'T EVEN--I TURNED MY BACK FOR ONE SECOND.
HEY, LITTLE ONE, WHAT ARE YOU--?

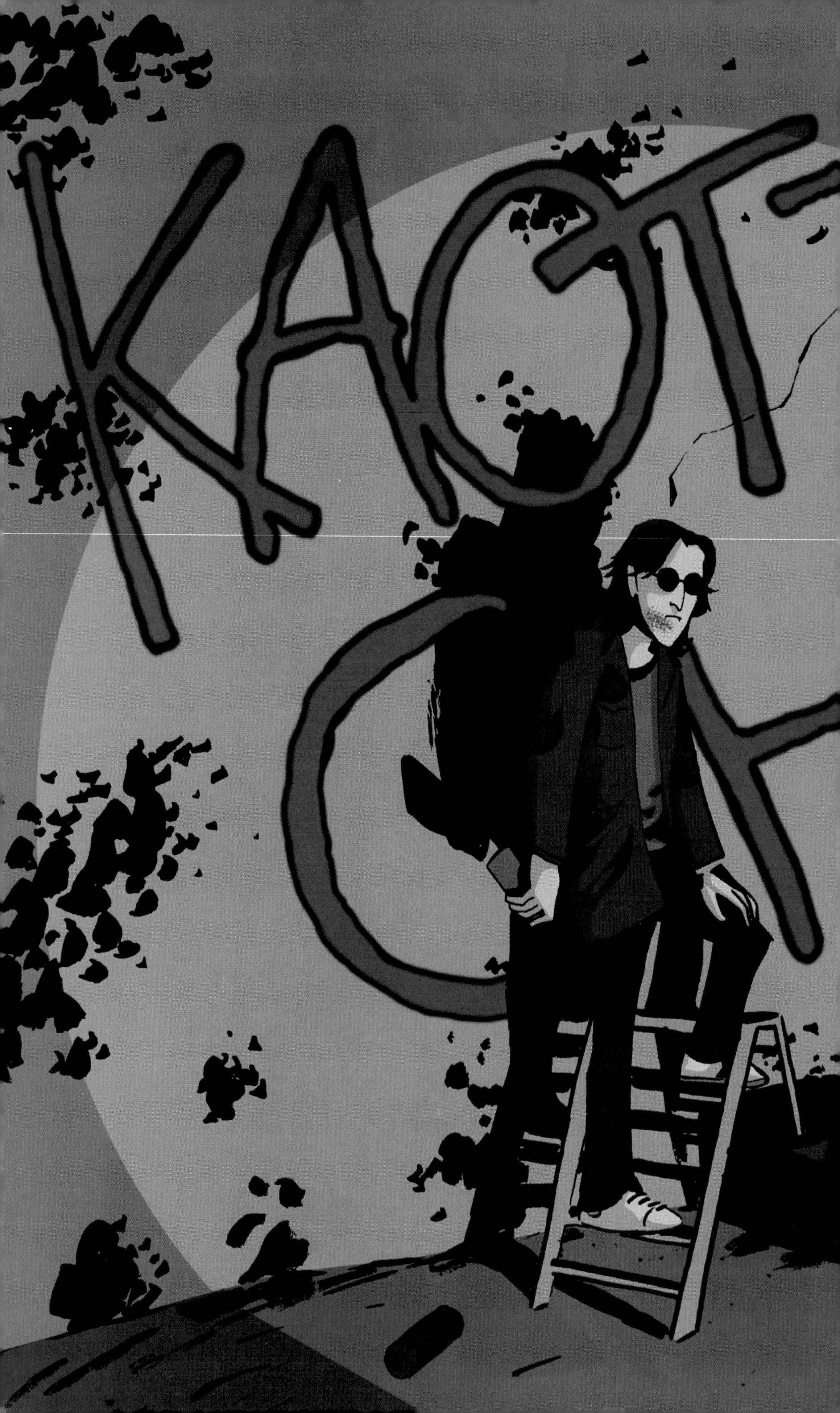

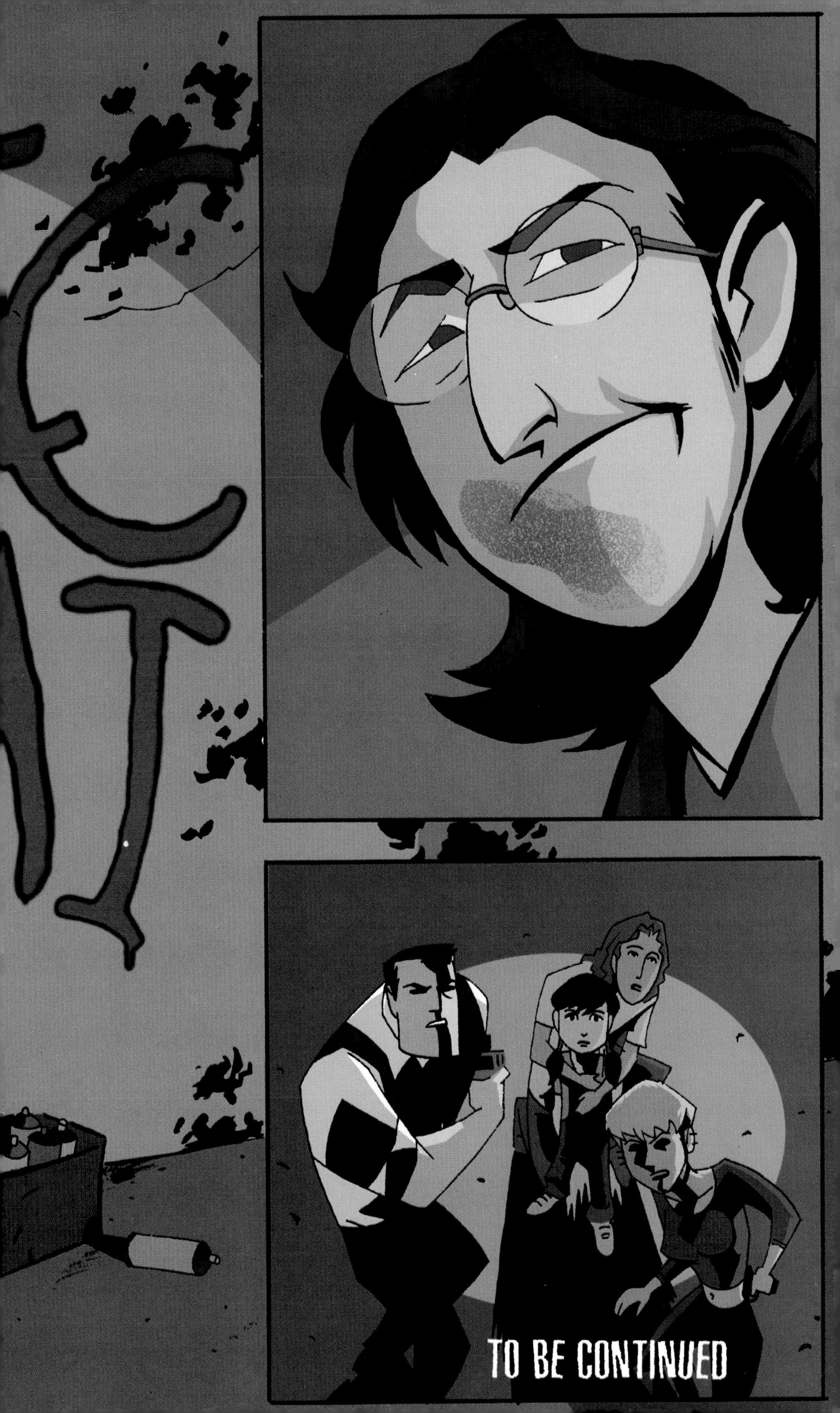
TO BE CONTINUED

AM I ON?
WELL, HOW LONG
WILL IT--?
HELLO??

OH MY! AHEM--
THIS IS COLLETTE
MCDANIEL. IT WAS
RIGHT HERE, ON THE
SOUTH SIDE OF THE
POLICE DEPARTMENT
ENTRANCE AT THE
THE DOWNTOWN
JUSTICE CENTER.

THAT--
JUST MOMENTS
AGO--DETECTIVE
CHRISTIAN WALKER
AND RELATIVE
NEWCOMER TO
THE HOMICIDE
DEPARTMENT
DETECTIVE
DEENA PILGRIM
BROUGHT AN
UNKNOWN
MAN INTO
CUSTODY.

THE MAN WAS APPREHENDED WHILE DEFACING POLICE PROPERTY WITH THIS GRAFFITI, JUST A FEW FEET AND AROUND THE CORNER FROM THE VERITABLE THRONG OF MEDIA THAT HAS BEEN CAMPED OUT HERE SINCE THIS TRAGEDY BEGAN.

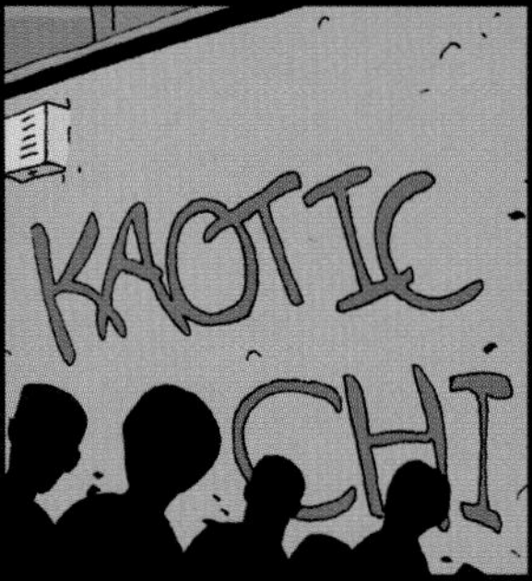
KAOTIC
CHI

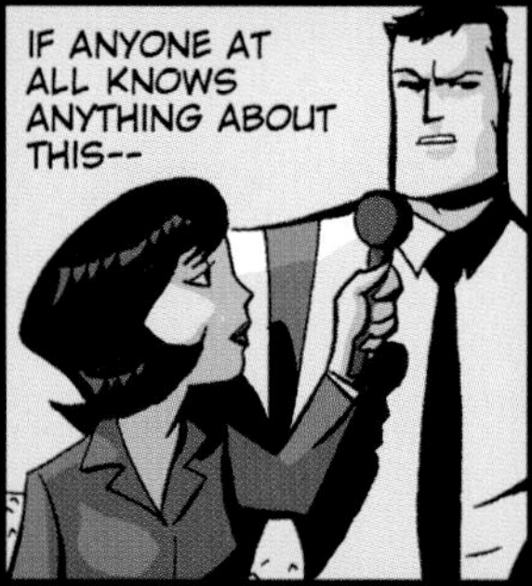
IF ANYONE AT ALL KNOWS ANYTHING ABOUT THIS--

KAOTIC CHIC-- THIS ODD GRAFFITI MATCHES THE GRAFFITI FOUND AT THE ***RETRO GIRL*** CRIME SCENE. IT WAS RIGHT HERE ON ***LIVE AT FIVE,*** EARLIER TODAY, THAT DETECTIVE WALKER PLEADED WITH OUR VIEWERSHIP FOR INFORMATION RELATED TO THE CRYPTIC MESSAGE.

OUR CAMERAS CAUGHT ONLY A GLIMPSE OF THE MAN. THERE HAS BEEN NO WORD AS YET TO THE IDENTITY OF THE MAN OR IF HE HAS IN FACT BEEN CHARGED IN THE RETRO GIRL MURDER.

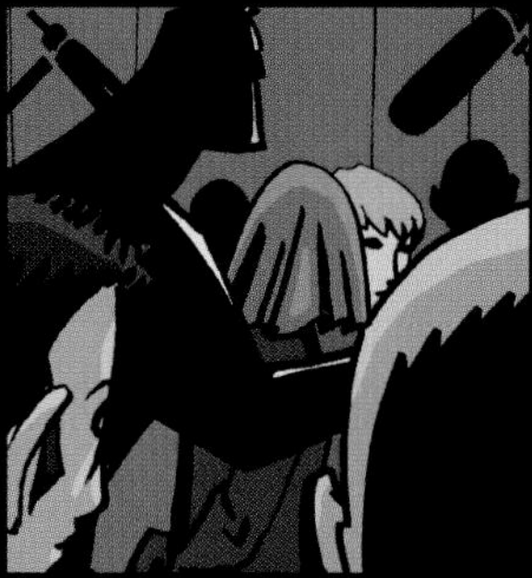

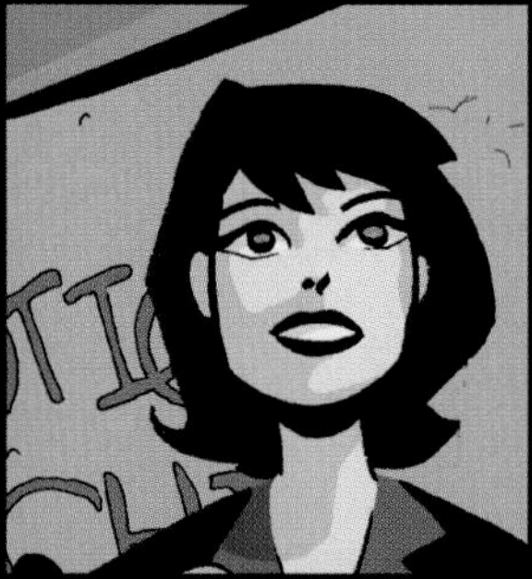

WE WILL STAY ON THE AIR WITH ROUND-THE-CLOCK COVERAGE UNTIL THE BLUE CODE OF SILENCE LIFTS HERE AT POLICE HEADQUARTERS.

WE CAN ONLY WAIT AND HOPE THAT THIS HORRIBLE TRAGEDY IS NEAR AN END.

BACK TO YOU IN THE STUDIO.

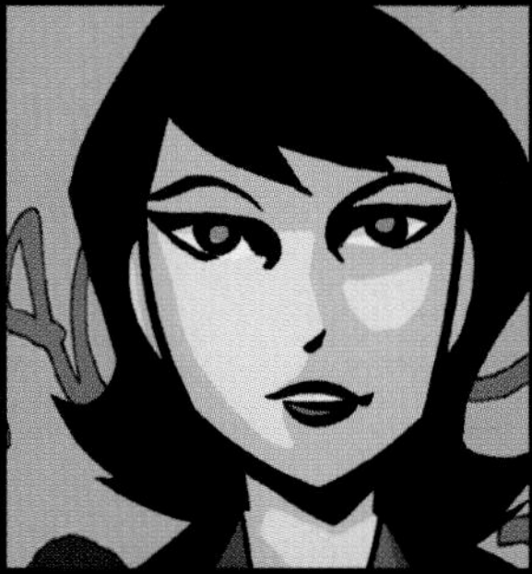

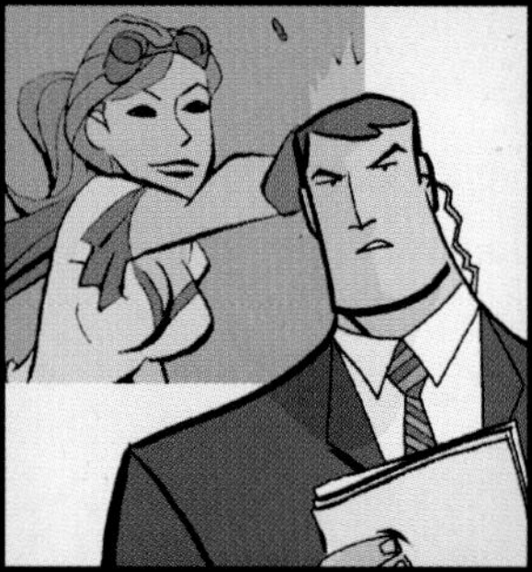

THANK YOU, COLLETTE.

FOR THOSE JUST JOINING US, THIS IS DAY TWO IN OUR WALL-TO-WALL LIVE COVERAGE OF... ***THE MURDER OF RETRO GIRL.***

WE'LL BE RIGHT BACK AFTER THIS STATION IDENTIFICATION.

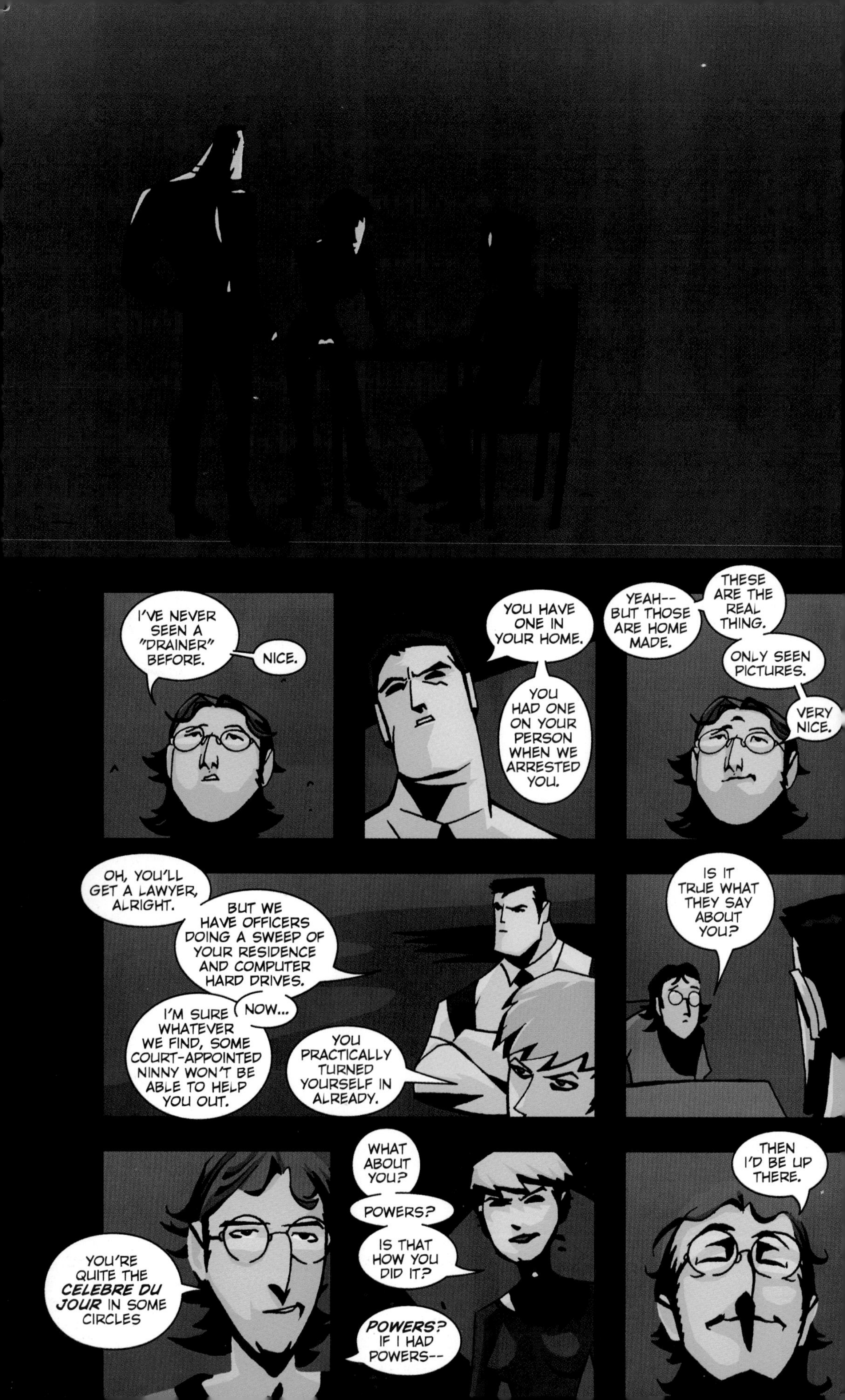
I'VE NEVER SEEN A "DRAINER" BEFORE.
NICE.
YOU HAVE ONE IN YOUR HOME.
YOU HAD ONE ON YOUR PERSON WHEN WE ARRESTED YOU.
YEAH-- BUT THOSE ARE HOME MADE.
THESE ARE THE REAL THING.
ONLY SEEN PICTURES.
VERY NICE.
OH, YOU'LL GET A LAWYER, ALRIGHT.
BUT WE HAVE OFFICERS DOING A SWEEP OF YOUR RESIDENCE AND COMPUTER HARD DRIVES.
NOW...
I'M SURE WHATEVER WE FIND, SOME COURT-APPOINTED NINNY WON'T BE ABLE TO HELP YOU OUT.
YOU PRACTICALLY TURNED YOURSELF IN ALREADY.
IS IT TRUE WHAT THEY SAY ABOUT YOU?
YOU'RE QUITE THE *CELEBRE DU JOUR* IN SOME CIRCLES
WHAT ABOUT YOU?
POWERS?
IS THAT HOW YOU DID IT?
POWERS? IF I HAD POWERS--
THEN I'D BE UP THERE.

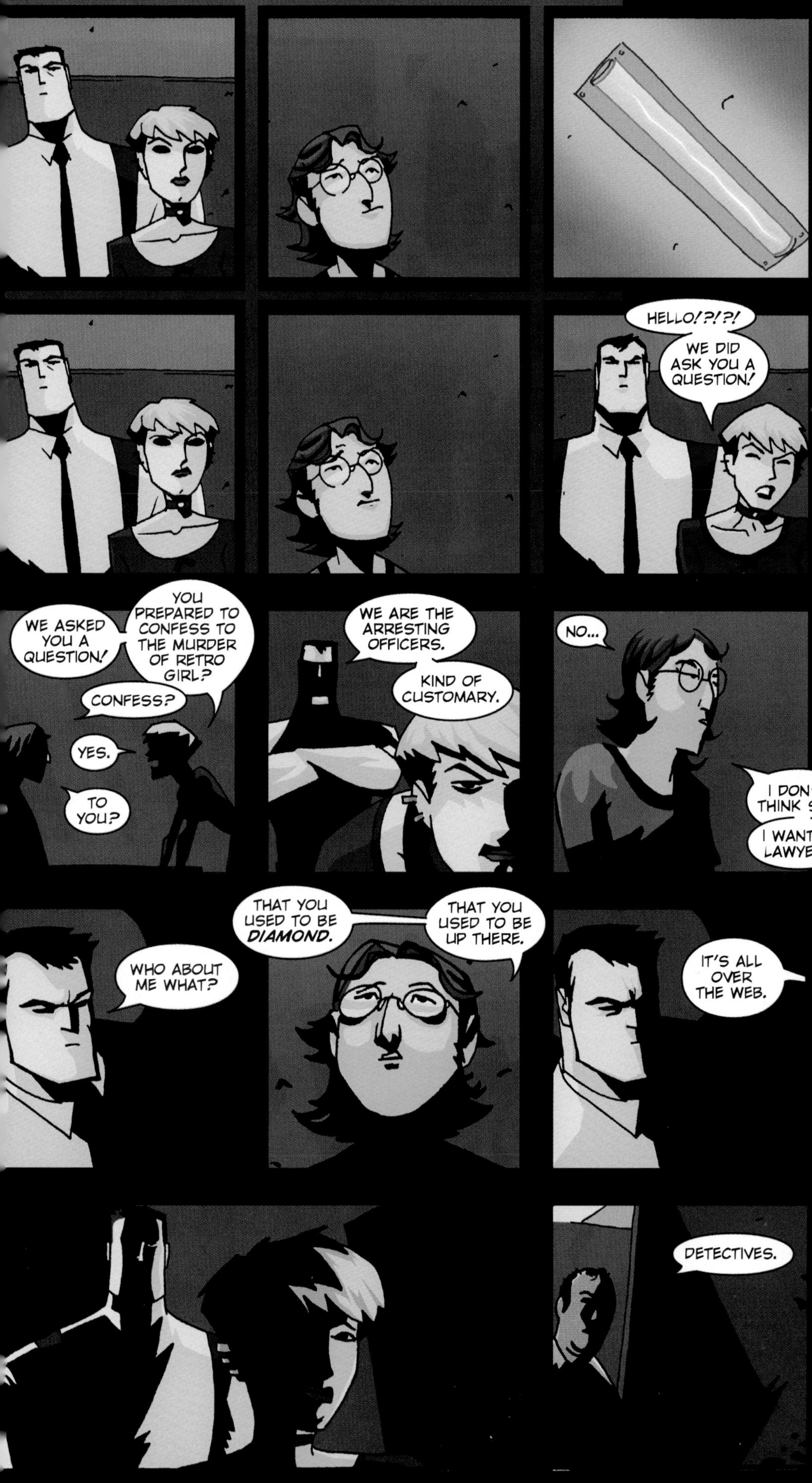

HELLO!?!?!
WE DID ASK YOU A QUESTION!
WE ASKED YOU A QUESTION!
YOU PREPARED TO CONFESS TO THE MURDER OF RETRO GIRL?
CONFESS?
YES.
TO YOU?
WE ARE THE ARRESTING OFFICERS.
KIND OF CUSTOMARY.
NO...
I DON'T THINK SO.
I WANT A LAWYER.
WHO ABOUT ME WHAT?
THAT YOU USED TO BE DIAMOND.
THAT YOU USED TO BE UP THERE.
IT'S ALL OVER THE WEB.
DETECTIVES.

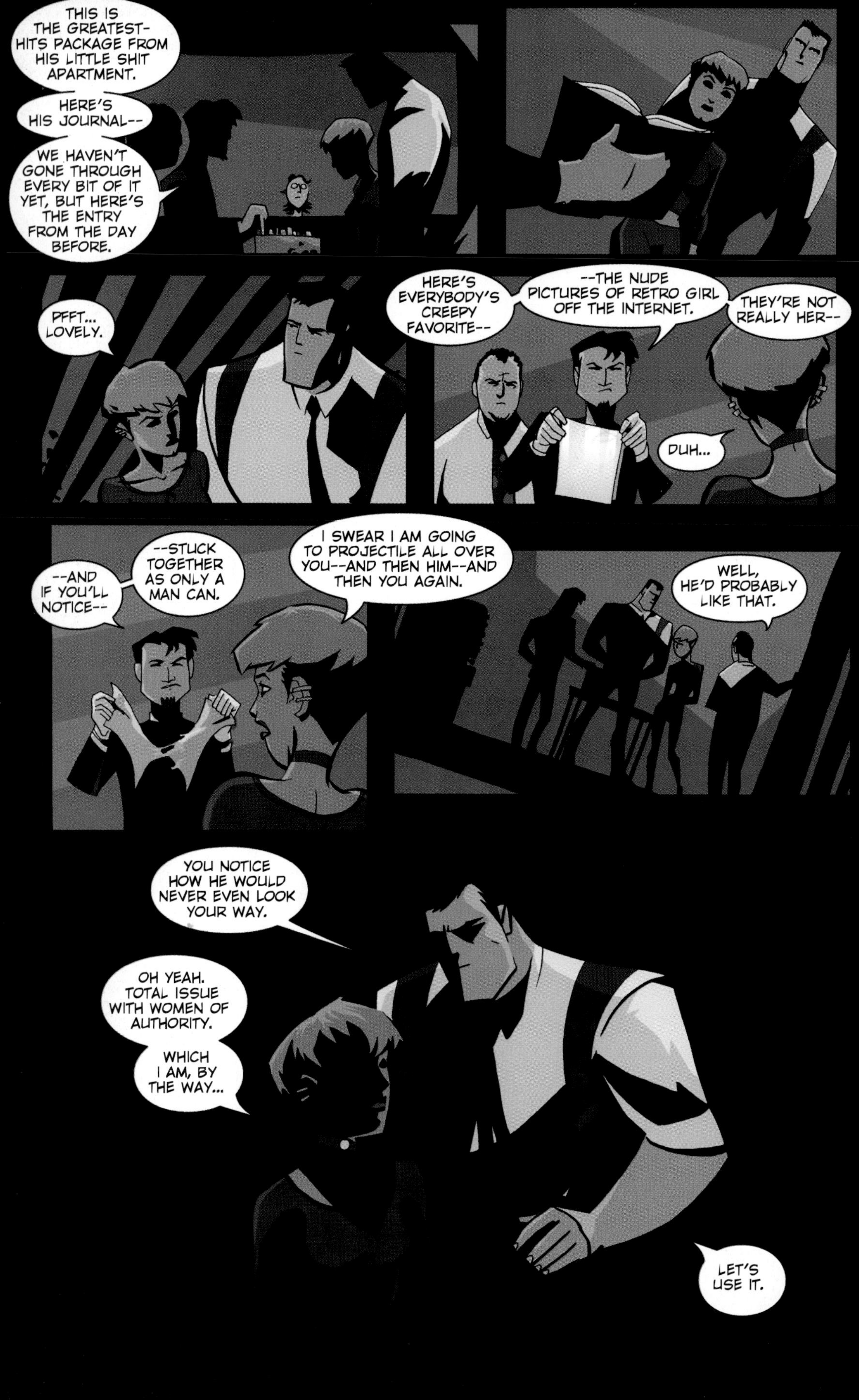
THIS IS THE GREATEST-HITS PACKAGE FROM HIS LITTLE SHIT APARTMENT.
HERE'S HIS JOURNAL--
WE HAVEN'T GONE THROUGH EVERY BIT OF IT YET, BUT HERE'S THE ENTRY FROM THE DAY BEFORE.
PFFT... LOVELY.
HERE'S EVERYBODY'S CREEPY FAVORITE--
--THE NUDE PICTURES OF RETRO GIRL OFF THE INTERNET.
THEY'RE NOT REALLY HER--
DUH...
--AND IF YOU'LL NOTICE--
--STUCK TOGETHER AS ONLY A MAN CAN.
I SWEAR I AM GOING TO PROJECTILE ALL OVER YOU--AND THEN HIM--AND THEN YOU AGAIN.
WELL, HE'D PROBABLY LIKE THAT.
YOU NOTICE HOW HE WOULD NEVER EVEN LOOK YOUR WAY.
OH YEAH. TOTAL ISSUE WITH WOMEN OF AUTHORITY.
WHICH I AM, BY THE WAY...
LET'S USE IT.

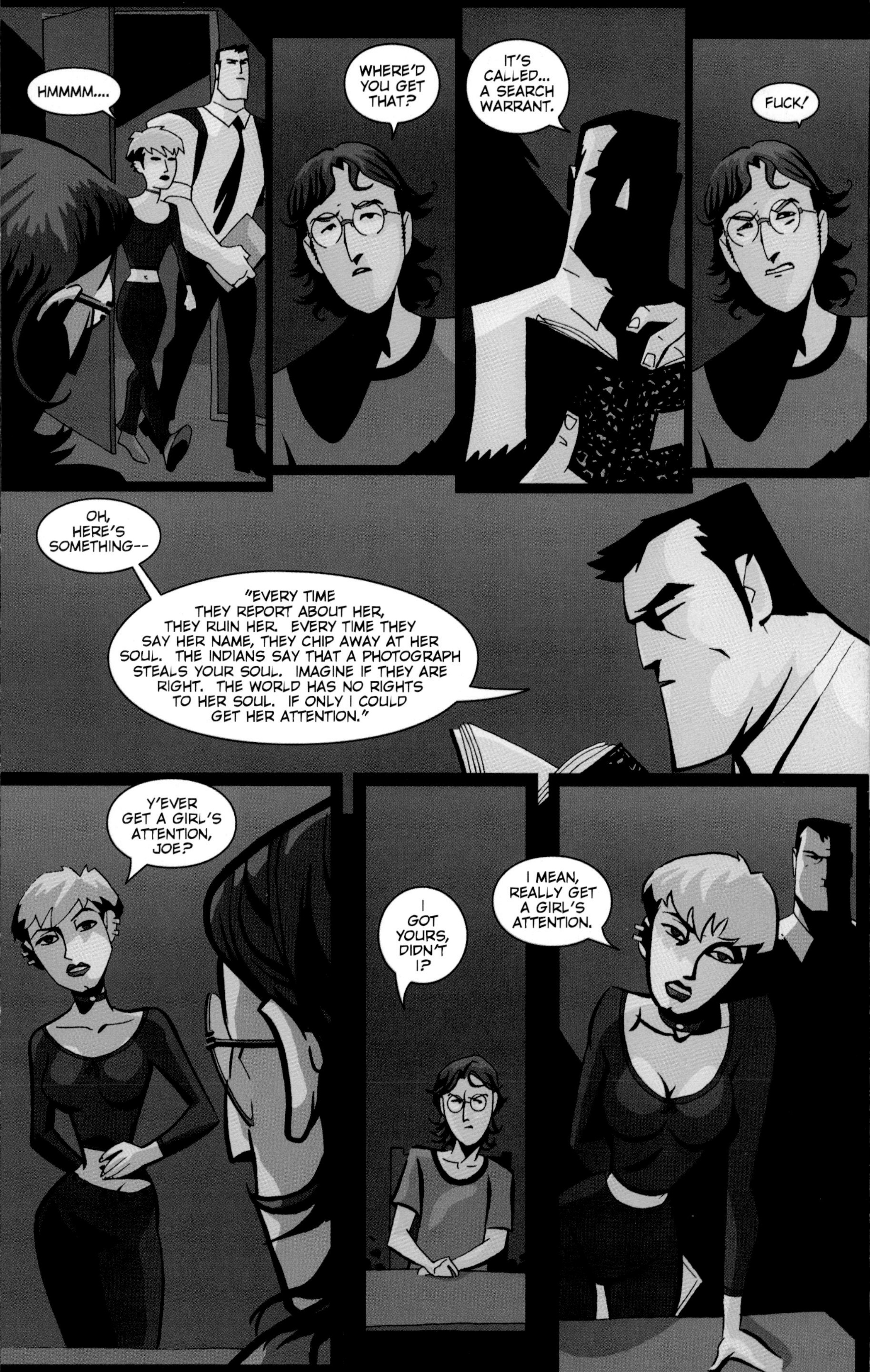
HMMMM....
WHERE'D YOU GET THAT?
IT'S CALLED... A SEARCH WARRANT.
FUCK!
OH, HERE'S SOMETHING--
"EVERY TIME THEY REPORT ABOUT HER, THEY RUIN HER. EVERY TIME THEY SAY HER NAME, THEY CHIP AWAY AT HER SOUL. THE INDIANS SAY THAT A PHOTOGRAPH STEALS YOUR SOUL. IMAGINE IF THEY ARE RIGHT. THE WORLD HAS NO RIGHTS TO HER SOUL. IF ONLY I COULD GET HER ATTENTION."
Y'EVER GET A GIRL'S ATTENTION, JOE?
I GOT YOURS, DIDN'T I?
I MEAN, REALLY GET A GIRL'S ATTENTION.

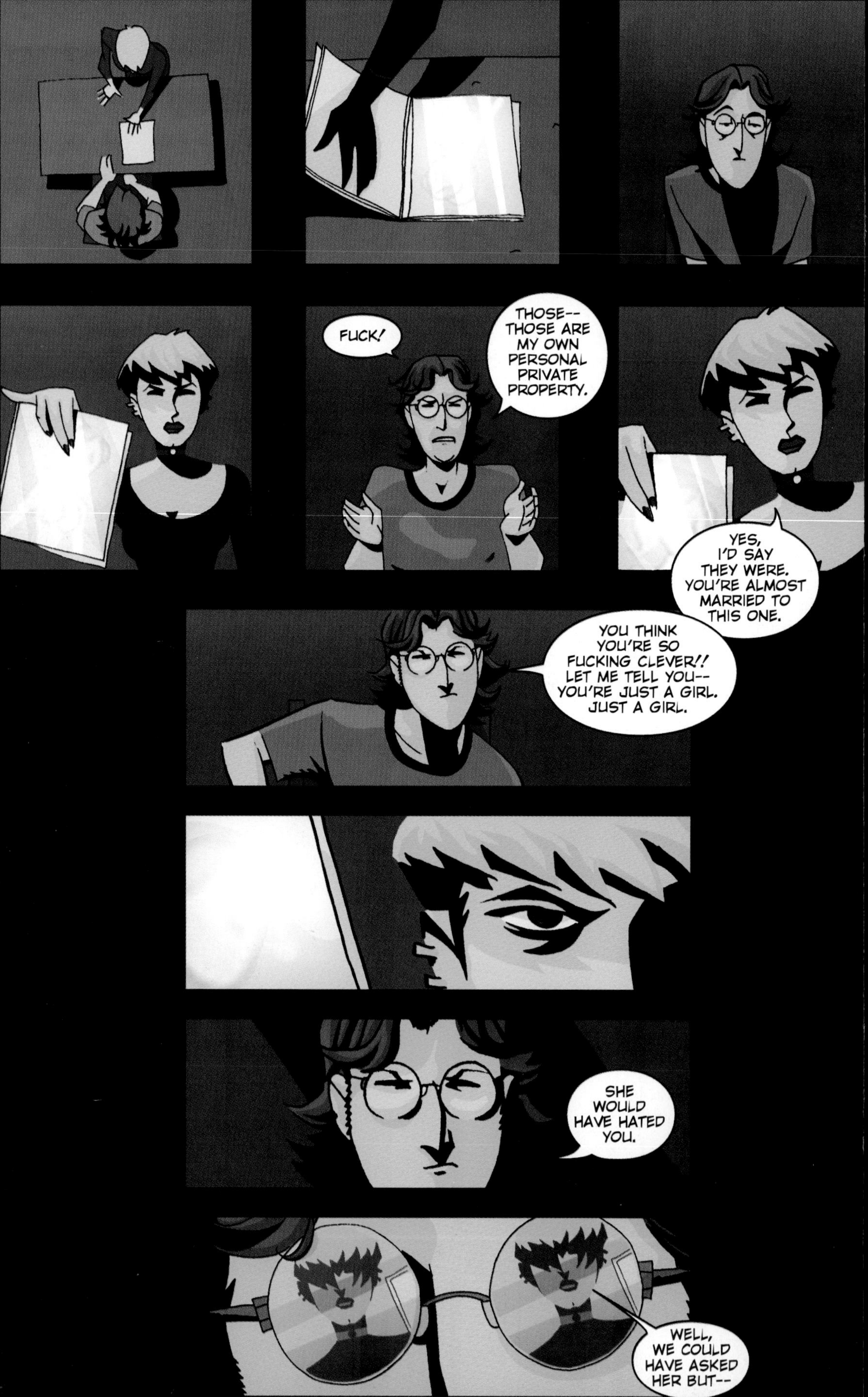
FUCK!
THOSE-- THOSE ARE MY OWN PERSONAL PRIVATE PROPERTY.
YES, I'D SAY THEY WERE. YOU'RE ALMOST MARRIED TO THIS ONE.
YOU THINK YOU'RE SO FUCKING CLEVER!! LET ME TELL YOU-- YOU'RE JUST A GIRL. JUST A GIRL.
SHE WOULD HAVE HATED YOU.
WELL, WE COULD HAVE ASKED HER BUT--

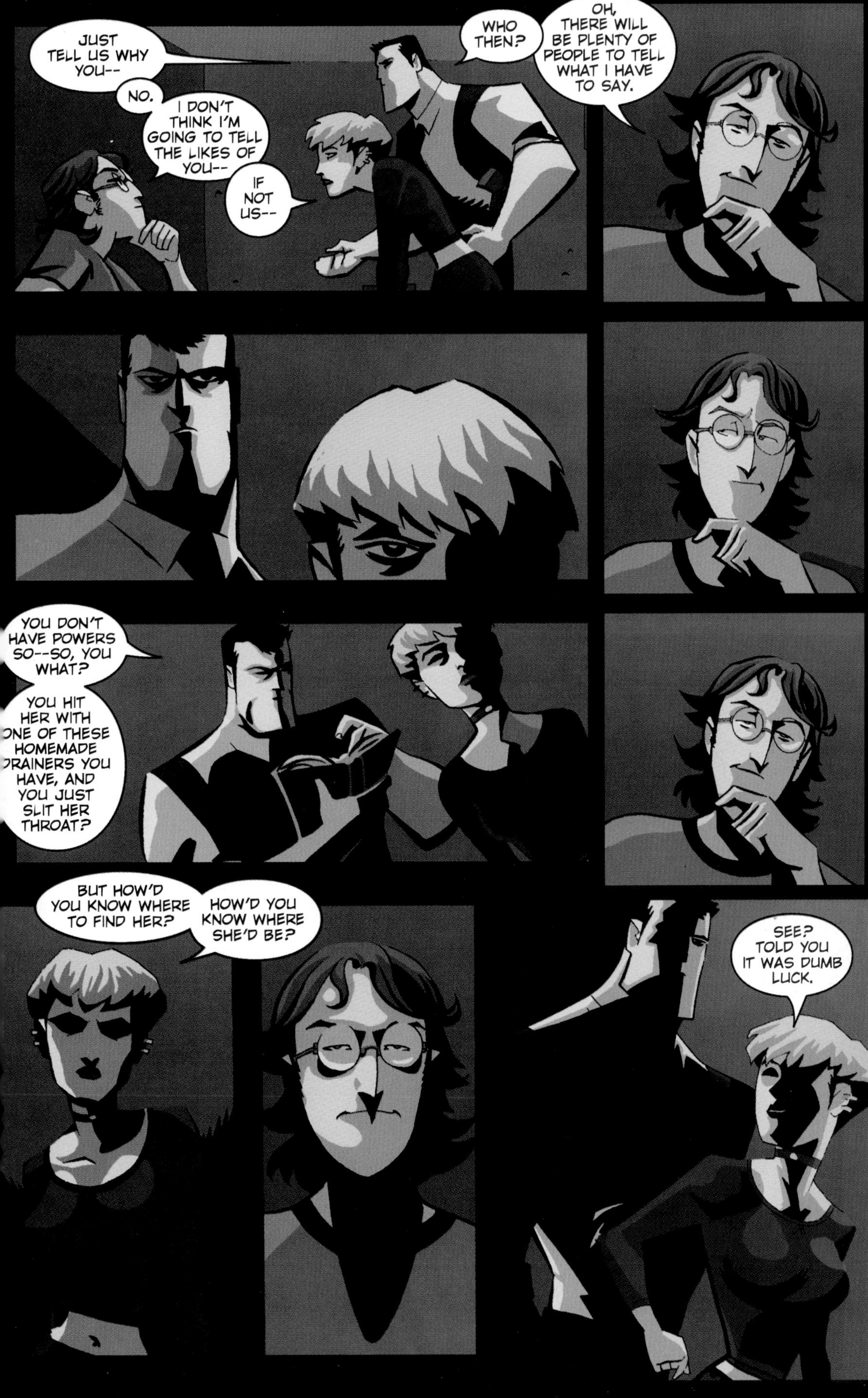
JUST TELL US WHY YOU--
NO.
I DON'T THINK I'M GOING TO TELL THE LIKES OF YOU--
IF NOT US--
WHO THEN?
OH, THERE WILL BE PLENTY OF PEOPLE TO TELL WHAT I HAVE TO SAY.
YOU DON'T HAVE POWERS SO--SO, YOU WHAT?
YOU HIT HER WITH ONE OF THESE HOMEMADE DRAINERS YOU HAVE, AND YOU JUST SLIT HER THROAT?
BUT HOW'D YOU KNOW WHERE TO FIND HER?
HOW'D YOU KNOW WHERE SHE'D BE?
SEE? TOLD YOU IT WAS DUMB LUCK.

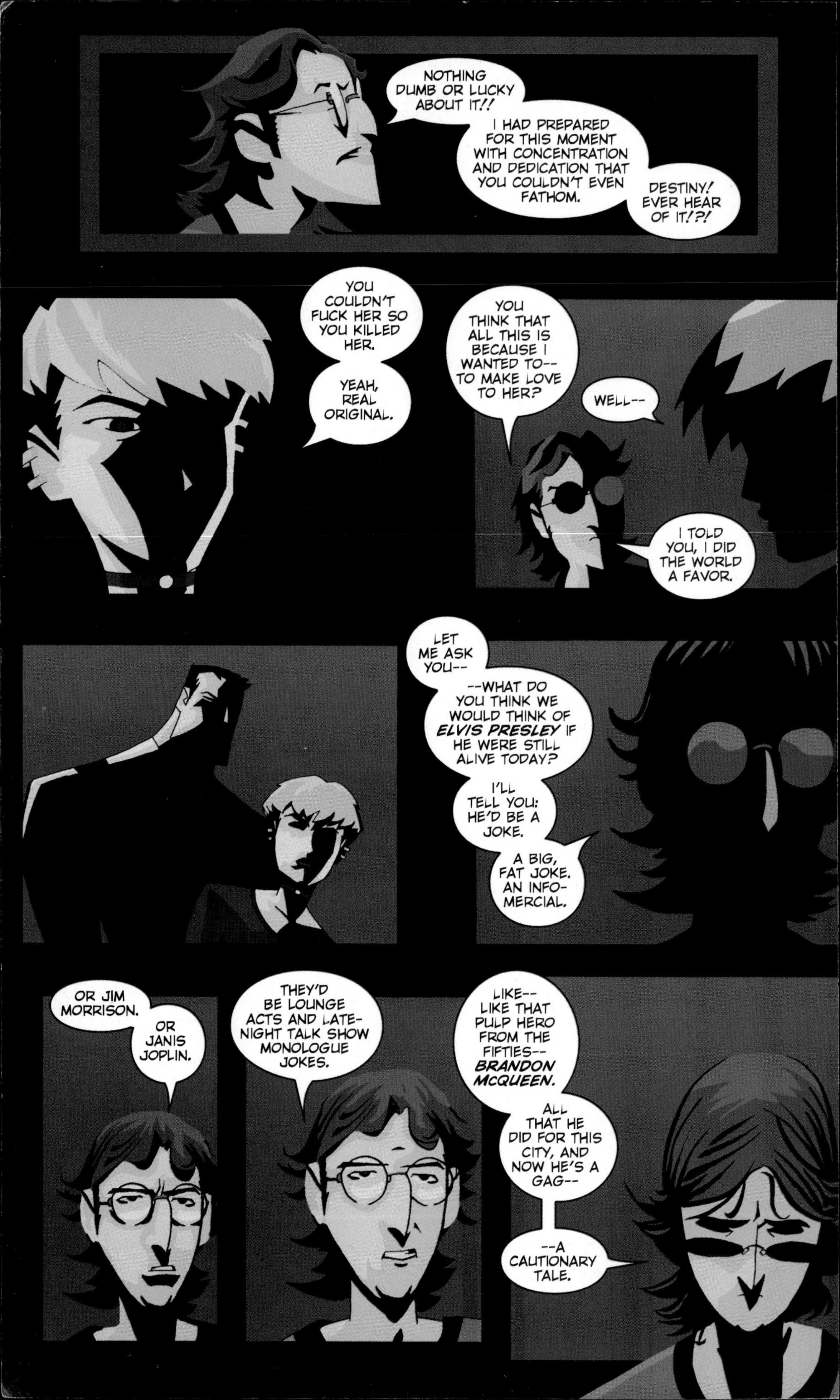
NOTHING DUMB OR LUCKY ABOUT IT!!
I HAD PREPARED FOR THIS MOMENT WITH CONCENTRATION AND DEDICATION THAT YOU COULDN'T EVEN FATHOM.
DESTINY! EVER HEAR OF IT!?!
YOU COULDN'T FUCK HER SO YOU KILLED HER.
YEAH, REAL ORIGINAL.
YOU THINK THAT ALL THIS IS BECAUSE I WANTED TO-- TO MAKE LOVE TO HER?
WELL--
I TOLD YOU, I DID THE WORLD A FAVOR.
LET ME ASK YOU--
--WHAT DO YOU THINK WE WOULD THINK OF ELVIS PRESLEY IF HE WERE STILL ALIVE TODAY?
I'LL TELL YOU: HE'D BE A JOKE.
A BIG, FAT JOKE. AN INFO-MERCIAL.
OR JIM MORRISON.
OR JANIS JOPLIN.
THEY'D BE LOUNGE ACTS AND LATE-NIGHT TALK SHOW MONOLOGUE JOKES.
LIKE-- LIKE THAT PULP HERO FROM THE FIFTIES-- BRANDON McQUEEN.
ALL THAT HE DID FOR THIS CITY, AND NOW HE'S A GAG--
--A CAUTIONARY TALE.

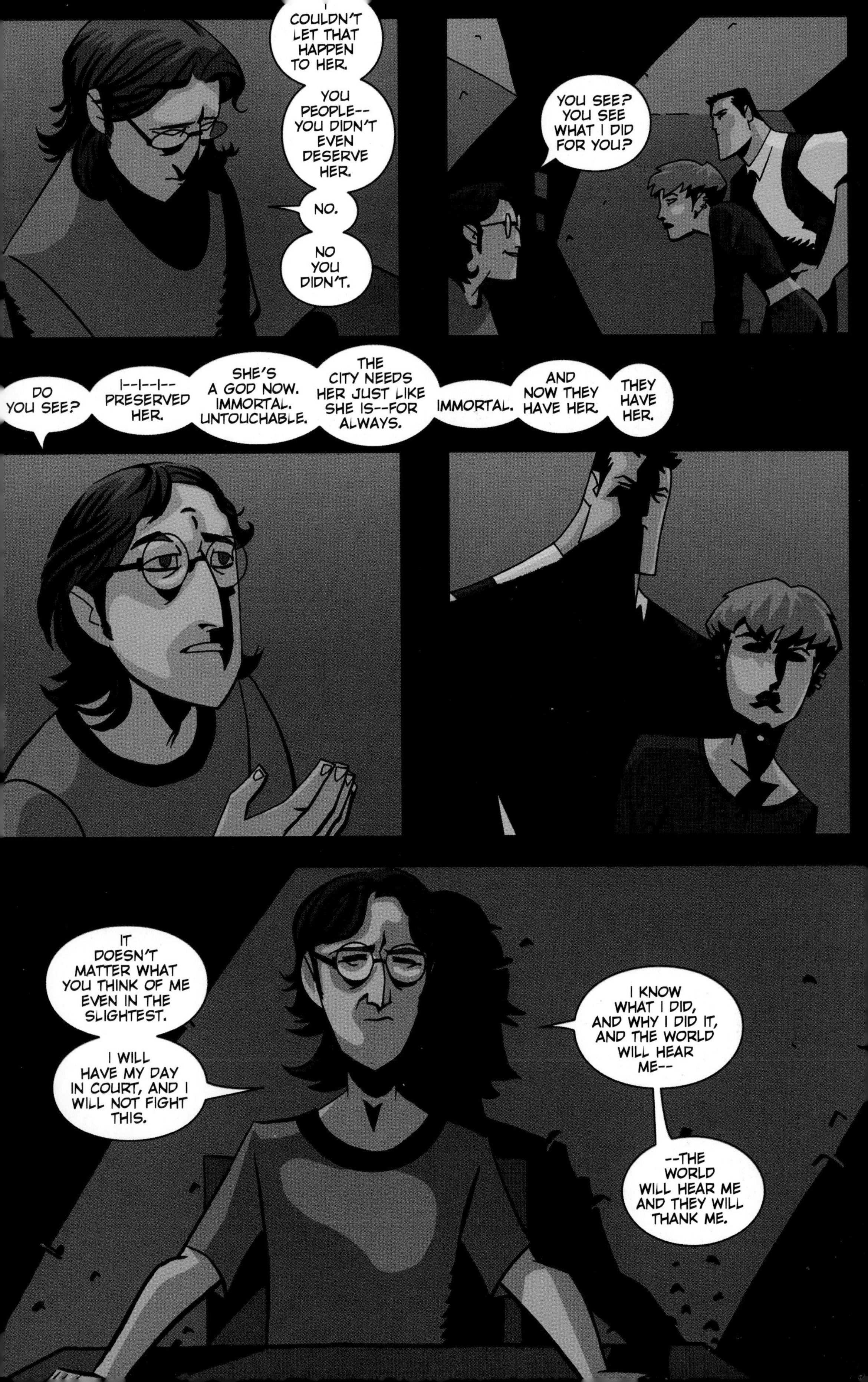
I COULDN'T LET THAT HAPPEN TO HER.
YOU PEOPLE-- YOU DIDN'T EVEN DESERVE HER.
NO.
NO YOU DIDN'T.
YOU SEE? YOU SEE WHAT I DID FOR YOU?
DO YOU SEE?
I--I--I-- PRESERVED HER.
SHE'S A GOD NOW. IMMORTAL. UNTOUCHABLE.
THE CITY NEEDS HER JUST LIKE SHE IS--FOR ALWAYS.
IMMORTAL.
AND NOW THEY HAVE HER.
THEY HAVE HER.
IT DOESN'T MATTER WHAT YOU THINK OF ME EVEN IN THE SLIGHTEST.
I WILL HAVE MY DAY IN COURT, AND I WILL NOT FIGHT THIS.
I KNOW WHAT I DID, AND WHY I DID IT, AND THE WORLD WILL HEAR ME--
--THE WORLD WILL HEAR ME AND THEY WILL THANK ME.

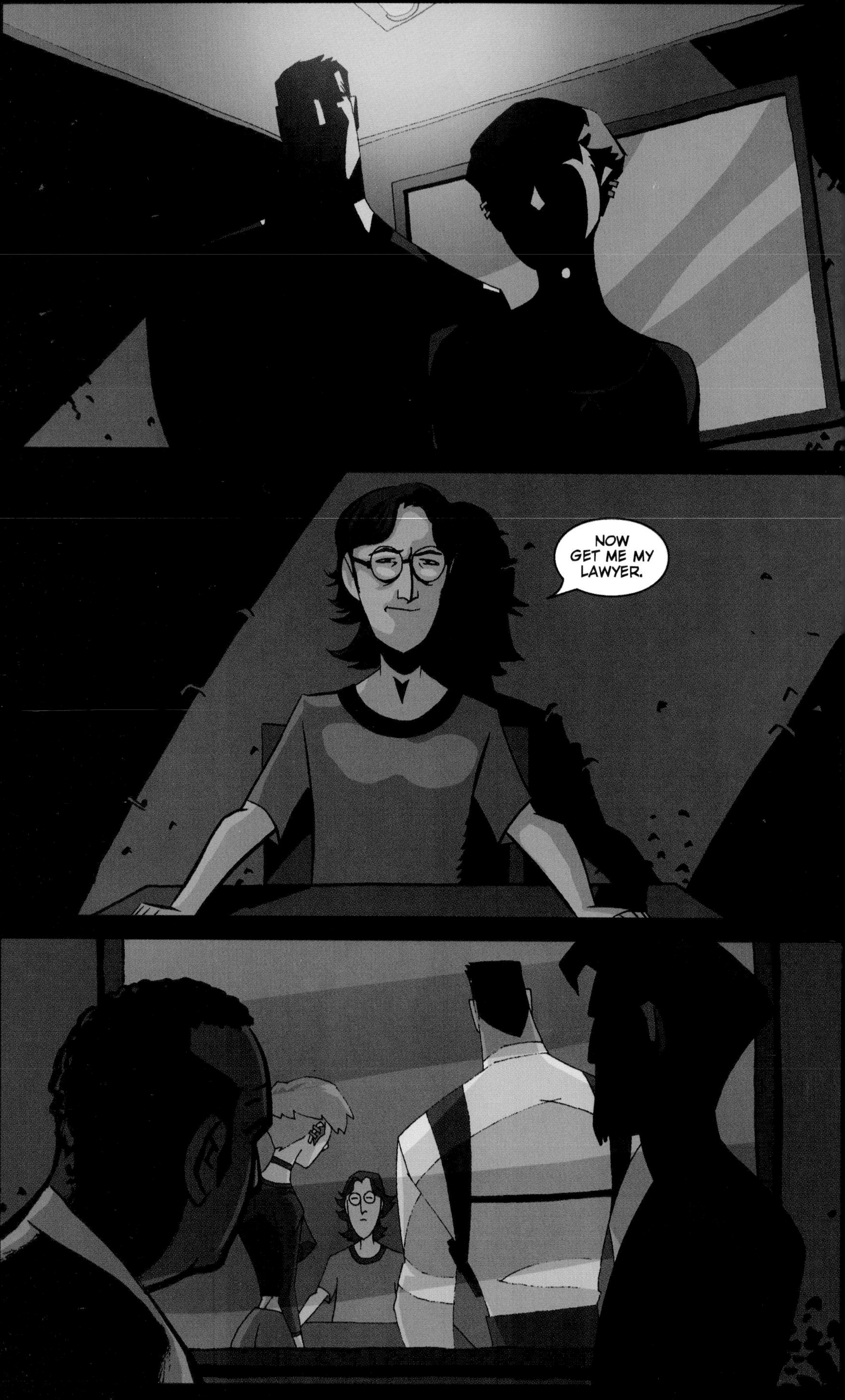
NOW GET ME MY LAWYER.

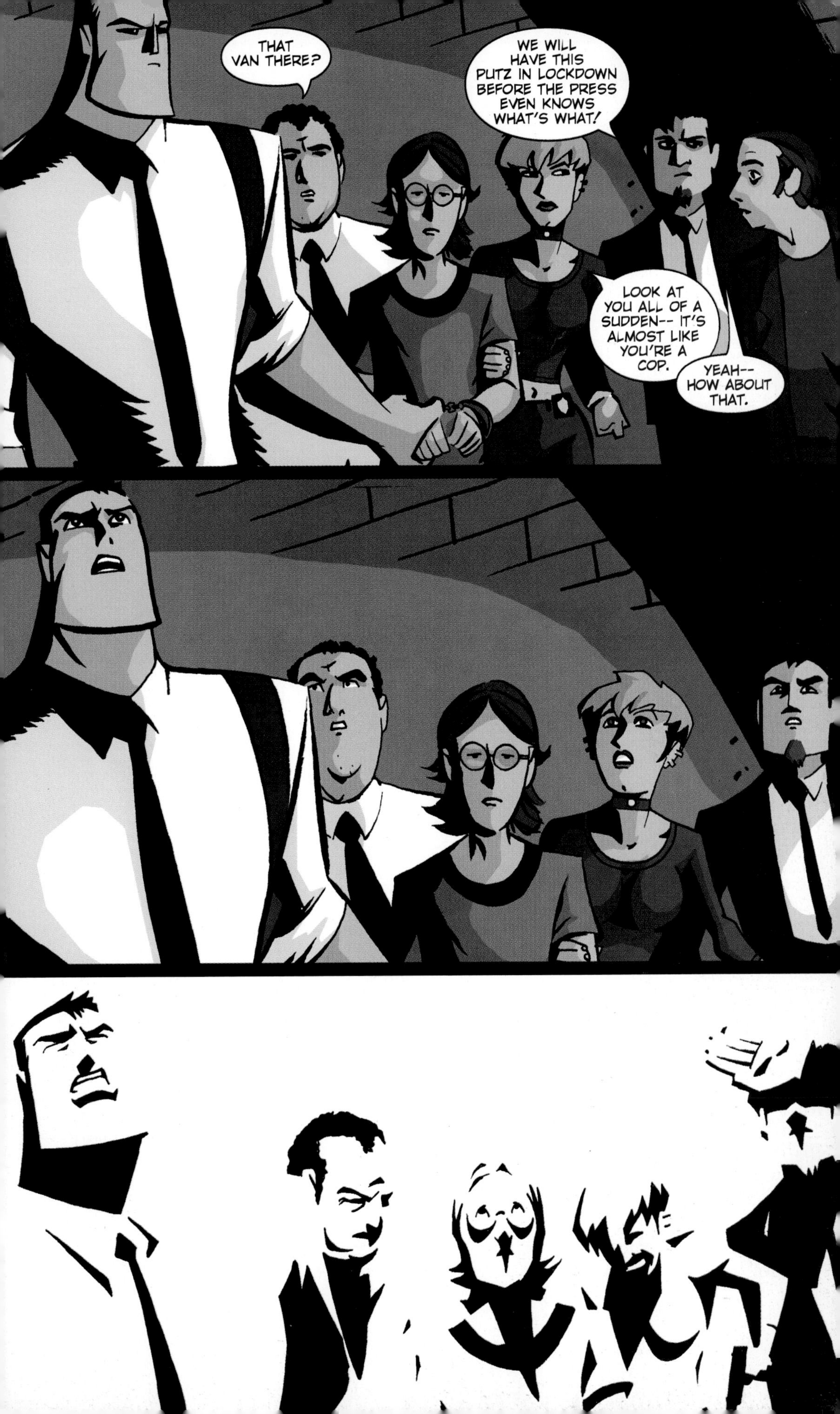
THAT VAN THERE?
WE WILL HAVE THIS PUTZ IN LOCKDOWN BEFORE THE PRESS EVEN KNOWS WHAT'S WHAT!
LOOK AT YOU ALL OF A SUDDEN-- IT'S ALMOST LIKE YOU'RE A COP.
YEAH-- HOW ABOUT THAT.

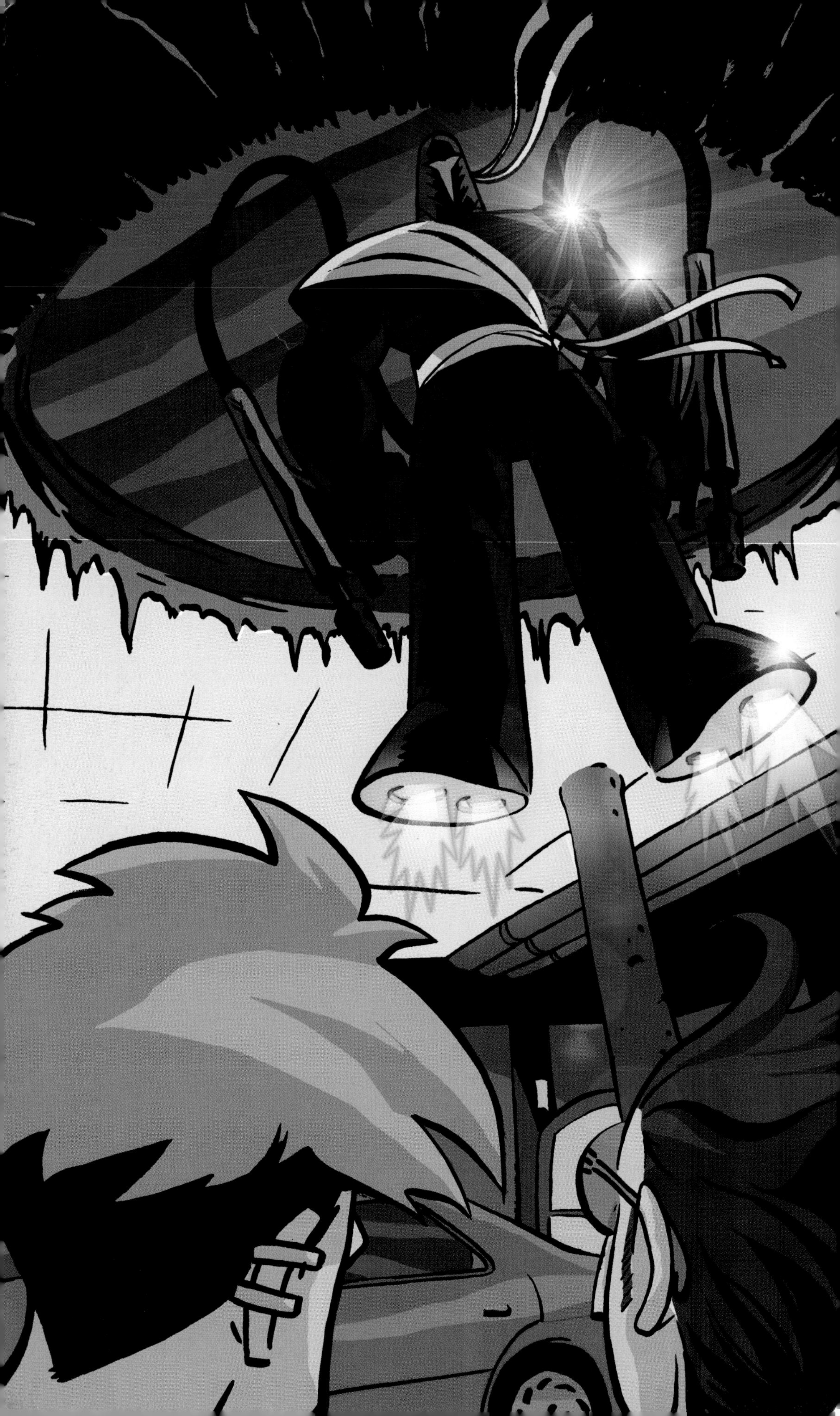

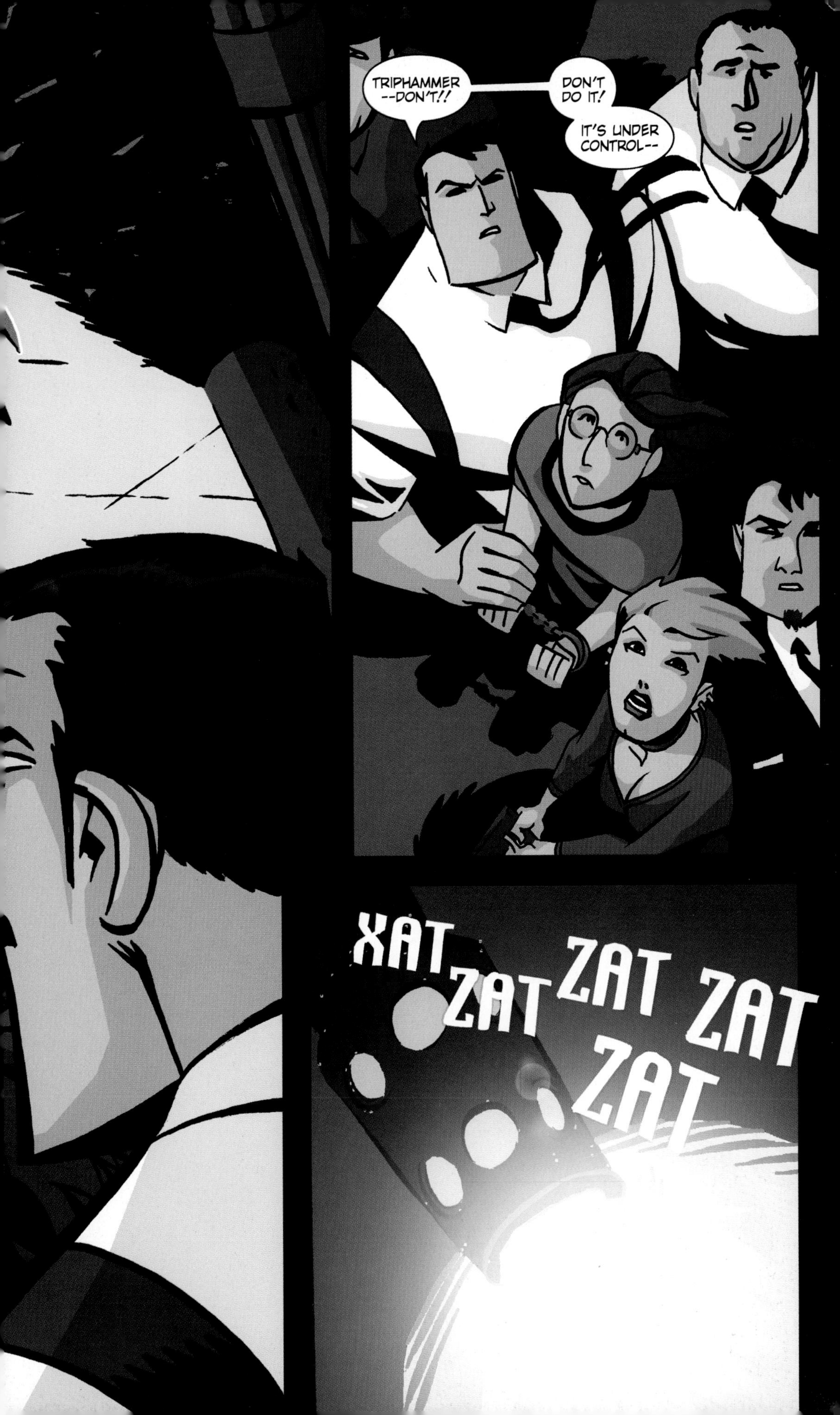
TRIPHAMMER --DON'T!!
DON'T DO IT!
IT'S UNDER CONTROL--
XAT ZAT ZAT ZAT ZAT ZAT

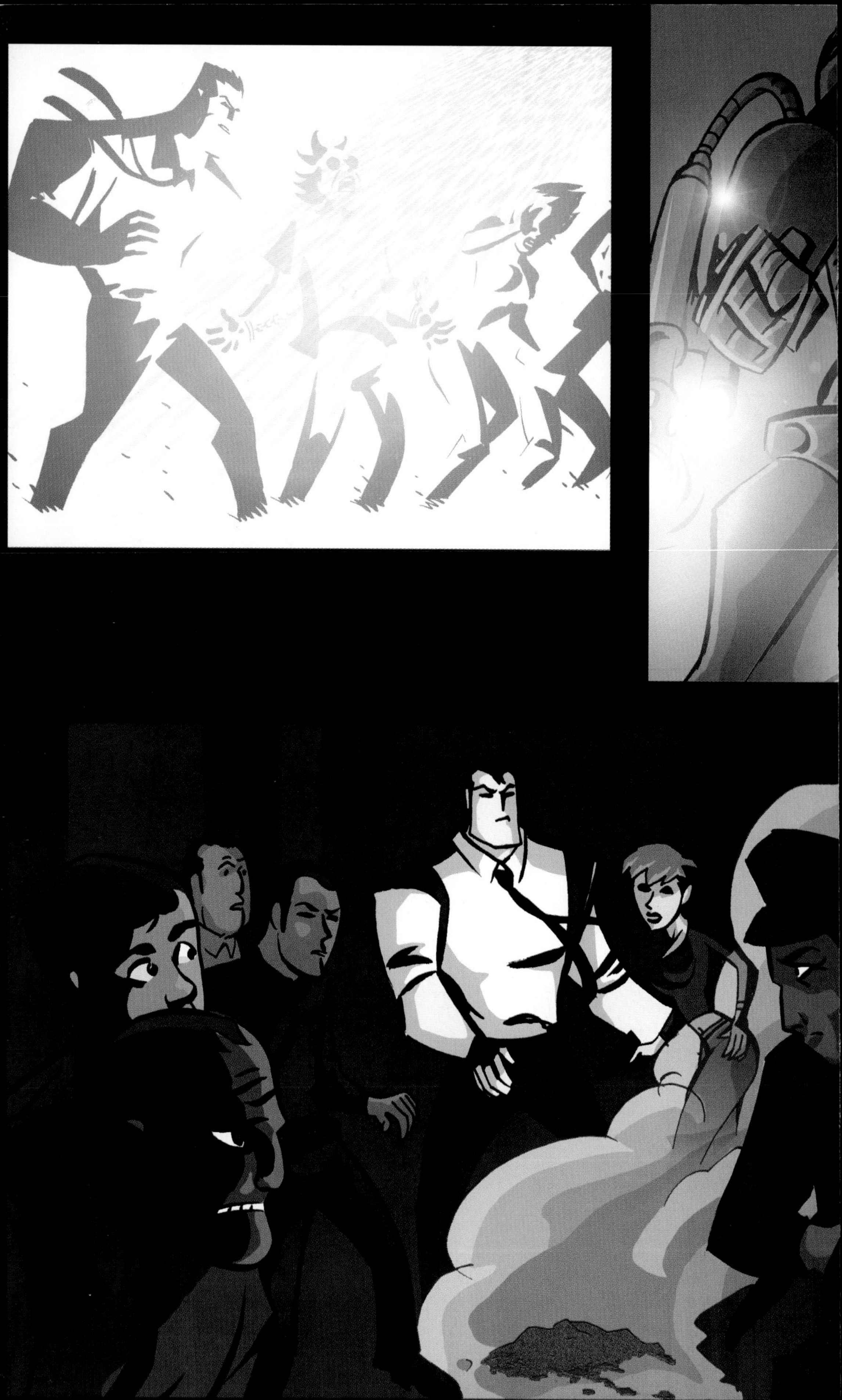

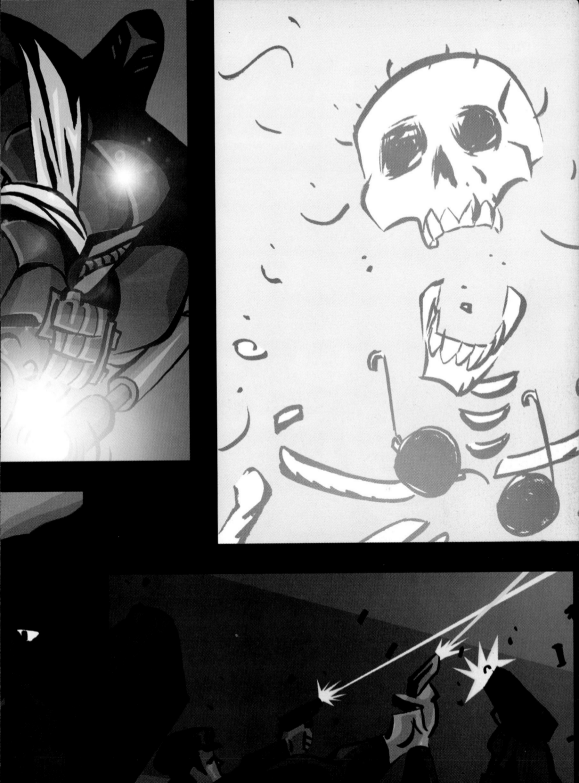

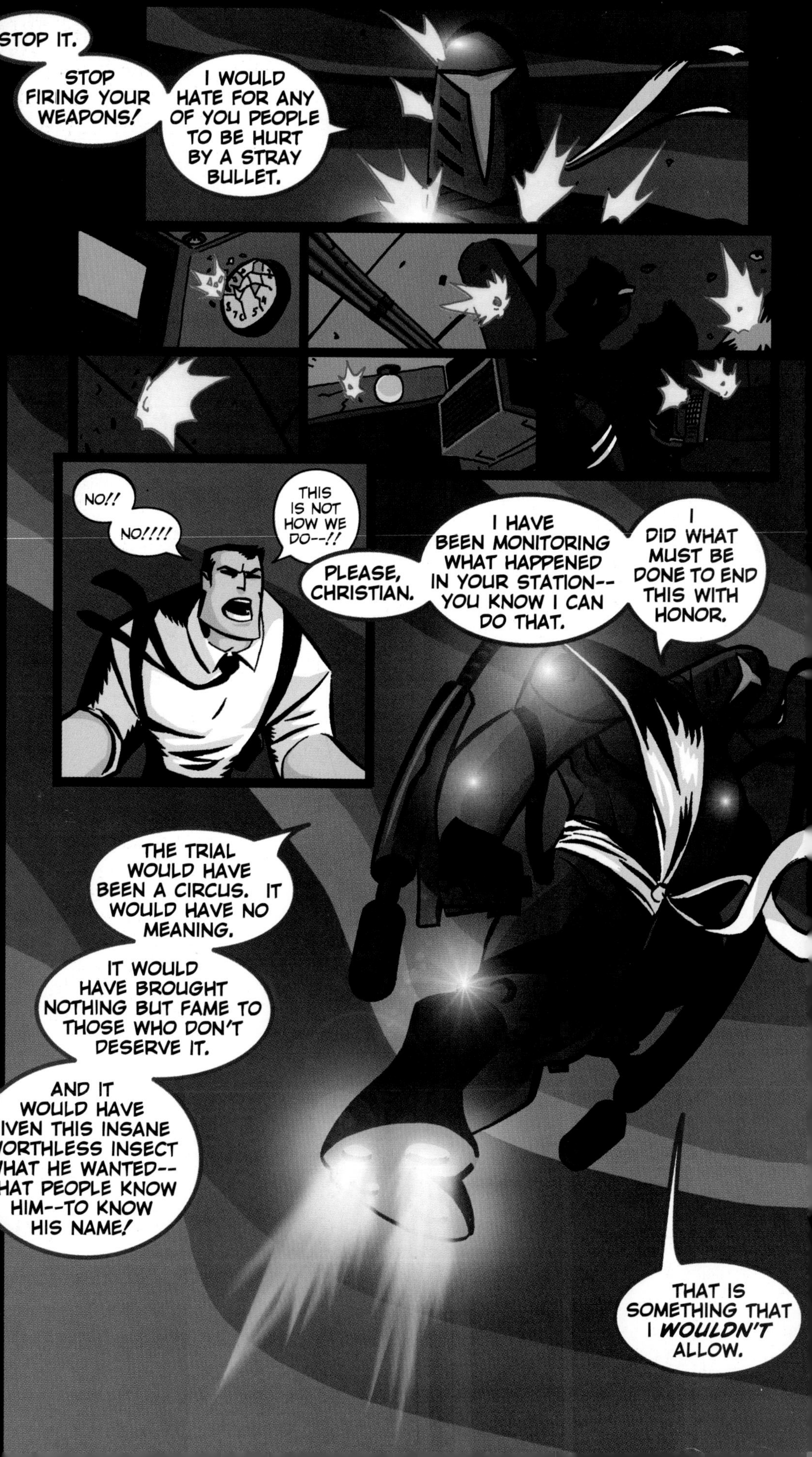

STOP IT.
STOP FIRING YOUR WEAPONS!
I WOULD HATE FOR ANY OF YOU PEOPLE TO BE HURT BY A STRAY BULLET.
NO!!
NO!!!!
THIS IS NOT HOW WE DO--!!
PLEASE, CHRISTIAN.
I HAVE BEEN MONITORING WHAT HAPPENED IN YOUR STATION--YOU KNOW I CAN DO THAT.
I DID WHAT MUST BE DONE TO END THIS WITH HONOR.
THE TRIAL WOULD HAVE BEEN A CIRCUS. IT WOULD HAVE NO MEANING.
IT WOULD HAVE BROUGHT NOTHING BUT FAME TO THOSE WHO DON'T DESERVE IT.
AND IT WOULD HAVE GIVEN THIS INSANE WORTHLESS INSECT WHAT HE WANTED--THAT PEOPLE KNOW HIM--TO KNOW HIS NAME!
THAT IS SOMETHING THAT I *WOULDN'T* ALLOW.

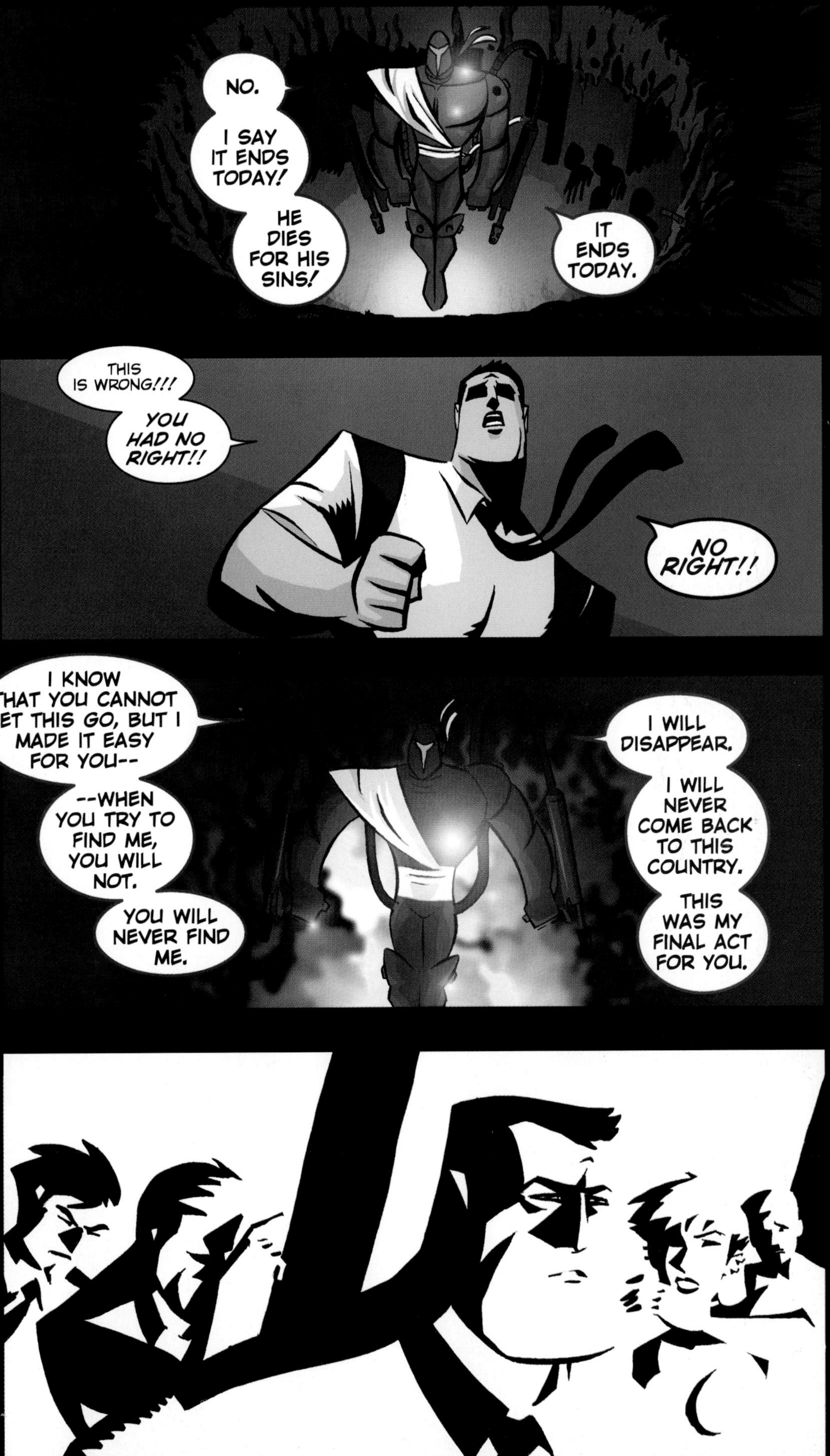
NO.
I SAY IT ENDS TODAY!
HE DIES FOR HIS SINS!
IT ENDS TODAY.
THIS IS WRONG!!!
YOU HAD NO RIGHT!!
NO RIGHT!!
I KNOW THAT YOU CANNOT LET THIS GO, BUT I MADE IT EASY FOR YOU--
--WHEN YOU TRY TO FIND ME, YOU WILL NOT.
YOU WILL NEVER FIND ME.
I WILL DISAPPEAR.
I WILL NEVER COME BACK TO THIS COUNTRY.
THIS WAS MY FINAL ACT FOR YOU.

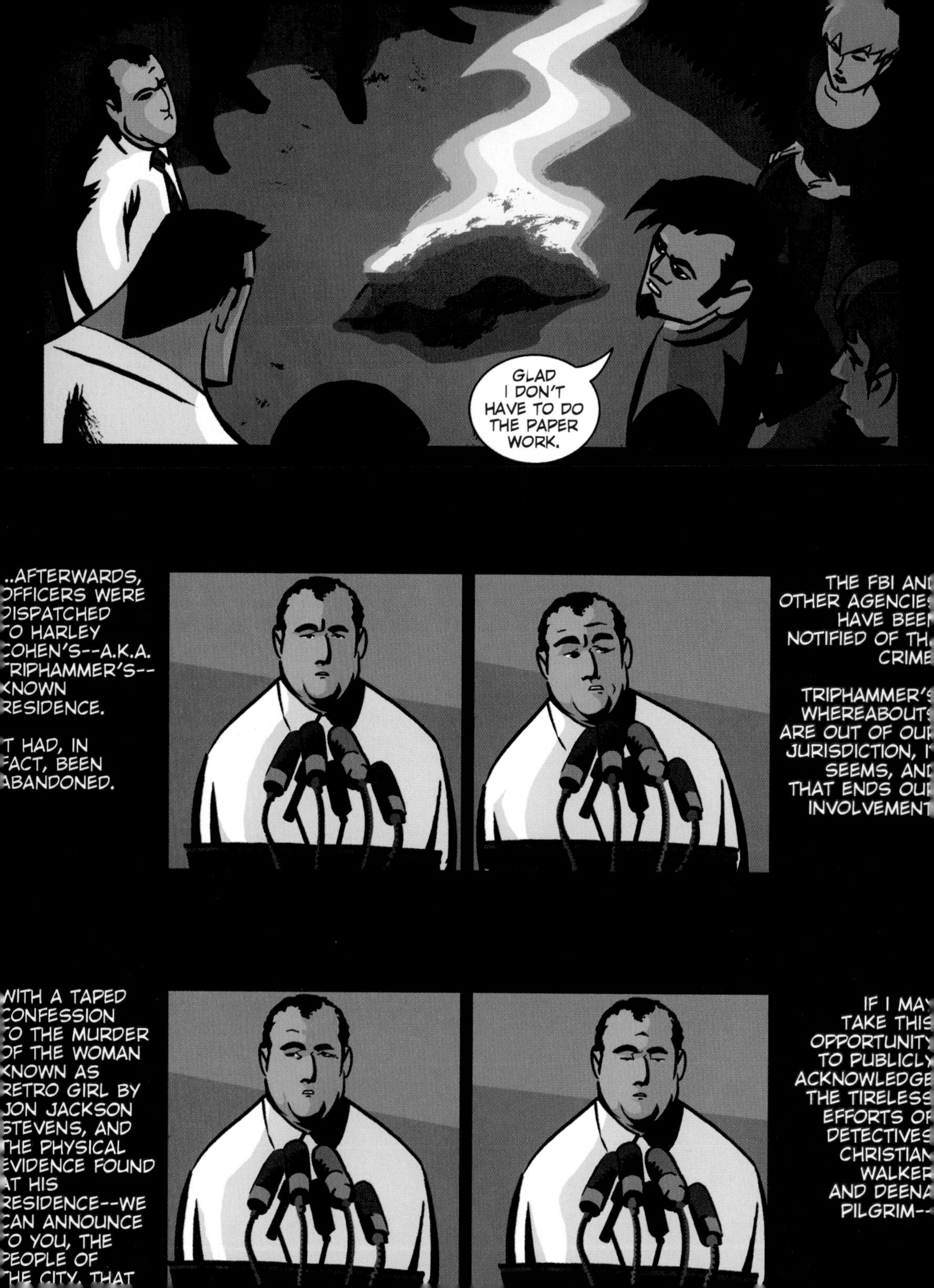
GLAD I DON'T HAVE TO DO THE PAPER WORK.
..AFTERWARDS, OFFICERS WERE DISPATCHED TO HARLEY COHEN'S--A.K.A. TRIPHAMMER'S--KNOWN RESIDENCE.
IT HAD, IN FACT, BEEN ABANDONED.
THE FBI AND OTHER AGENCIES HAVE BEEN NOTIFIED OF THE CRIME.
TRIPHAMMER'S WHEREABOUTS ARE OUT OF OUR JURISDICTION, IT SEEMS, AND THAT ENDS OUR INVOLVEMENT.
WITH A TAPED CONFESSION TO THE MURDER OF THE WOMAN KNOWN AS RETRO GIRL BY JON JACKSON STEVENS, AND THE PHYSICAL EVIDENCE FOUND AT HIS RESIDENCE--WE CAN ANNOUNCE TO YOU, THE PEOPLE OF THE CITY, THAT
IF I MAY TAKE THIS OPPORTUNITY TO PUBLICLY ACKNOWLEDGE THE TIRELESS EFFORTS OF DETECTIVES CHRISTIAN WALKER AND DEENA PILGRIM--

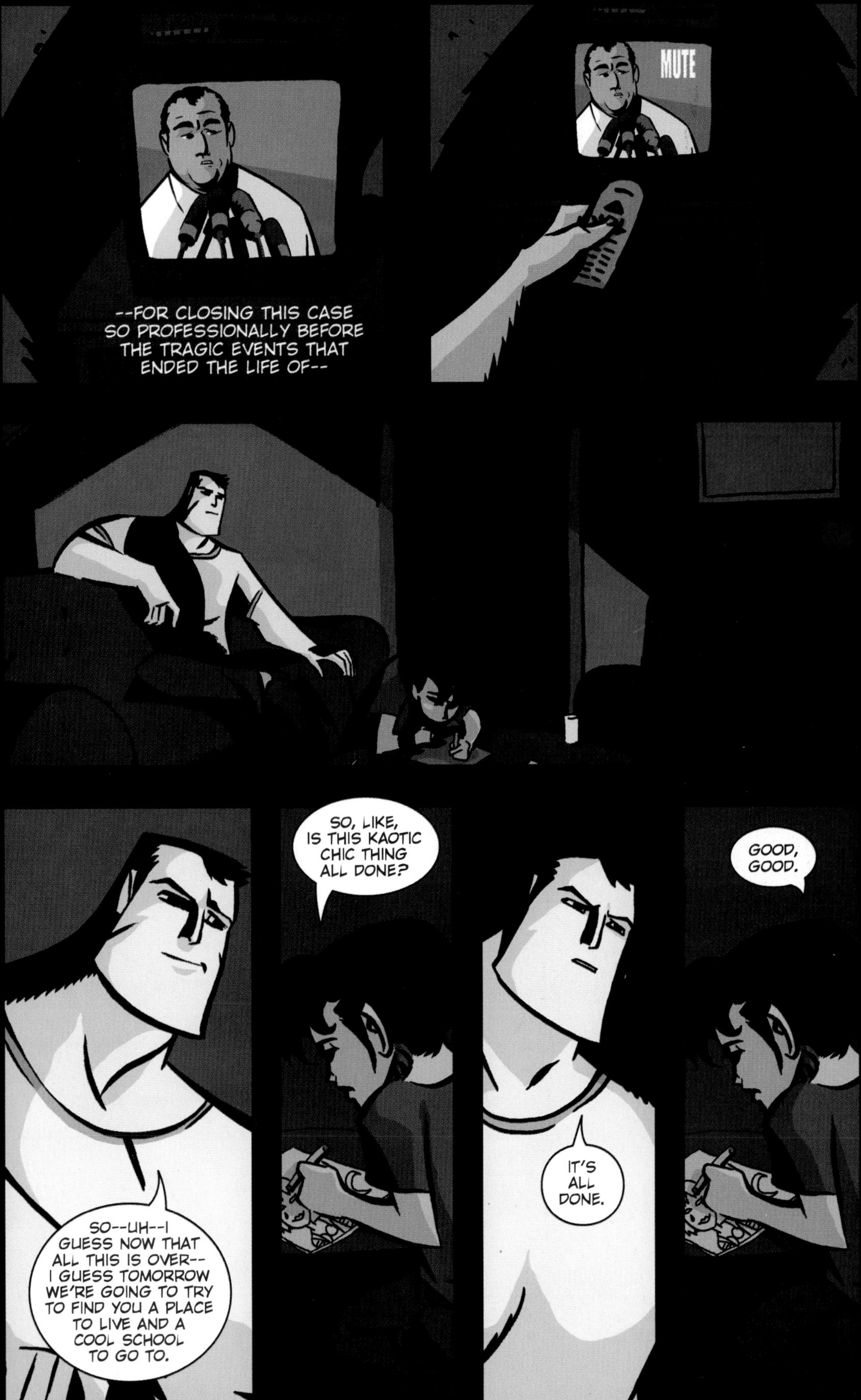
--FOR CLOSING THIS CASE SO PROFESSIONALLY BEFORE THE TRAGIC EVENTS THAT ENDED THE LIFE OF--
MUTE
SO--UH--I GUESS NOW THAT ALL THIS IS OVER-- I GUESS TOMORROW WE'RE GOING TO TRY TO FIND YOU A PLACE TO LIVE AND A COOL SCHOOL TO GO TO.
SO, LIKE, IS THIS KAOTIC CHIC THING ALL DONE?
IT'S ALL DONE.
GOOD, GOOD.

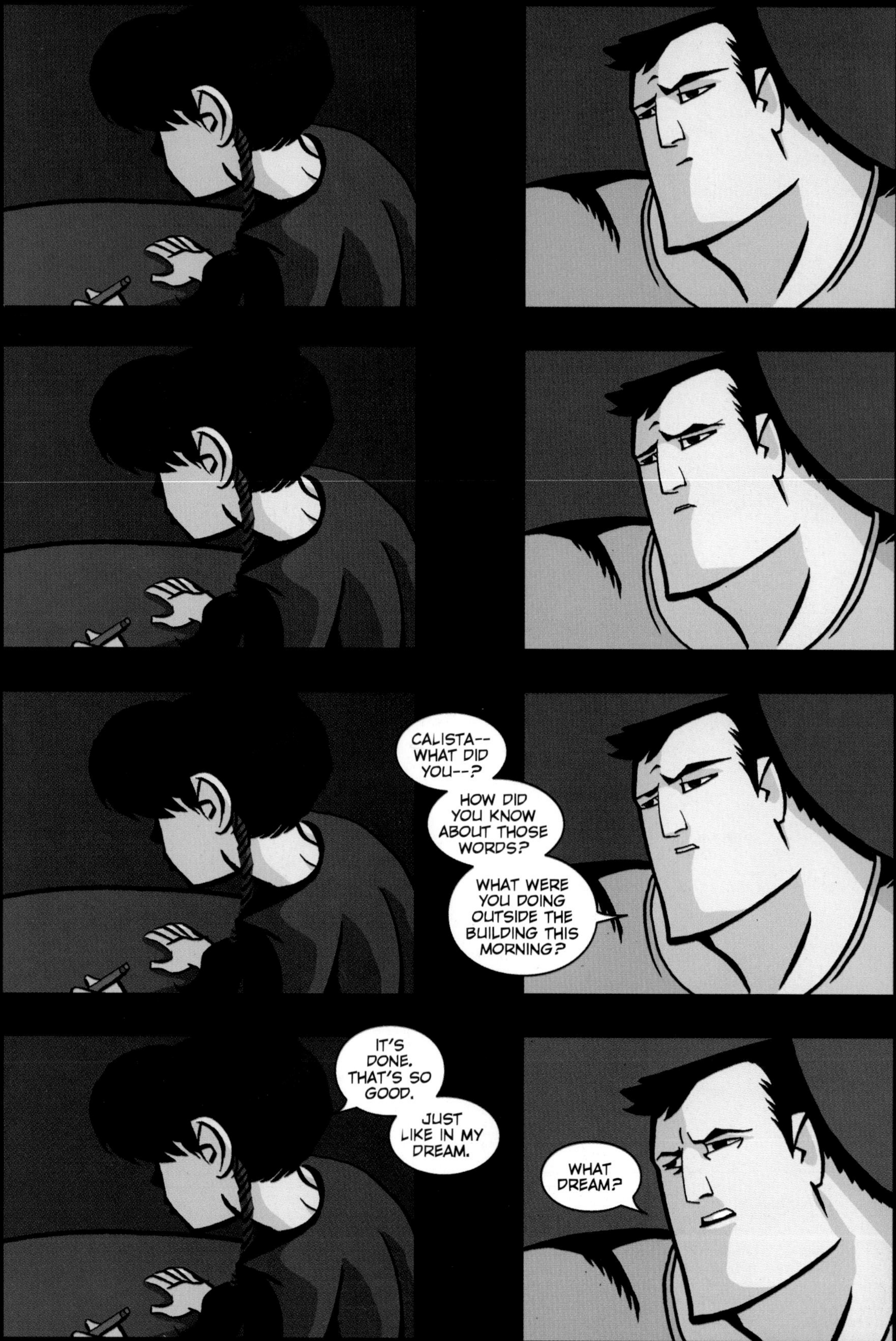
CALISTA-- WHAT DID YOU--?
HOW DID YOU KNOW ABOUT THOSE WORDS?
WHAT WERE YOU DOING OUTSIDE THE BUILDING THIS MORNING?
IT'S DONE. THAT'S SO GOOD.
JUST LIKE IN MY DREAM.
WHAT DREAM?

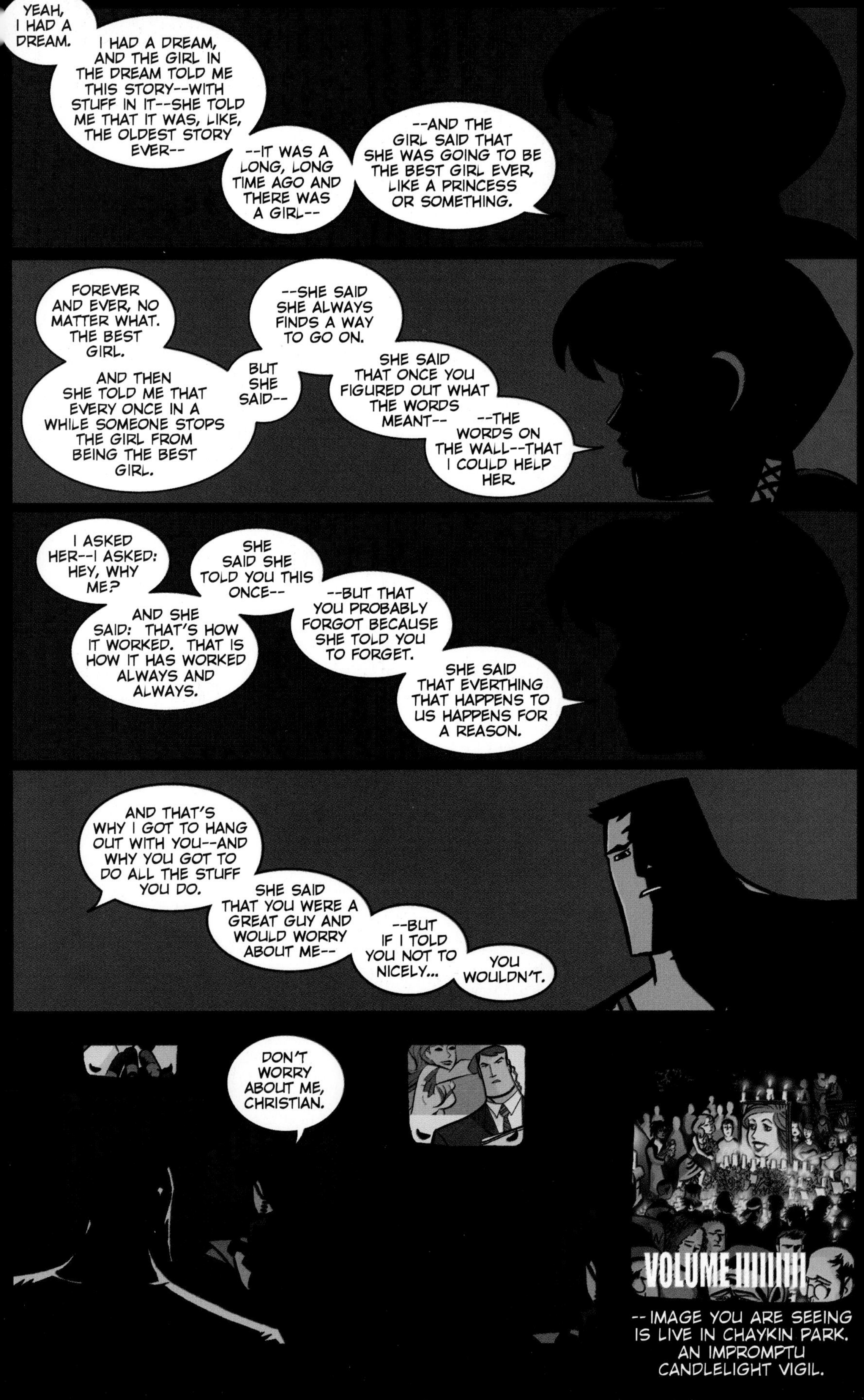
YEAH, I HAD A DREAM.
I HAD A DREAM, AND THE GIRL IN THE DREAM TOLD ME THIS STORY--WITH STUFF IN IT--SHE TOLD ME THAT IT WAS, LIKE, THE OLDEST STORY EVER--
--IT WAS A LONG, LONG TIME AGO AND THERE WAS A GIRL--
--AND THE GIRL SAID THAT SHE WAS GOING TO BE THE BEST GIRL EVER, LIKE A PRINCESS OR SOMETHING.
FOREVER AND EVER, NO MATTER WHAT. THE BEST GIRL.
AND THEN SHE TOLD ME THAT EVERY ONCE IN A WHILE SOMEONE STOPS THE GIRL FROM BEING THE BEST GIRL.
BUT SHE SAID--
--SHE SAID SHE ALWAYS FINDS A WAY TO GO ON.
SHE SAID THAT ONCE YOU FIGURED OUT WHAT THE WORDS MEANT--
--THE WORDS ON THE WALL--THAT I COULD HELP HER.
I ASKED HER--I ASKED: HEY, WHY ME?
AND SHE SAID: THAT'S HOW IT WORKED. THAT IS HOW IT HAS WORKED ALWAYS AND ALWAYS.
SHE SAID SHE TOLD YOU THIS ONCE--
--BUT THAT YOU PROBABLY FORGOT BECAUSE SHE TOLD YOU TO FORGET.
SHE SAID THAT EVERTHING THAT HAPPENS TO US HAPPENS FOR A REASON.
AND THAT'S WHY I GOT TO HANG OUT WITH YOU--AND WHY YOU GOT TO DO ALL THE STUFF YOU DO.
SHE SAID THAT YOU WERE A GREAT GUY AND WOULD WORRY ABOUT ME--
--BUT IF I TOLD YOU NOT TO NICELY...
YOU WOULDN'T.
DON'T WORRY ABOUT ME, CHRISTIAN.
VOLUME IIIIIIII
--IMAGE YOU ARE SEEING IS LIVE IN CHAYKIN PARK. AN IMPROMPTU CANDLELIGHT VIGIL.

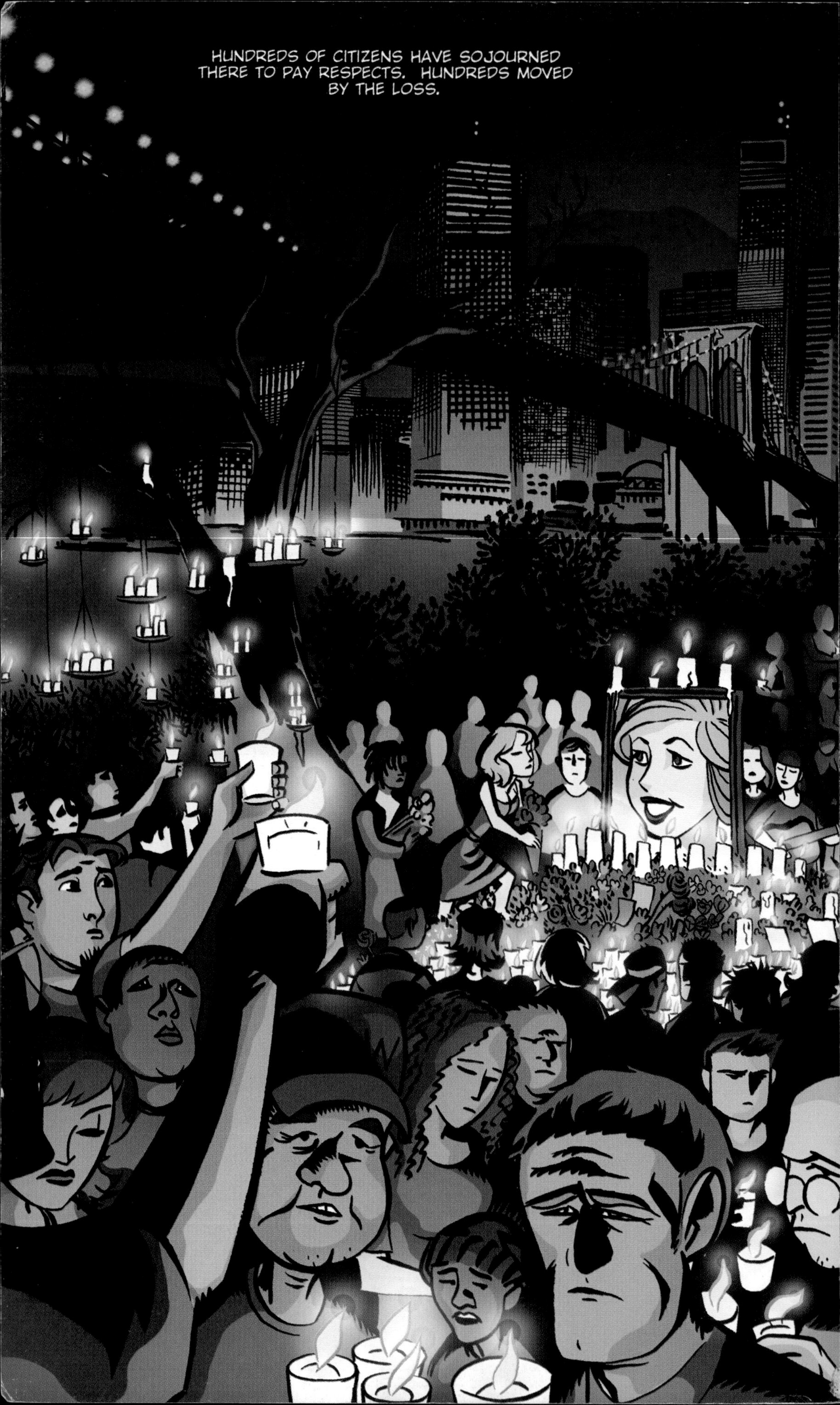
HUNDREDS OF CITIZENS HAVE SOJOURNED THERE TO PAY RESPECTS. HUNDREDS MOVED BY THE LOSS.

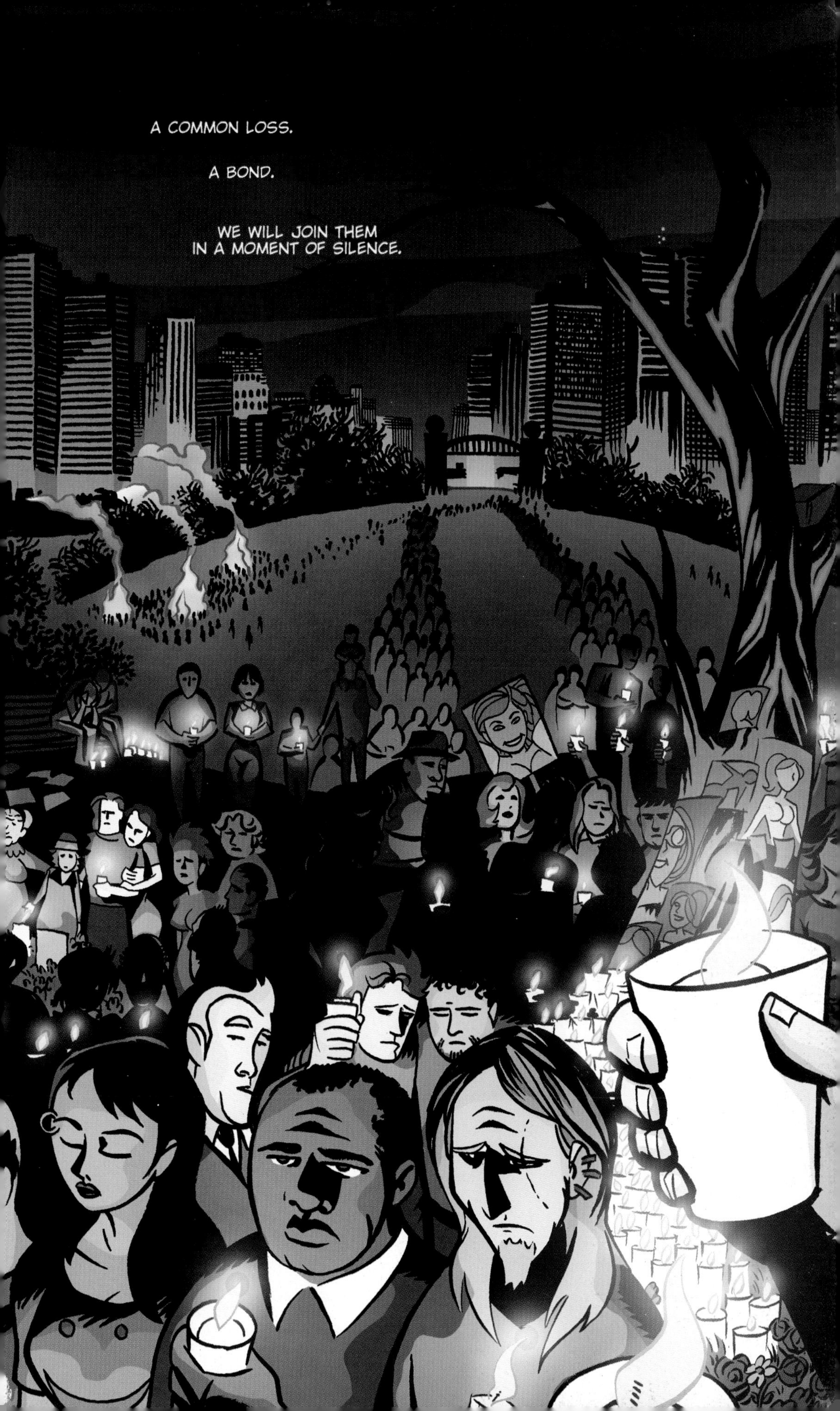
A COMMON LOSS.
A BOND.
WE WILL JOIN THEM IN A MOMENT OF SILENCE.

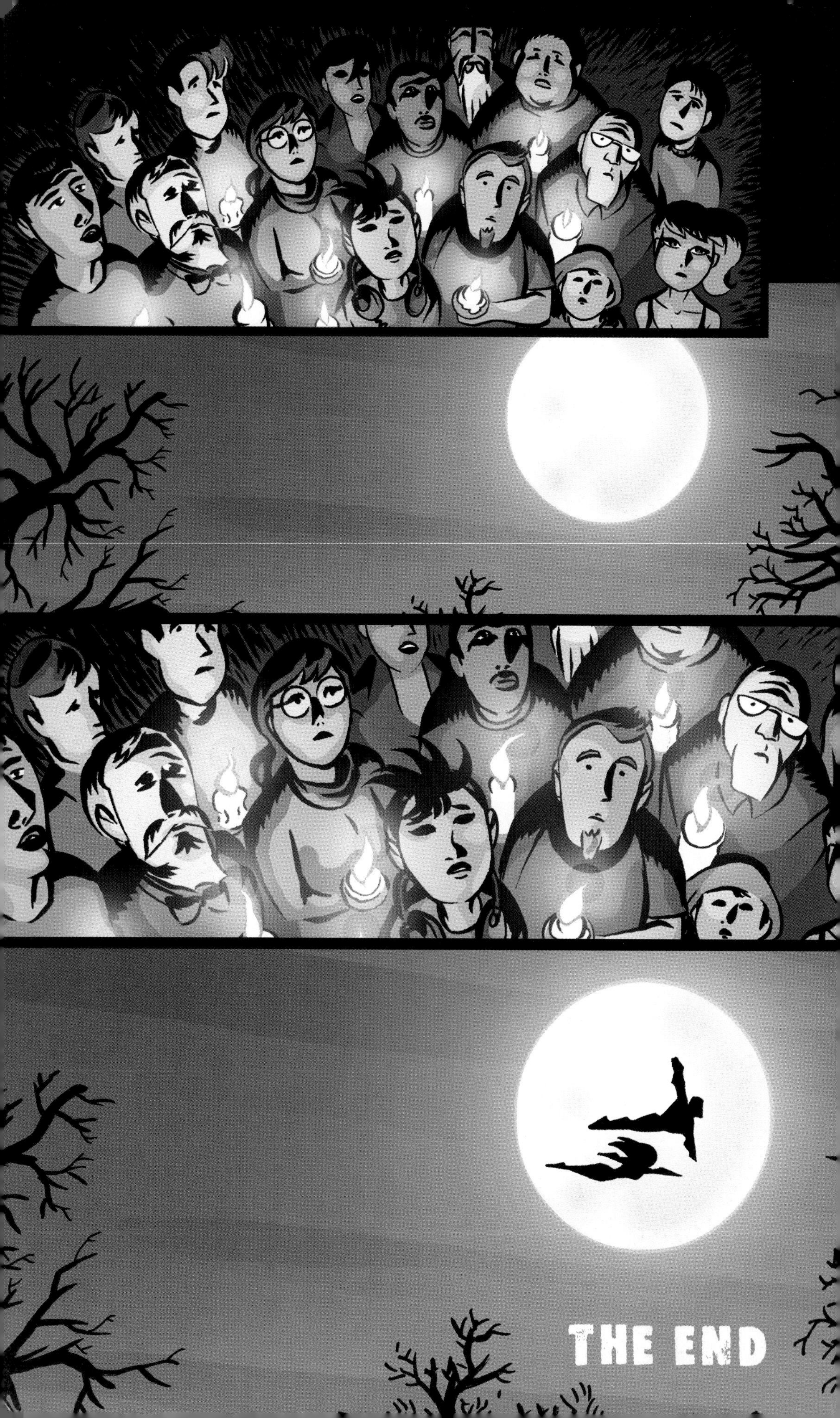
THE END

POWERS
THE CAMEOS

One of the best ideas we came up with for this book, and by 'best' I mean 'logistic nightmares,' was to ask well-known comic book creator friends of ours to lend us brand new super hero and villain creations to fill our cityscape.

This added an extra layer of fun to the whole thing. Many big name talents, talents people don't usually think of in this genre, were extremely generous by lending us their babies.

So, here on the following pages, for the first time, is a key to the identities of all the characters and their creators. Each character is copyright the creator named here. If no name is listed, that character is copyright Mike and myself and will be featured in an upcoming Powers storyarc.

We thank them all for being friends and pros.

DREI
DAVE JOHNSON

TWIGHLIGHT
DAVID MACK

THANKS AND DEDICATION

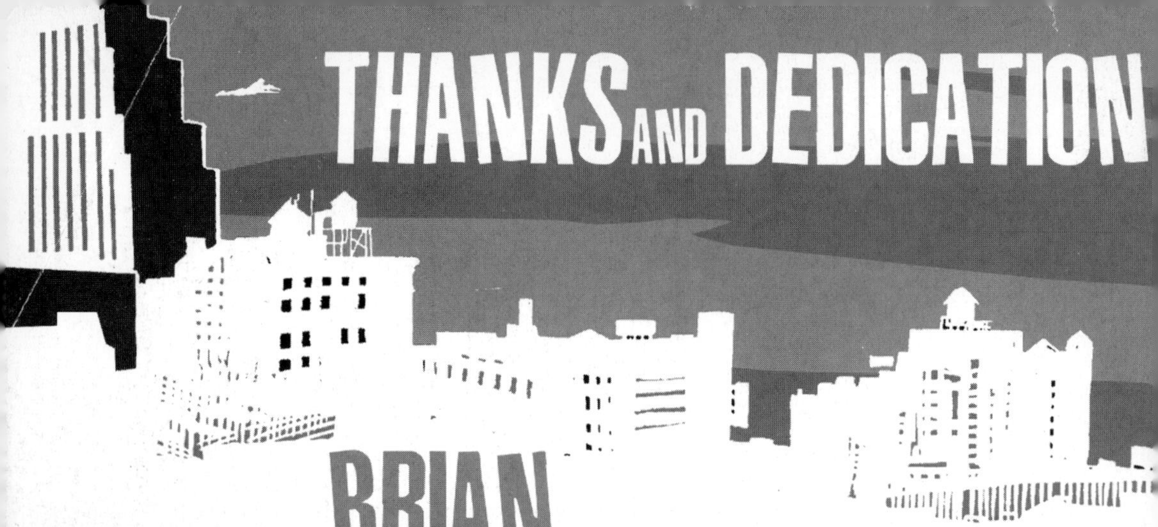

BRIAN

David Engel, Jim Valentino, Anthony Bozzi, Mace Neufeld, Brent Braun, Traci Hale, Joe Quesada, Bill Jemas, Kel Symons, Doug Belgrad, Jim McLaughlin, Randy Lander, Don Mcphereson, Jason Prichett, Justin Silvera, Chris Silberman, John Skrtic, Cliff Biggers, Ward Batty, Chris Lawrence, Warren Ellis, David Mack, James S. Rich, Joe Nozemack, Michael Dora Matt Brady, Joel Meadows, Jared Bendis, Pat, K.C., Mike, Alisa and the JINXWORLD messageboard.

MIKE

For Melissa and Ethan, the center of my world. Special thanks to Mom, Aunt Carol, Uncle Larry, Neil Vokes, the Bendis Board Posters and the Bordentown Police Department for all the support and help!

PAT

I'd like to thank the OCPStudios gents--Marshall Johnson, Josh Read, Mike Smith, James Dean Conklin, Tony Stocco, Ken Chang, and Scott Helmer. And I'd like to make sure to thank both my parents, 'cause I don't think I have thanked them previously in print.

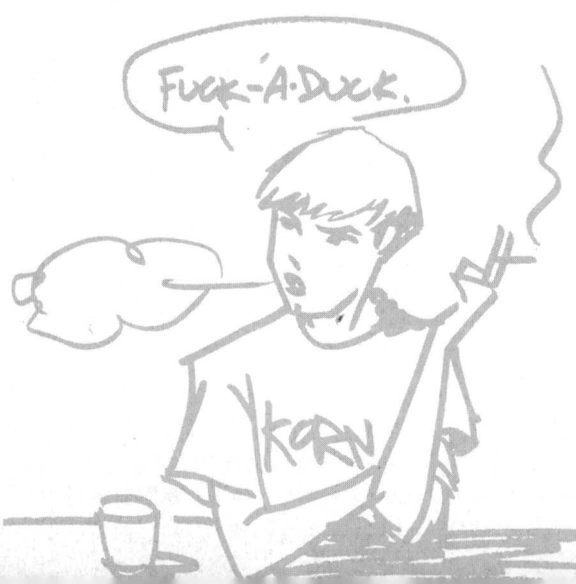
FUCK-A-DUCK.
KORN